Boulder's Masonic Pioneers 1867–1886

Members of Columbia Lodge No. 14
Boulder County, Colorado Territory

Compiled by Dina C. Carson

Boulder's Masonic Pioneers, 1867–1886

Members of Columbia Lodge No. 14
Boulder County, Colorado Territory

Compiled by Dina C. Carson

Published by: Iron Gate Publishing
on behalf of The Boulder Pioneers Project
P.O. Box 999
Niwot, CO 80544
http://www.boulderpioneers.com

Printed in the United States of America
ISBN 978-1-879579-57-6 1-879579-57-X

Cover Design by Robin R. Meetz
Imagination Technology, Inc.
www.imaginationtechnology.com

Publisher's Cataloging-in-Publication Data

Carson, Dina C, 1961 -

Boulder's Masonic Pioneers 1867–1886:
Members of Columbia Lodge No. 14
Boulder County, Colorado Territory

p. cm.
Includes index.
ISBN 978-1-879579-57-6 1-879579-57-X

1. Boulder (Colo.)—History.
2. Pioneers—Boulder (Colo.).
3. Masonic Lodges—Boulder (Colo.)—Records
4. Freemasons—Boulder (Colo.)—Members
5. Freemasons—Colorado—History I. Title.
F792.C6 2012
978.863 Car

Boulder's Masonic Pioneers, 1867–1886

Members of Columbia Lodge No. 14, Boulder County, Colorado Territory

TABLE OF CONTENTS

Boulder's Masonic Pioneers

1867–1886

Members of Columbia Lodge No. 14
Boulder County, Colorado Territory

Masons in Colorado have a history longer than the state itself. There were Masons among the earliest settlers in the new gold rush town of Auraria along the banks of the Platte River where it meets Cherry Creek. Henry Allen, among a group of gold seekers from Iowa, helped organize a group of seven Masons who would lay the foundation for the Grand Lodge of Colorado. Nineteen more Masons had joined the group by the time the first St. John's celebration was held on Dec. 27th, 1858 in a sixteen by sixteen foot cabin.

William N. Byers, the editor of the area's first newspaper, The Rocky Mountain News, attended a meeting of 40 Masons on the night of his arrival in April 1859. Before June was over, nearly 100 Masons had pre-empted a block of ground, leveled it using ox teams, dragged logs from the mountains and erected the first Masonic Temple in this part of the frontier. When the structure was finished, more than 200 visiting Masons, whose names were recorded on the Roll of Visitors, attended the first meeting. Although the initial Masonic Lodge was a crude log cabin, it was still a Masonic Temple. In the 1930s the Grand Lodge of Colorado acquired title to the ground where that temple once stood. Annual Grand Lodge pilgrimages are still made to the site.

On Aug 15, 1859 a dispensation was granted from the Grand Lodge of Kansas for the first recognized Lodge in the area. Henry Allen would serve as the first Master. On Oct 1, 1859, more than 40 Masons assembled on the upper floor of a new two-story building built on Ferry Street in Auraria. The success of the Auraria Lodge inspired new lodges in Golden City, Nevadaville, Parkville and Gold Hill.

On June 5, 1861, the Grand Lodge of Nebraska issued a charter to Rocky Mountain Lodge No. 8 at Gold Hill. By this time Colorado Territory had been recognized by the U.S. government, and the Lodges that had been organized under the Grand Lodges of Nebraska and Kansas were transferred to the newly formed Grand Lodge of Colorado.

Golden City became Lodge No. 1, Parkville Lodge No. 2 and Gold Hill Lodge No. 3. Gold Hill was the first lodge in Boulder County. In 1867 it would be joined by Columbia Lodge No. 14 organized near the "Old Columbia" mine in what is Ward today, followed by the St. Vrain Lodge No. 23 in 1873, and the Boulder Lodge No. 45 in 1881. Sometime in 1865 or 1866 a Lodge organized in Valmont east of Boulder. In

1868 when the Columbia Lodge petitioned to move from Columbia to Boulder, the Valmont Lodge dissolved and most members joined Columbia Lodge No. 14.

In 1907, Dr. Henly Wheaton Allen, one of the early members of the Columbia Lodge wrote down his recollections of what it was like to organize a Lodge in the developing communities of Boulder County and as importantly, what it was like to live in the area back then.

> "One of the striking differences in society between then (1861) and now (1907), is this, from 1860 to 1870 we had in Boulder county both a Vigilance committee and an organization called The Regulators. These two bodies did not always cultivate loving relations with each other. The purpose and work of these secret organizations is sufficiently evident to a western man without comment. It so happened that our fraternity was hereby somewhat divided. There were some things done very likely, which had better not have been done; there were some cases of capital punishment, and other chastisement inflicted, of which the law was kept in ignorance. Such things seem almost inevitable in a country so far from a settled civilization as Colorado was at that time. Perhaps you can yourselves more profitably fill up the hiatuses, I have hinted at, than for me to reproduce what is very unpleasant in memory, or anywhere else. ...
>
> An old time Mason, one of the earliest settlers in our country, told me only a few days ago, that for a long time after he came to Colorado, he dare not recognize any sign or token offered by a member of our order with whom he was not fairly well acquainted. Such a recognition was almost sure to expose him to imposition, swindle or robbery. I speak the more freely along this line, because I myself, had a very similar experience. ...
>
> Columbia Lodge room has been moved about as often as our Grand Master's remains. From Jan 3rd, 1867 till after Oct 8th, 1868, it was in the second story of Haswell & Henry's log store building, near the point where the two gulches unite, about a half mile down from "Old Columbia" (a mine). As near as I can remember the room was 20 x 30, possibly 40 feet. Flattened logs well chinked and mudded, in those days made a very comfortable place to live, do business or hold a Masonic Lodge. Fire long since wiped out the last vestige of this building in the second burning of Ward. ...
>
> October 24th, 1868, the Lodge was brought to our city and opened upstairs in the back part of the building at the south east corner of Pearl and Twelfth streets (Broadway). I remember we used to go up a flight of stairs, outdoors at the south end of the place. Here, and in adjoining rooms to the east, variously divided and fitted with improved paraphernalia, as the lodge grew stronger, Columbia did its work, till quite recently this Temple was built, and our home has been here ever since (he is referring to the Masonic building that used to stand at 14th & Pearl that was destroyed by fire in 1945). ...
>
> The first year of the life of this lodge was full of interest. Willhelm Sommers, William A. Corson, Henry Green, A. J. Stanton, W. C. Slater, A. E. Berger, E. P. McClure, H. B. Slaughter, George D. Cook and W. R. Blore all have left traces of their life work on the map of Boulder County. To attend Lodge these men went to Ward from Little Thompson, Gold Hill, Boulder and other places a distance varying from eight to forty miles. While the officers and members of

the Lodge traveled to Ward from Central City, Gold Dirt, Boulder, St. Vrain, Lower Boulder, Valmont, Coal Creek, Boulder City and other places at even greater distances. I well remember how David H. Nichols, David Parlin, T. J. Jones of Valmont and myself (Dr. Henley W. Allen) used often to start up to Ward after dinner, going by the ridge road from Gold Hill, or by the mouth of Left Hand Creek, we would arrive at A. A. Brookfield's hotel in time for such a meal as only Mrs. (Emma) Brookfield could prepare; thence without waiting for time we repaired to the Lodge room for work; generally remaining there till past low twelve, we returned to Brookfield's for a little sleep. In the morning after breakfast we hitched up, and drove home, arriving about noon. So that you can see it cost us the most of two days time, besides about five dollars in cash to attend the Lodge. More than all this, do not forget the roads through the mountains were new, and consequently very different from what they are now; to illustrate this, permit me to say I surveyed the trail from Black Hawk down to Middle Boulder Creek, and thence to Boulder City for James A. Maxwell, the father of Brother James P. Maxwell, who was then about to start a saw mill at the junction of the main Boulder (creek) with four mile creek, now called Orodell. There was no road opened up Boulder Creek to that point, but lumber and shingles were freighted over the "Gordon McHenry" road, a journey dangerous to both life and limb. What do you think of attending Lodge under such conditions? ...

In those early days Brother A. J. Macky established an enviable reputation as a first class carpenter, he built the first frame house erected in Boulder, and served successively as County Treasurer, Clerk of the District Court, and Post Master for many years. ...

Time would fail me to speak of the transportation used by all of us in coming to this country before the advent of the Union Pacific in 1868 (which only came as far as Cheyenne). Some came with cows yoked as oxen, some by bull train, some by horse or mule train, many walked and pushed a hand cart, a very few could pay the $300 price for a seat five days and nights in a crowded overland stage coach. ...

Many of these Brethren were for many years my most intimate friends. We endured the hardships of a frontier life together. We built up our homes, reared our families, and all together joined hands in laying the foundations of a new community. Of the handful of those early pioneers, there are left only myself and very few others."

Thank you for your attention,

H. W. Allen

Introduction Sources:

Carnegie Library, Clubs & Organizations Collection, 790 Box 2, Masons. "100th Anniversary, Grand Lodge, A.F. & A.M. of Colorado, Leon H Snyder, Grand Master.

Carnegie Library, Clubs & Organizations Collection, 790 Box 2, Masons. "Early History of Masonry in Northern Colorado" by Dr. H W Allen, M.A., Columbia Lodge No. 14, 1907.

Boulder Pioneers

Appearing in the Early Records of Columbia Lodge No. 14

The men, women and organizations who appear on this list are those who have settled in Boulder County, Colorado Territory prior to statehood in 1876. The names that appear with an asterisk are those for whom dates cannot be ascertained from these records.

Ackerman
Columbia Lodge No. 14 Minute Book Vol 1, 1867–1873

Adams
Columbia Lodge No. 14 Minute Book Vol 2, 1873–1879

Allen, Gay S
Columbia Lodge No. 14 Minute Book Vol 1, 1867–1873
Columbia Lodge No. 14 Minute Book Vol 2, 1873–1879

Allen, Henly Wheaton
Columbia Lodge No. 14 Minute Book Vol 1, 1867–1873
Columbia Lodge No. 14 Minute Book Vol 2, 1873–1879

***Allison, W H**
Columbia Lodge No. 14 Minute Book Vol 1, 1867–1873

Ambrook, Charles
Columbia Lodge No. 14 Minute Book Vol 1, 1867–1873

Ambrose
Columbia Lodge No. 14 Minute Book Vol 2, 1873–1879

***Ames, Leeman C**
Columbia Lodge No. 14 Minute Book Vol 1, 1867–1873

Amesburg
Columbia Lodge No. 14 Minute Book Vol 2, 1873–1879

Anderson, A A
Columbia Lodge No. 14 Minute Book Vol 2, 1873–1879
Columbia Lodge No. 14 Cash Book, 1875–1884

***Anderson, Daniel C**
Columbia Lodge No. 14 Minute Book Vol 1, 1867–1873

***Anderson, David B**
Columbia Lodge No. 14 Minute Book Vol 1, 1867–1873

Anderson, Erick J
Columbia Lodge No. 14 Minute Book Vol 1, 1867–1873

Anderson, J A
Columbia Lodge No. 14 Minute Book Vol 2, 1873–1879

Anderson, J S
Columbia Lodge No. 14 Minute Book Vol 1, 1867–1873

Andrews, Elijah H
Columbia Lodge No. 14 Minute Book Vol 1, 1867–1873
Columbia Lodge No. 14 Minute Book Vol 2, 1873–1879
Columbia Lodge No. 14 Cash Book, 1875–1884

Andrews, Wilber F
Columbia Lodge No. 14 Minute Book Vol 1, 1867–1873

Applewright
Columbia Lodge No. 14 Minute Book Vol 1, 1867–1873

Arnett, Williamette
Columbia Lodge No. 14 Minute Book Vol 1, 1867–1873

Atkinson, G W
Columbia Lodge No. 14 Minute Book Vol 2, 1873–1879

Austin, Eugene
Columbia Lodge No. 14 Minute Book Vol 1, 1867–1873

Austin, Samuel B
Columbia Lodge No. 14 Minute Book Vol 1, 1867–1873
Columbia Lodge No. 14 Minute Book Vol 2, 1873–1879

Austin, Schuyler D
Columbia Lodge No. 14 Minute Book Vol 1, 1867–1873
Columbia Lodge No. 14 Cash Book, 1875–1884
Columbia Lodge No. 14 Visitors Book, 1874–1886

Bader, Nicholas E
Columbia Lodge No. 14 Minute Book Vol 1, 1867–1873

Bailey
Columbia Lodge No. 14 Minute Book Vol 1, 1867–1873

Bailey, John
Columbia Lodge No. 14 Minute Book Vol 2, 1873–1879

Bailey, John C
Columbia Lodge No. 14 Minute Book Vol 1, 1867–1873
Columbia Lodge No. 14 Minute Book Vol 2, 1873–1879

Bailey, M
Columbia Lodge No. 14 Minute Book Vol 2, 1873–1879

***Balford, Frank D**
Columbia Lodge No. 14 Minute Book Vol 1, 1867–1873

Ballinger, William H
Columbia Lodge No. 14 Minute Book Vol 1, 1867–1873

Ballou, Mrs
Columbia Lodge No. 14 Minute Book Vol 1, 1867–1873

***Banks, F B**
Columbia Lodge No. 14 Minute Book Vol 1, 1867–1873

Banning, J A
Columbia Lodge No. 14 Minute Book Vol 2, 1873–1879

Bard, Richard
Columbia Lodge No. 14 Minute Book Vol 1, 1867–1873

Barker, Mrs
Columbia Lodge No. 14 Minute Book Vol 2, 1873–1879

Barkhurst, Ira C
Columbia Lodge No. 14 Minute Book Vol 1, 1867–1873

Barney, Royal Sigbert
Columbia Lodge No. 14 Minute Book Vol 1, 1867–1873
Columbia Lodge No. 14 Minute Book Vol 2, 1873–1879
Columbia Lodge No. 14 Cash Book, 1875–1884

Barney, William M
Columbia Lodge No. 14 Minute Book Vol 1, 1867–1873
Columbia Lodge No. 14 Minute Book Vol 2, 1873–1879
Columbia Lodge No. 14 Cash Book, 1875–1884

Barnhurst, George
Columbia Lodge No. 14 Minute Book Vol 2, 1873–1879

***Barrowman, William**
Columbia Lodge No. 14 Minute Book Vol 1, 1867–1873

***Bartels, Henry**
Columbia Lodge No. 14 Minute Book Vol 1, 1867–1873

Barter
Columbia Lodge No. 14 Minute Book Vol 1, 1867–1873

Barter, William
Columbia Lodge No. 14 Minute Book Vol 2, 1873–1879

Baum, Henry M
Columbia Lodge No. 14 Minute Book Vol 1, 1867–1873
Columbia Lodge No. 14 Minute Book Vol 2, 1873–1879
Columbia Lodge No. 14 Cash Book, 1875–1884

Baxter, William
Columbia Lodge No. 14 Minute Book Vol 2, 1873–1879

Belcher, Freeman
Columbia Lodge No. 14 Minute Book Vol 1, 1867–1873
Columbia Lodge No. 14 Minute Book Vol 2, 1873–1879

Belford
Columbia Lodge No. 14 Minute Book Vol 2, 1873–1879

Bently, W G
Columbia Lodge No. 14 Minute Book Vol 2, 1873–1879

Berdell, Theodore
Columbia Lodge No. 14 Minute Book Vol 2, 1873–1879

Berger, Andrew E
Columbia Lodge No. 14 Minute Book Vol 1, 1867–1873
Columbia Lodge No. 14 Cash Book, 1875–1884

Beveridge, James
Columbia Lodge No. 14 Minute Book Vol 1, 1867–1873
Columbia Lodge No. 14 Minute Book Vol 2, 1873–1879
Columbia Lodge No. 14 Cash Book, 1875–1884

Bigelow
Columbia Lodge No. 14 Minute Book Vol 2, 1873–1879

Bngham, Henry
Columbia Lodge No. 14 Minute Book Vol 2, 1873–1879

Bixby & Wilder
Columbia Lodge No. 14 Minute Book Vol 2, 1873–1879

Bixby, Amos
Columbia Lodge No. 14 Minute Book Vol 1, 1867–1873

Black, Harry E
Columbia Lodge No. 14 Minute Book Vol 1, 1867–1873

Blair, Charles H
Columbia Lodge No. 14 Minute Book Vol 1, 1867–1873

Blore, William R
Columbia Lodge No. 14 Minute Book Vol 1, 1867–1873

Bock, David
Columbia Lodge No. 14 Minute Book Vol 1, 1867–1873
Columbia Lodge No. 14 Minute Book Vol 2, 1873–1879
Columbia Lodge No. 14 Cash Book, 1875–1884

Bock, Mrs Malinda
Columbia Lodge No. 14 Minute Book Vol 1, 1867–1873
Columbia Lodge No. 14 Minute Book Vol 2, 1873–1879

Bosworth, R W
Columbia Lodge No. 14 Minute Book Vol 1, 1867–1873
Columbia Lodge No. 14 Minute Book Vol 2, 1873–1879

Boulder Chapter No. 7
Columbia Lodge No. 14 Minute Book Vol 2, 1873–1879
Columbia Lodge No. 14 Cash Book, 1875–1884

Boulder House
Columbia Lodge No. 14 Minute Book Vol 1, 1867–1873

Boulder News
Columbia Lodge No. 14 Minute Book Vol 2, 1873–1879

Boylan, John
Columbia Lodge No. 14 Minute Book Vol 1, 1867–1873

***Bradfield, Jack**
Columbia Lodge No. 14 Minute Book Vol 1, 1867–1873

Bradley
Columbia Lodge No. 14 Minute Book Vol 2, 1873–1879

Bradley & McClure
Columbia Lodge No. 14 Minute Book Vol 2, 1873–1879

Bradstreet
Columbia Lodge No. 14 Minute Book Vol 1, 1867–1873

Brainard, Thomas C
Columbia Lodge No. 14 Minute Book Vol 2, 1873–1879

Brainard, Thomas D
Columbia Lodge No. 14 Minute Book Vol 1, 1867–1873
Columbia Lodge No. 14 Cash Book, 1875–1884

Breath, Samuel M
Columbia Lodge No. 14 Minute Book Vol 1, 1867–1873
Columbia Lodge No. 14 Minute Book Vol 2, 1873–1879

Briggs, David
Columbia Lodge No. 14 Minute Book Vol 1, 1867–1873

Bristal, B J
Columbia Lodge No. 14 Minute Book Vol 1, 1867–1873

Brodie, John
Columbia Lodge No. 14 Minute Book Vol 1, 1867–1873
Columbia Lodge No. 14 Minute Book Vol 2, 1873–1879
Columbia Lodge No. 14 Cash Book, 1875–1884

Brookfield, Alfred A
Columbia Lodge No. 14 Minute Book Vol 1, 1867–1873
Columbia Lodge No. 14 Cash Book, 1875–1884

***Brown, Thomas J**
Columbia Lodge No. 14 Minute Book Vol 1, 1867–1873

Brush
Columbia Lodge No. 14 Minute Book Vol 1, 1867–1873

Buchanan, George W
Columbia Lodge No. 14 Minute Book Vol 1, 1867–1873
Columbia Lodge No. 14 Cash Book, 1875–1884

Budd, Sylvanus
Columbia Lodge No. 14 Minute Book Vol 1, 1867–1873
Columbia Lodge No. 14 Minute Book Vol 2, 1873–1879
Columbia Lodge No. 14 Cash Book, 1875–1884

Bunn, David
Columbia Lodge No. 14 Minute Book Vol 1, 1867–1873
Columbia Lodge No. 14 Minute Book Vol 2, 1873–1879
Columbia Lodge No. 14 Cash Book, 1875–1884

Buoss
Columbia Lodge No. 14 Minute Book Vol 1, 1867–1873

Bush, Arthur W
Columbia Lodge No. 14 Minute Book Vol 1, 1867–1873
Columbia Lodge No. 14 Minute Book Vol 2, 1873–1879
Columbia Lodge No. 14 Cash Book, 1875–1884

Buttles, John F
Columbia Lodge No. 14 Minute Book Vol 1, 1867–1873
Columbia Lodge No. 14 Cash Book, 1875–1884

Campbell, John H
Columbia Lodge No. 14 Minute Book Vol 1, 1867–1873

Campbell, John L
Columbia Lodge No. 14 Minute Book Vol 1, 1867–1873
Columbia Lodge No. 14 Minute Book Vol 2, 1873–1879
Columbia Lodge No. 14 Cash Book, 1875–1884

Campbell, L B
Columbia Lodge No. 14 Cash Book, 1875–1884

Campbell, Sanford B
Columbia Lodge No. 14 Minute Book Vol 1, 1867–1873
Columbia Lodge No. 14 Minute Book Vol 2, 1873–1879
Columbia Lodge No. 14 Cash Book, 1875–1884

Carmack, Thomas K
Columbia Lodge No. 14 Minute Book Vol 2, 1873–1879
Columbia Lodge No. 14 Visitors Book, 1874–1886

Canfield
Columbia Lodge No. 14 Minute Book Vol 1, 1867–1873

***Carmack, Thomas K**
Columbia Lodge No. 14 Minute Book Vol 1, 1867–1873

Carnahan, John
Columbia Lodge No. 14 Minute Book Vol 1, 1867–1873

Carrigan, D J
Columbia Lodge No. 14 Minute Book Vol 2, 1873–1879

Carrington, D J
Columbia Lodge No. 14 Minute Book Vol 2, 1873–1879

Carter, George W
Columbia Lodge No. 14 Minute Book Vol 1, 1867–1873
Columbia Lodge No. 14 Minute Book Vol 2, 1873–1879
Columbia Lodge No. 14 Cash Book, 1875–1884

***Chambers, John S**
Columbia Lodge No. 14 Minute Book Vol 1, 1867–1873

Champion, H W
Columbia Lodge No. 14 Minute Book Vol 1, 1867–1873
Columbia Lodge No. 14 Minute Book Vol 2, 1873–1879

Chapman, Joshua E
Columbia Lodge No. 14 Minute Book Vol 1, 1867–1873

Chase, George F
Columbia Lodge No. 14 Minute Book Vol 1, 1867–1873
Columbia Lodge No. 14 Minute Book Vol 2, 1873–1879
Columbia Lodge No. 14 Cash Book, 1875–1884

Clark, Dr. G A
Columbia Lodge No. 14 Minute Book Vol 1, 1867–1873
Columbia Lodge No. 14 Minute Book Vol 2, 1873–1879

Clawson, David
Columbia Lodge No. 14 Minute Book Vol 1, 1867–1873

Clayton, G W
Columbia Lodge No. 14 Minute Book Vol 1, 1867–1873

Cloud, E
Columbia Lodge No. 14 Minute Book Vol 1, 1867–1873

Clow, David
Columbia Lodge No. 14 Minute Book Vol 1, 1867–1873
Columbia Lodge No. 14 Minute Book Vol 2, 1873–1879

Clow, Richard
Columbia Lodge No. 14 Minute Book Vol 1, 1867–1873
Columbia Lodge No. 14 Minute Book Vol 2, 1873–1879
Columbia Lodge No. 14 Cash Book, 1875–1884
Columbia Lodge No. 14 Visitors Book, 1874–1886

Cluff, Chester P
Columbia Lodge No. 14 Minute Book Vol 1, 1867–1873
Columbia Lodge No. 14 Minute Book Vol 2, 1873–1879
Columbia Lodge No. 14 Cash Book, 1875–1884

Cluster, John A
Columbia Lodge No. 14 Minute Book Vol 1, 1867–1873

Cobb
Columbia Lodge No. 14 Minute Book Vol 1, 1867–1873

Coffman, E J
Columbia Lodge No. 14 Minute Book Vol 1, 1867–1873

Coffman, Enoch J
Columbia Lodge No. 14 Minute Book Vol 1, 1867–1873

Coin, Mrs J H
Columbia Lodge No. 14 Minute Book Vol 2, 1873–1879

Comb
Columbia Lodge No. 14 Minute Book Vol 2, 1873–1879

Conroy, Pierre
Columbia Lodge No. 14 Minute Book Vol 2, 1873–1879
Columbia Lodge No. 14 Cash Book, 1875–1884

***Conwell**
Columbia Lodge No. 14 Minute Book Vol 1, 1867–1873

Cook, George D
Columbia Lodge No. 14 Minute Book Vol 1, 1867–1873
Columbia Lodge No. 14 Minute Book Vol 2, 1873–1879
Columbia Lodge No. 14 Visitors Book, 1874–1886

Cook, William
Columbia Lodge No. 14 Minute Book Vol 1, 1867–1873

Corning, George C
Columbia Lodge No. 14 Minute Book Vol 1, 1867–1873
Columbia Lodge No. 14 Minute Book Vol 2, 1873–1879
Columbia Lodge No. 14 Cash Book, 1875–1884

Corson, William A
Columbia Lodge No. 14 Minute Book Vol 1, 1867–1873
Columbia Lodge No. 14 Minute Book Vol 2, 1873–1879
Columbia Lodge No. 14 Cash Book, 1875–1884

Cosgrove, John
Columbia Lodge No. 14 Minute Book Vol 2, 1873–1879

Coulborn, Joseph
Columbia Lodge No. 14 Minute Book Vol 2, 1873–1879
Columbia Lodge No. 14 Cash Book, 1875–1884

Coulson, C M
Columbia Lodge No. 14 Minute Book Vol 2, 1873–1879

Coulson, William Wallace
Columbia Lodge No. 14 Minute Book Vol 1, 1867–1873

Crosby, A B
Columbia Lodge No. 14 Minute Book Vol 1, 1867–1873

Crosby, Charles
Columbia Lodge No. 14 Minute Book Vol 1, 1867–1873

Crow, Richard
Columbia Lodge No. 14 Minute Book Vol 1, 1867–1873
Columbia Lodge No. 14 Minute Book Vol 2, 1873–1879
Columbia Lodge No. 14 Cash Book, 1875–1884

Curtis, W D
Columbia Lodge No. 14 Minute Book Vol 2, 1873–1879

Cullacott, John J F
Columbia Lodge No. 14 Minute Book Vol 1, 1867–1873

Cummins, Isaac
Columbia Lodge No. 14 Minute Book Vol 1, 1867–1873

Dabney & Russell
Columbia Lodge No. 14 Minute Book Vol 2, 1873–1879

Dabney, Charles
Columbia Lodge No. 14 Minute Book Vol 1, 1867–1873
Columbia Lodge No. 14 Minute Book Vol 2, 1873–1879

Daily & Smart
Columbia Lodge No. 14 Minute Book Vol 2, 1873–1879

Danforth, W T
Columbia Lodge No. 14 Minute Book Vol 1, 1867–1873
Columbia Lodge No. 14 Minute Book Vol 2, 1873–1879

***Davey, Joseph R J**
Columbia Lodge No. 14 Minute Book Vol 1, 1867–1873

***Davidson, Charles B**
Columbia Lodge No. 14 Minute Book Vol 1, 1867–1873

***Davidson, W__**
Columbia Lodge No. 14 Minute Book Vol 1, 1867–1873

Davis, B Y
Columbia Lodge No. 14 Minute Book Vol 2, 1873–1879

Davis, Benj
Columbia Lodge No. 14 Minute Book Vol 1, 1867–1873

Davis, David W
Columbia Lodge No. 14 Minute Book Vol 1, 1867–1873
Columbia Lodge No. 14 Minute Book Vol 2, 1873–1879

Davis, John M
Columbia Lodge No. 14 Minute Book Vol 1, 1867–1873
Columbia Lodge No. 14 Minute Book Vol 2, 1873–1879
Columbia Lodge No. 14 Cash Book, 1875–1884

Davis, Thomas
Columbia Lodge No. 14 Minute Book Vol 2, 1873–1879

Dawley, James M
Columbia Lodge No. 14 Minute Book Vol 1, 1867–1873
Columbia Lodge No. 14 Minute Book Vol 2, 1873–1879

Deardoff, Cyrus
Columbia Lodge No. 14 Minute Book Vol 1, 1867–1873

***Deitz, Henry**
Columbia Lodge No. 14 Minute Book Vol 1, 1867–1873

Denham, Thomas
Columbia Lodge No. 14 Minute Book Vol 2, 1873–1879
Columbia Lodge No. 14 Visitors Book, 1874–1886

Develine, Edward W
Columbia Lodge No. 14 Minute Book Vol 2, 1873–1879
Columbia Lodge No. 14 Visitors Book, 1874–1886

Dexter, W W
Columbia Lodge No. 14 Minute Book Vol 2, 1873–1879

Deyo, R H
Columbia Lodge No. 14 Minute Book Vol 1, 1867–1873
Columbia Lodge No. 14 Minute Book Vol 2, 1873–1879
Columbia Lodge No. 14 Cash Book, 1875–1884

Dickens, William H
Columbia Lodge No. 14 Minute Book Vol 1, 1867–1873

Dickerson, R E
Columbia Lodge No. 14 Visitors Book, 1874–1886

Dickinson
Columbia Lodge No. 14 Minute Book Vol 2, 1873–1879

Dickson, Lewis H
Columbia Lodge No. 14 Minute Book Vol 1, 1867–1873

Dimick, Erastus H
Columbia Lodge No. 14 Minute Book Vol 1, 1867–1873
Columbia Lodge No. 14 Minute Book Vol 2, 1873–1879
Columbia Lodge No. 14 Cash Book, 1875–1884

Dodge, Horace O
Columbia Lodge No. 14 Minute Book Vol 1, 1867–1873
Columbia Lodge No. 14 Minute Book Vol 2, 1873–1879

Dodge, Mrs Horace O
Columbia Lodge No. 14 Minute Book Vol 2, 1873–1879

Donald, William
Columbia Lodge No. 14 Minute Book Vol 2, 1873–1879

Donaldson, Charles B
Columbia Lodge No. 14 Minute Book Vol 1, 1867–1873
Columbia Lodge No. 14 Minute Book Vol 2, 1873–1879
Columbia Lodge No. 14 Cash Book, 1875–1884

Douglas, J & Bro
Columbia Lodge No. 14 Minute Book Vol 1, 1867–1873

Dow, J E
Columbia Lodge No. 14 Minute Book Vol 1, 1867–1873
Columbia Lodge No. 14 Minute Book Vol 2, 1873–1879
Columbia Lodge No. 14 Visitors Book, 1874–1886

***Dowell, C C**
Columbia Lodge No. 14 Minute Book Vol 1, 1867–1873

Downer, Benjamin F
Columbia Lodge No. 14 Minute Book Vol 1, 1867–1873

***Downer, S J**
Columbia Lodge No. 14 Minute Book Vol 1, 1867–1873

Drew
Columbia Lodge No. 14 Minute Book Vol 1, 1867–1873

***Drumm, Henry**
Columbia Lodge No. 14 Minute Book Vol 1, 1867–1873

Dunagan, Elijah
Columbia Lodge No. 14 Minute Book Vol 1, 1867–1873
Columbia Lodge No. 14 Minute Book Vol 2, 1873–1879
Columbia Lodge No. 14 Visitors Book, 1874–1886

Dunagan, Jackson J
Columbia Lodge No. 14 Minute Book Vol 1, 1867–1873
Columbia Lodge No. 14 Minute Book Vol 2, 1873–1879

Dunn, James
Columbia Lodge No. 14 Minute Book Vol 1, 1867–1873
Columbia Lodge No. 14 Minute Book Vol 2, 1873–1879
Columbia Lodge No. 14 Cash Book, 1875–1884

***Earhart, W R**
Columbia Lodge No. 14 Minute Book Vol 1, 1867–1873

Eldred
Columbia Lodge No. 14 Minute Book Vol 2, 1873–1879

Ellet
Columbia Lodge No. 14 Minute Book Vol 2, 1873–1879

Ellingham, Charles E
Columbia Lodge No. 14 Minute Book Vol 2, 1873–1879

Ellingham, John J
Columbia Lodge No. 14 Minute Book Vol 1, 1867–1873
Columbia Lodge No. 14 Minute Book Vol 2, 1873–1879
Columbia Lodge No. 14 Cash Book, 1875–1884

Ellingham, Robert
Columbia Lodge No. 14 Minute Book Vol 1, 1867–1873
Columbia Lodge No. 14 Minute Book Vol 2, 1873–1879

Ellis, Adelbert L
Columbia Lodge No. 14 Minute Book Vol 1, 1867–1873
Columbia Lodge No. 14 Minute Book Vol 2, 1873–1879
Columbia Lodge No. 14 Cash Book, 1875–1884

Emrick, H J
Columbia Lodge No. 14 Minute Book Vol 1, 1867–1873
Columbia Lodge No. 14 Minute Book Vol 2, 1873–1879

England, G A
Columbia Lodge No. 14 Minute Book Vol 2, 1873–1879

Esmond, Bart
Columbia Lodge No. 14 Minute Book Vol 1, 1867–1873

Euler, child
Columbia Lodge No. 14 Minute Book Vol 2, 1873–1879

Euler, Mr.
Columbia Lodge No. 14 Minute Book Vol 2, 1873–1879

Fairhurst, William
Columbia Lodge No. 14 Minute Book Vol 1, 1867–1873
Columbia Lodge No. 14 Visitors Book, 1874–1886

Farwell
Columbia Lodge No. 14 Minute Book Vol 2, 1873–1879

Foote, James B
Columbia Lodge No. 14 Minute Book Vol 2, 1873–1879

French, S M
Columbia Lodge No. 14 Minute Book Vol 1, 1867–1873
Columbia Lodge No. 14 Minute Book Vol 2, 1873–1879
Columbia Lodge No. 14 Visitors Book, 1874–1886

Fullerton, Mrs Mary S
Columbia Lodge No. 14 Minute Book Vol 2, 1873–1879

Fullerton, Robert E
Columbia Lodge No. 14 Minute Book Vol 2, 1873–1879

Gilbert, Clark W
Columbia Lodge No. 14 Minute Book Vol 1, 1867–1873
Columbia Lodge No. 14 Minute Book Vol 2, 1873–1879
Columbia Lodge No. 14 Cash Book, 1875–1884

Gillespie, Henry B
Columbia Lodge No. 14 Minute Book Vol 2, 1873–1879

***Gilliam, W H**
Columbia Lodge No. 14 Minute Book Vol 1, 1867–1873

Gillman, Walter
Columbia Lodge No. 14 Minute Book Vol 1, 1867–1873

Godwin, H H
Columbia Lodge No. 14 Minute Book Vol 1, 1867–1873

Goodall, Dania
Columbia Lodge No. 14 Minute Book Vol 1, 1867–1873

Goodall, David J
Columbia Lodge No. 14 Minute Book Vol 1, 1867–1873
Columbia Lodge No. 14 Minute Book Vol 2, 1873–1879
Columbia Lodge No. 14 Cash Book, 1875–1884

Goodwin, Harrison
Columbia Lodge No. 14 Minute Book Vol 1, 1867–1873

***Goodwin, M W**
Columbia Lodge No. 14 Minute Book Vol 1, 1867–1873

Gorman, Michael
Columbia Lodge No. 14 Minute Book Vol 2, 1873–1879
Columbia Lodge No. 14 Cash Book, 1875–1884

Goss, Abel
Columbia Lodge No. 14 Minute Book Vol 1, 1867–1873
Columbia Lodge No. 14 Minute Book Vol 2, 1873–1879

Goss, P D
Columbia Lodge No. 14 Minute Book Vol 1, 1867–1873
Columbia Lodge No. 14 Minute Book Vol 2, 1873–1879

Graham, George W
Columbia Lodge No. 14 Minute Book Vol 1, 1867–1873

Green, Henry
Columbia Lodge No. 14 Minute Book Vol 1, 1867–1873
Columbia Lodge No. 14 Minute Book Vol 2, 1873–1879
Columbia Lodge No. 14 Cash Book, 1875–1884

Green, Oscar Fitz Allen
Columbia Lodge No. 14 Visitors Book, 1874–1886

Green, William H
Columbia Lodge No. 14 Minute Book Vol 2, 1873–1879

Griffith, J S
Columbia Lodge No. 14 Minute Book Vol 1, 1867–1873
Columbia Lodge No. 14 Minute Book Vol 2, 1873–1879

Griffith, Joseph F
Columbia Lodge No. 14 Minute Book Vol 1, 1867–1873
Columbia Lodge No. 14 Minute Book Vol 2, 1873–1879

Groesbeck, John B
Columbia Lodge No. 14 Minute Book Vol 1, 1867–1873
Columbia Lodge No. 14 Minute Book Vol 2, 1873–1879
Columbia Lodge No. 14 Cash Book, 1875–1884

***Grund, John C**
Columbia Lodge No. 14 Minute Book Vol 1, 1867–1873

Guin, John T
Columbia Lodge No. 14 Minute Book Vol 1, 1867–1873

Guin, Mrs Spencer
Columbia Lodge No. 14 Minute Book Vol 2, 1873–1879

Guin, Spencer
Columbia Lodge No. 14 Minute Book Vol 1, 1867–1873
Columbia Lodge No. 14 Minute Book Vol 2, 1873–1879

Guin, Thomas J
Columbia Lodge No. 14 Minute Book Vol 1, 1867–1873

Gutterson, Charles L
Columbia Lodge No. 14 Minute Book Vol 1, 1867–1873
Columbia Lodge No. 14 Minute Book Vol 2, 1873–1879
Columbia Lodge No. 14 Cash Book, 1875–1884

Guyage, Julius
Columbia Lodge No. 14 Minute Book Vol 2, 1873–1879
Columbia Lodge No. 14 Cash Book, 1875–1884

Hall, T A
Columbia Lodge No. 14 Minute Book Vol 2, 1873–1879

Halverson, Christian
Columbia Lodge No. 14 Minute Book Vol 1, 1867–1873
Columbia Lodge No. 14 Minute Book Vol 2, 1873–1879
Columbia Lodge No. 14 Cash Book, 1875–1884

Hamblin, Oliver T
Columbia Lodge No. 14 Minute Book Vol 1, 1867–1873
Columbia Lodge No. 14 Minute Book Vol 2, 1873–1879

***Hanken, M F**
Columbia Lodge No. 14 Minute Book Vol 1, 1867–1873

Harden, Joseph
Columbia Lodge No. 14 Minute Book Vol 2, 1873–1879

Harker, Oliver H
Columbia Lodge No. 14 Minute Book Vol 2, 1873–1879

Harmon, George D
Columbia Lodge No. 14 Minute Book Vol 1, 1867–1873
Columbia Lodge No. 14 Minute Book Vol 2, 1873–1879
Columbia Lodge No. 14 Cash Book, 1875–1884

***Harmon, M D**
Columbia Lodge No. 14 Minute Book Vol 1, 1867–1873

Harney, Chris
Columbia Lodge No. 14 Cash Book, 1875–1884

Harrets, Myers B, see Harris, Myers B
Columbia Lodge No. 14 Minute Book Vol 1, 1867–1873

Harris & Woodward
Columbia Lodge No. 14 Minute Book Vol 1, 1867–1873

Harris, Addison W
Columbia Lodge No. 14 Minute Book Vol 1, 1867–1873
Columbia Lodge No. 14 Minute Book Vol 2, 1873–1879
Columbia Lodge No. 14 Cash Book, 1875–1884

Harris, John
Columbia Lodge No. 14 Minute Book Vol 1, 1867–1873
Columbia Lodge No. 14 Minute Book Vol 2, 1873–1879

Harris, Myers B
Columbia Lodge No. 14 Minute Book Vol 2, 1873–1879
Columbia Lodge No. 14 Cash Book, 1875–1884

Harrub, J M
Columbia Lodge No. 14 Minute Book Vol 2, 1873–1879

Hartley, Jessee
Columbia Lodge No. 14 Minute Book Vol 2, 1873–1879

Harvey, Christopher
Columbia Lodge No. 14 Minute Book Vol 1, 1867–1873
Columbia Lodge No. 14 Minute Book Vol 2, 1873–1879
Columbia Lodge No. 14 Cash Book, 1875–1884

Harvey, Mrs
Columbia Lodge No. 14 Minute Book Vol 1, 1867–1873

Haskins
Columbia Lodge No. 14 Minute Book Vol 2, 1873–1879

Haswell & Co
Columbia Lodge No. 14 Minute Book Vol 1, 1867–1873

Haswell & Henry
Columbia Lodge No. 14 Minute Book Vol 1, 1867–1873

Haswell, Theodore
Columbia Lodge No. 14 Minute Book Vol 1, 1867–1873
Columbia Lodge No. 14 Minute Book Vol 2, 1873–1879

Haswell, William
Columbia Lodge No. 14 Minute Book Vol 1, 1867–1873

Hathaway, Mark
Columbia Lodge No. 14 Minute Book Vol 1, 1867–1873
Columbia Lodge No. 14 Minute Book Vol 2, 1873–1879
Columbia Lodge No. 14 Cash Book, 1875–1884

Hawkins
Columbia Lodge No. 14 Minute Book Vol 2, 1873–1879

Hayden
Columbia Lodge No. 14 Cash Book, 1875–1884

Hayden, Joseph
Columbia Lodge No. 14 Minute Book Vol 2, 1873–1879

Hayden, Nathaniel
Columbia Lodge No. 14 Minute Book Vol 2, 1873–1879

***Hayward, D P**
Columbia Lodge No. 14 Minute Book Vol 1, 1867–1873

Heath, N H
Columbia Lodge No. 14 Minute Book Vol 1, 1867–1873

Henry & Metcalf
Columbia Lodge No. 14 Minute Book Vol 2, 1873–1879

Henry, Mrs
Columbia Lodge No. 14 Minute Book Vol 1, 1867–1873

Henry, Mrs Katie
Columbia Lodge No. 14 Minute Book Vol 1, 1867–1873

Henry, Oren H
Columbia Lodge No. 14 Minute Book Vol 1, 1867–1873
Columbia Lodge No. 14 Minute Book Vol 2, 1873–1879
Columbia Lodge No. 14 Cash Book, 1875–1884

Henry, Ormal E
Columbia Lodge No. 14 Minute Book Vol 1, 1867–1873
Columbia Lodge No. 14 Minute Book Vol 2, 1873–1879
Columbia Lodge No. 14 Cash Book, 1875–1884

Herman, Max
Columbia Lodge No. 14 Minute Book Vol 2, 1873–1879

Hernandez, Anthony
Columbia Lodge No. 14 Minute Book Vol 1, 1867–1873
Columbia Lodge No. 14 Minute Book Vol 2, 1873–1879
Columbia Lodge No. 14 Visitors Book, 1874–1886

***Herzinger**
Columbia Lodge No. 14 Minute Book Vol 1, 1867–1873

Hevelin, Benjamin
Columbia Lodge No. 14 Minute Book Vol 1, 1867–1873

Hewes, John M
Columbia Lodge No. 14 Minute Book Vol 1, 1867–1873

Hicks, John P
Columbia Lodge No. 14 Minute Book Vol 2, 1873–1879

Hill, Thomas J
Columbia Lodge No. 14 Minute Book Vol 1, 1867–1873
Columbia Lodge No. 14 Minute Book Vol 2, 1873–1879

Hinman, Porter M
Columbia Lodge No. 14 Minute Book Vol 1, 1867–1873

Hockaday, Charles N
Columbia Lodge No. 14 Minute Book Vol 1, 1867–1873
Columbia Lodge No. 14 Minute Book Vol 2, 1873–1879
Columbia Lodge No. 14 Cash Book, 1875–1884

Holly
Columbia Lodge No. 14 Minute Book Vol 1, 1867–1873

Holstein, Mark B
Columbia Lodge No. 14 Minute Book Vol 1, 1867–1873

Holstein, Moses
Columbia Lodge No. 14 Minute Book Vol 1, 1867–1873

***Holt**
Columbia Lodge No. 14 Minute Book Vol 1, 1867–1873

Honstine
Columbia Lodge No. 14 Minute Book Vol 1, 1867–1873

Hopkins, David L
Columbia Lodge No. 14 Minute Book Vol 1, 1867–1873
Columbia Lodge No. 14 Minute Book Vol 2, 1873–1879
Columbia Lodge No. 14 Cash Book, 1875–1884

Horner, John W
Columbia Lodge No. 14 Minute Book Vol 1, 1867–1873

Housel, Peter M
Columbia Lodge No. 14 Minute Book Vol 1, 1867–1873

Howard, Norman R
Columbia Lodge No. 14 Minute Book Vol 1, 1867–1873

Howell, William R
Columbia Lodge No. 14 Minute Book Vol 1, 1867–1873
Columbia Lodge No. 14 Minute Book Vol 2, 1873–1879
Columbia Lodge No. 14 Cash Book, 1875–1884

Howse, W J L
Columbia Lodge No. 14 Minute Book Vol 1, 1867–1873
Columbia Lodge No. 14 Minute Book Vol 2, 1873–1879
Columbia Lodge No. 14 Cash Book, 1875–1884

Hubbard, Horace W
Columbia Lodge No. 14 Minute Book Vol 1, 1867–1873

Hubbard, Mrs
Columbia Lodge No. 14 Minute Book Vol 2, 1873–1879

Hubbard, Mrs E
Columbia Lodge No. 14 Minute Book Vol 1, 1867–1873

Hubbard, Mrs S J
Columbia Lodge No. 14 Minute Book Vol 1, 1867–1873

Hunt, Fred A
Columbia Lodge No. 14 Minute Book Vol 1, 1867–1873
Columbia Lodge No. 14 Minute Book Vol 2, 1873–1879
Columbia Lodge No. 14 Cash Book, 1875–1884

Hunt, William A
Columbia Lodge No. 14 Minute Book Vol 2, 1873–1879
Columbia Lodge No. 14 Cash Book, 1875–1884

Hunter, Andrew
Columbia Lodge No. 14 Minute Book Vol 2, 1873–1879

Hupper, E A
Columbia Lodge No. 14 Minute Book Vol 1, 1867–1873

Hyder, David
Columbia Lodge No. 14 Minute Book Vol 2, 1873–1879

Inbody
Columbia Lodge No. 14 Minute Book Vol 2, 1873–1879

Insurance Company of North America
Columbia Lodge No. 14 Minute Book Vol 2, 1873–1879

***Irwin, Joseph**
Columbia Lodge No. 14 Minute Book Vol 1, 1867–1873
Columbia Lodge No. 14 Cash Book, 1875–1884

Jackson, G W
Columbia Lodge No. 14 Minute Book Vol 1, 1867–1873
Columbia Lodge No. 14 Minute Book Vol 2, 1873–1879

Jackson, John
Columbia Lodge No. 14 Minute Book Vol 1, 1867–1873
Columbia Lodge No. 14 Minute Book Vol 2, 1873–1879

Jacobs, Horatio H
Columbia Lodge No. 14 Minute Book Vol 1, 1867–1873

James, John
Columbia Lodge No. 14 Minute Book Vol 1, 1867–1873

James, T J
Columbia Lodge No. 14 Minute Book Vol 1, 1867–1873

***Janbom, C W**
Columbia Lodge No. 14 Minute Book Vol 1, 1867–1873

Jaynes
Columbia Lodge No. 14 Minute Book Vol 1, 1867–1873

***Jester, W H**
Columbia Lodge No. 14 Minute Book Vol 1, 1867–1873

Johns
Columbia Lodge No. 14 Minute Book Vol 2, 1873–1879

Johns, John H
Columbia Lodge No. 14 Minute Book Vol 1, 1867–1873
Columbia Lodge No. 14 Minute Book Vol 2, 1873–1879
Columbia Lodge No. 14 Cash Book, 1875–1884

Johns, Thomas J
Columbia Lodge No. 14 Minute Book Vol 1, 1867–1873

Johnson, Seymour
Columbia Lodge No. 14 Minute Book Vol 1, 1867–1873
Columbia Lodge No. 14 Minute Book Vol 2, 1873–1879
Columbia Lodge No. 14 Cash Book, 1875–1884

***Johnston, James J**
Columbia Lodge No. 14 Minute Book Vol 1, 1867–1873

***Johnston, U J**
Columbia Lodge No. 14 Minute Book Vol 1, 1867–1873

Jones, D E
Columbia Lodge No. 14 Minute Book Vol 1, 1867–1873

Jones, J M
Columbia Lodge No. 14 Minute Book Vol 2, 1873–1879

Jones, John
Columbia Lodge No. 14 Minute Book Vol 1, 1867–1873

Jones, Mrs
Columbia Lodge No. 14 Minute Book Vol 1, 1867–1873

Jones, Mrs S J
Columbia Lodge No. 14 Minute Book Vol 1, 1867–1873

Jones, Thomas J
Columbia Lodge No. 14 Minute Book Vol 1, 1867–1873
Columbia Lodge No. 14 Minute Book Vol 2, 1873–1879
Columbia Lodge No. 14 Cash Book, 1875–1884

Juneman, Frederick W
Columbia Lodge No. 14 Minute Book Vol 1, 1867–1873
Columbia Lodge No. 14 Minute Book Vol 2, 1873–1879
Columbia Lodge No. 14 Cash Book, 1875–1884

***K___se, _____**
Columbia Lodge No. 14 Minute Book Vol 1, 1867–1873

Kassler & Co
Columbia Lodge No. 14 Minute Book Vol 1, 1867–1873

Kassler, G W & Co
Columbia Lodge No. 14 Minute Book Vol 1, 1867–1873

Kavanaugh, A A
Columbia Lodge No. 14 Minute Book Vol 2, 1873–1879

Kellogg
Columbia Lodge No. 14 Minute Book Vol 2, 1873–1879

***Kemplor, James**
Columbia Lodge No. 14 Minute Book Vol 1, 1867–1873

Kerr, David
Columbia Lodge No. 14 Minute Book Vol 1, 1867–1873
Columbia Lodge No. 14 Minute Book Vol 2, 1873–1879
Columbia Lodge No. 14 Cash Book, 1875–1884

Kessler, Marion
Columbia Lodge No. 14 Minute Book Vol 1, 1867–1873
Columbia Lodge No. 14 Minute Book Vol 2, 1873–1879
Columbia Lodge No. 14 Cash Book, 1875–1884

King, Robert
Columbia Lodge No. 14 Minute Book Vol 1, 1867–1873
Columbia Lodge No. 14 Minute Book Vol 2, 1873–1879
Columbia Lodge No. 14 Cash Book, 1875–1884
Columbia Lodge No. 14 Visitors Book, 1874–1886

Kinney, Edward P
Columbia Lodge No. 14 Minute Book Vol 1, 1867–1873

Kiper
Columbia Lodge No. 14 Minute Book Vol 1, 1867–1873

Klein, Mrs Annie
Columbia Lodge No. 14 Minute Book Vol 2, 1873–1879

Kline, Marcus
Columbia Lodge No. 14 Minute Book Vol 1, 1867–1873
Columbia Lodge No. 14 Cash Book, 1875–1884

Knox, John
Columbia Lodge No. 14 Minute Book Vol 1, 1867–1873
Columbia Lodge No. 14 Minute Book Vol 2, 1873–1879
Columbia Lodge No. 14 Cash Book, 1875–1884

Kohler, Frederick W
Columbia Lodge No. 14 Minute Book Vol 1, 1867–1873
Columbia Lodge No. 14 Minute Book Vol 2, 1873–1879
Columbia Lodge No. 14 Cash Book, 1875–1884

***Kroll, Anson**
Columbia Lodge No. 14 Minute Book Vol 1, 1867–1873

LaPoint, George
Columbia Lodge No. 14 Minute Book Vol 1, 1867–1873
Columbia Lodge No. 14 Minute Book Vol 2, 1873–1879

Large, William Morton
Columbia Lodge No. 14 Minute Book Vol 2, 1873–1879

***Lawson, Alexander**
Columbia Lodge No. 14 Minute Book Vol 1, 1867–1873

Lawson, C C
Columbia Lodge No. 14 Minute Book Vol 1, 1867–1873

Lea, Alfred E
Columbia Lodge No. 14 Minute Book Vol 1, 1867–1873
Columbia Lodge No. 14 Minute Book Vol 2, 1873–1879
Columbia Lodge No. 14 Cash Book, 1875–1884

Lecturer, G
Columbia Lodge No. 14 Minute Book Vol 1, 1867–1873

***Lefoe, W F**
Columbia Lodge No. 14 Minute Book Vol 1, 1867–1873

Lelly, Eli
Columbia Lodge No. 14 Minute Book Vol 1, 1867–1873

Lennox, A
Columbia Lodge No. 14 Minute Book Vol 1, 1867–1873

Leonard, P A
Columbia Lodge No. 14 Minute Book Vol 2, 1873–1879

Letters
Columbia Lodge No. 14 Minute Book Vol 2, 1873–1879

Lewis, Augustus S
Columbia Lodge No. 14 Minute Book Vol 1, 1867–1873

Lewis, James
Columbia Lodge No. 14 Minute Book Vol 1, 1867–1873
Columbia Lodge No. 14 Minute Book Vol 2, 1873–1879

Leyner, Peter A
Columbia Lodge No. 14 Minute Book Vol 1, 1867–1873
Columbia Lodge No. 14 Minute Book Vol 2, 1873–1879
Columbia Lodge No. 14 Cash Book, 1875–1884

Logan, Mrs
Columbia Lodge No. 14 Minute Book Vol 1, 1867–1873

Logue
Columbia Lodge No. 14 Minute Book Vol 1, 1867–1873
Columbia Lodge No. 14 Minute Book Vol 2, 1873–1879

Logue, Wm O
Columbia Lodge No. 14 Minute Book Vol 1, 1867–1873

Longer, John
Columbia Lodge No. 14 Minute Book Vol 2, 1873–1879
Columbia Lodge No. 14 Cash Book, 1875–1884

***Luslich, James E**
Columbia Lodge No. 14 Minute Book Vol 1, 1867–1873

Luther, A O
Columbia Lodge No. 14 Minute Book Vol 2, 1873–1879

Luther, Henry E
Columbia Lodge No. 14 Minute Book Vol 2, 1873–1879

Luther, Mrs A O
Columbia Lodge No. 14 Minute Book Vol 2, 1873–1879

Lykins, David J
Columbia Lodge No. 14 Minute Book Vol 1, 1867–1873
Columbia Lodge No. 14 Minute Book Vol 2, 1873–1879

Lyons, Mrs
Columbia Lodge No. 14 Minute Book Vol 2, 1873–1879

Lytle, George
Columbia Lodge No. 14 Minute Book Vol 1, 1867–1873
Columbia Lodge No. 14 Minute Book Vol 2, 1873–1879
Columbia Lodge No. 14 Cash Book, 1875–1884

Mack, Henry
Columbia Lodge No. 14 Minute Book Vol 2, 1873–1879

Macky & Dabney Hall
Columbia Lodge No. 14 Minute Book Vol 1, 1867–1873

Macky, Andrew J
Columbia Lodge No. 14 Minute Book Vol 1, 1867–1873

***Madera, Shepherd L**
Columbia Lodge No. 14 Minute Book Vol 1, 1867–1873

***Madey**
Columbia Lodge No. 14 Minute Book Vol 1, 1867–1873

***Marck, T D**
Columbia Lodge No. 14 Minute Book Vol 1, 1867–1873

Masters, Thomas
Columbia Lodge No. 14 Minute Book Vol 2, 1873–1879

Martin, W
Columbia Lodge No. 14 Minute Book Vol 1, 1867–1873

Mason, Edward F
Columbia Lodge No. 14 Minute Book Vol 1, 1867–1873

Mathews
Columbia Lodge No. 14 Minute Book Vol 1, 1867–1873

Maxwell & Tyler
Columbia Lodge No. 14 Minute Book Vol 1, 1867–1873

Maxwell, James P
Columbia Lodge No. 14 Minute Book Vol 1, 1867–1873
Columbia Lodge No. 14 Minute Book Vol 2, 1873–1879
Columbia Lodge No. 14 Cash Book, 1875–1884

***Mayer, G F**
Columbia Lodge No. 14 Minute Book Vol 1, 1867–1873

***McAllister, J T**
Columbia Lodge No. 14 Minute Book Vol 1, 1867–1873

McCall, Nathaniel H
Columbia Lodge No. 14 Minute Book Vol 2, 1873–1879

McCarty
Columbia Lodge No. 14 Minute Book Vol 1, 1867–1873

McCaslin, Matthew L
Columbia Lodge No. 14 Minute Book Vol 1, 1867–1873
Columbia Lodge No. 14 Minute Book Vol 2, 1873–1879
Columbia Lodge No. 14 Cash Book, 1875–1884

McCleary, Troy
Columbia Lodge No. 14 Minute Book Vol 1, 1867–1873

McClure, Edward P
Columbia Lodge No. 14 Minute Book Vol 1, 1867–1873
Columbia Lodge No. 14 Minute Book Vol 2, 1873–1879
Columbia Lodge No. 14 Cash Book, 1875–1884

McClure, George M
Columbia Lodge No. 14 Minute Book Vol 2, 1873–1879

McCormick
Columbia Lodge No. 14 Minute Book Vol 2, 1873–1879

McCowan, J C
Columbia Lodge No. 14 Minute Book Vol 1, 1867–1873
Columbia Lodge No. 14 Minute Book Vol 2, 1873–1879

McDowell, John M
Columbia Lodge No. 14 Minute Book Vol 1, 1867–1873
Columbia Lodge No. 14 Minute Book Vol 2, 1873–1879
Columbia Lodge No. 14 Cash Book, 1875–1884

***McHant, William K**
Columbia Lodge No. 14 Minute Book Vol 1, 1867–1873

McIntosh & Van
Columbia Lodge No. 14 Minute Book Vol 2, 1873–1879

McIntosh, Lemuel
Columbia Lodge No. 14 Minute Book Vol 1, 1867–1873
Columbia Lodge No. 14 Minute Book Vol 2, 1873–1879
Columbia Lodge No. 14 Cash Book, 1875–1884

Mead, Marcus S
Columbia Lodge No. 14 Minute Book Vol 1, 1867–1873
Columbia Lodge No. 14 Minute Book Vol 2, 1873–1879
Columbia Lodge No. 14 Cash Book, 1875–1884

Meginnis, Daniel
Columbia Lodge No. 14 Minute Book Vol 1, 1867–1873
Columbia Lodge No. 14 Minute Book Vol 2, 1873–1879

***Messner, Charles E**
Columbia Lodge No. 14 Minute Book Vol 1, 1867–1873

Metcalf, Eli P
Columbia Lodge No. 14 Minute Book Vol 1, 1867–1873
Columbia Lodge No. 14 Minute Book Vol 2, 1873–1879
Columbia Lodge No. 14 Cash Book, 1875–1884

Meverson
Columbia Lodge No. 14 Minute Book Vol 1, 1867–1873

***Meyring, Henry**
Columbia Lodge No. 14 Minute Book Vol 1, 1867–1873

Michaud, Theodore
Columbia Lodge No. 14 Minute Book Vol 2, 1873–1879
Columbia Lodge No. 14 Cash Book, 1875–1884

Miller, David W
Columbia Lodge No. 14 Minute Book Vol 1, 1867–1873
Columbia Lodge No. 14 Minute Book Vol 2, 1873–1879

Miller, Lewis
Columbia Lodge No. 14 Minute Book Vol 2, 1873–1879

Mills, Abraham
Columbia Lodge No. 14 Minute Book Vol 1, 1867–1873
Columbia Lodge No. 14 Minute Book Vol 2, 1873–1879
Columbia Lodge No. 14 Cash Book, 1875–1884

***Minks, George W**
Columbia Lodge No. 14 Minute Book Vol 1, 1867–1873

Morgridge, A
Columbia Lodge No. 14 Minute Book Vol 2, 1873–1879

Morgridge, William O
Columbia Lodge No. 14 Minute Book Vol 1, 1867–1873

Morris
Columbia Lodge No. 14 Minute Book Vol 1, 1867–1873

Morris, Webb
Columbia Lodge No. 14 Minute Book Vol 2, 1873–1879

Morton, Richard
Columbia Lodge No. 14 Minute Book Vol 2, 1873–1879

Moser, Christopher
Columbia Lodge No. 14 Minute Book Vol 2, 1873–1879
Columbia Lodge No. 14 Cash Book, 1875–1884

Mulford, John Spencer
Columbia Lodge No. 14 Minute Book Vol 2, 1873–1879

Mulgrew, John H
Columbia Lodge No. 14 Minute Book Vol 1, 1867–1873

Mullen, Lauchu [??]
Columbia Lodge No. 14 Minute Book Vol 1, 1867–1873

Munson
Columbia Lodge No. 14 Minute Book Vol 2, 1873–1879

Mustin, Ed
Columbia Lodge No. 14 Minute Book Vol 2, 1873–1879

Neill, Thomas J
Columbia Lodge No. 14 Minute Book Vol 1, 1867–1873

Newnam, E R
Columbia Lodge No. 14 Minute Book Vol 1, 1867–1873

Newnam, Edward B
Columbia Lodge No. 14 Minute Book Vol 1, 1867–1873

Nichols, Charles L
Columbia Lodge No. 14 Minute Book Vol 1, 1867–1873
Columbia Lodge No. 14 Minute Book Vol 2, 1873–1879
Columbia Lodge No. 14 Cash Book, 1875–1884

Nichols, David H
Columbia Lodge No. 14 Minute Book Vol 1, 1867–1873
Columbia Lodge No. 14 Minute Book Vol 2, 1873–1879
Columbia Lodge No. 14 Cash Book, 1875–1884

Nichols, Ezra H
Columbia Lodge No. 14 Minute Book Vol 1, 1867–1873
Columbia Lodge No. 14 Minute Book Vol 2, 1873–1879
Columbia Lodge No. 14 Cash Book, 1875–1884

***Nicholson, John H**
Columbia Lodge No. 14 Minute Book Vol 1, 1867–1873
Columbia Lodge No. 14 Minute Book Vol 2, 1873–1879
Columbia Lodge No. 14 Cash Book, 1875–1884

***North, James M**
Columbia Lodge No. 14 Minute Book Vol 1, 1867–1873

O'Conner
Columbia Lodge No. 14 Minute Book Vol 2, 1873–1879

Odd Fellows
Columbia Lodge No. 14 Minute Book Vol 1, 1867–1873
Columbia Lodge No. 14 Minute Book Vol 2, 1873–1879
Columbia Lodge No. 14 Cash Book, 1875–1884

***O'Hara, William**
Columbia Lodge No. 14 Minute Book Vol 1, 1867–1873

Orahood, Harper M
Columbia Lodge No. 14 Minute Book Vol 1, 1867–1873
Columbia Lodge No. 14 Minute Book Vol 2, 1873–1879

Orey, Justice
Columbia Lodge No. 14 Minute Book Vol 1, 1867–1873

Owens, John
Columbia Lodge No. 14 Minute Book Vol 1, 1867–1873

Paige, John
Columbia Lodge No. 14 Minute Book Vol 1, 1867–1873

Parker, Charles E
Columbia Lodge No. 14 Minute Book Vol 1, 1867–1873
Columbia Lodge No. 14 Visitors Book, 1874–1886

Parlin, David
Columbia Lodge No. 14 Minute Book Vol 1, 1867–1873
Columbia Lodge No. 14 Minute Book Vol 2, 1873–1879
Columbia Lodge No. 14 Cash Book, 1875–1884

Parsons
Columbia Lodge No. 14 Minute Book Vol 2, 1873–1879

Parsons, E
Columbia Lodge No. 14 Minute Book Vol 2, 1873–1879

Patterson
Columbia Lodge No. 14 Minute Book Vol 1, 1867–1873
Columbia Lodge No. 14 Minute Book Vol 2, 1873–1879

Paul, Henry
Columbia Lodge No. 14 Minute Book Vol 1, 1867–1873
Columbia Lodge No. 14 Minute Book Vol 2, 1873–1879

Pell, William
Columbia Lodge No. 14 Minute Book Vol 1, 1867–1873

Peryam, William T
Columbia Lodge No. 14 Minute Book Vol 1, 1867–1873
Columbia Lodge No. 14 Minute Book Vol 2, 1873–1879
Columbia Lodge No. 14 Cash Book, 1875–1884

Peters, Anson W
Columbia Lodge No. 14 Minute Book Vol 1, 1867–1873
Columbia Lodge No. 14 Minute Book Vol 2, 1873–1879

Peterson
Columbia Lodge No. 14 Minute Book Vol 1, 1867–1873

Pettis & Co
Columbia Lodge No. 14 Minute Book Vol 2, 1873–1879

***Philippi, Frederick**
Columbia Lodge No. 14 Minute Book Vol 1, 1867–1873

Phillips Bros
Columbia Lodge No. 14 Minute Book Vol 2, 1873–1879

Phillips, Ives
Columbia Lodge No. 14 Minute Book Vol 2, 1873–1879
Columbia Lodge No. 14 Cash Book, 1875–1884

Phillips, M & Co
Columbia Lodge No. 14 Minute Book Vol 1, 1867–1873

Pierce, Oscar
Columbia Lodge No. 14 Minute Book Vol 1, 1867–1873

Pierce, S
Columbia Lodge No. 14 Minute Book Vol 1, 1867–1873

***Piteirub, Hiram R**
Columbia Lodge No. 14 Minute Book Vol 1, 1867–1873

***Pollirek, James R**
Columbia Lodge No. 14 Minute Book Vol 1, 1867–1873

Pomeroy, John W
Columbia Lodge No. 14 Minute Book Vol 1, 1867–1873

Poor, George
Columbia Lodge No. 14 Minute Book Vol 2, 1873–1879
Columbia Lodge No. 14 Cash Book, 1875–1884

Potter, S W
Columbia Lodge No. 14 Minute Book Vol 1, 1867–1873

Potter, Willie T
Columbia Lodge No. 14 Minute Book Vol 1, 1867–1873

***Pound, Charles**
Columbia Lodge No. 14 Minute Book Vol 1, 1867–1873

Quinn, John L
Columbia Lodge No. 14 Minute Book Vol 1, 1867–1873
Columbia Lodge No. 14 Minute Book Vol 2, 1873–1879

Quinn, T J
Columbia Lodge No. 14 Minute Book Vol 1, 1867–1873
Columbia Lodge No. 14 Minute Book Vol 2, 1873–1879

Ramsden, John N
Columbia Lodge No. 14 Minute Book Vol 1, 1867–1873

Renslow, Jerusha
Columbia Lodge No. 14 Minute Book Vol 2, 1873–1879

Renslow, Samuel
Columbia Lodge No. 14 Minute Book Vol 2, 1873–1879

Reynolds
Columbia Lodge No. 14 Minute Book Vol 2, 1873–1879

Reynolds, George D
Columbia Lodge No. 14 Visitors Book, 1874–1886

Reynolds, H G
Columbia Lodge No. 14 Minute Book Vol 1, 1867–1873

Rice
Columbia Lodge No. 14 Minute Book Vol 1, 1867–1873

Richards, William
Columbia Lodge No. 14 Minute Book Vol 2, 1873–1879

Richardson, John
Columbia Lodge No. 14 Minute Book Vol 1, 1867–1873

Ripley, Frank
Columbia Lodge No. 14 Minute Book Vol 2, 1873–1879

Ritchie, John W
Columbia Lodge No. 14 Minute Book Vol 1, 1867–1873
Columbia Lodge No. 14 Minute Book Vol 2, 1873–1879
Columbia Lodge No. 14 Cash Book, 1875–1884

Robbins, Roper & Nesbitt
Columbia Lodge No. 14 Minute Book Vol 2, 1873–1879

***Robertson, G B**
Columbia Lodge No. 14 Minute Book Vol 1, 1867–1873

Robinson, Daniel A
Columbia Lodge No. 14 Minute Book Vol 1, 1867–1873
Columbia Lodge No. 14 Minute Book Vol 2, 1873–1879
Columbia Lodge No. 14 Cash Book, 1875–1884

***Roen, Matt**
Columbia Lodge No. 14 Minute Book Vol 1, 1867–1873

Rompf, Charles
Columbia Lodge No. 14 Minute Book Vol 1, 1867–1873
Columbia Lodge No. 14 Minute Book Vol 2, 1873–1879

Rood, A
Columbia Lodge No. 14 Minute Book Vol 2, 1873–1879

Ross, M C
Columbia Lodge No. 14 Minute Book Vol 1, 1867–1873

***Rowen, William I**
Columbia Lodge No. 14 Minute Book Vol 1, 1867–1873

Rush [??]
Columbia Lodge No. 14 Minute Book Vol 1, 1867–1873

***Russell, C A**
Columbia Lodge No. 14 Minute Book Vol 1, 1867–1873

Russell, Horace M
Columbia Lodge No. 14 Minute Book Vol 1, 1867–1873

Rutherford
Columbia Lodge No. 14 Minute Book Vol 1, 1867–1873

Ryalls, Thomas
Columbia Lodge No. 14 Minute Book Vol 1, 1867–1873
Columbia Lodge No. 14 Minute Book Vol 2, 1873–1879
Columbia Lodge No. 14 Cash Book, 1875–1884

***Safely, Alexander Fenwick**
Columbia Lodge No. 14 Minute Book Vol 1, 1867–1873

***Samuels, H Clay**
Columbia Lodge No. 14 Minute Book Vol 1, 1867–1873

Sanderson
Columbia Lodge No. 14 Minute Book Vol 1, 1867–1873

Saunders
Columbia Lodge No. 14 Minute Book Vol 1, 1867–1873

Sawdey, Edgar
Columbia Lodge No. 14 Minute Book Vol 1, 1867–1873
Columbia Lodge No. 14 Minute Book Vol 2, 1873–1879
Columbia Lodge No. 14 Cash Book, 1875–1884

Sawyer, N F
Columbia Lodge No. 14 Visitors Book, 1874–1886

Schneider, Ed
Columbia Lodge No. 14 Minute Book Vol 2, 1873–1879

***Schriver, J D**
Columbia Lodge No. 14 Minute Book Vol 1, 1867–1873

Schwartzenberger, Lippman
Columbia Lodge No. 14 Minute Book Vol 1, 1867–1873

***Scorton, Samuel**
Columbia Lodge No. 14 Minute Book Vol 1, 1867–1873

Scott, Samuel
Columbia Lodge No. 14 Minute Book Vol 1, 1867–1873
Columbia Lodge No. 14 Minute Book Vol 2, 1873–1879
Columbia Lodge No. 14 Cash Book, 1875–1884

Sears, Frank
Columbia Lodge No. 14 Minute Book Vol 2, 1873–1879

Sears, William F
Columbia Lodge No. 14 Minute Book Vol 2, 1873–1879
Columbia Lodge No. 14 Visitors Book, 1874–1886

Secor, William W
Columbia Lodge No. 14 Minute Book Vol 2, 1873–1879

Seely, Eli
Columbia Lodge No. 14 Minute Book Vol 1, 1867–1873
Columbia Lodge No. 14 Minute Book Vol 2, 1873–1879

***Sermany, Isaac H**
Columbia Lodge No. 14 Minute Book Vol 1, 1867–1873

Shaffer, Phillip
Columbia Lodge No. 14 Minute Book Vol 1, 1867–1873

***Sharratt, Charles**
Columbia Lodge No. 14 Minute Book Vol 1, 1867–1873

Sheets, Henry W
Columbia Lodge No. 14 Minute Book Vol 1, 1867–1873
Columbia Lodge No. 14 Visitors Book, 1874–1886

Sherman
Columbia Lodge No. 14 Minute Book Vol 1, 1867–1873

Sherwood, Clarence A
Columbia Lodge No. 14 Minute Book Vol 1, 1867–1873
Columbia Lodge No. 14 Minute Book Vol 2, 1873–1879
Columbia Lodge No. 14 Cash Book, 1875–1884

Shortridge
Columbia Lodge No. 14 Minute Book Vol 1, 1867–1873
Columbia Lodge No. 14 Minute Book Vol 2, 1873–1879

Silver, S D
Columbia Lodge No. 14 Minute Book Vol 1, 1867–1873
Columbia Lodge No. 14 Minute Book Vol 2, 1873–1879
Columbia Lodge No. 14 Cash Book, 1875–1884

Simmons
Columbia Lodge No. 14 Minute Book Vol 2, 1873–1879

Simmons, John
Columbia Lodge No. 14 Visitors Book, 1874–1886

Simpson, John H
Columbia Lodge No. 14 Minute Book Vol 2, 1873–1879
Columbia Lodge No. 14 Visitors Book, 1874–1886

Slade, Charles E
Columbia Lodge No. 14 Minute Book Vol 1, 1867–1873

Slanton, A J
Columbia Lodge No. 14 Minute Book Vol 1, 1867–1873

Slater, William C
Columbia Lodge No. 14 Minute Book Vol 1, 1867–1873
Columbia Lodge No. 14 Minute Book Vol 2, 1873–1879
Columbia Lodge No. 14 Cash Book, 1875–1884

Slaughter, Benjamin H
Columbia Lodge No. 14 Minute Book Vol 1, 1867–1873
Columbia Lodge No. 14 Minute Book Vol 2, 1873–1879
Columbia Lodge No. 14 Cash Book, 1875–1884

Slifer, Esrom G
Columbia Lodge No. 14 Minute Book Vol 1, 1867–1873

Smith, Azon A
Columbia Lodge No. 14 Minute Book Vol 1, 1867–1873
Columbia Lodge No. 14 Minute Book Vol 2, 1873–1879
Columbia Lodge No. 14 Cash Book, 1875–1884

Smith, B F
Columbia Lodge No. 14 Minute Book Vol 1, 1867–1873

***Smith, Dr H**
Columbia Lodge No. 14 Minute Book Vol 1, 1867–1873

Smith, H
Columbia Lodge No. 14 Minute Book Vol 1, 1867–1873

Smith, J Alden
Columbia Lodge No. 14 Minute Book Vol 1, 1867–1873
Columbia Lodge No. 14 Minute Book Vol 2, 1873–1879

Smith, Marinus G
Columbia Lodge No. 14 Minute Book Vol 1, 1867–1873
Columbia Lodge No. 14 Minute Book Vol 2, 1873–1879
Columbia Lodge No. 14 Cash Book, 1875–1884

Smith, Walter H
Columbia Lodge No. 14 Minute Book Vol 1, 1867–1873
Columbia Lodge No. 14 Minute Book Vol 2, 1873–1879
Columbia Lodge No. 14 Cash Book, 1875–1884

Snedecor, Isaac D
Columbia Lodge No. 14 Minute Book Vol 2, 1873–1879

Snell, James
Columbia Lodge No. 14 Minute Book Vol 1, 1867–1873
Columbia Lodge No. 14 Minute Book Vol 2, 1873–1879

Snyder, Hanson
Columbia Lodge No. 14 Minute Book Vol 1, 1867–1873
Columbia Lodge No. 14 Minute Book Vol 2, 1873–1879
Columbia Lodge No. 14 Cash Book, 1875–1884

Solander, Daniel
Columbia Lodge No. 14 Minute Book Vol 1, 1867–1873
Columbia Lodge No. 14 Minute Book Vol 2, 1873–1879

Solander, Lane
Columbia Lodge No. 14 Minute Book Vol 2, 1873–1879

Sommers, Wilhelm
Columbia Lodge No. 14 Minute Book Vol 1, 1867–1873
Columbia Lodge No. 14 Minute Book Vol 2, 1873–1879
Columbia Lodge No. 14 Cash Book, 1875–1884

Sorrell, E J
Columbia Lodge No. 14 Minute Book Vol 2, 1873–1879

Soule, Albert G
Columbia Lodge No. 14 Minute Book Vol 1, 1867–1873

Southland, Judson D
Columbia Lodge No. 14 Minute Book Vol 2, 1873–1879
Columbia Lodge No. 14 Cash Book, 1875–1884

Southland, W J
Columbia Lodge No. 14 Minute Book Vol 1, 1867–1873
Columbia Lodge No. 14 Minute Book Vol 2, 1873–1879

***Spaulding, J F**
Columbia Lodge No. 14 Minute Book Vol 1, 1867–1873

***Spencer, Charles L**
Columbia Lodge No. 14 Minute Book Vol 1, 1867–1873

***Spengler**
Columbia Lodge No. 14 Minute Book Vol 1, 1867–1873

Squires, Frederick A
Columbia Lodge No. 14 Minute Book Vol 1, 1867–1873
Columbia Lodge No. 14 Minute Book Vol 2, 1873–1879

Squires, George C
Columbia Lodge No. 14 Minute Book Vol 1, 1867–1873
Columbia Lodge No. 14 Minute Book Vol 2, 1873–1879
Columbia Lodge No. 14 Cash Book, 1875–1884

Squires, Phineas L
Columbia Lodge No. 14 Minute Book Vol 2, 1873–1879

St Clair, Joel F T
Columbia Lodge No. 14 Minute Book Vol 1, 1867–1873
Columbia Lodge No. 14 Minute Book Vol 2, 1873–1879
Columbia Lodge No. 14 Visitors Book, 1874–1886

Stanley, Mr
Columbia Lodge No. 14 Minute Book Vol 1, 1867–1873

Stanton, John A
Columbia Lodge No. 14 Minute Book Vol 1, 1867–1873
Columbia Lodge No. 14 Minute Book Vol 2, 1873–1879
Columbia Lodge No. 14 Cash Book, 1875–1884
Columbia Lodge No. 14 Visitors Book, 1874–1886

Stanton, Mrs J A
Columbia Lodge No. 14 Minute Book Vol 1, 1867–1873

State Grange
Columbia Lodge No. 14 Minute Book Vol 2, 1873–1879

Stevens
Columbia Lodge No. 14 Minute Book Vol 2, 1873–1879

Stevens, George E
Columbia Lodge No. 14 Visitors Book, 1874–1886

Stevens, James
Columbia Lodge No. 14 Visitors Book, 1874–1886

Stewart, A R
Columbia Lodge No. 14 Minute Book Vol 1, 1867–1873

Stewart, Mrs
Columbia Lodge No. 14 Minute Book Vol 1, 1867–1873

Stewart, Thomas C
Columbia Lodge No. 14 Minute Book Vol 1, 1867–1873
Columbia Lodge No. 14 Minute Book Vol 2, 1873–1879
Columbia Lodge No. 14 Cash Book, 1875–1884

Stiles, Henry C
Columbia Lodge No. 14 Minute Book Vol 1, 1867–1873

***Strasburger, Mathias**
Columbia Lodge No. 14 Minute Book Vol 1, 1867–1873

Stone, W G
Columbia Lodge No. 14 Minute Book Vol 2, 1873–1879

Stratton
Columbia Lodge No. 14 Minute Book Vol 1, 1867–1873

Stuchell, C D
Columbia Lodge No. 14 Minute Book Vol 2, 1873–1879
Columbia Lodge No. 14 Visitors Book, 1874–1886

Sullivan, Jacob M
Columbia Lodge No. 14 Minute Book Vol 1, 1867–1873
Columbia Lodge No. 14 Minute Book Vol 2, 1873–1879

Sunshine Courier
Columbia Lodge No. 14 Minute Book Vol 2, 1873–1879

Sutherland, Datus E
Columbia Lodge No. 14 Minute Book Vol 1, 1867–1873
Columbia Lodge No. 14 Minute Book Vol 2, 1873–1879

Southerland, E D
Columbia Lodge No. 14 Minute Book Vol 1, 1867–1873

Taber, J F
Columbia Lodge No. 14 Minute Book Vol 1, 1867–1873

Talbot, Mrs
Columbia Lodge No. 14 Minute Book Vol 2, 1873–1879

Tallmann, Isaac T
Columbia Lodge No. 14 Minute Book Vol 1, 1867–1873
Columbia Lodge No. 14 Minute Book Vol 2, 1873–1879
Columbia Lodge No. 14 Visitors Book, 1874–1886

Tarvin, E M
Columbia Lodge No. 14 Minute Book Vol 2, 1873–1879
Columbia Lodge No. 14 Cash Book, 1875–1884

Taylor, C W
Columbia Lodge No. 14 Minute Book Vol 1, 1867–1873
Columbia Lodge No. 14 Minute Book Vol 2, 1873–1879

Taylor, Eugene
Columbia Lodge No. 14 Minute Book Vol 1, 1867–1873
Columbia Lodge No. 14 Minute Book Vol 2, 1873–1879

Thompson
Columbia Lodge No. 14 Minute Book Vol 1, 1867–1873

Thompson, H C
Columbia Lodge No. 14 Minute Book Vol 2, 1873–1879

Thompson, James M
Columbia Lodge No. 14 Minute Book Vol 1, 1867–1873

Thompson, Rev N
Columbia Lodge No. 14 Minute Book Vol 2, 1873–1879

***Thuy, Robert H**
Columbia Lodge No. 14 Minute Book Vol 1, 1867–1873

Tilney, Robert H
Columbia Lodge No. 14 Minute Book Vol 1, 1867–1873
Columbia Lodge No. 14 Minute Book Vol 2, 1873–1879
Columbia Lodge No. 14 Cash Book, 1875–1884

Tipple, George L
Columbia Lodge No. 14 Minute Book Vol 1, 1867–1873
Columbia Lodge No. 14 Visitors Book, 1874–1886

Titcomb, John S
Columbia Lodge No. 14 Minute Book Vol 1, 1867–1873
Columbia Lodge No. 14 Minute Book Vol 2, 1873–1879
Columbia Lodge No. 14 Cash Book, 1875–1884

***Todd, C D**
Columbia Lodge No. 14 Minute Book Vol 1, 1867–1873

Tourtellot & Squires
Columbia Lodge No. 14 Minute Book Vol 1, 1867–1873

Tourtellot, Mrs
Columbia Lodge No. 14 Minute Book Vol 1, 1867–1873

Trear, George
Columbia Lodge No. 14 Minute Book Vol 1, 1867–1873

Trevastator, Thomas J
Columbia Lodge No. 14 Minute Book Vol 2, 1873–1879

Tubbs, Octavius H
Columbia Lodge No. 14 Minute Book Vol 1, 1867–1873

Tuly
Columbia Lodge No. 14 Minute Book Vol 1, 1867–1873

Turner, Charles
Columbia Lodge No. 14 Minute Book Vol 2, 1873–1879
Columbia Lodge No. 14 Cash Book, 1875–1884

***Turney, Charles**
Columbia Lodge No. 14 Minute Book Vol 1, 1867–1873

Tuttle
Columbia Lodge No. 14 Minute Book Vol 1, 1867–1873

Tyrell, Norman J
Columbia Lodge No. 14 Minute Book Vol 1, 1867–1873
Columbia Lodge No. 14 Minute Book Vol 2, 1873–1879
Columbia Lodge No. 14 Cash Book, 1875–1884

Underwood, Henry M
Columbia Lodge No. 14 Minute Book Vol 2, 1873–1879

Van Deren, Archibald J
Columbia Lodge No. 14 Minute Book Vol 1, 1867–1873
Columbia Lodge No. 14 Minute Book Vol 2, 1873–1879

***Van Fleet, Charles G**
Columbia Lodge No. 14 Minute Book Vol 1, 1867–1873

Van Riper, Cornelius
Columbia Lodge No. 14 Minute Book Vol 1, 1867–1873
Columbia Lodge No. 14 Minute Book Vol 2, 1873–1879
Columbia Lodge No. 14 Cash Book, 1875–1884

Van Valkenberg, R J
Columbia Lodge No. 14 Minute Book Vol 1, 1867–1873
Columbia Lodge No. 14 Minute Book Vol 2, 1873–1879

Van, Clay M
Columbia Lodge No. 14 Minute Book Vol 1, 1867–1873
Columbia Lodge No. 14 Minute Book Vol 2, 1873–1879
Columbia Lodge No. 14 Cash Book, 1875–1884

***Viele, J B Jr**
Columbia Lodge No. 14 Minute Book Vol 1, 1867–1873

Wait, Mrs A L
Columbia Lodge No. 14 Minute Book Vol 2, 1873–1879

Walker, Thomas C
Columbia Lodge No. 14 Minute Book Vol 1, 1867–1873
Columbia Lodge No. 14 Minute Book Vol 2, 1873–1879
Columbia Lodge No. 14 Cash Book, 1875–1884

***Walker, Thomas J**
Columbia Lodge No. 14 Minute Book Vol 1, 1867–1873

Wallace
Columbia Lodge No. 14 Minute Book Vol 1, 1867–1873

***Wallace, George**
Columbia Lodge No. 14 Minute Book Vol 1, 1867–1873

Wallace, William J
Columbia Lodge No. 14 Minute Book Vol 1, 1867–1873
Columbia Lodge No. 14 Minute Book Vol 2, 1873–1879
Columbia Lodge No. 14 Cash Book, 1875–1884

Walter, M
Columbia Lodge No. 14 Minute Book Vol 1, 1867–1873

Walter, Thomas D
Columbia Lodge No. 14 Minute Book Vol 1, 1867–1873
Columbia Lodge No. 14 Minute Book Vol 2, 1873–1879

Ward, Ross
Columbia Lodge No. 14 Minute Book Vol 2, 1873–1879

Washburn, H E
Columbia Lodge No. 14 Minute Book Vol 1, 1867–1873

Webster, George W
Columbia Lodge No. 14 Minute Book Vol 1, 1867–1873
Columbia Lodge No. 14 Minute Book Vol 2, 1873–1879

Wellman, Luther C
Columbia Lodge No. 14 Minute Book Vol 1, 1867–1873
Columbia Lodge No. 14 Minute Book Vol 2, 1873–1879
Columbia Lodge No. 14 Cash Book, 1875–1884

Wellman, Sylvanus
Columbia Lodge No. 14 Minute Book Vol 1, 1867–1873
Columbia Lodge No. 14 Minute Book Vol 2, 1873–1879
Columbia Lodge No. 14 Cash Book, 1875–1884

Westlake
Columbia Lodge No. 14 Cash Book, 1875–1884

Westlake, M D
Columbia Lodge No. 14 Minute Book Vol 1, 1867–1873

Westlake, W B
Columbia Lodge No. 14 Minute Book Vol 2, 1873–1879

Wharton, Joseph J
Columbia Lodge No. 14 Minute Book Vol 1, 1867–1873
Columbia Lodge No. 14 Minute Book Vol 2, 1873–1879
Columbia Lodge No. 14 Cash Book, 1875–1884

White, David S
Columbia Lodge No. 14 Minute Book Vol 1, 1867–1873
Columbia Lodge No. 14 Minute Book Vol 2, 1873–1879

Whittemore
Columbia Lodge No. 14 Minute Book Vol 1, 1867–1873

Wigginton, John W
Columbia Lodge No. 14 Minute Book Vol 1, 1867–1873
Columbia Lodge No. 14 Minute Book Vol 2, 1873–1879
Columbia Lodge No. 14 Cash Book, 1875–1884

Wilder, Eugene
Columbia Lodge No. 14 Minute Book Vol 1, 1867–1873
Columbia Lodge No. 14 Minute Book Vol 2, 1873–1879
Columbia Lodge No. 14 Cash Book, 1875–1884

Wilkins, Cornelius
Columbia Lodge No. 14 Minute Book Vol 1, 1867–1873
Columbia Lodge No. 14 Minute Book Vol 2, 1873–1879
Columbia Lodge No. 14 Cash Book, 1875–1884

Williams, George W
Columbia Lodge No. 14 Minute Book Vol 2, 1873–1879

***Williams, John T**
Columbia Lodge No. 14 Minute Book Vol 1, 1867–1873

Williams, R H
Columbia Lodge No. 14 Visitors Book, 1874–1886

Wilson, Benjamin F
Columbia Lodge No. 14 Minute Book Vol 1, 1867–1873
Columbia Lodge No. 14 Minute Book Vol 2, 1873–1879
Columbia Lodge No. 14 Cash Book, 1875–1884

***Wilson, G W**
Columbia Lodge No. 14 Minute Book Vol 1, 1867–1873

Wilson, James L
Columbia Lodge No. 14 Minute Book Vol 1, 1867–1873

Wilson, John Milton
Columbia Lodge No. 14 Minute Book Vol 1, 1867–1873
Columbia Lodge No. 14 Minute Book Vol 2, 1873–1879
Columbia Lodge No. 14 Cash Book, 1875–1884

Wimer, John A
Columbia Lodge No. 14 Minute Book Vol 1, 1867–1873
Columbia Lodge No. 14 Minute Book Vol 2, 1873–1879
Columbia Lodge No. 14 Cash Book, 1875–1884

Wineberger
Columbia Lodge No. 14 Minute Book Vol 1, 1867–1873

***Wisner, John A**
Columbia Lodge No. 14 Minute Book Vol 1, 1867–1873

Witherow, Chase
Columbia Lodge No. 14 Minute Book Vol 1, 1867–1873

Wolff, Mrs
Columbia Lodge No. 14 Minute Book Vol 2, 1873–1879

Wood, Gardner P
Columbia Lodge No. 14 Minute Book Vol 1, 1867–1873
Columbia Lodge No. 14 Minute Book Vol 2, 1873–1879
Columbia Lodge No. 14 Cash Book, 1875–1884

Woodward, Robert J
Columbia Lodge No. 14 Minute Book Vol 1, 1867–1873
Columbia Lodge No. 14 Minute Book Vol 2, 1873–1879

Wright, Alpheus
Columbia Lodge No. 14 Minute Book Vol 1, 1867–1873
Columbia Lodge No. 14 Minute Book Vol 2, 1873–1879
Columbia Lodge No. 14 Cash Book, 1875–1884

Wynkoop, William C
Columbia Lodge No. 14 Minute Book Vol 1, 1867–1873

Yankee
Columbia Lodge No. 14 Minute Book Vol 2, 1873–1879

Yankee, William H
Columbia Lodge No. 14 Visitors Book, 1874–1886

***Yarvin, E M**
Columbia Lodge No. 14 Minute Book Vol 1, 1867–1873

***Yates, Isaiah**
Columbia Lodge No. 14 Minute Book Vol 1, 1867–1873

***Yates, Joseph**
Columbia Lodge No. 14 Minute Book Vol 1, 1867–1873

Yelita, Henry B
Columbia Lodge No. 14 Minute Book Vol 2, 1873–1879

Columbia Lodge No. 14

Minute Book Vol 1, 1867–1873

The Columbia Lodge No. 14 Ancient Free & Accepted Masons was formally established in the town of Columbia (now called Ward) in 1867. As the number suggests, there were 13 other Masonic lodges established before the Columbia Lodge in places like Golden City (Lodge No. 1), Nevada (Nevadaville - Lodge No. 4), Denver (Lodge No. 5), Central (Central City - Lodge No. 6), Empire (Lodge No. 8) and Black Hawk (Lodge No. 11).

In 1868, the Columbia Lodge petitioned the Grand Lodge to move the lodge to Boulder. There was a contemporary lodge in Valmont that disolved and many of the members of that lodge became members of the Columbia Lodge. In the 1870s, a new lodge opened up in Longmont (St. Vrain Lodge No. 23), and another lodge opened in Boulder (Boulder Lodge No. 45).

Access to the early records of the Columbia Lodge was gracious granted to the Boulder Pioneers Project by Bruce Yellen, current President of the Columbia Lodge. The Boulder Pioneers Project is trying to determine who all of the residents of Boulder County were before Colorado became a state in 1876. As a part of that project, we have reached out to groups like the Masons who were helping to create lasting communities within the Boulder Valley, for access to their records.

The Minute Book of the Columbia Lodge, Vol 1 1867-1873, contains not only references to the on-going activities of the Columbia Lodge, but mentions members of the community who provided services to the lodge; members of the community who were in need and were helped by the lodge; Masons from this lodge and others who died in Boulder and whose funerals were conducted by the lodge; the establishment of a cemetery in the community part of which was run by the Columbia Lodge, part of which was sold to the Odd Fellows, part of which was reserved for a potter's field; members of the community who purchased lots in the Masonic Cemetery; other organizations like the Odd Fellows who shared space and expenses with the Columbia Lodge, and much more. The Minute Book is a fascinating look at early life in Boulder.

As is to be expected, most of the mentions in the book pertain to the members of the lodge including who held which offices, who was present, who paid dues and who has asked for a "demit" and left the community for other places.

New members are often listed as visitors first along with the lodge where they were already a member. For the members, we have listed the offices they held, but not what role they played on each page where they were listed. Mostly, members were marked as "present" or shown as holding an office. Petitioners to the lodge often have their places of residence listed, and petitioners who are already Masons often have the name and number of their home lodges listed. These Masons often are listed as being "accompanied by a demit" meaning that they had been granted a release by their home lodge to apply to a new lodge in the place where they had settled.

Non-members' listings usually have more detail including the circumstances under which they were mentioned in the Minute Book, or where they might have been from. On occasion, motions were raised by members that contained interesting information about the community, and those tidbits are included.

Recording practices vary from Secretary to Secretary and accordingly, it is sometimes difficult to tell which Masons were simply visiting the lodge from out of town and which were members of the lodge who were present, but were not mentioned often. There is a note written within this Minute Book from 1956 which affirms that it was the practice of the early Masons to allow visiting Masons to take the seat of an officer as a courtesy to that visiting Mason which adds a bit to the confusion. The terms visiting and present were not used consistently.

Not all visiting members were listed as visiting either. Often they were listed among the other Columbia Lodge members as "present." There are also cases of Masons who were members of other lodges in other states who had moved to Boulder, but not affiliated with the Columbia Lodge who attended meetings as visitors.

Dates within the volume are listed year first, followed by month and day. This is an unconventional way to present dates, but it is the method that the Colorado State Archives uses in its databases and we have adopted the method here.

At the back of this Minute Book is a list of members that extends well into the 1880s. A part of that list contains no dates. The names of these Masons have been included in this index along with an asterisk denoting that a date cannot be determined.

Legend to the listings.

Members

Known members of the Columbia Lodge No. 14.

Possible Members

People who have attended meetings of the membership at the lodge, but who have very few records indicating that they might be a visiting Mason from another lodge. In the following list of Columbia Lodge Masons, those names which could not be determined for certain to have been members have an asterisk before them. There was a list hand-written in pencil that was stuck into the book. The names of these men are also considered possible members.

Boulder

People who were in Boulder but non-members such as members of the Valmont Lodge, St Vrain Lodge, wives of members, deceased Masons who were not members of the lodge, businesses, vendors who provided services to the lodge, etc.

Non-Boulder

These people were mentioned in a commmunication from another lodge and were not associated with the Columbia Lodge.

If there are listings where the correct spelling could not be determined, the listing will contain both spellings, such as **Imil [Imel], David.**

Every effort has been made to assure that these listings are correct, however, extracting hand-written records can be tricky, and some listings may contain inaccuracies. We hope you enjoy as much as we have the discoveries we have made about early Boulder.

— The Boulder Pioneers Project

Members List from Vol 1

*Ackerman
*Allen, Gay S
Allen, Henley Wheaton
Allison, William H
Allmon, Lee J
Ames, Leeman C
Anderson, Daniel C
Anderson, David B
Andrews, Elijah H
Angora, C E
Ashley, John K
Austin, Eugene A
Austin, Schuyler D
Bailey
Balford, Frank D
Banks, Francis B
Bard, Richard
Barkhurst, Ira C
Barney, Royal Sigbert
Barney, William M
Barrowman, William
Bartels, Henry
Barter, William
Baum, Henry M
Belcher, Freeman
Berger, Andrew E
Beveridge, James
Bierus, Miche F
Bigger, Robert A
Bixby, Amos
Black, Wolfe
Blair, Charles H
Blake, Frank O
Blore, William R
Bock, David
Border, Samuel B
Bosworth, R W
*Boylan, John
Bradfield, Jack (Zach)
Breath, Samuel M
Bresnahan, Edward N
*Bristal, B J
Brodie, John
Bromley, Wm C
Brookfield, Alfred A
Brown, J W
Brown, Thomas J
*Brush
Budd, Sylvanus
Bunn, David
Bunn, Samuel C
*Buoss
Bush, Arthur W
Buttles, John F
Campbell, John L
Campbell, Sanford B
*Canfield
Carmack, Thomas K
Carter, George W
Chambers, John S
Chapman, Joshua E
Chase, George F
Clark, Dr. G A
*Cloud, E
Clow, David
Clow, Richard
Cluff, Chester P
Cluster, John A
*Cobb
Coffman, Enoch J
Connell, John
*Conwell
Cook, George D
*Cook, William
Corning, George C
Corson, William A
Crosby, A B
*Crosby, Charles
Crow, Richard
Cullacott, John J F
Cummins, Isaac
Danforth, W T
Davey, Joseph R J
Davidson, Charles B
Davidson, W__
Davis, David
Davis, John
Davis, Joel
Dawley, James M
Deitz, Henry
Deyo, R H
Dimick, Erastus H
Dodge, Horace O
Dolloff, John W
Dow, J E
Dowell, C C
Downer, S J
*Drew
Drumm, Henry
Dunagan, Elijah
Dunagan, Jackson J
Dunn, James
Eagleston, James C
Earhart, W R
Edwards, Bruce V
Ellingham
Ellingham, John J
Ellingham, Robert
Ellingham, Will A
Ellis, Adelbert L
Emrick, H J
Esmond, Bart
*Fairhurst
Faurot, Chalres S
Fonda, George
Foote, James B
French, S M
Fullen, Hiram
Galusha, Simon S
Gilbert, Clark
Gilliam, W H
*Godwin, H H
Goodwin, M W [N W]
Goss, Abel
Goss, P D
Graham, George W
Green, Henry
Griffith, Joseph F
Groesbeck, John B
Grund, John C
Guin, John T
Guin, Spencer
Guin, Thomas J
Gutterson, Charles L
Haffner, Joseph
Hager, William
Halverson, Christian
Hamblin, Oliver T
Hanken, M F
Harmon, George D
Harmon, M D
Harrets, Myers B
Harris, Addison W
Harvey, Christopher
Haswell, Theodore
*Haswell, William
Hathaway, Mark
Hayward, D P
Hayward, Dan E
*Heath, N H
Henry, Oren H
Henry, Ormal E
Hernandez, Anthony
Herzinger
*Hevelin, Benjamin
Hill, Thomas J

Boulder's Pioneer Masons, 1867–1886

Hinkle, John P
Hinman, John
Hockaday, Charles N
*Holly
Holt
Holt, Matthew J
Honstine
Hopkins, David L
Horner, John W
Hoskinson, Charles G
Howard, Norman R
Howell, William R
Howse, W J L
Hoyle, Ed W
Hubbard, Horace W
Hunt, Fred A
Hupper, E A
Irwin, Joseph
Ivey, James
Jackson, George W
Jacobs, Horatio H
*James, T J
Janbom, C W
*Jaynes
Jeffers, Albert
Jeslin, John A
Jester, William H
Johns, John H
Johns, Thomas J
Johnson, Seymour
Johnson, Thomas C
Johnston, Frank
Johnston, James J
Johnston, William J
Jones, Thomas J
Juneman, Frederick W
K___se, _____
Kelley, James A
Kempton, James
Kerr, David
Kessler, Marion
King, Robert
*Kiper
Kline, Marcus
Kneale, Charles A
Knill, Thomas
Knox, John
Kohler, Frederick W
Krieketts, C
Kroll, Anson
Lafferty, L J
Lake, George E
LaPoint, George
Lawson, Alexander
Lea, Alfred E
Learmack, John T
Lebruler, Patrick
Lefoe, W F
*Lelly, Eli
Lewis, James
Leyner, Peter A
Lockwood, Fred L
Logue
Loomis, Isaac
Low, Theodore
Lowman, Ed E
Luscon, Joseph
Luslich, James E
Lykins, David J
Lytle, George
Madera, Shepherd L
*Madey
Martin, W
Mason, Edward F
*Mathews
Maxwell, James P
Mayer, Gottlieb F
McAllister, J T
McBride, R T
McCall, Nathaniel H
*McCarty
McCaslin, Matthew L
McCleary, Troy
McClure, Edward P
McDowell, John M
McHant, William K
McIntosh, Lemuel
Mead, Marcus S
Meginnis, Daniel
Messner, Charles E
Metcalf, Eli P
*Meverson
Meyring, Henry
Miller, David W
Mills, Abraham
Milton, William P
Minks, George W
Moffatt, J C
Monell, Heuer
Monell, Irv F
Mulford, J S
*Mulgrew, John H
*Mullen, Lauchu [??]
Newnam, Edward B
Nichols, Charles L
Nichols, David H
Nichols, Ezra H
Nicholson, John H
North, James M
O'Connor, Timothy
O'Hara, William
Orey, Justice
Owen, Thomas R, Jr
Parker, Charles E
Parlin, David
*Patterson
Patterson, G O
Paul, Henry
Peryam, William T
Peters, Anson W
*Peterson
Philippi, Frederick
Phillips, N M
Pierce, Ed F
Pierce, Oscar
*Pierce, S
Piteirub, Hiram R
Pollock, James R
*Pomeroy, John W
Pool, W H
*Potter, S W
Potter, Willie T
Pound, Charles
Quinn, [John L or T J]
Quinn, John L
Quinn, T J
Rankin, Arthur
Richardson, John
Ritchie, John W
Rittenwater, Alex Jr
Robertson, G B
Robinson, Daniel A
Roen, Matt
*Rompf, Charles
Ross, M C
Rowen, William I
*Rush [??]
Russell, C A
*Rutherford
Ryalls, Thomas
Safely, Alexander Fenwick
Samuels, H Clay
*Sanderson
*Saunders
Sawdey, Edgar
Schriver, J D
Schwartzenberger, Lippman
Scorton, Samuel
Seely, Eli
Sergeant, Ellis
Severance, Isaac H
Sheets, Henry W
*Sherman
Sherratt, Charles
Sherwood, Clarence A

Shires, Thomas
*Shortridge
Silver, S D
Simpson, John
*Slanton, A J
Slater, William C
Slaughter, Benjamin H
Slifer, Esrom G
Smith, Azon A
Smith, Dr H
*Smith, H
Smith, J Alden
Smith, J W
Smith, Marinus G
Smith, Walter H
Snyder, Hanson
Sommers, Wilhelm
Soule, Albert G
Southland, W J
*Spaulding, J F
Spencer, Charles L
*Spengler
Squires, George C
St Clair, Joel F T
Stanton, John A
Steinmetz, O C
Stevens, Rees Winfield
Stewart, Thomas
Stiles, Henry C
Strasburger, Mathias
*Stratton
Surbo, Zola
Sutherland, Datus E
Tallmann, Isaac T
Taylor, A W
Thome, S J
*Thompson
Thompson, G T
Thuy, Robert H
Tipple, George L
Titcomb, John S
*Todd, C D
Tremont, Hugh
Treppen, James
Tubbs, Octavius H
*Tuly
Turner, Charles
*Tuttle
Tyrell, Norman J
Van Deren, Archibald J
Van Fleet, Charles G
Van Riper, Cornelius
Van Valkenberg, R J
Van, Clay M
Viele, James B Jr
Walker, Ed S
Walker, Thomas C
*Walker, Thomas D
Walker, Thomas J
Wallace, George
Wallace, William J
*Walter, M
Washburn, Hiram E
Webster, George W
Wellman, Luther C
Wellman, Sylvanus
Wharton, Joseph J
White, David S
White, William W
Whitney, George H
Whittemore
Wigginton, John W
Wilder, Eugene
Wilkins, Cornelius
Williams, J O
Williams, James
Williams, John T
Williams, W J
Wilson, Benjamin F
Wilson, George W
*Wilson, James L
Wilson, James L F
Wilson, John Milton
Wimer, John A
*Wineberger
Wisner, John A
Withrow, Chase
Wood, Gardner P
Woodward, Robert J
Wright, Alpheus
Yarvin, E M
Yates, Isaiah
Yates, Joseph

__uelel, Ezra L
pg 362 (1870 Jan 22) El Paso Lodge No. 13

Abbott, Edward
pg 209 (1871 Nov 25) Washington Lodge No. 12

Ackerman
offices held: SW
pg 197 (1871 July 8)

Adams, Charles
pg 332 (1874 Apr 28) Doric Lodge U.D.

Adams, Henry D
pg 245 (1872 Oct 26); pg 336 (1872 Oct 19) Washington Lodge No. 12

Albaugh, J B
pg 135 (1870 Jan 22) Cheyenne Lodge No. 16

Albaugh, J B
pg 361 (1870 Jan 22) El Paso Lodge No. 13

Alleman, S H
pg 332 (1874 Aug 22) Denver Lodge No. 5

Allen, G S
pg 360 (1869 Feb 20) Cheyenne Lodge No. 16

Allen, Gay S
pg 267 (1873 Feb 8) petitioner

Allen, Henley Wheaton
appears as: Allen, H W
offices held: Secy
pg 55 (1867 Oct 26) visiting from Waverly Lodge No. 357 of WI; pg 60 (1867 Dec 29); pg 61 (1867 Dec 29)

Allison, William H
appears as: Allison, W H
pg 315 member

Allmon, Lee J
pg 317 (1888 Nov 24) member

Altman, H
appears as: Altman, H; Alltman, H; Altmon, H
pg 161 (1870 July 9) Larimer Lodge U.D,; pg 179 (1871 Jan 14) Laramie Lodge No. 18; pg 362 (1870 June 28) Laramie Lodge U.D.

Ambold, Robert A
pg 339 (1878 Oct 15) San Juan Lodge No. 33

Ambrook, Charles
appears as: Ambrook; Ambrook, Charles
pg 237 (1872 July 27); pg 244 (1872 Oct 26) of Carson Lodge No. 306 of MI; pg 248 (1872 Nov 23); pg 248 (1872 Nov 23)
*did not become a member of the Columbia Lodge

Ames, Leeman C
pg 315 member

Anderson, C W
pg 236 (1872 July 27) Nevada Lodge No. 4; pg 336 (1872 July 27) Nevada Lodge No. 4

Anderson, Daniel C
pg 315 member

Anderson, David B
pg 315 member

Anderson, Erick J
appears as: Anderson, Erick J; Anderson Erick; Anderson, E J
pg 109 (1869 May 22); pg 114 (1869 June 26); pg 114 (1869 June 26)*; pg 154 (1870 May 28) bill presented for making stakes for Masonic cemetery; pg 200 (1871 Aug 12) paid for work on cemetery
*did not become a member of the Columbia Lodge

Anderson, Henry
pg 356 (1867 May 18) Golden Lodge No. 1; pg 56 (1867 Oct 26) Golden Lodge No. 1

Anderson, J S
appears as: Anderson; Anderson, J S
pg 201 (1871 Sept 9) was taken care of by M G Smith while in Boulder; pg 214 (1871 Dec 23) late deceased; pg 218 (1872 Jan 27) communication from Washington Lodge No. 222, Chillicothe, IL, stating that Mr. J S Anderson had never been a member of that lodge; pg 220 (1872 Feb 10) deceased, boarded by Bro Squires

Andrew, Joseph
appears as: Andrew Joseph; Andrew, J
pg 7 (1867 Jan 24) Nevada Lodge No 4; pg 356 (1867 Jan 12) Nevada Lodge No. 4

Andrews, Elijah H
appears as: Andrews; Andrews, E H; Andrews, E
offices held: JW, JD, Secy, SS
pg 18 (1867 Apr 11); pg 24 (1867 May 9); pg 25

(1867 May 9); pg 37 (1867 July 24); pg 56 (1867 Oct 26); pg 56 (1867 Oct 26); pg 69 (1868 Sept 12); pg 69 (1868 Sept 12); pg 70 (1868 Sept 12); pg 70 (1868 Sept 12); pg 71 (1868 Oct 24); pg 75 (1868 Nov 28); pg 78 (1868 Dec 12); pg 80 (1868 Dec 14); pg 97 (1869 Feb 27); pg 99 (1869 Mar 13); pg 108 (1869 May 22); pg 110 (1869 May 22); pg 119 (1869 Sept 11); pg 119 (1869 Sept 11); pg 121 (1869 Sept 25); pg 126 (1869 Nov 27); pg 127 (1869 Dec 11); pg 128 (1869 Dec 11); pg 160 (1870 July 9); pg 161 (1870 July 9); pg 163 (1870 Aug 13); pg 181 (1871 Jan 28); pg 197 (1871 July 8); pg 205 (1871 Oct 5); pg 205 (1871 Oct 5); pg 241 (1872 Sept 28); pg 246 (1872 Oct 26); pg 313 member; pg 314 member

Andrews, Wilber F
pg 68 (1868 Aug 8) Valmont Lodge U.D.; pg 357 (1868 June 6) Valmont Lodge U.D.

Angora, C E
pg 317 (1888 Apr 19) member

Applewright
pg 251 (1872 Dec 14) visiting; pg 253 (1872 Dec 26) visiting; pg 257 (1873 Jan 4) present

Arnett, Joseph
pg 340 (1880 Dec 21) Las Animas Lodge No. 28

Arnett, Williamette
appears as: Arnett, Williamette; Arnette, Williamette
pg 255 (1872 Dec 28); pg 263 (1873 Jan 25); pg 263 (1873 Jan 25); pg 267 (1873 Feb 8) bill prsented for livery hire; pg 271 (1873 Feb 22) bill presented; pg 299 (1873 June 28) bill presented for livery hire pg 337 (1873 Feb 22)
*did not become a member of the Columbia Lodge

Arnold, W A
pg 359 (1868 Sept 19) Cheyenne Lodge U.D.

Ashcroft, Samuel P
appears as: Ashcroft, Samuel P; Ashcroft, S P
pg 42 (1867 Aug 25) Denver Lodge No. 5; pg 72 (1868 Oct 24) Denver Lodge No. 5; pg 356 (1867 Aug 17) Denver Lodge No. 5; pg 358 (1868 Aug 17); Denver Lodge No. 5

Ashley, John K
pg 341 (1885) member

Austin, [Eugene A or Schuyler D]
pg 241 (1872 Sept 28); pg 261 (1873 Jan 14); pg 279 (1873 Mar 20)

Austin, Eugene A
appears as: Austin, E; Austin, Eugene
offices held: JD, SD, JW
pg 250 (1872 Nov 30); pg 273 (1873 Mar 7); pg 287 (1873 May 1)

Austin, Olin
pg 340 (1880 Dec 24) Occidental Lodge No. 20

Austin, Samuel B
pg 180 (1871 Jan 14); pg 185 (1871 Feb 25); pg 185 (1871 Feb 25); pg 291 (1873 May 24); pg 337 (1873 Nov 8)
*did not become a member of Columbia Lodge

Austin, Schuyler D
appears as: Austin, S D; Austin, S; Austin, Schuyler D
offices held: JD
pg 187 (1871 Mar 11) visiting; pg 253 (1872 Dec 26); pg 258 (1873 Jan 8); pg 314 member

Ba[tes], Walter
pg 152 (1870 May 14) Washington Lodge No. 12

Bader, Nicholas E
pg 97 (1869 Feb 27); pg 101 (1869 Mar 27); pg 102 (1869 Mar 21); pg 158 (1870 June 25); pg 163 (1870 Aug 13); pg 163 (1870 Aug 13); pg 335 (1867 Aug 13); pg 360 (1869 Nov 27)
*did not become a member of Columbia Lodge

Bailey
pg 254 (1872 Dec 28); pg 255 (1872 Dec 28); pg 255 (1872 Dec 28); pg 255 (1872 Dec 28); pg 296 (1873 June 14)

Bailey, John C
pg 123 (1869 Nov 13); pg 128 (1869 Dec 11); pg 128 (1869 Dec 11); pg 361 (1869 Dec 11)
*did not become a member of Columbia Lodge

Balford, Frank D
pg 315 member

Ballinger, William H
appears as: Ballanger, Wm H; Ballinger, Wm H
pg 209 (1871 Nov 25); pg 217 (1872 Jan 13); pg

217 (1872 Jan 13); pg 335 (1872 Jan 5) *did not become a member of Columbia Lodge

Ballou, Mrs
pg 59 (1867 Dec 14) bill presented

Banks, Francis B
appears as: Banks, F B
pg 315 member

Bard, Richard
appears as: Bard, Richard; Bard
pg 75 (1868 Nov 28) visiting from Columbus Lodge No. 8 NE; pg 90 (1869 Jan 23); pg 96 (1869 Feb 24); pg 135 (1870 Jan 22); pg 231 (1872 May 16); pg 233 (1872 June 1); pg 272 (1873 Feb 22) deed to his lot in the cemetery donated to him; pg 274 (1873 Mar 8); pg 302 (1873 July 19); pg 355 (1868 Jan 23) visitor, Columbus Lodge No. 8, NE

Barius, J H
pg 335 (1870 Aug 20) Cheyenne Lodge No. 16

Barkhurst, Ira C
appears as: Barkhurst, Ira C; Barkhurst, Ira
pg 82 (1868 Dec 26); pg 92 (1869 Jan 25); pg 120 (1869 Sept 25); pg 355 (1868 Feb 25) visitor, Black Hawk Lodge No. 11

Barney, Royal Sigbert
pg 314 member

Barney, William M
appears as: Barney, Wm M; Barney; Barney William; Barney, W M
pg 71 (1868 Oct 24); pg 73 (1868 Oct 24); pg 74 (1868 Oct 24); pg 85 (1869 Jan 9); pg 90 (1869 Jan 23); pg 129 (1869 Dec 11); pg 171 (1870 Nov 12); pg 172 (1870 Nov 26); pg 180 (1871 Jan 14); pg 180 (1871 Jan 14); pg 313 member

Barret, John A
pg 167 (1870 Sept 10) Cheyenne Lodge No. 16

Barrett, George
pg 43 (1867 Sept 5) visiting

Barrowman, William
pg 315 member

Bartels, Henry
pg 315 member

Barter, WIlliam
appears as: Barter
pg 282 (1873 Apr 5) visiting; pg 287 (1873 May 3)

Barth, John
pg 195 (1871 June 11) Nevada Lodge No. 4

Bartlett, H C
pg 229 (1872 May 9) Washington Lodge No. 12; pg 336 (1872 May 9) Washington Lodge No. 12

Bartlett, John C
pg 255 (1872 Dec 28) Union Lodge No. 7

Bartlette, John C
pg 336 (1872 Dec 28) Central Lodge No. 6

Bates, Walter
pg 362 (1870 Apr 23) Washington Lodge No. 12

Baum, Henry M
pg 314; member

Baumback, J W
pg 139 (1870 Feb 26) Mount Moriah Lodge No. 15

Beardsley, Bruce H
pg 335 (1867 July 28) Washington Lodge No. 12

Beardsley, Isaac H
pg 163 (1870 Aug 13) Washington Lodge No. 12

Beaudry, D B
pg 340 (1880 Nov) Ionic Lodge No. 35

Bebee, Mack F
pg 68 (1868 Aug 8) Black Hawk Lodge No. 11; pg 357 (1868 June 6) Black Hawk Lodge No. 11

Beckenhaupt, J M
pg 105 (1869 Apr 24) Cheyenne Lodge No. 16

Beckenhoupt, J M
pg 360 (1869 Apr 3) Golden Lodge No. 1

Belcher, Freeman
appears as: Belcher; Belcher, F; Belcher, Freeman
pg 90 (1869 Jan 23); pg 91 (1869 Jan 23); pg 94 (1869 Feb 13); pg 100 (1869 Mar 13); pg 100 (1869 Mar 13); pg 100 (1869 Mar 13); pg 355 (1868 Jan 23)

Belcher, Oscar F
pg 240 (1872 Sept 14) Golden Lodge No. 1; pg 336 (1872 Sept 14) Golden Lodge No. 1

proposed Masonic Hall; pg 163 (1870 Aug 13); pg 164 (1870 Aug 27); pg 168 (1870 Sept 15); pg 169 (1870 Sept 24) unable to attend Grand Lodge at Central City; pg 174 (1870 Dec 10); pg 175 (1870 Dec 10); pg 178 (1871 Jan 4); pg 184 (1871 Feb 18); pg 185 (1871 Feb 25); pg 200 (1871 Aug 12); pg 203 (1871 Sept 23); pg 204 (1871 Sept 23); pg 205 (1871 Oct 5); pg 210 (1871 Dec 9); pg 222 (1872 Feb 24); pg 313 member

Bock, David
appears as: Bock; Bock, D; Bock, David
offices held: SD, Tiler, JD
pg 69 (1868 Sept 12) visiting from Bourbon Lodge No. 227 IN; pg 96 (1869 Feb 24); pg 97 (1869 Feb 27); pg 108 (1869 May 22); pg 109 (1869 May 22) from Burbon Lodge No. 227 of IN; pg 110 (1869 May 25); pg 115 (1869 Aug 14); pg 116 (1869 Aug 14); pg 117 (1869 Aug 14); pg 118 (1869 Aug 28); pg 119 (1869 Sept 11); pg 120 (1869 Sept 25); pg 123 (1869 Nov 13); pg 130 (1869 Dec 15); pg 134 (1870 Jan 15); pg 135 (1870 Jan 22); pg 138 (1870 Feb 19); pg 201 (1871 Sept 9); pg 206 (1871 Oct 8); pg 208 (1871 Nov 11); pg 215 (1871 Dec 23); pg 216 (1872 Jan 13); pg 222 (1872 Feb 24); pg 223 (1872 Mar 9); pg 225 (1872 Mar 23); pg 226 (1872 Apr 13); pg 226 (1872 Apr 27); pg 229 (1872 May 9); pg 231 (1872 May 25); pg 232 (1872 June 1); pg 233 (1872 June 8); pg 234 (1872 June 22); pg 235 (1872 June 29); pg 237 (1872 July 27); pg 238 (1872 Aug 24); pg 239 (1872 Aug 31); pg 240 (1872 Sept 14); pg 241 (1872 Sept 28); pg 243 (1872 Oct 4); pg 244 (1872 Oct 26); pg 245 (1872 Oct 26); pg 246 (1872 Nov 9); pg 247 (1872 Nov 23); pg 250 (1872 Nov 30); pg 251 (1872 Dec 14); pg 252 (1872 Dec 14); pg 253 (1872 Dec 26); pg 254 (1872 Dec 26); pg 254 (1872 Dec 28); pg 256 (1872 Dec 28); pg 257 (1873 Jan 4); pg 258 (1873 Jan 8); pg 258 (1873 Jan 8); pg 259 (1873 Jan 11); pg 261 (1873 Jan 14); pg 262 (1873 Jan 25); pg 263 (1873 Jan 25); pg 265 (1873 Feb 1); pg 266 (1873 Feb 8); pg 269 (1873 Feb 8); pg 269 (1873 Feb 12); pg 270 (1873 Feb 22); pg 273 (1873 Mar 1); pg 274 (1873 Mar 7); pg 274 (1873 Mar 8); pg 277 (1873 Mar 11); pg 277 (1873 Mar 12); pg 278 (1873 Mar 15); pg 279 (1873 Mar 20); pg 280 (1873 Mar 22); pg 281 (1873 Mar 22); pg 281 (1873 Mar 29); pg 282 (1873 Apr 5); pg 283 (1873 Apr 12); pg 284 (1873 Apr 19); pg 285 (1873 Apr 26); pg 288 (1873 May 10); pg 289 (1873 May 14); pg 290 (1873 May 19); pg 290 (1873 May 24); pg 291 (1873 May 24); pg 292 (1873 May 27); pg 294 (1873 May 31); pg 294 (1873 June 4); pg 296 (1873 June 14); pg 297 (1873 June 24); pg 298 (1873 June 28); pg 299 (1873 June 28); pg 300 (1873 July 2); pg 301 (1873 July 12); pg 302 (1873 July 19); pg 303 (1873 July 26); pg 304 (1873 Aug 9); pg 305 (1873 Aug 23); pg 306 (1873 Sept 13); pg 307 (1873 Sept 27); pg 308 (1873 Oct 11); pg 313 member; pg 355 (1868 Feb 13) visitor, Bourbon, IN; pg 355 (1868 Feb 27) visitor, Bourbon, IN

Bock, Mrs Malinda
appears as: Bock, Mrs; Bock, Mrs Malinda; Bock, Malinda
pg 226 (1872 Apr 13) bill presented; pg 234 (1872 June 22) bill presented; pg 242 (1872 Sept 28) bill presented; pg 280 (1873 Mar 22) bill presented

Bock, Otto
pg 105 (1869 Apr 24) Union Lodge No. 7

Boenback, J W
pg 361 (1870 Jan 15) Mount Moriah Lodge No. 15

Bolitha [Bolitho], John H
pg 216 (1872 Jan 13) Washington Lodge No. 12
pg 335 (1872 Jan 5) Washington Lodge No. 12

Border, Samuel B
pg 316 (1883 Dec 22) member

Bosworth, R W
appears as: Bosworth
offices held: JW, SW
pg 190 (1871 Apr 8); pg 200 (1871 Aug 12)

Boulder House
pg 126 (1869 Nov 27) to provide the festival supper for $4 per couple

Bowen, Nelson
pg 21 (1867 Apr 23) Chivington Lodge No. 6;
pg 356 (1867 Apr 10) Chivington Lodge No. 6

Feb 12); pg 137 (1870 Feb 12); pg 138 (1870 Feb 19); pg 152 (1870 May 14); pg 173 (1870 Dec 3); pg 181 (1871 Jan 28); pg 192 (1871 Apr 22); pg 216 (1872 Jan 13); pg 217 (1872 Jan 13); pg 229 (1872 May 9); pg 244 (1872 Oct 26); pg 246 (1872 Nov 9); pg 266 (1873 Feb 8); pg 269 (1873 Feb 8); pg 270 (1873 Feb 22); pg 273 (1873 Mar 1); pg 313 member

Buell, Oliver S
appears as: Buell, O S; Buell, Oliver S
pg 9 (1867 Feb 28) Chivington Lodge No. 6; pg 356 (1867 Feb 13) Chivington Lodge No. 6

Bullock, Charles B
pg 340 (1880 Oct 9) Washington Lodge No. 12

Bullock, J F
pg 360 (1869 Mar 27) Washington Lodge No. 12

Bullock, J L
pg 103 (1869 Apr 10) Black Hawk Lodge No. 11

Bullock, James
pg 359 (1869 Feb 27) Washington Lodge No. 12

Bullock, L J
pg 103 (1869 Apr 10) Black Hawk Lodge No. 11

Bullock, L J
pg 360 (1869 Mar 27) Washington Lodge No. 12

Bullock, T J
pg 359 (1869 Feb 27) Washington Lodge No. 12

Bunn, David
appears as: Bunn; Bunn, David
pg 283 (1873 Apr 12); pg 288 (1873 May 10); pg 289 (1873 May 14); pg 290 (1873 May 24); pg 291 (1873 May 24); pg 294 (1873 May 31); pg 296 (1873 June 14); pg 297 (1873 June 14); pg 297 (1873 June 24); pg 298 (1873 June 24); pg 299 (1873 June 28); pg 303 (1873 July 26); pg 308 (1873 Oct 11); pg 314 member

Bunn, Samuel C
pg 316 (1884 Oct 11) member

Buoss
office held: Tiler
pg 173 (1870 Dec 3)

Burley, John W
pg 72 (1868 Oct 24) Nevada Lodge No 4 ; pg 358 (1868 Sept 26) Nevada Lodge No. 4

Burney, Robert
pg 190 (1871 Apr 8) Black Hawk Lodge No. 11

Burns, Joseph F
pg 338 (1874 Mar 28) Cheyenne Lodge No. 16

Burns, Lewis R
pg 359 (1868 Oct 17) Cheyenne Lodge No. 16

Bush, Arthur W
pg 314 member

Buttles, John F
appears as: Buttles; Buttles, J H
offices held: JW
pg 177 (1870 Dec 29); pg 189 (1871 Mar 25); pg 192 (1871 Apr 22); pg 193 (1871 Apr 22); pg 194 (1871 May 27); pg 198 (1871 July 12); pg 313 member

Cain
pg 191 (1871 Apr 13) visiting

Cainukun [??], John
pg 316 (1884 Sept 13) offended [?]

Campbell, John H
pg 216 (1872 Jan 13); pg 220 (1872 Feb 10); pg 221 (1872 Feb 10); pg 336 (1872 Feb 24)
*he did not become a member of the Columbia Lodge

Campbell, John L
pg 314 member

Campbell, Sanford B
pg 314 gone [moved away]

Canfield
pg 243 (1872 Oct 4)

Canklin, Henry
pg 115 (1869 Aug 14) Cheyenne Lodge No. 16

Carmack, Thomas K
appears as: Carmack, T K
pg 314 member

Carnahan, John
pg 361 (1870 Feb 12)
*did not become a member of the Columbia Lodge

Carter, George W
appears as: Carter; Carter, G W; Carter, George W
offices held: Secy, SW

pg 1 (1867 Jan 3); pg 2 (1867 Jan 3); pg 5 (1867 Jan 10); pg 6 (1867 Jan 10); pg 7 (1867 Jan 24); pg 8 (1867 Feb 14); pg 9 (1867 Feb 14); pg 9 (1867 Feb 28); pg 11 (1867 Feb 28); pg 11 (1867 Mar 6); pg 12 (1867 Mar 14); pg 13 (1867 Mar 14); pg 13 (1867 Mar 15); pg 14 (1867 Mar 18); pg 14 (1867 Mar 28); pg 16 (1867 Mar 28); pg 16 (1867 Apr 1); pg 17 (1867 Apr 4); pg 17 (1867 Apr 11); pg 19 (1867 Apr 11); pg 19 (1867 Apr 15); pg 20 (1867 Apr 18); pg 20 (1867 Apr 23); pg 21 (1867 Apr 23); pg 22 (1867 Apr 23); pg 22 (1867 Apr 29); pg 23 (1867 Apr 29); pg 23 (1867 May 3); pg 24 (1867 May 9); pg 25 (1867 May 9); pg 25 (1867 May 13); pg 26 (1867 May 23); pg 27 (1867 May 23); pg 27 (1867 June 13); pg 28 (1867 June 13); pg 29 (1867 June 15); pg 29 (1867 June 27); pg 31 (1867 June 27); pg 32 (1867 July 6); pg 32 (1867 June 27); pg 33 (1867 July 11); pg 35 (1867 July 11); pg 35 (1867 July 13); pg 36 (1867 July 15); pg 36 (1867 July 17); pg 37 (1867 July 17); pg 37 (1867 July 24); pg 38 (1867 July 25); pg 39 (1867 Aug 7); pg 39 (1867 Aug 8); pg 41 (1867 Aug 8); pg 41 (1867 Aug 17); pg 42 (1867 Aug 25); pg 43 (1867 Aug 25); pg 43 (1867 Sept 5); pg 44 (1867 Sept 12); pg 45 (1867 Sept 12); pg 45 (1867 Sept 14); pg 46 (1867 Sept 26); pg 47 (1867 Sept 26); pg 58 (1867 Nov 23); pg 59 (1867 Nov 23); pg 69 (1868 Sept 12); pg 75 (1868 Nov 28); pg 78 (1868 Dec 12); pg 85 (1869 Jan 9); pg 99 (1869 Mar 13); pg 115 (1869 Aug 14); pg 117 (1869 Aug 14); pg 117 (1869 Aug 14); pg 119 (1869 Sept 11); pg 120 (1869 Sept 11); pg 123 (1869 Nov 13); pg 125 (1869 Nov 13); pg 313 member

Carter, John C
pg 110 (1869 May 25) visiting

Cathers, John
pg 340 (1880 Dec 15) Idaho Springs Lodge No. 26

Catteson, R C [B C]
appears as: Catteson, R C; Catteson, B C
pg 87 (1869 Jan 9) Washington Lodge No. 12; pg 358 (1868 Dec 12) Washington Lodge No. 12

Chaffee, A R
pg 203 (1871 Sept 23) Collins Lodge No. 19

Chamberlain, O
pg 332 (1874 Apr 10) Washington Lodge No. 12

Chambers, John S
pg 315 member

Champion, Benjamin
pg 18 (1867 Apr 11) Denver Lodge No. 5; pg 356 (1867 Apr 6) Denver Lodge No. 5

Champion, Benjamin
pg 359 (1868 June 6) Cheyenne Lodge U.D.

Champion, W H [H W]
pg 309 (1873 Oct 11); pg 337 (1873 Nov 22); pg 338 (1873 Dec 13)
*did not become a member of the Columbia Lodge

Chapman, George A
pg 72 (1868 Oct 24) Pueblo Lodge U.D.; pg 358 (1868 Aug 26) Pueblo Lodge U.D.

Chapman, Joshua E
appears as: Chapman; Chapman, J; Chapman, J E; Chapman, Joshua E
offices held: JS, Secy
pg 91 (1869 Jan 23);pg 97 (1869 Feb 27); pg 98 (1869 Feb 27);pg 99 (1869 Mar 6); pg 104 (1869 Apr 24); pg 105 (1869 Apr 24); pg 108 (1869 May 8); pg 125 (1869 Nov 27); pg 127 (1869 Nov 27); pg 132 (1870 Jan 8); pg 132 (1870 Jan 8); pg 149 (1870 Apr 23); pg 154 (1870 May 28); pg 169 (1870 Sept 24); pg 172 (1870 Nov 26); pg 173 (1870 Dec 3); pg 176 (1870 Dec 24); pg 180 (1871 Jan 14); pg 183 (1871 Feb 9); pg 185 (1871 Feb 25); pg 195 (1871 June 11); pg 207 (1871 Oct 28); pg 231 (1872 May 25); pg 243 (1872 Oct 4); pg 313 member

Chapman, V
pg 93 (1869 Feb 13) visiting; pg 355 (1868 Feb 13) visitor Manchester Lodge No. 48, MI

Chase, George F
appears as: Chase; Chase, Geo F; Chase, George F
offices held: Treas, SS, JS, SW, Tiler, JW, Secy
pg 72 (1868 Oct 24); pg 74 (1868 Oct 24); pg 75 (1868 Nov 28); pg 76 (1868 Nov 28); pg 81 (1868 Dec 5); pg 85 (1869 Jan 9); pg 85 (1869 Jan 9); pg 90 (1869 Jan 16); pg 92 (1869 Jan 25); pg 105 (1869 Apr 24); pg 105 (1869 Apr 24); pg 109 (1869 May 22); pg 110 (1869 May

25); pg 117 (1869 Aug 21); pg 119 (1869 Sept 11); pg 120 (1869 Sept 25); pg 121 (1869 Sept 25); pg 121 (1869 Sept 25); pg 121 (1869 Sept 25); pg 123 (1869 Nov 13); pg 125 (1869 Nov 27); pg 126 (1869 Nov 27) committee to survey and stake the burial ground; pg 128 (1869 Dec 11); pg 129 (1869 Dec 11); pg 134 (1870 Jan 15); pg 135 (1870 Jan 22); pg 136 (1870 Feb 12); pg 137 (1870 Feb 12); pg 138 (1870 Feb 19); pg 140 (1870 Mar 8); pg 141 (1870 Mar 12); pg 142 (1870 Mar 17); pg 144 (1870 Mar 26); pg 144 (1870 Mar 26); pg 146 (1870 Apr 2); pg 147 (1870 Apr 9); pg 148 (1870 Apr 9); pg 149 (1870 Apr 23); pg 149 (1870 Apr 23); pg 150 (1870 Apr 23); pg 151 (1870 May 7); pg 152 (1870 May 14); pg 154 (1870 May 28); pg 155 (1870 June 4); pg 156 (1870 June 11); pg 158 (1870 June 25); pg 160 (1870 July 2); pg 160 (1870 July 9); pg 161 (1870 July 9); pg 162 (1870 July 24); pg 163 (1870 Aug 13); pg 164 (1870 Aug 27); pg 167 (1870 Sept 10); pg 168 (1870 Sept 15); pg 169 (1870 Sept 24); pg 170 (1870 Oct 8); pg 171 (1870 Nov 12); pg 172 (1870 Nov 26) bill presented for surveying Masonic cemetery; pg 174 (1870 Dec 10); pg 175 (1870 Dec 10); pg 177 (1870 Dec 29); pg 179 (1871 Jan 14); pg 183 (1871 Feb 9); pg 184 (1871 Feb 18); pg 185 (1871 Feb 25); pg 187 (1871 Mar 11); pg 192 (1871 Apr 22); pg 194 (1871 May 27); pg 198 (1871 July 12); pg 199 (1871 July 22); pg 200 (1871 Aug 12); pg 201 (1871 Sept 9); pg 205 (1871 Oct 5); pg 207 (1871 Oct 28); pg 208 (1871 Nov 11); pg 209 (1871 Nov 25); pg 210 (1871 Dec 9); pg 213 (1871 Dec 9); pg 214 (1871 Dec 23) committee to investigate building a Masonic hall; pg 215 (1871 Dec 23); pg 216 (1872 Jan 13); pg 218 (1872 Jan 27); pg 219 (1872 Feb 10); pg 222 (1872 Feb 24); pg 223 (1872 Mar 9); pg 226 (1872 Apr 13); pg 226 (1872 Apr 27); pg 228 (1872 Apr 27); pg 231 (1872 May 16); pg 231 (1872 May 25); pg 232 (1872 June 1); pg 234 (1872 June 22); pg 235 (1872 June 29); pg 236 (1872 July 27); pg 237 (1872 July 27); pg 238 (1872 Aug 24); pg 239 (1872 Aug 31); pg 243 (1872 Oct 4); pg 243 (1872 Oct 19); pg 244 (1872 Oct 26); pg 246 (1872 Nov 9); pg 250 (1872 Dec 14); pg 252 (1872 Dec 14); pg 253 (1872 Dec 26); pg 254 (1872 Dec 26); pg 254 (1872 Dec 28); pg 255 (1872 Dec 28); pg 256 (1873 Jan 4); pg 258 (1873 Jan 8); pg 259 (1873 Jan 11); pg 260 (1873 Jan 11); pg 261 (1873 Jan 14); pg 262 (1873 Jan 25); pg 263 (1873 Jan 25); pg 265 (1873 Feb 1); pg 266 (1873 Feb 8); pg 273 (1873 Mar 1); pg 274 (1873 Mar 8); pg 277 (1873 Mar 11); pg 277 (1873 Mar 12); pg 278 (1873 Mar 15); pg 279 (1873 Mar 22); pg 281 (1873 Mar 29); pg 283 (1873 Apr 12); pg 284 (1873 Apr 19); pg 285 (1873 Apr 26); pg 287 (1873 May 3); pg 288 (1873 May 10); pg 289 (1873 May 14); pg 290 (1873 May 19); pg 290 (1873 May 24); pg 292 (1873 May 27); pg 294 (1873 May 31); pg 294 (1873 June 4); pg 296 (1873 June 14); pg 298 (1873 June 28); pg 300 (1873 July 2); pg 301 (1873 July 12); pg 302 (1873 July 19); pg 303 (1873 July 26); pg 304 (1873 Aug 9); pg 305 (1873 Aug 23); pg 306 (1873 Sept 13); pg 307 (1873 Sept 27); pg 308 (1873 Sept 27); pg 308 (1873 Oct 11); pg 309 (1873 Oct 11); pg 313 member

Chase, H H
pg 187 (1871 Mar 11) Washington Lodge No. 12

Chatfield, J W
pg 338 (1873 Dec 13); Weston Lodge No. 22

Childs, Munroe D
pg 203 (1871 Sept 23) Collins Lodge No. 19

Childsatt, H G
pg 332 (1874 June 27) Pueblo Lodge No. 17

Chubbuck, Theodore A
pg 203 (1871 Sept 23) Collins Lodge No. 19

Clapp, George H
pg 359 (1869 Jan 2) Cheyenne Lodge No. 16

Clark, Andrew C
pg 195 (1871 June 11) Washington Lodge No. 12

Clark, Dr. G A
appears as: Clark; Clarke, Dr G A
pg 290 (1873 May 19); pg 290 (1873 May 24); pg 294 (1873 May 31); pg 296 (1873 June 14); pg 315 member

Clark, William M
pg 183 (1871 Feb 9) Washington Lodge No. 12

Clause, Henry
pg 240 (1872 Sept 14) Cheyenne Lodge No. 16; pg 336 (1872 Sept 14) Cheyenne Lodge No. 16

Clawson, David
pg 128 (1869 Dec 11) petitioner
*no evidence that a David Clawson became a member of the Columbia Lodge, but this could be David Clow

Clayton, G W
pg 26 (1867 May 23) bill presented

Cloos, Henry
pg 338 (1874 Mar 14) Cheyenne Lodge No. 16

Cloud, E
pg 173 (1870 Dec 3)

Clow, David
appears as: Clow; Clow, David
pg 132 (1870 Jan 8); pg 133 (1870 Jan 8); pg 172 (1870 Nov 26); pg 176 (1870 Dec 24); pg 178 (1871 Jan 4); pg 185 (1871 Feb 25); pg 186 (1871 Feb 25); pg 195 (1871 June 11); pg 195 (1871 June 11); pg 196 (1871 June 11); pg 197 (1871 July 8); pg 207 (1871 Oct 28); pg 313 member; pg 361 (1870 Jan 8)

Clow, Richard
pg 314 member

Cluff, Chester P
pg 270 (1873 Feb 22); pg 283 (1873 Apr 12); pg 284 (1873 Apr 12); pg 314 member

Cluster, John A
pg 102 (1869 Mar 21) initiate from Eagle Lodge No 12. Keokuk, IA

Coad, J F
pg 332 (1874 May 9) Cheyenne Lodge No. 16

Cobb
pg 142 (1870 Mar 17)

Coffman, E J
pg 355 (1868 Feb 25) visitor, son of affilate

Coffman, Enoch J
appears as: Coffman; Coffman, E J; Coffman, Enoch J
offices held: SW, Treas
pg 55 (1867 Oct 26) visiting from Samuel H Davis Lodge No. 96 of IL; pg 121 (1869 Sept 25); pg 124 (1869 Nov 13); pg 124 (1869 Nov 13); pg 174 (1870 Dec 10); pg 181 (1871 Jan 28); pg 120 (1869 Sept 25); pg 122 (1869 Sept 25); pg 175 (1870 Dec 10); pg 216 (1872 Jan 13); pg 217 (1872 Jan 13); pg 233 (1872 June 8); pg 233 (1872 June 8) dispensation to form a new lodge in Longmont; pg 313 member

Collier & Hall
pg 76 (1868 Nov 28) bill presented (of Central City); pg 79 (1868 Dec 14) cash paid

Collins, L G [S G]
pg 232 (1872 May 25) Union Lodge No. 7; pg 336 (1872 May 25) Union Lodge No. 7

Conan, H
pg 187 (1871 Mar 11); Black Hawk Lodge No. 11

Conklin, Henry
pg 360 (1869 Aug 7) Cheyenne Lodge No. 16

Conklin, John D
pg 156 (1870 June 11) Cheyenne Lodge No. 16

Conklin, John H
pg 187 (1871 Mar 11) Cheyenne Lodge No. 16

Conklin, John R
pg 362 (1870 Apr 2) Cheyenne Lodge No. 16

Conlson, John C
pg 332 (1874 Sept 26) Idaho Lodge U.D.

Connaught, J V
pg 359 (1869 Feb 24) Pueblo Lodge No. 17

Connell, John
pg 317 (1887 Nov 26) member

Conwell
pg 318 (no date) pencil list

Cook, George D
appears as: Cook; Cook, G D; Cook George D
offices held: JW, JD, Tiler
pg 40 (1867 Aug 8); pg 44 (1867 Sept 12); pg 44 (1867 Sept 12); pg 45 (1867 Sept 14); pg 47 (1867 Sept 26); pg 54 (1867 Oct 14); pg 57 (1867 Nov 10); pg 57 (1867 Nov 10); pg 59 (1867 Dec 14); pg 58 (1867 Nov 23); pg 64 (1868 Mar 28); pg 69 (1868 Sept 12); pg 108 (1869 May 22); pg 110 (1869 May 22) asked demit to join Black Hawk Lodge No. 11; pg 115 (1869 Aug 14); pg 313 demitted

Cook, William
appears as: Cook, Wm
office held: JD
pg 277 (1873 Mar 11)

Cooper, E H
pg 260 (1873 Jan 11) Pueblo Lodge No. 17

Corman, John
pg 137 (1870 Feb 12) El Paso Lodge No. 13

Corning, George C
appears as: Corning; Corning, G C; Corning, George C
offices held: SD, Treas, SS,
pg 236 (1872 July 27); pg 238 (1872 Aug 24); pg 239 (1872 Aug 31); pg 240 (1872 Sept 14); pg 241 (1872 Sept 14); pg 241 (1872 Sept 28); pg 242 (1872 Sept 28); pg 243 (1872 Oct 19); pg 244 (1872 Oct 26); pg 246 (1872 Nov 9); pg 247 (1872 Nov 23); pg 248 (1872 Nov 23); pg 249 (1872 Nov 23) committee for St Johns Day festival; pg 249 (1872 Nov 27); pg 252 (1872 Dec 14); pg 254 (1872 Dec 26); pg 254 (1872 Dec 28); pg 255 (1872 Dec 28); pg 255 (1872 Dec 28); pg 256 (1873 Jan 4); pg 258 (1873 Jan 8); pg 259 (1873 Jan 11); pg 261 (1873 Jan 14); pg 262 (1873 Jan 25); pg 265 (1873 Feb 1); pg 266 (1873 Feb 8); pg 269 (1873 Feb 12); pg 270 (1873 Feb 22); pg 273 (1873 Mar 1); pg 277 (1873 Mar 11); pg 277 (1873 Mar 12); pg 279 (1873 Mar 20); pg 280 (1873 Mar 22); pg 281 (1873 Mar 22); pg 281 (1873 Mar 29); pg 282 (1873 Apr 5); pg 284 (1873 Apr 19); pg 288 (1873 May 10); pg 290 (1873 May 19); pg 292 (1873 May 27); resolution offered concerning the dec'd and that the resolutions be placed in the Boulder News and the Central and Black Hawk papers; pg 307 (1873 Sept 27); repaid for money paid to the Grand Lodge; pg 307 (1873 Sept 27); pg 308 (1873 Sept 27); motion to appoint a committee to secure lumber to repair the cemetery grand fence and erect a small tool house near the entrance gate; pg 313 member

Corson, William A
appears as: Corson; Corson, W A; Corson, Wm A
offices held: WM, SW, SS, Tiler, JW, SD, Secy
pg 7 (1867 Jan 24); pg 10 (1867 Feb 28); pg 22 (1867 Apr 23); pg 29 (1867 June 27); pg 30 (1867 June 27); pg 31 (1867 June 27); pg 32 (1867 June 27); pg 42 (1867 Aug 25); pg 43 (1867 Aug 25); pg 44 (1867 Sept 12); pg 49 (1867 Oct 12); pg 51 (1867 Oct 12); pg 55 (1867 Oct 26); pg 59 (1867 Dec 14); pg 60 (1867 Dec 14); pg 66 (1868 Apr 11); pg 67 (1868 Apr 11); pg 67 (1868 Aug 8); pg 69 (1868 Sept 12); pg 70 (1868 Sept 12) discussed the removal of Columbia Lodge No. 14 to Boulder City; pg 71 (1868 Oct 24); pg 72 (1868 Oct 24); pg 75 (1868 Nov 28); pg 76 (1868 Nov 28); pg 76 (1868 Nov 28); pg 78 (1868 Dec 12); pg 80 (1868 Dec 14); pg 81 (1868 Dec 5); pg 81 (1868 Dec 19); pg 82 (1868 Dec 26); pg 83 (1868 Dec 26); pg 84 (1868 Dec 28); pg 84 (1868 Dec 31); pg 85 (1869 Jan 9); pg 89 (1859 Jan 13); pg 89 (1869 Jan 16); pg 90 (1869 Jan 23); pg 91 (1869 Jan 23); pg 92 (1869 Jan 25); pg 92 (1869 Jan 29); pg 93 (1869 Feb 12); pg 93 (1869 Feb 13); pg 95 (1869 Feb 13); pg 95 (1869 Feb 15); pg 96 (1869 Feb 24); pg 97 (1869 Feb 27); pg 98 (1869 Mar 6); pg 99 (1869 Mar 13); pg 101 (1869 Mar 13); pg 101 (1869 Mar 27); pg 103 (1869 Apr 10); pg 103 (1869 Apr 10); pg 104 (1869 Apr 24); pg 106 (1869 May 7); pg 107 (1869 May 8); pg 107 (1869 May 8); pg 108 (1869 May 22); pg 110 (1869 May 25); pg 111 (1869 June 12); pg 111 (1869 May 25); pg 112 (1869 June 12); pg 113 (1869 June 26); pg 114 (1869 June 26); pg 116 (1869 Aug 14); pg 118 (1869 Aug 28); pg 120 (1869 Sept 25); pg 121 (1869 Sept 25); pg 121 (1869 Sept 25); pg 123 (1869 Nov 13); pg 124 (1869 Nov 13) festival committee; pg 125 (1869 Nov 27); pg 126 (1869 Nov 27); pg 126 (1869 Nov 27) committee to survey and stake the burial ground; pg 127 (1869 Dec 11); pg 128 (1869 Dec 11); pg 129 (1869 Dec 11); pg 130 (1869 Dec 15); pg 131 (1869 Dec 15); pg 132 (1870 Jan 8); pg 134 (1870 Jan 15); pg 135 (1870 Jan 22); pg 136 (1870 Feb 12); pg 138 (1870 Feb 19); pg 139 (1870 Feb 26); pg 140 (1870 Feb 26); pg 140 (1870 Mar 8); pg 141 (1870 Mar 12); pg 142 (1870 Mar 17); pg 142 (1870 Mar 24); pg 143 (1870 Mar 25); pg 144 (1870 Mar 26); pg 147 (1870 Apr 9); pg 148 (1870 Apr 9) motion to fence in the burying ground on or before the 13th of June; pg 149 (1870 Apr 23); pg 150 (1870 Apr 23) motion that the SW quarter of block C by reserved as potters field; pg 150 (1870 Apr 23) motion to reserve Blocks A, B C and D in the cemetery for members only; pg 151 (1870 May 11); pg 151 (1870 May 7); pg 152

(1870 May 14); pg 154 (1870 May 28); pg 155 (1870 June 4); pg 157 (1870 June 11) committee to build the proposed Masonic Hall; pg 159 (1870 June 25) motion to reserve Blocks A, B C and D in the cemetery for members only; pg 159 (1870 June 25) motion that the SW quarter of block C by reserved as potters field; pg 160 (1870 July 2); pg 160 (1870 July 9); pg 161 (1870 July 9); pg 162 (1870 July pg 163 (1870 Aug 13); pg 164 (1870 Aug 27); pg 166 (1870 Sept 3); pg 167 (1870 Sept 10); pg 168 (1870 Sept 15); pg 169 (1870 Sept 24); pg 171 (1870 Nov 12); pg 172 (1870 Nov 26) bill presented for surveying Masonic cemetery; pg 173 (1870 Dec 3); pg 174 (1870 Dec 10); pg 175 (1870 Dec 10); pg 176 (1870 Dec 24); pg 177 (1870 Dec 29); pg 179 (1871 Jan 14); pg 180 (1871 Jan 14); pg 181 (1871 Jan 28); pg 183 (1871 Feb 9); pg 185 (1871 Feb 25); pg 187 (1871 Mar 11); pg 189 (1871 Mar 25); pg 190 (1871 Apr 8); pg 191 (1871 Apr 13); pg 192 (1871 Apr 22); pg 194 (1871 May 27); pg 199 (1871 July 22); pg 200 (1871 Aug 12); pg 200 (1871 Aug 12); pg 206 (1871 Oct 8); pg 207 (1871 Oct 28); pg 208 (1871 Nov 11); pg 209 (1871 Nov 25); pg 210 (1871 Dec 9); pg 213 (1871 Dec 9); pg 213 (1871 Dec 9); pg 214 (1871 Dec 23); pg 214 (1871 Dec 23); pg 216 (1872 Jan 13); pg 218 (1872 Jan 27); pg 219 (1872 Feb 10); pg 222 (1872 Feb 24); pg 223 (1872 Mar 9); pg 225 (1872 Apr 6); pg 225 (1872 Mar 23); pg 225 (1872 Mar 23); pg 226 (1872 Apr 13); pg 226 (1872 Apr 27); pg 229 (1872 May 9); pg 231 (1872 May 16); pg 231 (1872 May 25); pg 232 (1872 June 1); pg 233 (1872 June 8); pg 234 (1872 June 22); pg 235 (1872 June 29); pg 236 (1872 July 27); pg 237 (1872 July 27); pg 238 (1872 Aug 24); pg 239 (1872 Aug 31); pg 240 (1872 Sept 14); pg 242 (1872 Oct 4); pg 243 (1872 Oct 19); pg 244 (1872 Oct 26); pg 245 (1872 Oct 26); pg 247 (1872 Nov 23); pg 249 (1872 Nov 27); pg 250 (1872 Dec 14); pg 250 (1872 Nov 30); pg 250 (1872 Nov 30); pg 253 (1872 Dec 26); pg 262 (1873 Jan 25); pg 263 (1873 Jan 25); pg 267 (1873 Feb 8); pg 268 (1873 Feb 8); pg 268 (1873 Feb 8); pg 268 (1873 Feb 8); pg 277 (1873 Mar 12); pg 278 (1873 Mar 12); pg 281 (1873 Mar 29); pg 282 (1873 Apr 5); pg 283 (1873 Apr 12); pg 291 (1873 May 24); pg 299 (1873 June 28); pg 300 (1873 June 28); pg 301 (1873 July 12); pg 308 (1873 Sept 27) requested to write to H M Russell to present his bill for bringing furniture from Denver; pg 308 (1873 Oct 11); pg 309 (1873 Oct 11) member; pg 313 member

Corwin, John
pg 187 (1871 Mar 11) Black Hawk Lodge No. 11

Coulson, William Wallace
appears as: Coulson, W W
pg 91 (1869 Jan 23); pg 97 (1869 Feb 27); pg 98 (1869 Feb 27); pg 183 (1871 Feb 9); pg 187 (1871 Mar 11); pg 188 (1871 Mar 11); pg 195 (1871 June 11) bill presented for recording deeds of the cemetery and plat of the same; pg 358 (1869 Feb 27)
*did not become a member of the Columbia Lodge

Coulter, John A
pg 332 (1874 Nov 14) Washington Lodge No. 12

Cowgill
pg 307 (1873 Sept 27) visiting

Cox, James M
pg 361 (1869 Sept 25) Nevada Lodge No. 4

Cox, S M
pg 245 (1872 Oct 26) Mount Moriah Lodge No. 15

Cox, Thomas M
pg 139 (1870 Feb 26) Nevada Lodge No 4

Crawley, Daniel
pg 280 (1873 Mar 22) Collins Lodge No. 19; pg 337 (1873 Mar 22) Collins Lodge No. 19

Crofford, S W J [W S J]
pg 115 (1869 Aug 14) Washington Lodge No. 12; pg 361 (1869 June 26) Washington Lodge No. 12

Crolye, Lubyen
pg 179 (1871 Jan 14) Denver Lodge No. 5

Crosby, A B
offices held: JW, SW
pg 82 (1868 Dec 26) visiting from Liconic Lodge No. 144 ME; pg 85 (1868 Dec 31) visiting from Liconic Lodge No. 144 ME; pg 90 (1869 Jan 23; pg 140 (1870 Mar 8); pg 142 (1870 Mar

24); pg 149 (1870 Apr 23) bill presented for staking and plating the Masonic Cemetery; pg 166 (1870 Sept 3); pg 167 (1870 Sept 10); pg 168 (1870 Sept 15); pg 355 (1868 Jan 23) visitor, Leconic Lodge No. 144, ME

Crosby, Charles
offices held: JW
pg 6 (1867 Jan 10)

Crow, Richard
appears as: Crow; Crow, Ricahrd
pg 267 (1873 Feb 8); pg 275 (1873 Mar 8); pg 276 (1873 Mar 8); pg 278 (1873 Mar 12); pg 278 (1873 Mar 12); pg 290 (1873 May 24); pg 291 (1873 May 24); pg 291 (1873 May 24); pg 292 (1873 May 24); pg 296 (1873 June 14); pg 297 (1873 June 14); pg 297 (1873 June 14); pg 297 (1873 June 14); pg 305 (1873 Aug 23); pg 309 (1873 Oct 11); pg 314 member

Crowe, Price
pg 361 (1870 Jan 15) Denver Lodge No. 5

Cullacott, John J F
pg 315 member

Cummins, Isaac
appears as: Cummins; Cummins, Isaac
offices held: Treas
pg 29 (1867 June 27) visiting; pg 35 (1867 July 13) visiting; pg 32 (1867 July 6) ; pg 33 (1867 July 11); pg 41 (1867 Aug 17) visiting; pg 42 (1867 Aug 25) visiting; pg 43 (1867 Sept 5) visiting

Dabney, Charles
pg 42 (1867 Aug 25); pg 46 (1867 Sept 26); pg 47 (1867 Sept 26); pg 87 (1869 Jan 9) given ticket to the Festival; pg 301 (1873 July 12); pg 338 (1874 Mar 28); pg 356 (1867 Sept 26) *did not become a member of the Columbia Lodge

Daigne, Henry
pg 72 (1868 Oct 24) Pueblo Lodge U.D.; pg 358 (1868 Aug 26) Pueblo Lodge U.D.

Dailey, Baker and Smart
pg 226 (1872 Apr 13) printers of blank deeds, Denver, CO; pg 234 (1872 June 22) bill presented for printing blank deeds to cemetery lots

Dailey, John
pg 332 (1874 June 27) Washington Lodge No. 12

Danforth, W T
appears as: Danforth; Danforth, W T
offices held: Secy
pg 273 (1873 Mar 1); pg 274 (1873 Mar 7); pg 283 (1873 Apr 12); pg 284 (1873 Apr 19); pg 285 (1873 Apr 26); pg 290 (1873 May 24); pg 294 (1873 June 4); pg 296 (1873 June 14); pg 298 (1873 June 28); pg 300 (1873 July 2)

Davey, Joseph R J
pg 315 member

Davidson, Charles B
pg 315 member

Davidson, D
pg 226 (1872 Apr 13) Union Lodge No. 7; pg 336 (1872 Apr 13) Union Lodge No. 7

Davidson, W__
pg 315 member

Davis, Benj
pg 332 (1874 Apr 10) St Vrain Lodge No. 23

Davis, David
appears as: Davis, D
pg 314 member

Davis, J J
pg 132 (1870 Jan 8) El Paso Lodge No. 13; pg 361 (1869 Oct 9) El Paso Lodge No. 13

Davis, John
appears as: Davis; David; Davis, J; Davis, John
offices held: JS, JD, Tiler
pg 63 (1868 Feb 8); pg 65 (1868 Mar 28); pg 65 (1868 Mar 28); pg 66 (1868 Apr 11); pg 67 (1868 Apr 11); pg 69 (1868 Sept 12); pg 69 (1868 Sept 12); pg 69 (1868 Sept 12); pg 70 (1868 Sept 12); pg 90 (1869 Jan 23); pg 92 (1869 Jan 25); pg 93 (1869 Feb 13); pg 93 (1869 Feb 13); pg 95 (1869 Feb 13); pg 96 (1869 Feb 24); pg 96 (1869 Feb 24); pg 104 (1869 Apr 24); pg 111 (1869 June 12); pg 113 (1869 June 26); pg 118 (1869 Aug 28); pg 127 (1869 Dec 11); pg 127 (1869 Dec 11); pg 129 (1869 Dec 11); pg 130 (1869 Dec 15); pg 132 (1870 Jan 8); pg 132 (1870 Jan 8); pg 132 (1870 Jan 8); pg 135 (1870 Jan 22); pg 137 (1870 Feb 12); pg 154 (1870 May 28); pg 169 (1870 Sept

24); pg 171 (1870 Nov 12); pg 172 (1870 Nov 26); pg 180 (1871 Jan 14); pg 185 (1871 Feb 25); pg 185 (1871 Feb 25); pg 187 (1871 Mar 11); pg 192 (1871 Apr 22); pg 206 (1871 Oct 8); pg 207 (1871 Oct 28); pg 210 (1871 Nov 25); pg 210 (1871 Dec 9); pg 201 (1871 Sept 9); pg 209 (1871 Nov 25); pg 237 (1872 July 27); pg 253 (1872 Dec 14); pg 272 (1873 Feb 22); pg 278 (1873 Mar 15); pg 283 (1873 Apr 12); pg 308 (1873 Oct 11); pg 308 (1873 Sept 27); pg 313 member

Davis, Joel
pg 317 (1887 Mar 26) member

Davis, S A
pg 161 (1870 July 9) Larimer Lodge U.D,

Dawley, J[ames] M
pg 314 member

Day, W J
pg 185 (1871 Feb 25) Pueblo Lodge No. 17

Deardoff, Cyrus
pg 194 (1871 May 27) bill presented for building a gate and fence at the cemetery

Decker, Layman
pg 163 (1870 Aug 13) Black Hawk Lodge No. 11

Deitz, Henry
pg 315 member

DeKaes, T W
pg 161 (1870 July 9) Larimer Lodge U.D,

Dekey, T W
pg 362 (1870 May 25) Laramie Lodge U.D.

Delano, Milton M
appears as: Delano, M M; Delano, Milton M
pg 42 (1867 Aug 25) Denver Lodge No. 5; pg 72 (1868 Oct 24) Denver Lodge No. 5; pg 356 (1867 Aug 17) Denver Lodge No. 5; pg 358 (1868 Aug 17) Denver Lodge No. 5

Demars, Joseph
pg 283 (1873 Apr 12) Laramie Lodge No. 18; pg 337 (1873 Apr 12) Laramie Lodge No. 18

Dennison, B W [W W]
pg 68 (1868 Aug 8) Union Lodge No. 7; pg 357 (1868 Apr 11) Union Lodge No. 7

Deusman [Duesman], Geo
appears as Duesman, George; Deusman, George
pg 216 (1872 Jan 13) Washington Lodge No. 12; pg 335 (1872 Jan 5) Washington Lodge No. 12

Deyo, R H
pg 314 gone [moved]

Dickens, William H
pg 86 (1869 Jan 9); pg 94 (1869 Feb 13); pg 95 (1869 Feb 13); pg 358 (1869 Feb 13)
*did not become a member of the Columbia Lodge

Dickson, Lewis H
appears as: Dickson, L H
pg 86 (1869 Jan 9); pg 94 (1869 Feb 13); pg 95 (1869 Feb 13); pg 358 (1869 Feb 13)
*did not become a member of the Columbia Lodge

Dimick, E C
pg 340 (1881 Jan 15) Collins Lodge No. 19

Dimick, Erastus H
appears as: Dimick, E H
pg 314 member

Doane, George
pg 209 (1871 Nov 25) Washington Lodge No. 12

Dodge, Horace O
pg 315 member

Dolan, John
pg 359 (1868 Dec 5) Cheyenne Lodge No. 16

Dolloff, John W
appears as: Dolluff, J W
pg 316 (1883 June 23) member

Dolluff, see Dolloff, John W

Dolph, A
pg 170 (1870 Oct 8) Union Lodge No. 7

Donald
pg 253 (1872 Dec 26) visiting

Donaldson, Charles B
pg 332 (1874 July 25)
*did not become a member of the Columbia Lodge

Donnelly, George M
pg 51 (1867 Oct 12) Nevada Lodge No 4; pg 356 (1867 Sept 28) Nevada Lodge No. 4

Douglas, J & Bro
pg 51 (1867 Oct 12) bill presented

Douglas, W W
pg 203 (1871 Sept 23) Mount Moriah Lodge No. 15

Dow, A J House
pg 187 (1871 Mar 11) Occidental Lodge U.D.

Dow, J E
pg 315 member

Dowell, C C
pg 315 member

Down, John
pg 332 (1874 Aug 8) Black Hawk Lodge No. 11

Downer, Benjamin F
appears as: Downer, B F; Downer, Benjamin F
pg 94 (1869 Feb 13); pg 100 (1869 Mar 13); pg 100 (1869 Mar 13); pg 355 (1868 Feb 27) visitor, Denver Lodge No. 5, Colo
*did not become a member of the Columbia Lodge

Downer, S J
pg 315 member

Dreckman, Adolph
pg 115 (1869 Aug 14) Cheyenne Lodge No. 16; pg 360 (1869 July 17) Cheyenne Lodge No. 16

Drew
pg 269 (1873 Feb 12); pg 288 (1873 May 10)

Drumm, Henry
pg 315 member

Duesman, see Deusman, George

Dullen, J A
pg 161 (1870 July 9) Larimer Lodge U.D,

Dunagan, Elijah
appears as: Dunagan, E
pg 315 member

Dunagan, Jackson J
appears as: Dunigan, J J; Dunagan, J J
offices held: Tiler, SS, JW, SD
pg 1 (1867 Jan 3); pg 7 (1867 Jan 24); pg 8 (1867 Feb 14); pg 9 (1867 Feb 28); pg 11 (1867 Mar 6); pg 12 (1867 Mar 14); pg 13 (1867 Mar 15); pg 14 (1867 Mar 18); pg 14 (1867 Mar 28); pg 16 (1867 Apr 1);pg 17 (1867 Apr 11);pg 17 (1867 Apr 4); pg 19 (1867 Apr 15);pg 20 (1867 Apr 18);pg 20 (1867 Apr 23); pg 22 (1867 Apr 29); pg 23 (1867 May 3);pg 24 (1867 May 9); pg 25 (1867 May 13); pg 26 (1867 May 23); pg 27 (1867 June 13); pg 29 (1867 June 15); pg 29 (1867 June 27);pg 32 (1867 July 6);pg 33 (1867 July 11);pg 35 (1867 July 13); pg 36 (1867 July 15); pg 36 (1867 July 17); pg 38 (1867 July 25); pg 39 (1867 Aug 7); pg 41 (1867 Aug 17); pg 42 (1867 Aug 25); pg 43 (1867 Sept 5); pg 45 (1867 Sept 14)

Dunn, James
pg 267 (1873 Feb 8); pg 275 (1873 Mar 8); pg 276 (1873 Mar 8); pg 278 (1873 Mar 12); pg 278 (1873 Mar 12); pg 290 (1873 May 24); pg 291 (1873 May 24); pg 291 (1873 May 24); pg 292 (1873 May 24); pg 298 (1873 June 28); pg 299 (1873 June 28); pg 300 (1873 June 28); pg 314 member

Dunnigan, see Dunagan, Jackson J

Duran, J G
pg 362 (1870 May 25) Laramie Lodge U.D.

Duval, John
pg 340 (1880 Nov) Ionic Lodge No. 35

Dyer, Timothy
appears as: Dyer, Tim; Dyer, Timothy
pg 128 (1869 Dec 11) Cheyenne Lodge No. 16; pg 187 (1871 Mar 11) Cheyenne Lodge No. 16; pg 361 (1869 Dec 7) Cheyenne Lodge No. 16; pg 359 (1868 Oct 17) Cheyenne Lodge No. 16

Dyre
pg 234 (1872 June 22) visiting; pg 307 (1873 Sept 27) visiting

Eagleston, James C
pg 341 (1885) member

Earhart, W R
pg 315 member

Ebers, James
pg 358 (1869 Jan 23) Washington Lodge No. 12

Eddy, Edward
pg 332 (1874 Apr 10) Washington Lodge No. 12

Fairhurst
pg 318 pencil list

Fairhurst, James
pg 162 (1870 July 24) Pueblo Lodge No. 17; pg 335 (1867 July 4) Pueblo Lodge No. 17

Farmun, H H Jr
pg 15 (1867 Mar 28) Chivington Lodge No. 6; pg 356 (1867 Mar 13) Chivington Lodge No. 6

Farrer, Fisk
pg 219 (1872 Feb 10) Union Lodge No. 7; pg 335 (1872 Feb 11) Union Lodge No. 7

Farwell, Cyrus D
pg 68 (1868 Aug 8) Union Lodge No. 7; pg 357 (1868 July 25) Union Lodge No. 7

Faurot, Chalres S
pg 317 (1888 Mar 19) member

Fein, J J
pg 362 (1870 Apr 25) Laramie Lodge U.D.

Feshler, Maris
pg 332 (1874 Oct 11) Black Hawk Lodge No. 11

Fickler, M
pg 246 (1872 Nov 9) Nevada Lodge No. 4; pg 336 (1872 Nov 9) Nevada Lodge No. 4

Finch, L J
pg 360 (1869 Mar 27) Washington Lodge No. 12

Fishler, Moriarty
pg 195 (1871 June 11) Nevada Lodge No. 4

Fitzgerald, John
pg 147 (1870 Apr 9) Cheyenne Lodge No. 16; pg 362 (1870 Mar 19) Cheyenne Lodge No. 16

Fitzsimmons, George N
pg 338 (1878 Aug 22) Black Hawk Lodge No. 11

Fleming, W H
pg 291 (1873 May 24) Washington Lodge No. 12; pg 337 (1873 May 24) Washington Lodge No. 12

Fonda, George
pg 316 (1883 Aug 11) member

Foote, James B
pg 316 (1884 Aug 9); member

Foster, James A
pg 149 (1870 Apr 23) Pueblo Lodge No. 17; pg 362 (1870 Apr 14) Pueblo Lodge No. 17

Fowler, Wm R
pg 245 (1872 Oct 26) Mount Moriah Lodge No. 15

French, S M
pg 315 member

Freund, George
pg 101 (1869 Mar 27) Cheyenne Lodge No. 16; pg 360 (1869 Nov 20) Cheyenne Lodge No. 16

Fry, Wm H
pg 69 (1868 Sept 12) visiting from Keystone Lodge No. 271, A Y M Penn

Fullen, Hiram
pg 317 (1889 June 8) member

Fuller, Samuel G
pg 332 (1874 Oct 11) Occidental Lodge No. 20

Gallagher, Joseph
pg 333 (1874 Nov 28) Nevada Lodge No. 4

Galusha, Simon S
pg 318 (1889 Oct 12) member

Gamble, Rufus E
pg 56 (1867 Oct 26) Golden Lodge No. 1; pg 356 (1867 May 4) Golden Lodge No. 1

Gardner
pg 99 (1869 Mar 13) visiting

Gardner, Charles
pg 258 (1873 Jan 8) visiting

Gardner, E H
pg 219 (1872 Feb 10) Union Lodge No. 7

Gates, F A
pg 359 (1868 Dec 5) Cheyenne Lodge No. 16

Gates, Frank
pg 121 (1869 Sept 25) Pueblo Lodge No. 17

Gilbert, Clark
pg 314 member

Gilbert, Joseph
pg 338 (1878 Aug 22) Black Hawk Lodge No. 11

Gilbert, Richard
pg 226 (1872 Apr 13) Central Lodge No. 6; pg 336 (1872 Apr 13) Central Lodge No. 6

Gilliam, W H
pg 315 member

Gillinger, Joseph
pg 339 (1878 Aug 22) Black Hawk Lodge No. 11

Gillman, Walter
pg 245 (1872 Oct 26) bill presented for playing in the band and his expenses while staying for that purpose

Glass, Daniel
pg 275 (1873 Mar 8) Washington Lodge No. 12; pg 337 (1873 Mar 8) Washington Lodge No. 12

Gleen, O S
pg 42 (1867 Aug 25) Denver Lodge No. 5

Glenden & Brewer
pg 121 (1869 Sept 25) bill presented (of Central City)

Glenn, O S
pg 356 (1867 Aug 3) Denver Lodge No. 5

Gobesthurler, John W
pg 113 (1869 June 26) Union Lodge No. 7; pg 360 (1869 June 14) Union Lodge No. 7

Godwin, H H
pg 355 (1868 Jan 23) visitor, demitted from Westfield Lodge No. 115, IN

Goff, Lorin S
pg 69 (1868 Sept 12) Germania Lodge, U.D.; pg 358 (1868 Aug 17) Germania Lodge, U.D.

Goldenworthy, John
pg 332 (1874 June 27) Empire Lodge No. 8

Good Templar's Lodge
pg 31 (1867 June 27) petition to hold their meetings in the Masonic Lodge

Goodall, Dania
pg 121 (1869 Sept 25) bill presented

Goodall, David J
appears as: Goodail, D J; Goodail, David J
pg 114 (1869 June 26) bill presented; pg 338 (1873 Dec 13)
*did not become a member of the Columbia Lodge

Goodail, see Goodall, Dania, Goodall, David J

Goodrich, W W
pg 340 (1880 Oct 23) Union Lodge No. 7

Goodwin, Harrison
appears as: Goodwin; Goodwin, Dr; Goodwin, H; Goodwin, Harrison
pg 90 (1869 Jan 23); pg 91 (1869 Jan 23); pg 97 (1869 Feb 27); pg 98 (1869 Feb 27); pg 99 (1869 Mar 13); pg 246 (1872 Nov 9)
*did not become a member of the Columbia Lodge

Goodwin, M W [N W]
pg 315 member

Goodwin, Oliver P
pg 251 (1872 Dec 14) Collins Lodge No. 19; pg 336 (1872 Dec 14) Collins Lodge No. 19

Goss, [Abel or P D]
pg 226 (1872 Apr 13); pg 231 (1872 May 25); pg 232 (1872 June 1); pg 233 (1872 June 8); pg 234 (1872 June 22); pg 235 (1872 June 29); pg 236 (1872 July 27); pg 237 (1872 July 27); pg 238 (1872 Aug 24); pg 239 (1872 Aug 31); pg 243 (1872 Oct 19); pg 244 (1872 Oct 26); pg 269 (1873 Feb 12); pg 297 (1873 June 24); pg 301 (1873 July 12); pg 302 (1873 July 19)

Goss, Abel
offices held: Tiler
pg 71 (1868 Oct 24); pg 85 (1868 Dec 31) visiting from Parumsic Lodge No. 27 VT; pg 314 member

Goss, P D
offices held: Secy, JD, JS, Treas
pg 178 (1871 Jan 4); pg 178 (1871 Jan 4); pg 225 (1872 Apr 6); pg 235 (1872 June 29); pg 236 (1872 July 27); pg 240 (1872 Sept 14); pg 269 (1873 Feb 12)

Goulding, W E
pg 338 (1874 Mar 28) Cheyenne Lodge No. 16

Graham, George W
appears as: Graham; Graham, G W; Graham, George W
offices held: JW, SS, Tiler, SW
pg 7 (1867 Jan 24); pg 8 (1867 Feb 14); pg 9 (1867 Feb 28); pg 11 (1867 Mar 6); pg 12 (1867 Mar 14); pg 13 (1867 Mar 15); pg 14 (1867 Mar 28); pg 16 (1867 Apr 1); pg 17 (1867 Apr 11); pg 17 (1867 Apr 4); pg 19 (1867 Apr 15); pg

20 (1867 Apr 18); pg 20 (1867 Apr 23); pg 22 (1867 Apr 29); pg 23 (1867 May 3); pg 24 (1867 May 9); pg 25 (1867 May 13); pg 26 (1867 May 23); pg 27 (1867 June 13); pg 29 (1867 June 15); pg 29 (1867 June 27); pg 33 (1867 July 11); pg 35 (1867 July 13); pg 36 (1867 July 15); pg 36 (1867 July 17); pg 37 (1867 July 24); pg 38 (1867 July 25); pg 42 (1867 Aug 25); pg 43 (1867 Sept 5); pg 44 (1867 Sept 12); pg 45 (1867 Sept 14); pg 46 (1867 Sept 26); pg 49 (1867 Oct 12); pg 51 (1867 Oct 12); pg 52 (1867 Oct 14); pg 54 (1867 Oct 16); pg 55 (1867 Oct 26); pg 57 (1867 Nov 10)

Graham, Joseph
pg 359 (1868 Nov 27) Cheyenne Lodge No. 16

Grant, Dewitt C
appears as: Grant, D C; Grant, Dewitt, C
pg 72 (1868 Oct 24) Nevada Lodge No 4; pg 116 (1869 Aug 14) Nevada Lodge No 4; pg 358 (1868 July 25) Nevada Lodge No. 4; pg 360 (1869 June 12) Nevada Lodge No. 4

Grant, M N
pg 332 (1874 Nov 28) Laramie Lodge No. 18

Gravestrock, John
pg 113 (1869 June 26) Mount Maria Lodge No. 15; pg 360 (1869 June 18) Mount Moriah Lodge No. 15

Gray, John
pg 262 (1873 Jan 25) Denver Lodge No. 5

Gray, W S
pg 101 (1869 Mar 21) communication from Keokuk, IA that John A Cluster was initiated in 1862

Green, Henry
appears as: Green; Green, H; Green, Henry
offices held: JS, JD. SD. SS
pg 27 (1867 June 13); pg 34 (1867 July 11); pg 34 (1867 July 11); pg 37 (1867 July 24); pg 41 (1867 Aug 17); pg 44 (1867 Sept 12); pg 45 (1867 Sept 12); pg 46 (1867 Sept 26); pg 47 (1867 Sept 26); pg 49 (1867 Oct 12); pg 55 (1867 Oct 26); pg 57 (1867 Nov 10); pg 59 (1867 Dec 14); pg 60 (1867 Dec 14); pg 60 (1867 Dec 14); pg 66 (1868 Apr 11); pg 67 (1868 Aug 8); pg 78 (1868 Dec 12); pg 80 (1868 Dec 14); pg 81 (1868 Dec 19); pg 82 (1868 Dec 26); pg 84 (1868 Dec 28); pg 85 (1868 Dec 31); pg 89 (1859 Jan 13); pg 90 (1869 Jan 23); pg 92 (1869 Jan 25); pg 92 (1869 Jan 29); pg 95 (1869 Feb 15); pg 96 (1869 Feb 24); pg 97 (1869 Feb 27); pg 98 (1869 Mar 6); pg 99 (1869 Mar 13); pg 101 (1869 Mar 27); pg 104 (1869 Apr 24); pg 108 (1869 May 22); pg 110 (1869 May 25); pg 113 (1869 June 26); pg 127 (1869 Dec 11); pg 129 (1869 Dec 11); pg 130 (1869 Dec 15); pg 133 (1870 Jan 8); pg 135 (1870 Jan 22); pg 139 (1870 Feb 26); pg 142 (1870 Mar 17); pg 144 (1870 Mar 26); pg 149 (1870 Apr 23); pg 151 (1870 May 7); pg 151 (1870 May 11); pg 155 (1870 June 4); pg 156 (1870 June 11); pg 163 (1870 Aug 13); pg 168 (1870 Sept 15); pg 172 (1870 Nov 26); pg 174 (1870 Dec 10); pg 181 (1871 Jan 28); pg 190 (1871 Apr 8); pg 192 (1871 Apr 22); pg 194 (1871 May 27); pg 210 (1871 Dec 9); pg 214 (1871 Dec 23); pg 218 (1872 Jan 27); pg 219 (1872 Feb 10); pg 221 (1872 Feb 10); pg 222 (1872 Feb 24); pg 223 (1872 Mar 9); pg 225 (1872 Mar 23); pg 225 (1872 Apr 6); pg 237 (1872 July 27); pg 243 (1872 Oct 19); pg 246 (1872 Nov 9); pg 247 (1872 Nov 23); pg 249 (1872 Nov 23); pg 249 (1872 Nov 27); pg 250 (1872 Dec 14); 253 (1872 Dec 14); pg 254 (1872 Dec 26); pg 262 (1873 Jan 25); pg 263 (1873 Jan 25); pg 265 (1873 Feb 1); pg 266 (1873 Feb 8); pg 267 (1873 Feb 8); pg 269 (1873 Feb 12); pg 277 (1873 Mar 12); pg 278 (1873 Mar 15); pg 287 (1873 May 3); pg 292 (1873 May 27); 306 (1873 Sept 13); pg 313 member

Greenlief, L N
pg 51 (1867 Oct 12); Junior Grand Master

Gregory, A J
pg 338 (1874 Mar 14) Laramie Lodge No. 18

Griffith, J S
pg 332 (1874 Aug 22) St Vrain Lodge No. 23

Griffith, Joseph F
appears as: Griffith, Joseph; Griffith, Joseph F; Griffith, Joseph L
pg 255 (1872 Dec 28); pg 263 (1873 Jan 25); pg 264 (1873 Jan 25); pg 337 (1873 Feb 22)
*did not become a member of the Columbia Lodge

(1871 Jan 14); pg 223 (1872 Feb 24); pg 253 (1872 Dec 14); pg 259 (1873 Jan 11); pg 313 member

Hammond
pg 154 (1870 May 28) visiting; pg 155 (1870 June 4) visiting

Hampton, James
pg 141 (1870 Mar 12) Washington Lodge No. 12

Hancock, John
pg 246 (1872 Nov 9) Nevada Lodge No. 4; pg 336 (1872 Nov 9) Nevada Lodge No. 4

Hanken, M F
pg 314 member

Hanson, H P
pg 124 (1869 Nov 13) Cheyenne Lodge No. 16; pg 361 (1869 Nov 6) Cheyenne Lodge No. 16

Harkell, Hubbard B
pg 141 (1870 Mar 12) Union Lodge No. 7

Harmon, George D
appears as: Harmon; Harmon, G D; Harmon, George D
pg 107 (1869 May 8); pg 110 (1869 May 25); pg 103 (1869 Apr 10); pg 134 (1870 Jan 15); pg 274 (1873 Mar 8); pg 275 (1873 Mar 8); pg 280 (1873 Mar 22); pg 281 (1873 Mar 22); pg 283 (1873 Apr 12); pg 284 (1873 Apr 12); pg 285 (1873 Apr 26); pg 286 (1873 Apr 26); pg 286 (1873 Apr 26); pg 286 (1873 Apr 26); pg 298 (1873 June 28); pg 298 (1873 June 28); pg 299 (1873 June 28); pg 300 (1873 July 2)

Harmon, M D
pg 314 member

Harper, J W
pg 115 (1869 Aug 14) Washington Lodge No. 12; pg 361 (1869 June 26) Washington Lodge No. 12

Harrets, Myers B
appears as: Harrets, M B; Harrets, Myers B, Harris; Harris, Myers; Marris, M;
*later changed his name to Myers B Harris
offices held: Tiler
pg 44 (1867 Sept 12); pg 85 (1869 Jan 9); pg 97 (1869 Feb 27); pg 99 (1869 Mar 13); pg 123 (1869 Nov 13); pg 125 (1869 Nov 13); pg 128 (1869 Dec 11); pg 149 (1870 Apr 23); pg 154 (1870 May 28); pg 155 (1870 May 28); pg 155 (1870 June 4); pg 156 (1870 June 4); pg 164 (1870 Aug 27); pg 165 (1870 Aug 27); pg 166 (1870 Sept 3); pg 167 (1870 Sept 10); pg 167 (1870 Sept 10); pg 168 (1870 Sept 15); pg 175 (1870 Dec 10); pg 176 (1870 Dec 24); pg 177 (1870 Dec 29); pg 178 (1871 Jan 4); pg 179 (1871 Jan 14); pg 181 (1871 Jan 28); pg 183 (1871 Feb 9); pg 184 (1871 Feb 18); pg 185 (1871 Feb 25); pg 194 (1871 May 27); pg 195 (1871 June 11); pg 197 (1871 July 8); pg 198 (1871 July 12); pg 199 (1871 July 22); pg 200 (1871 Aug 12); pg 200 (1871 Aug 12); pg 201 (1871 Sept 9); pg 203 (1871 Sept 23); pg 207 (1871 Oct 28); pg 208 (1871 Nov 11); pg 209 (1871 Nov 25); pg 210 (1871 Dec 9); pg 211 (1871 Dec 9); pg 214 (1871 Dec 23); pg 216 (1872 Jan 13); pg 217 (1872 Jan 13); pg 218 (1872 Jan 27); pg 219 (1872 Feb 10); pg 220 (1872 Feb 10); pg 230 (1872 May 9); pg 231 (1872 May 16); pg 233 (1872 June 8); pg 243 (1872 Oct 19); pg 245 (1872 Oct 26); pg 246 (1872 Nov 9); pg 248 (1872 Nov 23); pg 249 (1872 Nov 27); pg 260 (1873 Jan 11); pg 265 (1873 Feb 1); pg 296 (1873 June 14); pg 313 member; pg 361 (1869 Dec 11)

Harris & Woodward
pg 234 (1872 June 22) bill presented for gloves

Harris, Addison W
appears as: Harris, A W; Harris, Addison W; Harrison, Addison W
offices held: Tiler, JS, Steward, SD, JW, SW
pg 26 (1867 May 23); pg 30 (1867 June 27); pg 31 (1867 June 27); pg 72 (1868 Oct 24); pg 74 (1868 Oct 24); pg 75 (1868 Nov 28); pg 76 (1868 Nov 28); pg 77 (1868 Nov 28); pg 78 (1868 Dec 12); pg 80 (1868 Dec 14); pg 81 (1868 Dec 19); pg 81 (1868 Dec 19); pg 82 (1868 Dec 26); pg 83 (1868 Dec 26); pg 84 (1868 Dec 28); pg 85 (1868 Dec 31); pg 89 (1859 Jan 13); pg 89 (1869 Jan 16); pg 92 (1869 Jan 25); pg 93 (1869 Feb 12); pg 93 (1869 Feb 13); pg 96 (1869 Feb 24); pg 98 (1869 Mar 6); pg 104 (1869 Apr 24); pg 106 (1869 May 7); pg 107 (1869 May 8); pg 108 (1869 May 22); pg 110 (1869 May 25); pg 117 (1869 Aug 21); pg 120 (1869 Sept 25); pg 121 (1869 Sept 25); pg 122 (1869 Sept 25); pg 129 (1869 Dec 11); pg

170 (1870 Oct 8); pg 187 (1871 Mar 11); pg 205 (1871 Oct 5); pg 233 (1872 June 8); pg 313 member; pg 356 (1867 June 27)

Harris, Albert
pg 361 (1869 Dec 23); Black Hawk Lodge No. 11

Harris, Jacob C
pg 338 (1874 Mar 28) Cheyenne Lodge No. 16

Harris, John
pg 333 (1874 June 27)
*did not become a member of the Columbia Lodge

Harris, Robert
pg 139 (1870 Feb 26) Black Hawk Lodge No. 11; pg 165 (1870 Aug 27) Black Hawk Lodge No. 11; pg 335 (1867 Dec 13) Black Hawk Lodge No. 11

Harris, William L
pg 183 (1871 Feb 9) El Paso Lodge No. 13

Hart, Thomas C
pg 192 (1871 Apr 22) Pueblo Lodge No. 17

Harter, G W
pg 360 (1869 Mar 15) Black Hawk Lodge No. 11

Harvey, Christopher
appears as: Harvey; Harvey, Christopher
pg 288 (1873 May 10); pg 314 member

Harvey, Mrs
pg 245 (1872 Oct 26) bill presented
*probably Mrs Christopher Harvey

Haskell, Hickford B
pg 362 (1870 Mar 1) Union Lodge No. 7

Haskins, M R
pg 357 (1868 Jan 11) Washington Lodge No. 12

Haskins, Phillip S
pg 62 (1868 Jan 25) Washington Lodge No. 12; pg 357 (1868 Jan 11) Washington Lodge No. 12

Haskins, W R
pg 62 (1868 Jan 25) Washington Lodge No. 12

Hass, H
pg 115 (1869 Aug 14) Cheyenne Lodge No. 16

Hasse, H
pg 360 (1869 Aug 7) Cheyenne Lodge No. 16

Haswell & Co
pg 15 (1867 Mar 28) bill presented; pg 30 (1867 June 27) cash draft; pg 34 (1867 July 11) bill presented; pg 47 (1867 Sept 26) bill presented; pg 59 (1867 Dec 14) bill presented; pg 79 (1868 Dec 14) cash paid

Haswell & Henry
pg 66 (1868 Apr 11) bill presented; pg 78 (1868 Dec 12) bill presented

Haswell, Theodore
appears as: Haswell; Haswell, T; Haswell, Theo; Haswell, Theodore
offices held: SW, WM
pg 1 (1867 Jan 3); pg 2 (1867 Jan 3); pg 7 (1867 Jan 24); pg 8 (1867 Feb 14); pg 9 (1867 Feb 28); pg 11 (1867 Mar 6); pg 12 (1867 Mar 14); pg 13 (1867 Mar 15); pg 14 (1867 Mar 18); pg 14 (1867 Mar 28); pg 16 (1867 Mar 28); pg 16 (1867 Apr 1); pg 17 (1867 Apr 4); pg 17 (1867 Apr 11); pg 19 (1867 Apr 15); pg 20 (1867 Apr 18); pg 20 (1867 Apr 23); pg 22 (1867 Apr 29); pg 23 (1867 May 3); pg 24 (1867 May 9); pg 25 (1867 May 13); pg 26 (1867 May 23); pg 27 (1867 May 23); pg 27 (1867 June 13); pg 29 (1867 June 15); pg 29 (1867 June 27); pg 31 (1867 June 27); pg 32 (1867 July 6); pg 33 (1867 July 11); pg 35 (1867 July 13); pg 36 (1867 July 15); pg 36 (1867 July 17); pg 37 (1867 July 24); pg 38 (1867 July 25); pg 39 (1867 Aug 7); pg 39 (1867 Aug 8); pg 41 (1867 Aug 17); pg 42 (1867 Aug 25); pg 43 (1867 Sept 5); pg 44 (1867 Sept 12); pg 45 (1867 Sept 14); pg 46 (1867 Sept 26); pg 49 (1867 Oct 8); pg 49 (1867 Oct 12); pg 50 (1867 Oct 12); pg 52 (1867 Oct 14); pg 54 (1867 Oct 16); pg 55 (1867 Oct 26); pg 57 (1867 Nov 10); pg 58 (1867 Nov 23); pg 59 (1867 Dec 14); pg 60 (1867 Dec 14); pg 62 (1868 Jan 25); pg 63 (1868 Feb 8); pg 63 (1868 Jan 25); pg 64 (1868 Mar 28); pg 66 (1868 Apr 11); pg 130 (1869 Dec 15); pg 313 member

Haswell, William
office held: JW
pg 187 (1871 Mar 11) visiting; pg 199 (1871 July 22)

Hathaway, Mark
pg 298 (1873 June 28);pg 314 member

Hattenbach, Isaac
pg 51 (1867 Oct 12) Chivington Lodge No. 6; pg 356 (1867 Sep 25) Chivington Lodge No. 6

Hays
pg 185 (1871 Feb 25) visiting

Hays, B E
pg 65 (1868 Mar 28) Chivington Lodge No. 6; pg 357 (1868 Mar 11) Chivington Lodge No. 6

Hayward, D P
pg 318 pencil list

Hayward, Dan E
pg 318 (1890 Mar 22) member

Heat, Charles
pg 332 (1874 May 9) Cheyenne Lodge No. 16

Heath, N H
office held: Tiler
pg 7 (1867 Jan 24) visiting; pg 8 (1867 Feb 14) Tiler; pg 9 (1867 Feb 28) visiting; pg 11 (1867 Mar 6) Tiler

Heckey, James S
pg 179 (1871 Jan 14) Laramie Lodge No. 18

Heinman, see Hinman, P M

Helm, Thomas
pg 94 (1869 Feb 13) Central Lodge No. 6; pg 358 (1869 Jan 27) Central Lodge No. 6

Helm, W A
pg 359 (1869 Feb 5) Mount Moriah Lodge No. 15

Helpiatine, Henry H
pg 332 (1874 June 27) Cheyenne Lodge No. 16

Hendershott, F F [T F]
pg 76 (1868 Nov 28) Black Hawk Lodge No. 11; pg 358 (1868 Nov 21) Black Hawk Lodge No. 11

Henderson, W M
pg 360 (1869 Mar 27) Washington Lodge No. 12

Henderson, William H
pg 135 (1870 Jan 22) Washington Lodge No. 12; pg 361 (1870 Jan 17) Washington Lodge No. 12

Heney, Henry
pg 358 (1869 Jan 27) Pueblo Lodge No. 17

Henninger, Michael
pg 65 (1868 Mar 28) Germania Lodge, U.D.; pg 357 (1868 Mar 16) Germania Lodge, U.D.

Henry, [Oren H or Ormal E]
pg 176 (1870 Dec 24); pg 194 (1871 May 27); pg 199 (1871 July 22); pg 208 (1871 Nov 11); pg 209 (1871 Nov 25); pg 219 (1872 Feb 10); pg 236 (1872 July 27); pg 255 (1872 Dec 28)

Henry, Mrs
pg 30 (1867 June 27) cash draft

Henry, Mrs Katie
pg 72 (1868 Oct 24) bill presented

Henry, Oren H
appears as: Henry; Henry, O H
offices held: WM, SD, JD, SD, SW, JW, Secy
pg 1 (1867 Jan 3); pg 1 (1867 Jan 3); pg 2 (1867 Jan 3); pg 6 (1867 Jan 10); pg 6 (1867 Jan 10); pg 8 (1867 Feb 14); pg 9 (1867 Feb 28); pg 9 (1867 Feb 28); pg 11 (1867 Mar 6); pg 12 (1867 Mar 14); pg 13 (1867 Mar 15); pg 14 (1867 Mar 28); pg 15 (1867 Mar 28); pg 16 (1867 Apr 1); pg 17 (1867 Apr 11); pg 17 (1867 Apr 4); pg 19 (1867 Apr 15); pg 20 (1867 Apr 18); pg 20 (1867 Apr 23); pg 22 (1867 Apr 29); pg 23 (1867 May 3); pg 24 (1867 May 9); pg 24 (1867 May 9); pg 25 (1867 May 13); pg 26 (1867 May 23); pg 27 (1867 June 13); pg 29 (1867 June 15); pg 29 (1867 June 27); pg 32 (1867 July 6); pg 33 (1867 July 11); pg 35 (1867 July 13); pg 36 (1867 July 15); pg 36 (1867 July 17); pg 37 (1867 July 24); pg 38 (1867 July 25); pg 39 (1867 Aug 7); pg 39 (1867 Aug 8); pg 42 (1867 Aug 25); pg 43 (1867 Sept 5); pg 44 (1867 Sept 12); pg 46 (1867 Sept 26); pg 49 (1867 Oct 12); pg 51 (1867 Oct 12); pg 52 (1867 Oct 14); pg 54 (1867 Oct 16); pg 55 (1867 Oct 26); pg 56 (1867 Oct 26); pg 57 (1867 Nov 10); pg 58 (1867 Nov 23); pg 59 (1867 Dec 14); pg 60 (1867 Dec 14); pg 61 (1868 Jan 11); pg 62 (1868 Jan 25); pg 63 (1868 Feb 8); pg 64 (1868 Mar 28); pg 66 (1868 Apr 11); pg 67 (1868 Aug 8); pg 75 (1868 Nov 28); pg 77 (1868 Dec 12); pg 80 (1868 Dec 14); pg 81 (1868 Dec 19); pg 81 (1868 Dec 5); pg 82 (1868 Dec 26); pg 84 (1868 Dec 28); pg 84 (1868 Dec 31); pg 85 (1869 Jan 9); pg 87 (1869 Jan 9); pg 88 (1869 Jan 9); pg 89 (1859 Jan 13); pg 89 (1869 Jan 16); pg 103 (1869 Apr

10); pg 115 (1869 Aug 14); pg 117 (1869 Aug 21); pg 118 (1869 Aug 28); pg 118 (1869 Sept 11); pg 120 (1869 Sept 25); pg 121 (1869 Sept 25); pg 121 (1869 Sept 25) motion to appoint a committee to locate a burying ground for the use of Columbia Lodge; pg 123 (1869 Nov 13); pg 125 (1869 Nov 27); acting pg 126 (1869 Nov 27); pg 127 (1869 Dec 11); pg 128 (1869 Dec 11) motion to allow IOOF to hold meetings in the lodge; pg 129 (1869 Dec 11); pg 130 (1869 Dec 15); pg 132 (1870 Jan 8); pg 134 (1870 Jan 15); pg 135 (1870 Jan 22); pg 136 (1870 Feb 12); pg 138 (1870 Feb 19); pg 139 (1870 Feb 26); pg 141 (1870 Mar 12); pg 142 (1870 Mar 17); pg 143 (1870 Mar 25); pg 144 (1870 Mar 26); pg 146 (1870 Apr 2); pg 147 (1870 Apr 9); pg 149 (1870 Apr 23); pg 151 (1870 May 7); pg 154 (1870 May 28); pg 155 (1870 June 4); pg 156 (1870 June 11); pg 158 (1870 June 25); pg 160 (1870 July 2); pg 160 (1870 July 9); pg 162 (1870 July 24); pg 164 (1870 Aug 27); pg 166 (1870 Sept 3); pg 167 (1870 Sept 10); pg 168 (1870 Sept 15); pg 169 (1870 Sept 24); pg 170 (1870 Oct 8); pg 171 (1870 Nov 12); pg 172 (1870 Nov 26); pg 173 (1870 Dec 3); pg 174 (1870 Dec 10); pg 175 (1870 Dec 10); pg 175 (1870 Dec 10); pg 176 (1870 Dec 24); pg 177 (1870 Dec 29); pg 178 (1871 Jan 4); pg 179 (1871 Jan 14); pg 181 (1871 Jan 28); pg 183 (1871 Feb 9); pg 184 (1871 Feb 18); pg 185 (1871 Feb 25); pg 187 (1871 Mar 11); pg 189 (1871 Mar 25); pg 190 (1871 Apr 8); pg 192 (1871 Apr 22); pg 194 (1871 May 27); pg 195 (1871 June 11); pg 197 (1871 July 8); pg 198 (1871 July 12); pg 199 (1871 July 22); pg 201 (1871 Sept 9); pg 203 (1871 Sept 23); pg 205 (1871 Oct 5); pg 206 (1871 Oct 8); pg 207 (1871 Oct 28); pg 208 (1871 Nov 11); pg 209 (1871 Nov 25); pg 209 (1871 Nov 25) bill presented for lumber for the burying ground; pg 210 (1871 Dec 9); pg 211 (1871 Dec 9); pg 212 (1871 Dec 9); pg 213 (1871 Dec 9); pg 214 (1871 Dec 23); pg 216 (1872 Jan 13); pg 217 (1872 Jan 13) added to committee on building Masonic Lodge; pg 218 (1872 Jan 27); pg 220 (1872 Feb 10); pg 221 (1872 Feb 10); pg 222 (1872 Feb 24); pg 223 (1872 Mar 9); pg 224 (1872 Mar 9); pg 225 (1872 Apr 6); pg 230 (1872 May 9) motion to ask Odd Fellows if they wanted to join in renting and furnishing the Lodge; pg 232 (1872 June 1); pg 233 (1872 June 8); pg 234 (1872 June 22); pg 235 (1872 June 29); pg 236 (1872 July 27); pg 241 (1872 Sept 14) motion to lay the corner stone; pg 241 (1872 Sept 28); pg 244 (1872 Oct 26); pg 246 (1872 Nov 9); pg 252 (1872 Dec 14); pg 253 (1872 Dec 14); pg 254 (1872 Dec 26); pg 254 (1872 Dec 28); pg 255 (1872 Dec 28); pg 255 (1872 Dec 28); pg 256 (1872 Dec 28) resolution that members wear slippers in the lodge room and that tobacco be prohibited; pg 267 (1873 Feb 8); pg 268 (1873 Feb 8); pg 271 (1873 Feb 22); pg 272 (1873 Feb 22); pg 273 (1873 Mar 1) motion to host a sociable next Thursday evening; pg 276 (1873 Mar 8); pg 277 (1873 Mar 11); pg 277 (1873 Mar 12); pg 279 (1873 Mar 20); pg 279 (1873 Mar 22); pg 280 (1873 Mar 22); pg 282 (1873 Apr 5); pg 289 (1873 May 14); pg 294 (1873 June 4); pg 304 (1873 Aug 9); pg 307 (1873 Sept 27); pg 307 (1873 Sept 27); pg 308 (1873 Oct 11); pg 313 member

Henry, Ormal E

appears as: Henry; Henry, O E; Henry, Ormal E
offices held: JD, SS, SW, SD, Tiler, JW, JS, Tiler
pg 132 (1870 Jan 8); pg 133 (1870 Jan 8); pg 127 (1869 Dec 11); pg 134 (1870 Jan 15); pg 134 (1870 Jan 15); pg 144 (1870 Mar 26); pg 145 (1870 Mar 26); pg 156 (1870 June 4); pg 156 (1870 June 4); pg 166 (1870 Sept 3); pg 167 (1870 Sept 10); pg 167 (1870 Sept 10); pg 173 (1870 Dec 3); pg 173 (1870 Dec 3); pg 184 (1871 Feb 18); pg 189 (1871 Mar 25); pg 191 (1871 Apr 13); pg 195 (1871 June 11); pg 205 (1871 Oct 5); pg 209 (1871 Nov 25); pg 215 (1871 Dec 23); pg 216 (1872 Jan 13); pg 216 (1872 Jan 13); pg 216 (1872 Jan 13); pg 222 (1872 Feb 24); pg 226 (1872 Apr 13); pg 229 (1872 May 9); pg 233 (1872 June 8); pg 234 (1872 June 22); pg 239 (1872 Aug 31); pg 250 (1872 Nov 30); pg 253 (1872 Dec 14); pg 253 (1872 Dec 26); pg 254 (1872 Dec 26); pg 256 (1873 Jan 4); pg 259 (1873 Jan 11); pg 260 (1873 Jan 11); pg 261 (1873 Jan 14); pg 262 (1873 Jan 25); pg 265 (1873 Feb 1); pg 266 (1873 Feb 8); pg 267 (1873 Feb 8); pg 268 (1873 Feb 8) to procure hooks to hang the chandeliers; pg 269 (1873 Feb 8); pg 273 (1873 Mar 1); pg 274 (1873 Mar 8); pg 277 (1873 Mar 11); pg 277

(1873 Mar 12); pg 278 (1873 Mar 15); pg 279 (1873 Mar 20); pg 279 (1873 Mar 22); pg 282 (1873 Apr 5); pg 283 (1873 Apr 12); pg 285 (1873 Apr 26) bill presented for freight on the organ from Denver; pg 285 (1873 Apr 26); pg 287 (1873 May 3) pg 288 (1873 May 10); pg 289 (1873 May 10); pg 290 (1873 May 19); pg 290 (1873 May 24); pg 292 (1873 May 27); pg 294 (1873 June 4); pg 297 (1873 June 24); pg 298 (1873 June 28); pg 300 (1873 July 2); pg 301 (1873 July 12); pg 303 (1873 July 26); pg 308 (1873 Oct 11); pg 313 member

Hepburn, G W
pg 101 (1869 Mar 27) Pueblo Lodge No. 17; pg 360 (1869 Mar 10) Pueblo Lodge No. 17

Hepburn, Henry
pg 9 (1867 Feb 28) Chivington Lodge No. 6; pg 356 (1867 Feb 13) Chivington Lodge No. 6

Hernandez, Anthony
pg 315 member

Herrington, H M
pg 21 (1867 Apr 23) Union Lodge No. 7; pg 356 (1867 Apr 13) Union Lodge No. 7

Herzinger
pg 318 pencil list

Hevelin, Benjamin
offices held: Tiler
pg 6 (1867 Jan 10); pg 7 (1867 Jan 24)

Hewes, John M
pg 91 (1869 Jan 23); pg 97 (1869 Feb 27); pg 98 (1869 Feb 27); pg 358 (1869 Feb 27)
*did not become a member of the Columbia Lodge

Hill, S M
pg 359 (1869 Jan 2) Cheyenne Lodge No. 16

Hill, Thomas J
appears as: Hill, T J; Hill, Thomas J
pg 78 (1868 Dec 12); pg 91 (1869 Jan 23); pg 93 (1869 Feb 13); pg 99 (1869 Mar 13); pg 100 (1869 Mar 13); pg 141 (1870 Mar 12); pg 109 (1869 May 22); pg 292 (1873 May 27) deceased; pg 300 (1873 June 28) estate to receive bill for livery from Williamette Arnett; pg 305 (1873 Aug 9) motion to present the bill for livery to the estate was countermanded by vote of the lodge

Hilliard, J B
pg 340 (1881 Jan 8) El Paso Lodge No 13

Hilton, George F
appears as: Hilton, G F; Hilton, George F
pg 201 (1871 Sept 9) Laramie Lodge No. 18; pg 240 (1872 Sept 14) Laramie Lodge No. 18

Hiney, Henry
pg 94 (1869 Feb 13) Pueblo Lodge No. 17

Hinkle, John P
pg 317 (1887 Mar 26) member

Hinman, John
pg 317 (1886 June12) member

Hinman, Porter M
appears as: Heinman, P M; Hinman, P M
pg 123 (1869 Nov 13); pg 128 (1869 Dec 11); pg 361 (1869 Dec 11)
*did not become a memeber of the Columbia Lodge

Hitchcock, David M
pg 139 (1870 Feb 26) Union Lodge No. 7

Ho___, Wolf
pg 362 (1870 Feb 19) Cheyenne Lodge No. 16

Hoagam, Martin
pg 124 (1869 Nov 13) Cheyenne Lodge No. 16

Hockaday, Charles N
appears as: Hockaday; Hockaday, C N; Hockaday, Charles N
offices held: JD
pg 78 (1868 Dec 12); pg 86 (1869 Jan 9); pg 88 (1869 Jan 9); pg 88 (1869 Jan 9); pg 135 (1870 Jan 22); pg 135 (1870 Jan 22); pg 140 (1870 Mar 8); pg 147 (1870 Apr 9); pg 148 (1870 Apr 9); pg 151 (1870 May 11); pg 154 (1870 May 28); pg 175 (1870 Dec 10); pg 178 (1871 Jan 4); pg 199 (1871 July 22); pg 218 (1872 Jan 27); pg 231 (1872 May 25); pg 305 (1873 Aug 23); pg 309 (1873 Oct 11); pg 313 member

Hodges, G E
pg 361 (1870 Jan 1) Golden Lodge No. 1

Hogan, Martin
pg 361 (1869 Oct 2) Cheyenne Lodge No. 16

214 (1871 Dec 23); pg 219 (1872 Feb 10); pg 222 (1872 Feb 24); pg 226 (1872 Apr 13); pg 229 (1872 May 9); pg 231 (1872 May 16); pg 231 (1872 May 25); pg 237 (1872 July 27); pg 238 (1872 Aug 24); pg 242 (1872 Oct 4); pg 243 (1872 Oct 19); pg 246 (1872 Nov 9); pg 249 (1872 Nov 27); pg 250 (1872 Dec 14); pg 251 (1872 Dec 14); pg 251 (1872 Dec 14); pg 252 (1872 Dec 14); pg 253 (1872 Dec 14); pg 253 (1872 Dec 26); pg 254 (1872 Dec 26); pg 254 (1872 Dec 28); pg 256 (1873 Jan 4); pg 258 (1873 Jan 8); pg 259 (1873 Jan 11); pg 261 (1873 Jan 14); pg 262 (1873 Jan 25); pg 265 (1873 Feb 1); pg 266 (1873 Feb 8); pg 270 (1873 Feb 22); pg 273 (1873 Mar 1); pg 273 (1873 Mar 7); pg 274 (1873 Mar 8); pg 278 (1873 Mar 15); pg 281 (1873 Mar 29); pg 282 (1873 Apr 5); pg 285 (1873 Apr 26); pg 287 (1873 May 3); pg 290 (1873 May 19); pg 292 (1873 May 27) presiding over the tribute to dec'd Brother Thomas J Hill; pg 292 (1873 May 27); pg 296 (1873 June 14); pg 297 (1873 June 24); pg 298 (1873 June 28); pg 304 (1873 Aug 9); pg 305 (1873 Aug 23); pg 306 (1873 Sept 13); pg 307 (1873 Sept 27); pg 313 member; pg 355 (1868 Jan 23) visitor, Golden City Lodge No. 1, Colo

Howes, see Howse, W J L

Howse, W J L
appears as Howes, W J L; Howse; Howse, W J L
offices held: SS, JS, Treas, JD, Tiler
pg 244 (1872 Oct 26); petitioner; pg 248 (1872 Nov 23); pg 248 (1872 Nov 23); pg 249 (1872 Nov 27); pg 250 (1872 Nov 27); pg 251 (1872 Dec 14); pg 252 (1872 Dec 14); pg 253 (1872 Dec 26); pg 254 (1872 Dec 26); pg 259 (1873 Jan 11); pg 261 (1873 Jan 11); pg 261 (1873 Jan 14); pg 261 (1873 Jan 14); pg 267 (1873 Feb 8); pg 268 (1873 Feb 8); pg 270 (1873 Feb 22); pg 274 (1873 Mar 7); pg 277 (1873 Mar 12); pg 281 (1873 Mar 29); pg 282 (1873 Apr 5); pg 283 (1873 Apr 12); pg 284 (1873 Apr 19); pg 285 (1873 Apr 26); pg 287 (1873 May 1); pg 287 (1873 May 3); pg 289 (1873 May 14); pg 290 (1873 May 24); pg 291 (1873 May 24); pg 301 (1873 July 12); pg 302 (1873 July 12); pg 302 (1873 July 19); pg 314 member

Hoyle, Ed W
pg 317 (1886 Jan 9) member

Hubbard, Horace W
appears as: Hubbard; Hubbard, H W
offices held: Treas, JS, JD, Secy
pg 81 (1868 Dec 19); pg 82 (1868 Dec 26); pg 84 (1868 Dec 28); pg 89 (1869 Jan 13); pg 93 (1869 Feb 12); pg 95 (1869 Feb 15); pg 96 (1869 Feb 15); pg 96 (1869 Feb 24)

Hubbard, Mrs E
pg 94 (1869 Feb 13) bill presented

Hubbard, Mrs S J
pg 133 (1870 Jan 8) bill presented

Hugh, Thomas M
pg 267 (1873 Feb 8) Laramie Lodge No. 18

Hughes, Hugh
pg 59 (1867 Dec 14) Denver Lodge No. 5; pg 357 (1867 Dec 7) Denver Lodge No. 5

Hugill, W George
pg 26 (1867 May 23) Nevada Lodge No 4; pg 356 (1867 May 11) Nevada Lodge No. 4

Hunt, Fred A
pg 314 member

Hupper, E A
appears as: Hupper; Hupper, E A; Huppert, E A
offices held: JD
pg 1 (1867 Jan 3); pg 6 (1867 Jan 10); pg 7 (1867 Jan 24); pg 8 (1867 Feb 14); pg 9 (1867 Feb 28); pg 8 (1867 Feb 14); pg 9 (1867 Feb 28); pg 11 (1867 Mar 6); pg 12 (1867 Mar 14); pg 13 (1867 Mar 15); pg 14 (1867 Mar 18); pg 14 (1867 Mar 28); pg 16 (1867 Apr 1); pg 17 (1867 Apr 11); pg 17 (1867 Apr 4); pg 18 (1867 Apr 11); pg 19 (1867 Apr 15); pg 20 (1867 Apr 18); pg 20 (1867 Apr 23); pg 21 (1867 Apr 23); pg 22 (1867 Apr 29); pg 23 (1867 May 3); pg 24 (1867 May 9); pg 25 (1867 May 13); pg 26 (1867 May 23); pg 27 (1867 June 13); pg 29 (1867 June 15); pg 29 (1867 June 27); pg 32 (1867 July 6); pg 33 (1867 July 11); pg 35 (1867 July 13); pg 36 (1867 July 15); pg 36 (1867 July 17); pg 37 (1867 July 24); pg 38 (1867 July 25); pg 39 (1867 Aug 7); pg 39 (1867 Aug 8); pg 40 (1867 Aug 8); pg 41 (1867 Aug 17); pg 42 (1867 Aug 25); pg 43 (1867 Sept 5); pg 45 (1867 Sept 14); pg 46 (1867 Sept 26)

Hurlbut, G T
pg 341 (1885)
*did not become a member of the Columbia Lodge

Imil [Imel], David
pg 28 (1867 June 13) Chivington Lodge No. 6; pg 356 (1867 May 22) Chivington Lodge No. 6

Irwin, J H
pg 30 (1867 June 27) Union Lodge No. 7 ; pg 356 (1867 June 8) Union Lodge No. 7

Irwin, Joseph
pg 315 member

Israel, James H
pg 333 (1874 Mar 14) Collins Lodge No. 19; pg 338 (1874 Mar 14) Collins Lodge No. 19

Ivey, James
pg 318 (1889 Aug 24) member

Jackson, George W
appears as: Jackson, G W
pg 314 member

Jackson, John
pg 255 (1872 Dec 28); pg 263 (1873 Jan 25); pg 264 (1873 Jan 25); pg 337 (1873 Feb 22)
*did not become a member of the Columbia Lodge

Jackson, Stephen D
pg 192 (1871 Apr 22) Washington Lodge No. 12

Jacobs, Horatio H
appears as: Jacobs, H H; Jacobs, Horatio H
offices held: Secy
pg 73 (1868 Oct 23); pg 107 (1869 May 8); pg 85 (1869 Jan 9); pg 92 (1869 Jan 29); pg 92 (1869 Jan 29); pg 97 (1869 Feb 27); pg 108 (1869 May 8); pg 355 (1868 Feb 27) visitor, Dunlap Lodge, IL; pg 355 (1868 Jan 9) visitor, Dunlap Lodge, IL

James, John
pg 104 (1869 Apr 10)
*did not become a member of the Columbia Lodge

James, Joseph
pg 361 (1869 Sept 25) Nevada Lodge No. 4

James, T J
pg 138 (1870 Feb 19) present

Janbom, C W
pg 319 member

Jay, W F
pg 283 (1873 Apr 12) Union Lodge No. 7; pg 337 (1873 Apr 12) Union Lodge No. 7

Jaynes
pg 222 (1872 Feb 24) present

Jeffers, Albert
pg 316 (1884 Mar 8) member

Jeslin, John A
pg 316 (1885 Sept 12) member

Jester, William H
appears as: Jester, W H
pg 315 member

Johns, John B
pg 185 (1871 Feb 25) Washington Lodge No. 12

Johns, John H
pg 314 member

Johns, Stephen
pg 338 (1878 Aug 22) Black Hawk Lodge No. 11

Johns, Thomas J
appears as: Johns, T J; Johns, Thomas J
offices held: JW, WM,
pg 1 (1867 Jan 3); pg 2 (1867 Jan 3); pg 4 (1867 Jan 10); pg 6 (1867 Jan 10); pg 7 (1867 Jan 24); pg 8 (1867 Feb 14); pg 9 (1867 Feb 28); pg 39 (1867 Aug 8);pg 41 (1867 Aug 17);pg 49 (1867 Oct 8); pg 50 (1867 Oct 12); pg 51 (1867 Oct 12)

Johns, William
pg 291 (1873 May 24) Washington Lodge No. 12; pg 337 (1873 May 24) Washington Lodge No. 12

Johnson, Charles A
pg 194 (1871 May 27) Cheyenne Lodge No. 16

Johnson, John W
pg 209 (1871 Nov 25) Pueblo Lodge No. 17

Johnson, Seymour
pg 315 member

Johnson, Thomas C
appears as: Johnson, T C
pg 316 (1884 July 26) member

Johnson, W B
pg 15 (1867 Mar 28) Chivington Lodge No. 6; pg 356 (1867 Mar 13) Chivington Lodge No. 6

Johnston, Frank
pg 318 (1889 June 15) member

Johnston, James J
pg 315 member

Johnston, William J
appears as: Johnston, W J
pg 315 member

Jones, A M
pg 17 (1867 Apr 4) visiting from Nevada Lodge No. 4; pg 51 (1867 Oct 12) Senior Grand Master

Jones, D E
pg 113 (1869 June 26) bill presented

Jones, J S
pg 267 (1873 Feb 8) Weston Lodge No. 22

Jones, John
pg 99 (1869 Mar 13); pg 103 (1869 Apr 10); pg 360 (1869 Apr 10)
*did not become a member of the Columbia Lodge

Jones, John S
pg 298 (1873 June 28) Denver Lodge No. 5

Jones, Joseph
pg 139 (1870 Feb 26) Nevada Lodge No 4

Jones, Mrs
pg 91 (1869 Jan 23) donation made

Jones, Mrs S J
pg 87 (1869 Jan 9) note held for monies owed by several former members of the Valmont Lodge U.D.

Jones, Thomas J
appears as: Jones, T J; Jones, Thomas J
offices held: JS, Tiler, SD, Treas, JD, JW
pg 66 (1868 Apr 11) visiting Valmont Lodge U.D.; pg 71 (1868 Oct 24); pg 73 (1868 Oct 23); pg 73 (1868 Oct 24); pg 74 (1868 Oct 24); pg 75 (1868 Nov 28); pg 78 (1868 Dec 12); pg 80 (1868 Dec 14); pg 81 (1868 Dec 5); pg 82 (1868 Dec 26); pg 84 (1868 Dec 28); pg 85 (1868 Dec 31); pg 85 (1869 Jan 9); pg 89 (1869 Jan 16); pg 90 (1869 Jan 23); pg 92 (1869 Jan 25); pg 92 (1869 Jan 29); pg 93 (1869 Feb 13); pg 95 (1869 Feb 15); pg 96 (1869 Feb 24); pg 97 (1869 Feb 27); pg 99 (1869 Mar 13); pg 101 (1869 Mar 27); pg 103 (1869 Apr 10); pg 104 (1869 Apr 24); pg 105 (1869 Apr 24); pg 107 (1869 May 8); pg 111 (1869 June 12); pg 113 (1869 June 26); pg 119 (1869 Sept 11); pg 123 (1869 Nov 13); pg 127 (1869 Dec 11); pg 130 (1869 Dec 15); pg 130 (1869 Dec 15); pg 136 (1870 Feb 12); pg 145 (1870 Mar 26); pg 170 (1870 Oct 8); pg 181 (1871 Jan 28); pg 185 (1871 Feb 25); pg 195 (1871 June 11); pg 207 (1871 Oct 28); pg 219 (1872 Feb 10); pg 251 (1872 Dec 14); pg 273 (1873 Mar 1); pg 299 (1873 June 28) member; pg 313 member

Jones, William W
pg 338 (1874 Mar 28) Mount Moriah Lodge No. 15

Judd, Cyrus T
pg 139 (1870 Feb 26) El Paso Lodge No. 13

Judson, Charles
pg 338 (1874 Mar 28) Doric Lodge U.D.

June, James
pg 161 (1870 July 9) Larimer Lodge U.D,

Juneman, Frederick W
appears as: Juneman; Juneman, F W
pg 307 (1873 Sept 27); pg 314 member

Junrium, J W
pg 341 (1885)
*did not become a member of the Columbia Lodge

K__se, _____
pg 315 member

Kassler & Co
pg 30 (1867 June 27) cash draft

Kassler, G W & Co
pg 26 (1867 May 23) bill presented

Keer, see Kerr, David

Kelley, Charles W
pg 332 (1874 May 9) Cheyenne Lodge No. 16

Kelley, James A
pg 316 (1883 May 26) member

Kelley, William A
pg 359 (1868 Dec 5) Cheyenne Lodge No. 16

Lake, John E
pg 333 (1874 Nov 28) Washington Lodge No. 12

Lander, Fred
pg 338 (1874 Mar 14) Cheyenne Lodge No. 16

LaPoint, George
appears as: LaPoint; LaPoint, George
pg 78 (1868 Dec 12); pg 86 (1869 Jan 9); pg 88 (1869 Jan 9); pg 91 (1869 Jan 23); pg 110 (1869 May 25); pg 103 (1869 Apr 10); pg 104 (1869 Apr 10); pg 108 (1869 May 8); pg 109 (1869 May 22); pg 110 (1869 May 25); pg 213 (1871 Dec 9); pg 313 member

Lawson, A
pg 338 (1874 Mar 14) Cheyenne Lodge No. 16

Lawson, Alexander
pg 315 member

Lawson, C C
pg 125 (1869 Nov 27); pg 130 (1869 Dec 15); pg 131 (1869 Dec 15); pg 361 (1869 Dec 25)
*did not become a member of the Columbia Lodge

Lea, Alfred E
appears as: Lea; Lea, A E; Lee, Alfred E
offices held: JS, JD
pg 238 (1872 Aug 24); pg 244 (1872 Oct 26); pg 248 (1872 Nov 23); pg 249 (1872 Nov 27); pg 250 (1872 Nov 27); pg 259 (1873 Jan 11); pg 260 (1873 Jan 11); pg 261 (1873 Jan 14); pg 266 (1873 Feb 8); pg 268 (1873 Feb 8); pg 269 (1873 Feb 8); pg 274 (1873 Mar 7); pg 294 (1873 June 4); pg 301 (1873 July 12); pg 314 member

Lea, R M
pg 332 (1874 June 27) Weston Lodge No. 22

Learmack, John T
pg 317 (1889 Apr 20) member

Lebruler, Patrick
pg 316 (1885 Sept 26) member

Lecturer, G
pg 61 (1867 Dec 29) brethren at Valmont

Lee, Richard M
pg 337 (1873 Nov 8) Weston Lodge No. 22

Lees, James
pg 115 (1869 Aug 14) Washington Lodge No. 12; pg 361 (1869 June 26) Washington Lodge No. 12

Lefoe, W F
pg 316 member

Lein, J J
pg 161 (1870 July 9) Larimer Lodge U.D,

Lelly, Eli
office held: JS
pg 249 (1872 Nov 27)

Lemen, Louis E
pg 333 (1874 Nov 28) Washington Lodge No. 12

Lennox, A
pg 76 (1868 Nov 28) bill presented (deceased); pg 83 (1868 Dec 26) deceased

Lewis, Augustus S
appears as: Lewis, A S; Lewis, Augustus S
pg 75 (1868 Nov 28); pg 77 (1868 Nov 28); pg 82 (1868 Dec 26); pg 83 (1868 Dec 26); pg 84 (1868 Dec 28); pg 85 (1869 Jan 9); pg 86 (1869 Jan 9); pg 88 (1869 Jan 9)
*did not become a member of the Columbia Lodge

Lewis, James
pg 314 member

Lewis, W A
pg 296 (1873 June 14) Washington Lodge No. 12; pg 337 (1873 June 14) Washington Lodge No. 12

Leymore, George
pg 165 (1870 Aug 27) Cheyenne Lodge No. 16; pg 335 (1870 Aug 6) Cheyenne Lodge No. 16

Leyner, Peter A
appears as: Leyner; Leyner, P A; Leyner, Peter A
offices held: JD
pg 91 (1869 Jan 23) visiting from the Denver Lodge No. 5; pg 97 (1869 Feb 27); pg 98 (1869 Feb 27); pg 100 (1869 Mar 13); pg 108 (1869 May 22); pg 109 (1869 May 22); pg 111 (1869 June 12); pg 112 (1869 June 12); pg 113 (1869 June 26); pg 134 (1870 Jan 15); pg 163 (1870 Aug 13); pg 164 (1870 Aug 27); pg 125 (1869 Nov 27); pg 160 (1870 July 9); pg 161 (1870 July 9); pg 171 (1870 Nov 12); pg 255 (1872 Dec 28);

Manetell, Phillip
pg 179 (1871 Jan 14) Laramie Lodge No. 18

Marck, T D
pg 315 crossed out

Mares, J N
pg 161 (1870 July 9) Larimer Lodge U.D,

Marsh, C H
pg 280 (1873 Mar 22) Laramie Lodge No. 18; pg 337 (1873 Mar 22) Laramie Lodge No. 18

Marshall, William
pg 161 (1870 July 9) Larimer Lodge U.D,; pg 362 (1870 May 25) Laramie Lodge U.D.

Martin, J K
pg 210 (1871 Dec 9) Cheyenne Lodge No. 16

Martin, W
pg 140 (1870 Feb 26) motion to survey the new burial ground; pg 261 (1873 Jan 14)

Marx, Sigemond
appears as: Marx, Sigemond; Marx, Sigmund
pg 267 (1873 Feb 8) Occidental Lodge No. 20; pg 332 (1874 June 27) Occidental Lodge No. 20; pg 337 (1873 Feb 8) Occidental Lodge No. 20

Mason, Edward F
appears as: Mason; Mason, E F; Mason, Edward F (*changed his name from Tubbs, Octavius H)
office held: Treas
pg 61 (1868 Jan 11); pg 64 (1868 Mar 28); pg 65 (1868 Mar 28) changed his name from Octavins H Tubbs to Edward F Mason; pg 313 deceased?

Mathews
pg 290 (1873 May 19) present

Mattison, Menzo C
pg 338 (1874 Mar 28) Occidental Lodge No. 20

Maxon, W W
pg 262 (1873 Jan 25) Denver Lodge No. 5

Maxwell and Tyler
pg 230 (1872 May 9) proposal to rent the Maxwell and Tyler building for Masonic Lodge for a term of 3 years with an option for an additional 5

Maxwell, James P
appears as: Maxwell; Maxwell, J P; Maxwell, James P
offices held: JS, JD, Secy, JW, SD, SW
pg 78 (1868 Dec 12); pg 86 (1869 Jan 9); pg 88 (1869 Jan 9); pg 92 (1869 Jan 29); pg 117 (1869 Aug 21); pg 104 (1869 Apr 24); pg 115 (1869 Aug 14); pg 116 (1869 Aug 14); pg 117 (1869 Aug 14); pg 127 (1869 Dec 11); pg 128 (1869 Dec 11); pg 129 (1869 Dec 11); pg 132 (1870 Jan 8); pg 155 (1870 June 4); pg 156 (1870 June 11); pg 180 (1871 Jan 14); pg 192 (1871 Apr 22); pg 192 (1871 Apr 22); pg 195 (1871 June 11); pg 197 (1871 July 8); pg 200 (1871 Aug 12); pg 201 (1871 Sept 9); pg 203 (1871 Sept 23); pg 204 (1871 Sept 23); pg 206 (1871 Oct 8); pg 207 (1871 Oct 28); pg 214 (1871 Dec 23) bill presented for taking Bro Anderson late deceased to Denver; pg 217 (1872 Jan 13); pg 222 (1872 Feb 24); pg 223 (1872 Mar 9); pg 226 (1872 Apr 13); pg 226 (1872 Apr 27); pg 229 (1872 May 9); pg 231 (1872 May 16); pg 231 (1872 May 25); pg 233 (1872 June 8); pg 235 (1872 June 29); pg 237 (1872 July 27); pg 238 (1872 Aug 24); pg 239 (1872 Aug 31); pg 240 (1872 Sept 14); pg 241 (1872 Sept 28); pg 250 (1872 Nov 30); pg 250 (1872 Dec 14); pg 252 (1872 Dec 14); pg 255 (1872 Dec 28); pg 253 (1872 Dec 26); pg 254 (1872 Dec 26); pg 254 (1872 Dec 28); pg 256 (1873 Jan 4); pg 259 (1873 Jan 11); pg 261 (1873 Jan 14); pg 265 (1873 Feb 1); pg 266 (1873 Feb 8); pg 267 (1873 Feb 8); pg 268 (1873 Feb 8); pg 269 (1873 Feb 12); pg 270 (1873 Feb 22); pg 273 (1873 Mar 1); pg 274 (1873 Mar 8); pg 278 (1873 Mar 15); pg 283 (1873 Apr 12); pg 285 (1873 Apr 26) bill presented for rent of the lodge room; pg 287 (1873 May 3); pg 288 (1873 May 10); pg 290 (1873 May 19); pg 292 (1873 May 27); pg 294 (1873 June 4); pg 294 (1873 May 31); pg 296 (1873 June 14); pg 297 (1873 June 24); pg 298 (1873 June 28); pg 299 (1873 June 28); pg 300 (1873 July 2); pg 302 (1873 July 19); pg 303 (1873 July 26); pg 304 (1873 Aug 9); pg 307 (1873 Sept 27); pg 308 (1873 Oct 11); pg 309 (1873 Oct 11); pg 313 member

Mayer, Gottlieb F
appears as: Mayer, G F
pg 315 member

McIntosh, Lemuel
appears as: McIntosh; McIntosh, Lemuel
offices held: JW, Secy, Tiler, SD
pg 33 (1867 July 11); pg 40 (1867 Aug 8); pg 41 (1867 Aug 17); pg 55 (1867 Oct 26); pg 56 (1867 Oct 26); pg 66 (1868 Apr 11); pg 67 (1868 Apr 11); pg 67 (1868 Aug 8); pg 81 (1868 Dec 19); pg 82 (1868 Dec 26); pg 93 (1869 Feb 13); pg 96 (1869 Feb 24); pg 101 (1869 Mar 27); pg 104 (1869 Apr 24); pg 107 (1869 May 8); pg 108 (1869 May 22); pg 125 (1869 Nov 27); pg 127 (1869 Nov 27); pg 130 (1869 Dec 15); pg 160 (1870 July 9); pg 161 (1870 July 9); pg 172 (1870 Nov 26); pg 173 (1870 Dec 3); pg 175 (1870 Dec 10); pg 176 (1870 Dec 24); pg 189 (1871 Mar 25); pg 223 (1872 Mar 9); pg 243 (1872 Oct 19); pg 313 member

McKenzie, Neal D
appears as McKenzie, Neal D; McKinzie, Neal D
pg 68 (1868 Aug 8) Black Hawk Lodge No. 11; pg 357 (1868 July 4) Black Hawk Lodge No. 11; pg 360 (1869 Mar 25) Black Hawk Lodge No. 11

McKinney, A L
pg 65 (1868 Mar 28) Black Hawk Lodge No. 11; pg 357 (1868 Feb 15) Black Hawk Lodge No. 11

McKinzie, see McKenzie, Neal D

McLaughlin, James B
pg 181 (1871 Jan 28) Cheyenne Lodge No. 16

McLemore, C C
pg 21 (1867 Apr 23) Union Lodge No. 7; pg 356 (1867 Apr 13) Union Lodge No. 7

McLeod, John M
pg 359 (1868 Dec 5) Cheyenne Lodge No. 16

McMullen, John
pg 124 (1869 Nov 13) Cheyenne Lodge No. 16; pg 162 (1870 July 24) Cheyenne Lodge No. 16; pg 335 (1867 July 16) Cheyenne Lodge No. 16; pg 361 (1869 Sept 18) Cheyenne Lodge No. 16

McWinne, Neal D
pg 103 (1869 Apr 10) Black Hawk Lodge No. 11

Mead, Marcus S
appears as: Mead, M S
pg 314 member

Meginnis, Daniel
pg 267 (1873 Feb 8) bill presented for repairing furniture; pg 281 (1873 Mar 22) made the stand purchased by Bro Bock; pg 291 (1873 May 24) bill presented; pg 304 (1873 Aug 9) bill presented for a step ladder; pg 315 member

Melanger, Edward
pg 24 (1867 May 9); Denver Lodge No. 5; pg 356 (1867 May 4) Denver Lodge No. 5

Messner, Charles E
pg 315 member

Metcalf, Eli P
appears as: Metcalf; Metcalf, Eli P
offices held: JS, SS
pg 262 (1873 Jan 25); pg 271 (1873 Feb 22); pg 273 (1873 Mar 1); pg 274 (1873 Mar 8); pg 275 (1873 Mar 8); pg 277 (1873 Mar 11); pg 280 (1873 Mar 22); pg 281 (1873 Mar 22); pg 281 (1873 Mar 29); pg 282 (1873 Mar 29); pg 287 (1873 May 1); pg 291 (1873 May 24); pg 303 (1873 July 26); pg 290 (1873 May 19); pg 314 member; pg 316 (1883 May 15) member

Meverson
pg 174 (1870 Dec 10) present

Meyring, Henry
pg 315 member

Miller, David F
pg 332 (1874 Apr 28) Doric Lodge U.D.

Miller, David W
appears as: Miller; Miller, David W; Miller, D W
offices held: Secy
pg 97 (1869 Feb 27); pg 101 (1869 Mar 27); pg 102 (1869 Mar 21); pg 144 (1870 Mar 26); pg 153 (1870 May 14); pg 153 (1870 May 14); pg 154 (1870 May 28); pg 164 (1870 Aug 27); pg 165 (1870 Aug 27); pg 181 (1871 Jan 28); pg 182 (1871 Jan 28); pg 184 (1871 Feb 18); pg 189 (1871 Mar 25); pg 231 (1872 May 25); pg 232 (1872 May 25); pg 243 (1872 Oct 4); pg 313 member; pg 360 (1869 Nov 27)

Miller, Tobias
pg 219 (1872 Feb 10) Collins Lodge No. 19; pg 335 (1872 Feb 11) Collins Lodge No. 19

Mullen, L
pg 177 (1870 Dec 29) visiting

Mullen, Lauchu [??]
offices held: JW
pg 191 (1871 Apr 13)

Mullin, Charles M
pg 139 (1870 Feb 26) Union Lodge No. 7

Muncell, Thomas
pg 66 (1868 Apr 11) Washington Lodge No. 12; pg 357 (1868 Mar 14) Washington Lodge No. 12

Munshower, G W W
pg 301 (1873 July 12) Denver Lodge No. 5; pg 337 (1873 July 12) Denver Lodge No. 5

Munshower, George W H
pg 335 (1870 Sept 24) Union Lodge No. 7

Munstrawn, George W
pg 170 (1870 Oct 8) Union Lodge No. 7

Munstrawn, Solomon
pg 170 (1870 Oct 8) Union Lodge No. 7

Murray [Murry], M H
pg 111 (1869 June 12) Pueblo Lodge No. 17; pg 360 (1869 May 26) Pueblo Lodge No. 17

Myles, Thomas
pg 174 (1870 Dec 10) Nevada Lodge No 4

Naphyes, Benj F
pg 332 (1874 June 27) Washington Lodge No. 12

Nathan, Casper
pg 359 (1869 Jan 2) Cheyenne Lodge No. 16

Nations, W C
pg 209 (1871 Nov 25) Pueblo Lodge No. 17

Neidminger, James J
pg 72 (1868 Oct 24) Black Hawk Lodge No. 11

Neill, Thomas J
offices held: Secy
pg 106 (1869 May 7); pg 109 (1869 May 22)

Nerdinger, Joseph J
pg 358 (1868 Sept 19) Black Hawk Lodge No. 11

Newland, D P
pg 236 (1872 July 27) Black Hawk Lodge No. 11; pg 336 (1872 July 27) Black Hawk Lodge No. 11

Newnam, E R
pg 355 (1868 Feb 25) visitor, son of affilate

Newnam, Edward B
appears as: Newnam, E B; Newnam, Edward B
offices held: JD, JW
pg 55 (1867 Oct 26) visiting from Nevada Lodge No. 4; pg 120 (1869 Sept 25); pg 121 (1869 Sept 25); pg 122 (1869 Sept 25); pg 124 (1869 Nov 13); pg 125 (1869 Nov 13); pg 175 (1870 Dec 10); pg 194 (1871 May 27); pg 214 (1871 Dec 23); pg 216 (1872 Jan 13); pg 217 (1872 Jan 13); pg 232 (1872 May 25); pg 313 member; pg 355 (1868 Feb 27) visitor, Nevada Lodge No. 4, Colo

Nicholas, Stephen
pg 229 (1872 May 9) Nevada Lodge No. 4; pg 336 (1872 May 9) Nevada Lodge No. 4

Nichols, Charles L
appears as: Nichols, C L
pg 314 member

Nichols, David H
appears as Nichols; Nichols, D H;
offices held: JW, JD, Secy, SW, Marshall
pg 78 (1868 Dec 12) formerly of Valmont Lodge U.D.; pg 82 (1868 Dec 26) visiting; pg 136 (1870 Jan 22) Proffitstown Lodge No 137 - granted permission to affiliate, having formerly belonged to Valmont Lodge under dispensation; pg 136 (1870 Feb 12); pg 137 (1870 Feb 12); pg 138 (1870 Feb 19); pg 141 (1870 Mar 12); pg 143 (1870 Mar 25); pg 144 (1870 Mar 26); pg 145 (1870 Mar 26); pg156 (1870 June 11); pg 158 (1870 June 25); pg 164 (1870 Aug 27); pg 165 (1870 Aug 27); pg 171 (1870 Nov 12); pg 173 (1870 Dec 3); pg 175 (1870 Dec 10); pg 185 (1871 Feb 25); pg 189 (1871 Mar 25); pg 203 (1871 Sept 23); pg 208 (1871 Nov 11); pg 209 (1871 Nov 25); pg 210 (1871 Dec 9); pg 213 (1871 Dec 9); pg 214 (1871 Dec 23) committee to investigate building a Masonic hall; pg 215 (1871 Dec 23); pg 216 (1872 Jan 13); pg 217 (1872 Jan 13); pg 218 (1872 Jan 27); pg 219 (1872 Feb 10); pg 221 (1872 Feb 10); pg 222 (1872 Feb 24); pg 223 (1872 Feb 24); pg 225 (1872 Mar 23) appointed to a committee to work with the Odd Fellows to repair chairs; pg 225 (1872 Apr 6); pg 226 (1872 Apr 6); pg 226 (1872 Apr 13); pg 226 (1872 Apr 27); pg 229 (1872 Apr 27); pg 229 (1872 May 9); pg 230 (1872 May 9); pg

O'Hara, William
appears as: Ohare, William
pg 315 member

Oleson, Hans U
pg 340 (1880 Nov) Ionic Lodge No. 35

Olson, John
pg 179 (1871 Jan 14) Laramie Lodge No. 18

Orahood, Harper M
appears as: Orahood, H M; Orahood, Harper M
pg 61 (1867 Dec 29) brethren at Valmont; pg 88 (1869 Jan 9) bill for services rendered Valmont Lodge

Orey, Justice
pg 121 (1869 Sept 25); pg 123 (1869 Nov 13); pg 124 (1869 Nov 13); pg 125 (1869 Nov 13)

Owen, D P
pg 359 (1869 Feb 5) Mount Moriah Lodge No. 15

Owen, Thomas R, Jr
pg 316 (1884 July 26) member

Owens, John
pg 338 (1874 Mar 14) St Vrain Lodge No. 23

Padew, B
pg 195 (1871 June 11) Black Hawk Lodge No. 11

Paige, John
pg 247 (1872 Nov 23) St Vrain Lodge No. 23; pg 336 (1872 Nov 23) St Vrain Lodge No. 23

Palew [??], Robert
pg 174 (1870 Dec 10) Nevada Lodge No 4

Palmer, Thomas
pg 340 (1880 Oct 9) Washington Lodge No. 12

Parker
pg 160 (1870 July 9) visiting; pg 163 (1870 Aug 13) visiting; pg 233 (1872 June 1) visiting

Parker, Charles E
appears as: Parker, C E; Parker, Charles; Parker, Charles E
offices held: Tiler, JD, SS
pg 151 (1870 May 11); pg 151 (1870 May 7); pg 158 (1870 June 25); pg 355 (1868 Apr 23) visitor, Stewart Lodge No. 92, IL

Parker, L E [S E]
pg 234 (1872 June 22) Occidental Lodge No. 20; pg 336 (1872 June 10) Occidental Lodge No. 20

Parlan, see Parlin, David

Parlin, David
appears as: Parlan; Parlan, David; Parlin, David
offices held: SD, JD, JW, SS, SW
pg 46 (1867 Sept 26) visiting; pg 55 (1867 Oct 26) visiting from Denver Lodge No. 5; pg 57 (1867 Nov 10); visiting from Denver Lodge No. 5; pg 71 (1868 Oct 24); pg 73 (1868 Oct 23); pg 73 (1868 Oct 24); pg 74 (1868 Oct 24); pg 75 (1868 Nov 28); pg 78 (1868 Dec 12); pg 81 (1868 Dec 5); pg 82 (1868 Dec 26); pg 84 (1868 Dec 28); pg 85 (1868 Dec 31); pg 85 (1869 Jan 9); pg 89 (1859 Jan 13); pg 89 (1869 Jan 16); pg 90 (1869 Jan 23); pg 92 (1869 Jan 25); pg 92 (1869 Jan 29); pg 93 (1869 Feb 13); pg 95 (1869 Feb 15); pg 96 (1869 Feb 24); pg 97 (1869 Feb 27); pg 99 (1869 Mar 13); pg 101 (1869 Mar 27); pg 104 (1869 Apr 24); pg 107 (1869 May 8); pg 110 (1869 May 25); pg 111 (1869 June 12); pg 115 (1869 Aug 14); pg 118 (1869 Sept 11); pg 119 (1869 Sept 11); pg 123 (1869 Nov 13); pg 124 (1869 Nov 13); pg 125 (1869 Nov 27); pg 126 (1869 Nov 27); pg 127 (1869 Dec 11); pg 132 (1870 Jan 8); pg 134 (1870 Jan 15); pg 142 (1870 Mar 17); pg 144 (1870 Mar 26); pg 145 (1870 Mar 26); pg 146 (1870 Apr 2); pg 147 (1870 Apr 9); pg 148 (1870 Apr 9) motion to appoint a committee to fence in the cemetery; pg 150 (1870 Apr 23) motion to appoint a committee to secure a contract to fence the cemetery before the 10th of June next (1870); pg 151 (1870 May 11); pg 153 (1870 May 14); pg 157 (1870 June 11) motion to pay M G Smith the rest of the price for the cemetery ground on 1 Oct 1870; pg 160 (1870 July 2); pg 163 (1870 Aug 13); pg 173 (1870 Dec 3); pg 215 (1871 Dec 23); pg 218 (1872 Jan 27); pg 220 (1872 Feb 10); pg 222 (1872 Feb 24) charges read; pg 222 (1872 Feb 24); pg 224 (1872 Mar 9); pg 313 member

Parmelee, Ed C
appears as: Parmelee, Ed C; Parnelle, Ewel C
pg 51 (1867 Oct 12) Grand Secretary; pg 57 (1867 Nov 10) Grand Secretary; pg 71 (1868 Oct 7) Grand Secretary granted permission

for the lodge to move to Boulder City; pg 174 (1870 Dec 10) Grand Secretary; pg 224 (1872 Mar 9) Grand Secretary

Parnelle, see Parmelee, Ed C

Parsons, J M
pg 15 (1867 Mar 28) Chivington Lodge No. 6; pg 356 (1867 Mar 13) Chivington Lodge No. 6

Pascoe, Edward
pg 339 (1878 Oct 12) Washington Lodge No. 12

Patrick, J A
pg 338 (1874 Mar 14) Laramie Lodge No. 18

Patterson
pg 148 (1870 Apr 9) petitioner from Fort Collins, Larimer County, Colorado Territory

Patterson
pg 167 (1870 Sept 10) visiting; pg 234 (1872 June 22) visiting

Patterson, G O
pg 341 (1885) member

Paugh, W W
pg 338 (1874 Mar 14) Union Lodge No. 7

Paul, Henry
appears as: Paul; Paul, Henry
offices held: Secy, SW, JS, Tiler, Treas
pg 9 (1867 Feb 28); pg 15 (1867 Mar 28); pg 16 (1867 Apr 1); pg 17 (1867 Apr 11); pg 18 (1867 Apr 11); pg 20 (1867 Apr 18); pg 21 (1867 Apr 23); pg 22 (1867 Apr 23); pg 23 (1867 Apr 29); pg 24 (1867 May 9); pg 41 (1867 Aug 17); pg 43 (1867 Sept 5); pg 44 (1867 Sept 12); pg 45 (1867 Sept 14); pg 46 (1867 Sept 26); pg 49 (1867 Oct 12); pg 51 (1867 Oct 12); pg 52 (1867 Oct 12); pg 52 (1867 Oct 14); pg 54 (1867 Oct 14); pg 54 (1867 Oct 16); pg 55 (1867 Oct 16); pg 55 (1867 Oct 26); pg 56 (1867 Oct 26); pg 57 (1867 Nov 10); pg 58 (1867 Nov 10); pg 59 (1867 Dec 14); pg 60 (1867 Dec 14); pg 61 (1868 Jan 11); pg 62 (1868 Jan 11); pg 62 (1868 Jan 25); pg 63 (1868 Jan 25); pg 63 (1868 Feb 8); pg 64 (1868 Feb 8); pg 64 (1868 Mar 28); pg 65 (1868 Mar 28); pg 66 (1868 Apr 11); pg 67 (1868 Apr 11); pg 67 (1868 Aug 8); pg 68 (1868 Aug 8); pg 69 (1868 Sept 12); pg 70 (1868 Sept 12); pg 71 (1868 Oct 24); pg 74 (1868 Oct 24); pg 75 (1868 Nov 28); pg 77 (1868 Nov 28); pg 77 (1868 Dec 12); pg 79 (1868 Dec 14); pg 80 (1868 Dec 14); pg 84 (1868 Dec 31); pg 85 (1868 Dec 31); pg 85 (1869 Jan 9); pg 89 (1869 Jan 9); pg 90 (1869 Jan 23); pg 91 (1869 Jan 23); pg 92 (1869 Jan 25); pg 93 (1869 Feb 13); pg 95 (1869 Feb 13); pg 97 (1869 Feb 27); pg 98 (1869 Feb 27); pg 101 (1869 Mar 27); pg 102 (1869 Mar 21); pg 120 (1869 Sept 25); pg 122 (1869 Sept 25); pg 127 (1869 Dec 11); pg 129 (1869 Dec 11); pg 129 (1869 Dec 11); pg 131 (1869 Dec 15); pg 173 (1870 Dec 3); pg 177 (1870 Dec 29); pg 256 (1872 Dec 28); pg 259 (1873 Jan 11); pg 313 member

Peabody, Willam L
pg 340 (1880 Oct 9) Washington Lodge No. 12

Pearce, Frank L
pg 333 (1874 Nov 28) Washington Lodge No. 12

Pearce, see Pierce, Oscar

Pell, William
pg 175 (1870 Dec 10); pg 180 (1871 Jan 14) *did not become a member of the Columbia Lodge

Peltan, Samuel
pg 217 (1872 Jan 13) Black Hawk Lodge No. 11; pg 335 (1872 Jan 5) Black Hawk Lodge No. 11

Pelton, Ben H
pg 340 (1880 Nov) Ionic Lodge No. 35

Pelton, Samuel
pg 305 (1873 Aug 23) Central Lodge No. 6; pg 337 (1873 Aug 23) Central Lodge No. 6

Peryam, William T
appears as: Peryam, W J; Peryam, William T
pg 255 (1872 Dec 28); pg 256 (1872 Dec 28); pg 257 (1873 Jan 4); pg 257 (1873 Jan 4); pg 301 (1873 July 12); pg 302 (1873 July 19); pg 314 member

Peters, Anson W
appears as: Peters; Peters, A W; Peters, Anson W
offices held: Steward, Tiler, JD, Secy, SS, JS, JW, SD
pg 51 (1867 Oct 12); pg 58 (1867 Nov 23); pg 58 (1867 Nov 23); pg 61 (1867 Dec 29); pg 67 (1868 Aug 8); pg 68 (1868 Aug 8); pg 71 (1868

Raif, John
pg 332 (1874 July 11) Laramie Lodge No. 18

Ramsden, John N
pg 61 (1868 Jan 11); pg 64 (1868 Feb 8); pg 79 (1868 Dec 14); pg 357 (1868 Feb 8)
*did not become a member of the Columbia Lodge

Randlschlor [??], John M
pg 174 (1870 Dec 10) Pueblo Lodge No. 17

Rankin, Arthur
pg 341 (1885) member

Rankin, Sandy
pg 359 (1868 June 20) Cheyenne Lodge U.D.

Rannal, Rudolph
pg 357 (1868 Mar 1) Black Hawk Lodge No. 11

Rawson, George C
pg 234 (1872 June 22) Washington Lodge No. 12; pg 336 (1872 June 8) Washington Lodge No. 12

Raymond, Albert L
pg 296 (1873 June 14) Collins Lodge No. 19; pg 337 (1873 June 14) Collins Lodge No. 19

Raynor, George W
pg 49 (1867 Oct 12) visiting from Chivington Temple No. 6, Colo. Terr.

Reet, Lewellyn
pg 360 (1869 Feb 20) Cheyenne Lodge No. 16

Reilty, Thomas H
pg 362 (1870 Mar 5) Cheyenne Lodge No. 16

Resemond, Henry
pg 362 (1870 Feb 15) Black Hawk Lodge No. 11

Retallick, William P
pg 62 (1868 Jan 25) Nevada Lodge No 4; pg 357 (1868 Jan 11) Nevada Lodge No. 4

Reynolds & Son
pg 52 (1867 Oct 12) of Springfield, IL, order placed

Reynolds, H G
pg 167 (1870 Sept 10) bill presented

Reynolds, William F
pg 260 (1873 Jan 11) Washington Lodge No. 12; pg 336 (1873 Jan 11) Washington Lodge No. 12

Rice
pg 231 (1872 May 16) visiting; pg 241 (1872 Sept 28)

Rice, Robert D
pg 170 (1870 Oct 8) Pueblo Lodge No. 17; pg 335 (1870 Sept 7) Pueblo Lodge No. 17

Rich, Samuel
pg 338 (1874 Mar 14) Pueblo Lodge No. 17

Richardson, John
appears as: Richardson; Richardson, J; Richardson John
offices held: Tiler, JS
pg 1 (1867 Jan 3); pg 32 (1867 July 6); pg 35 (1867 July 13); pg 36 (1867 July 17); pg 38 (1867 July 25); pg 42 (1867 Aug 25); pg 44 (1867 Sept 12); pg 45 (1867 Sept 14); pg 36 (1867 July 15); pg 42 (1867 Aug 25); pg 43 (1867 Sept 5); pg 46 (1867 Sept 26)

Richardson, M
pg 301 (1873 July 12) Washington Lodge No. 12; pg 337 (1873 July 12) Washington Lodge No. 12

Richie, see Ritchie, John W

Rick, Herman
pg 359 (1868 Sept 19) Cheyenne Lodge U.D.

Riels, A H
pg 338 (1874 Mar 14) Cheyenne Lodge No. 16

Ritchie, John W
appears as: Richie; Richie, J; Richie John W; Ritchie; Ritchie, J W; Ritchie, John; Ritchie, John W
offices held: JW, Secy, SW
pg 66 (1868 Apr 11) visiting SW of Valmont Lodge; pg 71 (1868 Oct 24); pg 72 (1868 Oct 24); pg 73 (1868 Oct 24); pg 74 (1868 Oct 24); pg 75 (1868 Nov 28); pg 76 (1868 Nov 28); pg 78 (1868 Dec 12); pg 96 (1869 Feb 24); pg 82 (1868 Dec 26); pg 84 (1868 Dec 28); pg 85 (1869 Jan 9); pg 100 (1869 Mar 13) bill presented for Valmont Lodge U.D.; pg 101 (1869 Mar 27); pg 111 (1869 June 12); pg 130 (1869 Dec 15); pg 117 (1869 Aug 21); pg 118 (1869 Sept 11); pg 130 (1869 Dec 15); pg 143 (1870 Mar 25); pg 147 (1870 Apr 9); pg 152 (1870 May 14); pg 170 (1870 Oct 8) communication stating that he was unable to attend the lodge on account that he did not

(1873 Feb 22) motion that a notice be put in the next issue of the Boulder News that the deeds to the cemetery lots are ready for delivery; pg 273 (1873 Mar 1); pg 273 (1873 Mar 7); pg 274 (1873 Mar 8); pg 277 (1873 Mar 11); pg 277 (1873 Mar 12); pg 278 (1873 Mar 15); pg 279 (1873 Mar 20); pg 279 (1873 Mar 22); pg 281 (1873 Mar 29); pg 282 (1873 Apr 5); pg 283 (1873 Apr 12); pg 284 (1873 Apr 19); pg 285 (1873 Apr 26); pg 286 (1873 May 1); pg 287 (1873 May 3); pg 288 (1873 May 10); pg 289 (1873 May 14); pg 290 (1873 May 19); pg 290 (1873 May 24); pg 292 (1873 May 27); pg 294 (1873 May 31); pg 294 (1873 June 4); pg 295 (1873 June 4) as acting WM, gave a tribute of respect to Brother Lipman Schwarzenberger dec'd; pg 296 (1873 June 14); pg 297 (1873 June 24); pg 298 (1873 June 28); pg 300 (1873 July 2); pg 301 (1873 July 12); pg 302 (1873 July 19); pg 303 (1873 July 26); pg 304 (1873 Aug 9); pg 305 (1873 Aug 23); pg 307 (1873 Sept 27); pg 308 (1873 Oct 11); pg 313 member

Robinson, John
pg 68 (1868 Aug 8) Union Lodge No. 7; pg 357 (1868 June 13) Union Lodge No. 7

Rock, David
pg 90 (1869 Jan 23) visiting; pg 93 (1869 Feb 13) visiting

Rodgers, Henry
pg 360 (1869 Mar 27) Washington Lodge No. 12

Roen, Matt
pg 315 member

Rogers, Henry
pg 103 (1869 Apr 10) Washington Lodge No. 12

Rompf, Charles
pg 248 (1872 Nov 23); pg 251 (1872 Dec 14); pg 260 (1873 Jan 11)

Rood, M L
pg 42 (1867 Aug 25) Denver Lodge No. 5; pg 65 (1868 Mar 28) Denver Lodge No. 5; pg 105 (1869 Apr 24) Golden Lodge No. 1; pg 356 (1867 Aug 3) Denver Lodge No. 5; pg 357 (1868 Feb 15) Denver Lodge No. 5; pg 360 (1869 Apr 10) Union Lodge No. 7

Root, D W C
pg 201 (1871 Sept 9) Occidental Lodge U.D.; pg 338 (1874 Mar 14) El Paso Lodge No. 13

Root, M H
pg 58 (1867 Nov 23) Chivington Lodge No. 6; 356 (1867 Nov 13) Chivington Lodge No. 6

Rosemond, Henry
pg 76 (1868 Nov 28) Black Hawk Lodge No. 11; pg 358 (1868 Nov 7) Black Hawk Lodge No. 11

Rosenbloom, Isaac
pg 337 (1873 Dec 13) Central Lodge No. 6

Rosenbloom, J
pg 222 (1872 Feb 24) Union Lodge No. 7

Rosmound, Harry
pg 144 (1870 Mar 26) Black Hawk Lodge No. 11

Ross, M C
appears as: Ross; Ross, M C
offices held: JD, Tiler, JS
pg 141 (1870 Mar 12); pg 146 (1870 Apr 2); pg 147 (1870 Apr 9); pg 149 (1870 Apr 23); pg 155 (1870 June 4); pg 156 (1870 June 11); pg 158 (1870 June 25); pg 160 (1870 July 9); pg 162 (1870 July 24); pg 167 (1870 Sept 10); pg 168 (1870 Sept 15); pg 169 (1870 Sept 24); pg 170 (1870 Oct 8); pg 171 (1870 Nov 12); pg 174 (1870 Dec 10); pg 177 (1870 Dec 29); pg 183 (1871 Feb 9); pg 187 (1871 Mar 11); pg 189 (1871 Mar 25); pg 190 (1871 Apr 8); pg 191 (1871 Apr 13); pg 192 (1871 Apr 22)

Ross, William A
pg 339 (1878 Aug 17) Idaho Springs Lodge No. 26

Rowen, William I
pg 315 member

Ruhl
pg 177 (1870 Dec 29) visiting

Rush [??]
pg 136 (1870 Feb 12) present

Russell, C A
pg 316 member

Russell, Horace M
appears as: Russell, H M; Russell, Horace M
pg 75 (1868 Nov 28); pg 77 (1868 Nov 28); pg 83 (1868 Dec 26); pg 308 (1873 Sept 27)

Seabring, A F
pg 203 (1871 Sept 23) Pueblo Lodge No. 17

Sears, Mathew A
pg 132 (1870 Jan 8) Nevada Lodge No 4

Sears, Nathan A
pg 361 (1869 Dec 11) Nevada Lodge No. 4

Seely, Eli
appears as: Seely; Seely, Eli
pg 240 (1872 Sept 14) contractor for school district No. 3 that the lodge lay the corner stone of the new school house being built; pg 271 (1873 Feb 22) bill presented; pg 279 (1873 Mar 20); pg 281 (1873 Mar 29); pg 287 (1873 May 1)

Sergeant, Ellis
pg 341 (1885) member

Session, Fred
pg 336 (1872 Nov 27) Central Lodge No. 6

Sessler, Fred
pg 228 (1872 Apr 27) Central Lodge No. 6

Severance, Isaac H
pg 315 member

Sevier
pg 17 (1867 Apr 4) visiting Grand Warden

Shackman, Isaac
pg 359 (1868 Apr 18) Cheyenne Lodge U.D.

Shaffenburg, M A
pg 68 (1868 Aug 8) Union Lodge No. 7; pg 357 (1868 July 25) Union Lodge No. 7

Shaffer, Phillip
appears as: Shaffer; Shaffer, Phillip
offices held: Treas
pg 42 (1867 Aug 25) visiting; pg 67 (1868 Aug 8); pg 90 (1869 Jan 23) visiting; pg 97 (1869 Feb 27) visiting; pg 103 (1869 Apr 10); pg 355 (1868 Feb 27) visitor, Jamestown Lodge, WI

Shaw, D J
pg 359 (1868 Nov 7) Cheyenne Lodge No. 16

Sheet, George
pg 135 (1870 Jan 22) Cheyenne Lodge No. 16

Sheets, Henry W
pg 315 member

Sheets, Jesse
pg 361 (1870 Jan 17) Cheyenne Lodge No. 16

Shellabarger, W S
pg 181 (1871 Jan 28) Black Hawk Lodge No. 11

Shelly
pg 226 (1872 Apr 13) visiting

Sherman
pg 281 (1873 Mar 29); pg 282 (1873 Apr 5) visiting; pg 284 (1873 Apr 19)

Sherman, J
pg 21 (1867 Apr 23) Union Lodge No. 7; pg 356 (1867 Apr 13) Union Lodge No. 7

Sherman, W H
pg 338 (1878 Aug 22) Black Hawk Lodge No. 11

Sherratt, Charles
pg 315 member

Sherwood, Clarence A
pg 314 member

Shields, Robert C
pg 340 (1881 Jan 5) Del Norte Lodge No. 29

Shires, Thomas
pg 318 (1889 July 27) member

Short, Thomas
pg 128 (1869 Dec 11) Central Lodge No. 6; pg 361 (1869 Nov 24) Central Lodge No. 6

Shortreed, E
pg 333 (1874 Dec 6) Cheyenne Lodge No. 16

Shortridge
pg 265 (1873 Feb 1) present

Silver, S D
appears as: Silver; Silver, S D
pg 234 (1872 June 22) visiting; pg 274 (1873 Mar 7); pg 314 member

Silverstein, H
pg 161 (1870 July 9) Larimer Lodge U.D,; pg 362 (1870 Apr 25) Laramie Lodge U.D.

Simmons, L
pg 66 (1868 Apr 11) Washington Lodge No. 12

Simpson, John
pg 341 (1885) member

Slade, Charles E
pg 291 (1873 May 24); pg 299 (1873 June 28);

pg 337 (1873 June 28)
*did not become a member of the Columbia Lodge

Slanton, A J
office held: JD
pg 63 (1868 Feb 8); pg 64 (1868 Mar 28)

Slater, William C
appears as: Slater; Slater, Wm C; Slater, William C; Slater, W C
offices held: JD, Tiler, SS, JW, SD, JS, Tiler
pg 12 (1867 Mar 14); pg 18 (1867 Apr 11); pg 20 (1867 Apr 23); pg 21 (1867 Apr 23); pg 23 (1867 Apr 29); pg 24 (1867 May 9); pg 25 (1867 May 9); pg 25 (1867 May 13); pg 26 (1867 May 23); pg 27 (1867 June 13); pg 29 (1867 June 15); pg 29 (1867 June 27); pg 33 (1867 July 11); pg 35 (1867 July 13); pg 36 (1867 July 15); pg 36 (1867 July 17); pg 37 (1867 July 24); pg 38 (1867 July 25); pg 39 (1867 Aug 7); pg 39 (1867 Aug 8); pg 41 (1867 Aug 17); pg 42 (1867 Aug 25); pg 43 (1867 Sept 5); pg 44 (1867 Sept 12); pg 45 (1867 Sept 14); pg 46 (1867 Sept 26); pg 49 (1867 Oct 12); pg 53 (1867 Oct 14); pg 54 (1867 Oct 16); pg 55 (1867 Oct 26); pg 57 (1867 Nov 10); pg 58 (1867 Nov 23); pg 59 (1867 Dec 14); pg 60 (1867 Dec 14); pg 60 (1867 Dec 29); pg 61 (1868 Jan 11); pg 62 (1868 Jan 25); pg 63 (1868 Feb 8); pg 64 (1868 Mar 28); pg 66 (1868 Apr 11); pg 67 (1868 Aug 8); pg 69 (1868 Sept 12); pg 71 (1868 Oct 24); pg 77 (1868 Dec 12); pg 80 (1868 Dec 14); pg 82 (1868 Dec 26); pg 84 (1868 Dec 28); pg 84 (1868 Dec 31); pg 89 (1869 Jan 16); pg 90 (1869 Jan 23); pg 92 (1869 Jan 25); pg 96 (1869 Feb 24); pg 97 (1869 Feb 27); pg 142 (1870 Mar 24); pg 143 (1870 Mar 25); pg 144 (1870 Mar 26); pg 313 member

Slaughter, Benjamin H
appears as: Slaughter; Slaughter, B H; Slaughter, Benjamin H
offices held: JS, Tiler, Steward
pg 42 (1867 Aug 25); pg 46 (1867 Sept 26); pg 47 (1867 Sept 26); pg 52 (1867 Oct 12); pg 53 (1867 Oct 14); pg 54 (1867 Oct 14); pg 54 (1867 Oct 16); pg 56 (1867 Oct 26) application for demit; pg 69 (1868 Sept 12); pg 71 (1868 Oct 24); pg 75 (1868 Nov 28); pg 76 (1868 Nov 28); pg 77 (1868 Nov 28); pg 93 (1869 Feb 12); pg 93 (1869 Feb 13); pg 96 (1869 Feb 24); pg 107 (1869 May 8); pg 110 (1869 May 25); pg 119 (1869 Sept 11); pg 121 (1869 Sept 25); pg 122 (1869 Sept 25); pg 160 (1870 July 2); pg 210 (1871 Nov 25); pg 273 (1873 Mar 1); pg 313 member; pg 313 demitted

Slifer, Esrom G
appears as: Slifer, E G; Slifer, Esrom G
pg 71 (1868 Oct 24); pg 73 (1868 Oct 24); pg 74 (1868 Oct 24); pg 117 (1869 Aug 14); pg 129 (1869 Dec 11); pg 210 (1871 Nov 25); pg 313 member

Smith, Azon A
pg 314 member

Smith, B F
pg 207 (1871 Oct 28); pg 211 (1871 Dec 9); pg 210 (1871 Dec 9)
*did not become a member of the Columbia Lodge

Smith, Dr H
pg 313 member

Smith, Elias
pg 359 (1868 Dec 19) Cheyenne Lodge No. 16

Smith, Fred
pg 359 (1868 Nov 7) Cheyenne Lodge No. 16

Smith, George
pg 236 (1872 July 27) Cheyenne Lodge No. 16; pg 336 (1872 July 27) Cheyenne Lodge No. 16

Smith, H
pg 27 (1867 June 13) petitioner

Smith, Henry S
pg 201 (1871 Sept 9) Denver Lodge No. 5

Smith, J Alden
pg 314 member

Smith, J W
pg 316 (1884 Feb 23) member

Smith, John H
pg 121 (1869 Sept 25) Cheyenne Lodge No. 16

Smith, Marinus G
appears as: Smith; Smith, M G
offices held: Treas, JW, Marshall, SS, SW, JD, SD
pg 1 (1867 Jan 3); pg 2 (1867 Jan 3); pg 26 (1867 May 23); pg 29 (1867 June 27); pg 39

(1867 Aug 8); pg 42 (1867 Aug 25); pg 46 (1867 Sept 26); pg 57 (1867 Nov 10); pg 64 (1868 Mar 28); pg 67 (1868 Apr 11); pg 67 (1868 Aug 8); pg 75 (1868 Nov 28); pg 80 (1868 Dec 14); pg 81 (1868 Dec 5); pg 81 (1868 Dec 19); pg 82 (1868 Dec 26); pg 83 (1868 Dec 26); pg 84 (1868 Dec 28); pg 84 (1868 Dec 31); pg 85 (1869 Jan 9); pg 89 (1859 Jan 13); pg 89 (1869 Jan 16); pg 90 (1869 Jan 16); pg 90 (1869 Jan 23); pg 92 (1869 Jan 25); pg 92 (1869 Jan 29); pg 93 (1869 Feb 12); pg 93 (1869 Feb 13); pg 95 (1869 Feb 15); pg 96 (1869 Feb 24); pg 97 (1869 Feb 27); pg 98 (1869 Mar 6); pg 99 (1869 Mar 13); pg 101 (1869 Mar 27); pg 103 (1869 Apr 10); pg 103 (1869 Apr 10); pg 104 (1869 Apr 24); pg 106 (1869 May 7); pg 107 (1869 May 8) motion to petition the Grand Lodge to allow the Columbia Lodge No. 14 to admit the remaining members of the Valmont Lodge; pg 107 (1869 May 8); pg 108 (1869 May 22); pg 110 (1869 May 22); pg 110 (1869 May 25); pg 111 (1869 June 12); pg 113 (1869 June 26); pg 115 (1869 Aug 14); pg 116 (1869 Aug 14); pg 117 (1869 Aug 21); pg 118 (1869 Aug 28); pg 118 (1869 Sept 11); pg 120 (1869 Sept 25); pg 121 (1869 Sept 25); pg 123 (1869 Nov 13); pg 123 (1869 Nov 13); pg 124 (1869 Nov 13); pg 125 (1869 Nov 27); pg 125 (1869 Nov 27); pg 126 (1869 Nov 27) lodge purchased 10 acres for $20/acre to be made in 2 payments for use as a cemetery; pg 126 (1869 Nov 27) land on his farm suitable for a burial ground which can be purchased for $20/acre; pg 127 (1869 Dec 11); pg 128 (1869 Dec 11); pg 129 (1869 Dec 11); pg 130 (1869 Dec 15); pg 132 (1870 Jan 8); pg 134 (1870 Jan 15); pg 135 (1870 Jan 22); pg 136 (1870 Feb 12); pg 138 (1870 Feb 19); pg 139 (1870 Feb 26); pg 140 (1870 Mar 8); pg 141 (1870 Mar 12); pg 142 (1870 Mar 17); pg 142 (1870 Mar 24); pg 143 (1870 Mar 25); pg 144 (1870 Mar 26); pg 145 (1870 Mar 26); pg 146 (1870 Apr 2); pg 147 (1870 Apr 9); pg 148 (1870 Apr 9); pg 149 (1870 Apr 23); pg 150 (1870 Apr 23); pg 151 (1870 May 11); pg 151 (1870 May 7); pg 152 (1870 May 14); pg 154 (1870 May 28); pg 155 (1870 June 4); pg 156 (1870 June 11); pg 157 (1870 June 11) bill presented for the cemetery grounds and for setting 280 posts around the land; pg 158 (1870 June 25); pg 160 (1870 July 2); pg 160 (1870 July 9); pg 162 (1870 July 24); pg 163 (1870 Aug 13); pg 164 (1870 Aug 27); pg 165 (1870 Aug 27) motion that the lodge sell one fourth of the Masonic Cemetery to the Odd Fellows Lodge of Boulder - deed ordered; pg 166 (1870 Sept 3); pg 167 (1870 Sept 10); pg 168 (1870 Sept 15); pg 169 (1870 Sept 24); pg 171 (1870 Nov 12); pg 172 (1870 Nov 26) bill presented for surveying Masonic cemetery; pg 172 (1870 Nov 26); pg 173 (1870 Dec 3); pg 174 (1870 Dec 10); pg 175 (1870 Dec 10); pg 176 (1870 Dec 24); pg 177 (1870 Dec 29); pg 178 (1871 Jan 4); pg 179 (1871 Jan 14); pg 181 (1871 Jan 28); pg 183 (1871 Feb 9); pg 184 (1871 Feb 18); pg 185 (1871 Feb 25); pg 187 (1871 Mar 11); pg 187 (1871 Mar 11); pg 189 (1871 Mar 25); pg 190 (1871 Apr 8); pg 191 (1871 Apr 13); pg 192 (1871 Apr 22); pg 194 (1871 May 27); pg 195 (1871 June 11); pg 197 (1871 July 8); pg 198 (1871 July 12); pg 199 (1871 July 22); pg 200 (1871 Aug 12); pg 201 (1871 Sept 9); pg 203 (1871 Sept 23); pg 205 (1871 Oct 5); pg 206 (1871 Oct 8); pg 207 (1871 Oct 28); pg 209 (1871 Nov 25); pg 210 (1871 Dec 9); pg 213 (1871 Dec 9); pg 214 (1871 Dec 23) committee to investigate building a Masonic hall; pg 216 (1872 Jan 13); pg 219 (1872 Feb 10); pg 224 (1872 Mar 9); pg 225 (1872 Mar 23); pg 226 (1872 Apr 6); pg 226 (1872 Apr 27); pg 228 (1872 Apr 27); pg 229 (1872 May 9); pg 231 (1872 May 16); pg 235 (1872 June 29); pg 236 (1872 July 27); pg 237 (1872 July 27) bill pesented for cash paid for repairing cemetery fence; pg 238 (1872 Aug 24); pg 239 (1872 Aug 31); pg 241 (1872 Sept 28); pg 244 (1872 Oct 26); pg 244 (1872 Oct 26); pg 246 (1872 Nov 9); pg 247 (1872 Nov 23); pg 249 (1872 Nov 23); pg 249 (1872 Nov 27); pg 250 (1872 Nov 30); pg 251 (1872 Dec 14); pg 255 (1872 Dec 28); pg 257 (1873 Jan 4); pg 258 (1873 Jan 8); pg 260 (1873 Jan 11); pg 262 (1873 Jan 25); pg 263 (1873 Jan 25); pg 265 (1873 Feb 1); pg 269 (1873 Feb 12); pg 271 (1873 Feb 22); pg 274 (1873 Mar 7); pg 274 (1873 Mar 8); pg 277 (1873 Mar 11); pg 277 (1873 Mar 12); pg 278 (1873 Mar 15); pg 279 (1873 Mar 20); pg 281 (1873 Mar 29); pg

8); pg 41 (1867 Aug 17); pg 42 (1867 Aug 25); pg 43 (1867 Sept 5); pg 44 (1867 Sept 12); pg 46 (1867 Sept 26); pg 49 (1867 Oct 12); pg 51 (1867 Oct 12); pg 53 (1867 Oct 14); pg 54 (1867 Oct 16); pg 55 (1867 Oct 26); pg 58 (1867 Nov 23); pg 59 (1867 Dec 14); pg 60 (1867 Dec 14); pg 60 (1867 Dec 29); pg 63 (1868 Feb 8); pg 66 (1868 Apr 11); pg 61 (1868 Jan 11); pg 64 (1868 Feb 8); pg 71 (1868 Oct 24); pg 75 (1868 Nov 28); pg 78 (1868 Dec 12); pg 80 (1868 Dec 14); pg 81 (1868 Dec 5); pg 81 (1868 Dec 19); pg 82 (1868 Dec 26); pg 84 (1868 Dec 28); pg 89 (1859 Jan 13); pg 90 (1869 Jan 23); pg 92 (1869 Jan 29); pg 93 (1869 Feb 12); pg 97 (1869 Feb 27); pg 98 (1869 Mar 6); pg 99 (1869 Mar 6); pg 101 (1869 Mar 27); pg 106 (1869 May 7); pg 107 (1869 May 8); pg 113 (1869 June 26); pg 115 (1869 Aug 14); pg 117 (1869 Aug 21); pg 118 (1869 Aug 28); pg 127 (1869 Dec 11); pg 129 (1869 Dec 11); pg 132 (1870 Jan 8); pg 134 (1870 Jan 15); pg 135 (1870 Jan 22); pg 136 (1870 Feb 12); pg 138 (1870 Feb 19); pg 139 (1870 Feb 26); pg 140 (1870 Mar 8); pg 142 (1870 Mar 17); pg 143 (1870 Mar 25); pg 144 (1870 Mar 26); pg 149 (1870 Apr 23); pg 163 (1870 Aug 13); pg 173 (1870 Dec 3); pg 174 (1870 Dec 10); pg 175 (1870 Dec 10); pg 177 (1870 Dec 29); pg 179 (1871 Jan 14); pg 183 (1871 Feb 9); pg 187 (1871 Mar 11); pg 191 (1871 Apr 13); pg 192 (1871 Apr 22); pg 198 (1871 July 12); pg 198 (1871 July 12); pg 223 (1872 Mar 9); pg 225 (1872 Mar 23); pg 225 (1872 Apr 6); pg 226 (1872 Apr 27); pg 228 (1872 Apr 27); pg 229 (1872 May 9); pg 239 (1872 Aug 31); pg 242 (1872 Oct 4); pg 287 (1873 May 3); pg 290 (1873 May 19); pg 290 (1873 May 24); pg 297 (1873 June 24); pg 313 member

Soule, Albert G
pg 161 (1870 July 9); pg 163 (1870 Aug 13); pg 335 (1867 Aug 13)
*did not become a member of the Columbia Lodge

Soule, Albert G
appears as: Soule, Alf
pg 316 (1883 Oct 27) member

Southerland, see Sutherland, Datus E

Southland, W J
pg 314 member

Spaulding, J F
pg 1 (1867 Jan 3) petitioner

Spencer, Charles L
pg 315 member

Spencer, S W
pg 65 (1868 Mar 28) Denver Lodge No. 5; pg 357 (1868 Mar 7) Denver Lodge No. 5

Spengler
pg 318 pencil list

Spraina, D A
pg 195 (1871 June 11) Black Hawk Lodge No. 11

Squires, Frederick A
appears as: Squires, F A
pg 157 (1870 June 11) proposed builder; pg 190 (1871 Apr 8) bill presented; pg 237 (1872 July 27) bill presented; pg 283 (1873 Apr 12) bill presented

Squires, George C
appears as: Squires; Squires, G C; Squires, George E
offices held: SD, Secy, SW, JD
pg 78 (1868 Dec 12); pg 86 (1869 Jan 9); pg 87 (1869 Jan 9); pg 88 (1869 Jan 9); pg 89 (1869 Jan 13); pg 90 (1869 Jan 23); pg 91 (1869 Jan 23); pg 92 (1869 Jan 25); pg 93 (1869 Feb 12); pg 93 (1869 Feb 13); pg 95 (1869 Feb 13); pg 95 (1869 Feb 15); pg 96 (1869 Feb 24); pg 97 (1869 Feb 27); pg 98 (1869 Mar 6); pg 99 (1869 Mar 13); pg 103 (1869 Apr 10); pg 106 (1869 May 7); pg 107 (1869 May 8); pg 108 (1869 May 22); pg 110 (1869 May 25); pg 113 (1869 June 26); pg 115 (1869 Aug 14); pg 118 (1869 Aug 28); pg 119 (1869 Sept 11); pg 129 (1869 Dec 11); pg 132 (1870 Jan 8); pg 134 (1870 Jan 15); pg 139 (1870 Feb 26); pg 140 (1870 Mar 8); pg 142 (1870 Mar 17); pg 142 (1870 Mar 24); pg 143 (1870 Mar 25); pg 144 (1870 Mar 26); pg 146 (1870 Apr 2); pg 147 (1870 Apr 9); pg 151 (1870 May 7); pg 151 (1870 May 11); pg 152 (1870 May 14); pg 154 (1870 May 28); pg 155 (1870 June 4); pg 156 (1870 June 11); pg 158 (1870 June 25); pg 160 (1870 July 2); pg 174 (1870 Dec 10); pg 213 (1871 Dec 9); pg 210 (1871 Dec 9); pg 220 (1872 Feb 10);

pg 222 (1872 Feb 24) bill presented for taking care of J S Anderson; pg 251 (1872 Dec 14); pg 313 member

St Clair, Joel F T
appears as: St Clair, J F T
pg 314 member

Stanley, Mr
pg 256 (1872 Dec 28) bill presented

Stanton, John A
appears as: Stanton; Stanton, A J, Stanton, J A
offices held: Tiler, JD, JS, Treas, SS
pg 4 (1867 Jan 10); pg 5 (1867 Jan 10); pg 8 (1867 Feb 14); pg 9 (1867 Feb 28); pg 10 (1867 Feb 28); pg 11 (1867 Mar 6); pg 12 (1867 Mar 14); pg 13 (1867 Mar 14); pg 14 (1867 Mar 18); pg 14 (1867 Mar 28); pg 15 (1867 Mar 28); pg 16 (1867 Apr 1); pg 17 (1867 Apr 4); pg 17 (1867 Apr 11); pg 19 (1867 Apr 15); pg 20 (1867 Apr 18); pg 20 (1867 Apr 23); pg 21 (1867 Apr 23); pg 22 (1867 Apr 29); pg 23 (1867 May 3); pg 24 (1867 May 9); pg 24 (1867 May 9); pg 25 (1867 May 13); pg 26 (1867 May 23); pg 27 (1867 June 13); pg 29 (1867 June 15); pg 29 (1867 June 27); pg 32 (1867 July 6); pg 33 (1867 July 11); pg 35 (1867 July 13); pg 36 (1867 July 15); pg 36 (1867 July 17); pg 37 (1867 July 24); pg 38 (1867 July 25); pg 39 (1867 Aug 7); pg 39 (1867 Aug 8); pg 41 (1867 Aug 17); pg 42 (1867 Aug 25); pg 43 (1867 Sept 5); pg 44 (1867 Sept 12); pg 45 (1867 Sept 14); pg 46 (1867 Sept 26); pg 49 (1867 Oct 12); pg 51 (1867 Oct 12); pg 53 (1867 Oct 14); pg 54 (1867 Oct 16); pg 55 (1867 Oct 26); pg 57 (1867 Nov 10); pg 58 (1867 Nov 23); pg 59 (1867 Dec 14); pg 60 (1867 Dec 14); pg 60 (1867 Dec 29); pg 61 (1868 Jan 11); pg 62 (1868 Jan 11); pg 62 (1868 Jan 25); pg 64 (1868 Feb 8); pg 66 (1868 Apr 11); pg 67 (1868 Aug 8); pg 77 (1868 Dec 12); pg 79 (1868 Dec 14); pg 129 (1869 Dec 11); pg 313 member

Stanton, Mrs J A
pg 46 (1867 Sept 26) bill presented

Steinmetz, O C
pg 317 (1889 Feb 9) member

Stevens, Rees Winfield
pg 317 (1888 June 4) member

Stewart, A R
pg 304 (1873 Aug 9) bill presented for coal oil

Stewart, Henry
pg 139 (1870 Feb 26) Denver Lodge No. 5; pg 361 (1870 Feb 5) Denver Lodge No. 5

Stewart, Joseph
appears as: Stewart, J; Stewart, Joseph
pg 103 (1869 Apr 10) Washington Lodge No. 12; pg 360 (1869 Mar 27) Washington Lodge No. 12; pg 360 (1869 Feb 27) Washington Lodge No. 12

Stewart, Mrs
pg 245 (1872 Oct 26) bill presented

Stewart, Thomas
pg 231 (1872 May 16) visiting; pg 235 (1872 June 29); pg 237 (1872 July 27) ; pg 314 member

Stiles, Henry C
appears as: Stiles; Stiles, Henry C; Stites; Stites, H C, Stites, Henry C
pg 180 (1871 Jan 14); pg 183 (1871 Feb 9); pg 184 (1871 Feb 18); pg 189 (1871 Mar 25); pg 189 (1871 Mar 25); pg 192 (1871 Apr 22); pg 193 (1871 Apr 22); pg 200 (1871 Aug 12); pg 232 (1872 May 25); pg 243 (1872 Oct 4); pg 274 (1873 Mar 8); pg 304 (1873 Aug 9); pg 313 member

Stokes, T T
pg 97 (1869 Feb 27) Central Lodge No. 6; pg 358 (1869 Feb 10) Central Lodge No. 6

Stoners [??], C P
pg 174 (1870 Dec 10) Nevada Lodge No 4

Strasburg, John
pg 359 (1869 Jan 2) Cheyenne Lodge No. 16; pg 359 (1868 June 6) Cheyenne Lodge U.D.

Strasburger, Mathias
pg 315 member

Stratton
pg 270 (1873 Feb 22) present

Stroup, Peter A
pg 167 (1870 Sept 10) Denver Lodge No. 5; pg 335 (1870 Aug 6) Denver Lodge No. 5

Studinsley, W
pg 203 (1871 Sept 23) Pueblo Lodge No. 17

Sturfield, Levi
pg 179 (1871 Jan 14) Denver Lodge No. 5

Sullivan, Jacob M
pg 83 (1868 Dec 26) bill presented to make a coffin for brother A Lennox; pg 113 (1869 June 26) bill presented

Summer, J R
pg 360 (1869 Feb 6) Cheyenne Lodge No. 16

Summonds, T F
pg 357 (1868 Mar 14) Washington Lodge No. 12

Surbo, Zola
pg 341 (1885) member

Sutherland, Datus E
appears as: Southerland, D E; Sutherland; Sutherland, D E, Sutherland, Dorcas
offices held: WM, JW, SW
pg 60 (1867 Dec 29); pg 71 (1868 Oct 24); pg 72 (1868 Oct 24); pg 73 (1868 Oct 23); pg 73 (1868 Oct 24); pg 74 (1868 Oct 24); pg 75 (1868 Nov 28); pg 76 (1868 Nov 28); pg 77 (1868 Dec 12); pg 80 (1868 Dec 14); pg 81 (1868 Dec 5); pg 82 (1868 Dec 26); pg 84 (1868 Dec 31); pg 85 (1869 Jan 9); pg 88 (1869 Jan 9) paid the final $15 left in the treasury of the Valmont Lodge when it surrendered its dispensation; pg 89 (1869 Jan 13); pg 90 (1869 Jan 23); pg 92 (1869 Jan 25); pg 92 (1869 Jan 29); pg 93 (1869 Feb 12); pg 93 (1869 Feb 13); pg 95 (1869 Feb 15); pg 96 (1869 Feb 24); pg 97 (1869 Feb 27); pg 98 (1869 Mar 6); pg 99 (1869 Mar 13); pg 101 (1869 Mar 27); pg 103 (1869 Apr 10); pg 104 (1869 Apr 24); pg 106 (1869 May 7); pg 107 (1869 May 8); pg 110 (1869 May 25); pg 111 (1869 June 12); pg 113 (1869 June 26); pg 121 (1869 Sept 25); pg 123 (1869 Nov 13); pg 123 (1869 Nov 13); pg 125 (1869 Nov 27); pg 126 (1869 Nov 27); pg 127 (1869 Dec 11); pg 130 (1869 Dec 15); pg 132 (1870 Jan 8); pg 193 (1871 Apr 22); pg 225 (1872 Mar 23) application for a demit; pg 269 (1873 Feb 12); pg 313 member

Southerland, E D
pg 66 (1868 Apr 11) visiting WM of Valmont Lodge

Sutherland, Dorcas, see Sutherland, Datus E

Sutphin, Daniel O
pg 66 (1868 Apr 11) Black Hawk Lodge No. 11; pg 357 (1868 Mar 21) Black Hawk Lodge No. 11

Swop, D
pg 226 (1872 Apr 13) Central Lodge No. 6; pg 336 (1872 Apr 13) Central Lodge No. 6

T___tly, Fred L
pg 362 (1870 May 21) Cheyenne Lodge No. 16

Taber, J F
appears as: Taber; Taber, J F; Tabor, J F
pg 10 (1867 Feb 28); pg 30 (1867 June 27); pg 31 (1867 June 27); pg 356 (1867 Feb 28)
*does not become a member of the Columbia Lodge

Tallmann, Isaac T
pg 314 member

Tannall, Jackson
pg 65 (1868 Mar 28) Black Hawk Lodge No. 11; pg 357 (1868 Mar 1) Black Hawk Lodge No. 11

Tannall, Rudolph
pg 65 (1868 Mar 28) Black Hawk Lodge No. 11

Tannat, E O
pg 359 (1869 Jan 2) Cheyenne Lodge No. 16

Taylor, A D
pg 355 (1868 Apr 23) visitor, Souhegan Lodge No. 67, NH

Taylor, A W
pg 341 (1885) member

Taylor, C W
pg 299 (1873 June 28) certificate of membership from Waynesburg Lodge No. 153, state of Pennsylvania with a request for aid; pg 309 (1873 Oct 11) being cared for by Robert Ellingham

Taylor, Eugene
pg 333 (1874 Dec 12)
*did not become a member of the Columbia Lodge

Taylor, R S
pg 338 (1873 Dec 27) El Paso Lodge No. 13

Taylor, Samuel
pg 195 (1871 June 11) Washington Lodge No. 12

Teller, Henry M
appears as: Teller, Henry M; Teller, H M
offices held: Most Worshipful Grand Master of Colorado
pg 53 (1867 Oct 14); pg 73 (1868 Oct 23); pg 80 (1868 Dec 14); pg 138 (1870 Feb 19); pg 179 (1871 Jan 14); pg 230 (1872 May 9); pg 135 (1870 Jan 22); pg 136 (1870 Jan 22)

Thomas, Henry F
pg 69 (1868 Sept 12) Chivington Lodge No. 6; pg 357 (1868 Aug 12) Chivington Lodge No. 6

Thome, S J
pg 316 (1884 June 14) member

Thompson
pg 251 (1872 Dec 14) present

Thompson, Charles H
pg 339 (1878 Oct 12) Washington Lodge No. 12

Thompson, G T
pg 317 (1887 Apr 20) member

Thompson, Henry
pg 339 (1878 Oct 12) Washington Lodge No. 12

Thompson, James M
pg 185 (1871 Feb 25); pg 192 (1871 Apr 22); pg 193 (1871 Apr 22)
*did not become a member of the Columbia Lodge

Thuy, Robert H
pg 314 member

Tiffany, J W
pg 68 (1868 Aug 8) Chivington Lodge No. 6; pg 357 (1868 May 13) Chivington Lodge No. 6

Tiffany, W W
pg 65 (1868 Mar 28) Chivington Lodge No. 6; pg 357 (1868 Mar 11) Chivington Lodge No. 6

Tilney, Robert H
pg 132 (1870 Jan 8); pg 140 (1870 Feb 26); pg 362 (1870 Feb 25)
*did not become a member of the Columbia Lodge

Tippet, George
pg 181 (1871 Jan 28) Black Hawk Lodge No. 11

Tipple, George L
pg 315 member

Titcomb, John S
appears as: Titcomb; Titcomb, John S
offices held: JD
pg 279 (1873 Mar 20); pg 280 (1873 Mar 22); pg 282 (1873 Apr 5); pg 314 member

Todd, C D
pg 318 pencil list

Tourtellot & Squires
pg 72 (1868 Oct 24); pg 76 (1868 Nov 28); pg 79 (1868 Dec 14); pg 87 (1869 Jan 9); pg 103 (1869 Apr 10)

Tourtellot, Mrs
pg 245 (1872 Oct 26) bill presented

Towner, B F
pg 355 (1868 Jan 23) visitor, Denver Lodge No. 5, Colo

Travel, Elijah
pg 128 (1869 Dec 11) Central Lodge No. 6

Trear, George
pg 8 (1867 Feb 14); pg 12 (1867 Mar 14); pg 30 (1867 June 27); pg 31 (1867 June 27); pg 356 (1867 Mar 4)
*did not become a member of the Columbia Lodge

Tremont, Hugh
pg 341 (1885) member

Treppen, James
pg 341 (1885) member

Trevarsen, Richard
pg 87 (1869 Jan 9) Nevada Lodge No 4; pg 358 (1868 Dec 26) Nevada Lodge No. 4

Trezise, James
pg 123 (1869 Nov 13) visiting from Nevada Lodge

Trezise, John
pg 338 (1874 Mar 14) Nevada Lodge No. 4; pg 355 (1868 Mar 13) visitor, Nevada Lodge No. 4, Colo

Tubbs, Octavius H
appears as: Tubbs; Tubbs, O H; Tubbs, Octavius H (*changed his name to Edward F Mason)
offices held: Tiler, JS, Treas
pg 6 (1867 Jan 10); pg 8 (1867 Feb 14); pg 9 (1867 Feb 14); pg 9 (1867 Feb 28); pg 10 (1867

Feb 28); pg 11 (1867 Mar 6); pg 12 (1867 Mar 14); pg 13 (1867 Mar 14); pg 13 (1867 Mar 15); pg 14 (1867 Mar 18); pg 14 (1867 Mar 28); pg 15 (1867 Mar 28); pg 16 (1867 Apr 1); pg 17 (1867 Apr 11); pg 17 (1867 Apr 4); pg 19 (1867 Apr 15); pg 20 (1867 Apr 18); pg 22 (1867 Apr 29); pg 24 (1867 May 9); pg 27 (1867 June 13); pg 26 (1867 May 23); pg 27 (1867 June 13); pg 38 (1867 July 25); pg 39 (1867 Aug 8); pg 46 (1867 Sept 26); pg 59 (1867 Dec 14); pg 313 deceased?

Tuly
pg 270 (1873 Feb 22); pg 277 (1873 Mar 12)

Turner, Charles
pg 314 member

Tuttle
pg 280 (1873 Mar 22) present

Tyrell, Norman J
appears as: Tyrell; Tyrell, N J; Tyrell, Norman J
pg 255 (1872 Dec 28); pg 263 (1873 Jan 25); pg 264 (1873 Jan 25); pg 265 (1873 Jan 25); pg 274 (1873 Mar 8); pg 275 (1873 Mar 8); pg 277 (1873 Mar 11); pg 284 (1873 Apr 19); pg 288 (1873 May 10); pg 290 (1873 May 19); pg 290 (1873 May 19); pg 314 member

Uren, William
pg 69 (1868 Sept 12) Chivington Lodge No. 6; pg 357 (1868 Aug 12) Chivington Lodge No. 6

Van Camp, A
pg 87 (1869 Jan 9) Central Lodge No. 6; pg 358 (1868 Dec 9) Central Lodge No. 6

Van Deren, Archibald J
appears as: Van Deren, A J; Van Deren, Archibald, J
offices held: WM
pg 1 (1867 Jan 3); pg 2 (1867 Jan 3)

Van Fleet, Charles G
pg 315 member

Van Houston, John P
pg 167 (1870 Sept 10) Union Lodge No. 7; pg 335 (1870 Aug 27) Union Lodge No. 7

Van Riper, Cornelius
appears as: Van Riper, C
pg 307 (1873 Sept 27) visiting; pg 314 member

Van Valkenburg, R J
pg 120 (1869 Sept 25) visiting; pg 246 (1872 Nov 9); pg 255 (1872 Dec 28); pg 274 (1873 Mar 8); pg 355 (1868 Feb 25) visitor, Warren Lodge No. 240, PA

Van, Clay M
appeared as: Van; Van, C M;
offices held: JS, JD, SW, SS, JW
pg 255 (1872 Dec 28); pg 263 (1873 Jan 25); pg 264 (1873 Jan 25); pg 265 (1873 Jan 25); pg 266 (1873 Feb 8); pg 268 (1873 Feb 8); pg 269 (1873 Feb 12); pg 270 (1873 Feb 22); pg 271 (1873 Feb 22); pg 274 (1873 Mar 7); pg 277 (1873 Mar 11); pg 277 (1873 Mar 12); pg 279 (1873 Mar 20); pg 279 (1873 Mar 22); pg 281 (1873 Mar 29); pg 282 (1873 Apr 5); pg 283 (1873 Apr 12); pg 284 (1873 Apr 19); pg 285 (1873 Apr 26); pg 287 (1873 May 1); pg 287 (1873 May 3); pg 288 (1873 May 10); pg 289 (1873 May 14); pg 290 (1873 May 24); pg 294 (1873 May 31); pg 296 (1873 June 14); pg 298 (1873 June 28); pg 300 (1873 July 2); pg 301 (1873 July 12); pg 302 (1873 July 19); pg 303 (1873 July 26); pg 305 (1873 Aug 23); pg 308 (1873 Oct 11); pg 314 member; pg 315

Viele, James B Jr
pg 315 member

Viere, James
pg 267 (1873 Feb 8) Laramie Lodge No. 18; pg 337 (1873 Feb 8) Laramie Lodge No. 18

Wadsworth, T H
pg 219 (1872 Feb 10) Black Hawk Lodge No. 11; pg 336 (1872 Feb 10) Black Hawk Lodge No. 11

Waggoner, A A
pg 162 (1870 July 24) El Paso Lodge No. 13; pg 335 (1867 July 9) El Paso Lodge No. 13

Wagner, Thomas S
pg 161 (1870 July 9) Larimer Lodge U.D,

Wait, D G
pg 94 (1869 Feb 13) Central Lodge No. 6; pg 358 (1869 Jan 27) Central Lodge No. 6

Walker, Ed S
pg 317 (1886 May 8) member

Walker, Thomas C
pg 314 member

pg 287 (1873 May 1); pg 313 member; pg 355 (1868 Jan 9) visitor, Denver Lodge No. 5, Colo

Weeks, Nicholas
pg 156 (1870 June 11) Cheyenne Lodge No. 16; pg 362 (1870 May 7) Cheyenne Lodge No. 16

Wellman, [Luther C or Sylvanus]
pg 240 (1872 Sept 14); pg 241 (1872 Sept 28); pg 243 (1872 Oct 19); pg 257 (1873 Jan 4); pg 259 (1873 Jan 11); pg 277 (1873 Mar 12); pg 280 (1873 Mar 22); pg 285 (1873 Apr 26); pg 303 (1873 July 26)

Wellman, Luther C
appears as: Wellman, L C; Wellman, Luther C
offices held: JS
pg 132 (1870 Jan 8); pg 140 (1870 Feb 26); pg 228 (1872 Apr 27); pg 232 (1872 May 25); pg 232 (1872 May 25); pg 233 (1872 June 1); pg 234 (1872 June 22); pg 235 (1872 June 22); pg 235 (1872 June 29); pg 238 (1872 Aug 24); pg 239 (1872 Aug 24); pg 253 (1872 Dec 14); pg 270 (1873 Feb 22); pg 289 (1873 May 14); pg 294 (1873 May 31); pg 313 member; pg 362 (1870 Feb 25)

Wellman, Sylvanus
appears as: Wellman, S; Wellman, Sylvanus
offices held: JD, SS
pg 136 (1870 Feb 12); pg 141 (1870 Mar 12); pg 141 (1870 Mar 12); pg 142 (1870 Mar 17); pg 152 (1870 May 14); pg 153 (1870 May 14); pg 158 (1870 June 25); pg 159 (1870 June 25); pg 160 (1870 July 2); pg 171 (1870 Nov 12); pg 173 (1870 Dec 3); pg 175 (1870 Dec 10); pg 195 (1871 June 11); pg 203 (1871 Sept 23); pg 204 (1871 Sept 23); pg 210 (1871 Dec 9); pg 214 (1871 Dec 23); pg 216 (1872 Jan 13); pg 223 (1872 Mar 9); pg 224 (1872 Mar 9); pg 226 (1872 Apr 27); pg 229 (1872 May 9); pg 231 (1872 May 25); pg 232 (1872 June 1); pg 234 (1872 June 22); pg 235 (1872 June 29); pg 238 (1872 Aug 24); pg 241 (1872 Sept 28); pg 253 (1872 Dec 14); pg 259 (1873 Jan 11); pg 261 (1873 Jan 14); pg 270 (1873 Feb 22); pg 280 (1873 Mar 22); pg 313 member

Wells, Frank P
pg 339 (1878 Aug 22) Black Hawk Lodge No. 11

Wells, William
pg 338 (1874 Jan 10) Union Lodge No. 7

Wendt, Frederick
pg 224 (1872 Mar 9) Nevada Lodge No. 4; pg 275 (1873 Mar 8) Nevada Lodge No. 4

Westlake, M D
pg 33 (1867 July 11); pg 40 (1867 Aug 8); pg 356 (1867 Aug 8)
*did not become a member of the Columbia Lodge

Wharton, Joseph J
appears as: Wharton, J J; Wharton, Joseph J
pg 272 (1873 Feb 22); pg 276 (1873 Mar 8); pg 255 (1872 Dec 28); pg 263 (1873 Jan 25); pg 264 (1873 Jan 25); pg 265 (1873 Feb 1); pg 266 (1873 Feb 1); pg 270 (1873 Feb 22); pg 271 (1873 Feb 22); pg 272 (1873 Feb 22); pg 274 (1873 Mar 8); pg 276 (1873 Mar 8); pg 304 (1873 Aug 9); pg 314 member

Wheeler, John C
pg 149 (1870 Apr 23) Black Hawk Lodge No. 11

White, David S
pg 314 member; pg 315 member

White, William W
pg 316 (1884 Mar 15) member

Whitehead, Edward
pg 338 (1873 Dec 13) Union Lodge No. 7

Whitford, A H
pg 139 (1870 Feb 26) Black Hawk Lodge No. 11; pg 335 (1870 June 12) Black Hawk Lodge No. 11

Whitney, George H
pg 316 (1884 Oct 25) member

Whittemore
pg 237 (1872 July 27) present

Whitwell, G B
pg 361 (1870 Jan 15) Black Hawk Lodge No. 11

Whurles, John A
pg 362 (1870 Apr 14) Black Hawk Lodge No. 11

Widford, R H
pg 165 (1870 Aug 27) Black Hawk Lodge No. 11

Wigginton, John W
appears as: Wigginton; Wigginton, J W; Wigginton, John W
offices held: JS, Tiler
pg 9 (1867 Feb 28); pg 15 (1867 Mar 28); pg 16 (1867 Apr 1); pg 17 (1867 Apr 11); pg 18 (1867 Apr 11); pg 19 (1867 Apr 15); pg 20 (1867 Apr 18); pg 21 (1867 Apr 23); pg 21 (1867 Apr 23); pg 23 (1867 Apr 29); pg 23 (1867 May 3); pg 24 (1867 May 9); pg 25 (1867 May 13); pg 37 (1867 July 24); pg 38 (1867 July 25); pg 42 (1867 Aug 25); pg 43 (1867 Sept 5); pg 44 (1867 Sept 12); pg 55 (1867 Oct 26); pg 58 (1867 Nov 23); pg 63 (1868 Jan 25); pg 210 (1871 Nov 25); pg 266 (1873 Feb 8); pg 313 member

Wilder
pg 253 (1872 Dec 26) visiting

Wilder, Eugene
pg 314 member

Wilkins, Cornelius
pg 314 member

Wilkins, George
pg 240 (1872 Sept 14) Cheyenne Lodge No. 16; pg 336 (1872 Sept 14) Cheyenne Lodge No. 16

Wille, John
pg 105 (1869 Apr 24) Golden Lodge No. 1

Williams, George T
pg 209 (1871 Nov 25) Cheyenne Lodge No. 16

Williams, J O
pg 317 (1889 Jan 26) member

Williams, James
pg 317 (1888 Mar 12) member

Williams, John
pg 217 (1872 Jan 13) Pueblo Lodge No. 17

Williams, John H
pg 340 (1880 Nov 14) Black Hawk Lodge No. 11

Williams, John T
pg 315 member

Williams, John T
pg 335 (1872 Jan 5) Pueblo Lodge No. 17

Williams, W J
pg 318 (1889 Nov 9) member

Willie, John G
pg 360 (1869 Apr 3) Cheyenne Lodge No. 16

Willoughby, E A
pg 65 (1868 Mar 28) Union Lodge No. 7; pg 357 (1868 Feb 22) Union Lodge No. 7

Wilson, Benjamin F
pg 314 member

Wilson, George W
pg 316 member

Wilson, James L
pg 82 (1868 Dec 26) visiting; pg 93 (1869 Feb 12); pg 133 (1870 Jan 8)

Wilson, James L F
pg 317 (1888 Mar 10) member

Wilson, John Milton
appears as: Willson; Willson, J M; Willson, John
offices held: SD, SW, JW, Treas, Tiler, JD, SS
pg 200 (1871 Aug 12); pg 203 (1871 Sept 23); pg 225 (1872 Mar 23); pg 225 (1872 Apr 6); pg 226 (1872 Apr 13); pg 226 (1872 Apr 6); pg 226 (1872 Apr 27); pg 229 (1872 May 9); pg 231 (1872 May 16); pg 232 (1872 June 1); pg 233 (1872 June 1); pg 233 (1872 June 8); pg 234 (1872 June 22); pg 235 (1872 June 29); pg 236 (1872 July 27); pg 238 (1872 Aug 24); pg 239 (1872 Aug 31); pg 240 (1872 Sept 14); pg 241 (1872 Sept 28); pg 242 (1872 Oct 4); pg 243 (1872 Oct 19); pg 244 (1872 Oct 26) petitioner of Live Oak Lodge No. 128 of Missouri; pg 247 (1872 Nov 23); pg 248 (1872 Nov 23); pg 249 (1872 Nov 23); pg 250 (1872 Nov 30); pg 254 (1872 Dec 28); pg 255 (1872 Dec 28); pg 256 (1873 Jan 4); pg 258 (1873 Jan 8); pg 261 (1873 Jan 14); pg 263 (1873 Jan 25); pg 269 (1873 Feb 12); pg 270 (1873 Feb 22); pg 274 (1873 Mar 7); pg 279 (1873 Mar 20); pg 279 (1873 Mar 22); pg 282 (1873 Apr 5); pg 284 (1873 Apr 19); pg 287 (1873 May 3); pg 288 (1873 May 10); pg 289 (1873 May 14); pg 294 (1873 May 31); pg 297 (1873 June 24); pg 300 (1873 July 2); pg 301 (1873 July 12); pg 302 (1873 July 19); pg 303 (1873 July 26); pg 306 (1873 Sept 13); pg 313 member

Wimer, John A
appears as: Wymer, John; Wymer; Wymer, John A

offices held: Tiler, JS
pg 274 (1873 Mar 8); pg 276 (1873 Mar 8); pg 277 (1873 Mar 11); pg 282 (1873 Apr 5); pg 284 (1873 Apr 19); pg 287 (1873 May 1); pg 289 (1873 May 14); pg 300 (1873 July 2); pg 306 (1873 Sept 13)

Windt, Fred
pg 337 (1873 Mar 8) Nevada Lodge No. 4

Wineberger
pg 266 (1873 Feb 8) present

Wise, Charles
pg 98 (1869 Feb 27) Washington Lodge No. 12

Wise, Charles
pg 358 (1869 Feb 10) Central Lodge No. 6

Wisebart, B W
pg 28 (1867 June 13) Grand Lecturer

Wisner, John A
pg 314 member

Withrow, Chase
appears as: Witherow, Chase; Withrow, Chase; Withrow
offices held: Grand Master
pg 142 (1870 Mar 24) Grand Lecturer; pg 2 (1867 Jan 3) Grand Master of the Black Hawk Lodge; pg 3 (1866 Dec 17) Grand Master of the Grand Lodge; pg 28 (1867 June 13) Grand Master; pg 51 (1867 Oct 12) Grand Master; pg 143 (1870 Mar 24) addressed the lodge; pg 144 (1870 Mar 26) Grand Lecturer; pg 185 (1871 Feb 25) PM visiting

Wood, Frank J
pg 195 (1871 June 11) Washington Lodge No. 12

Wood, Gardner P
appears as: Wood; Wood, G P; Wood, Gardner P
offices held: JD
pg 285 (1873 Apr 26); pg 195 (1871 June 11); pg 298 (1873 June 28) petitioner from Aurora Lodge No. ___ State of Massachusetts; pg 303 (1873 July 26); pg 303 (1873 July 26); pg 303 (1873 July 26); pg 314 member

Woodbray, see Woodbury, W C

Woodbury, Benjamin
pg 338 (1878 Aug 22) Black Hawk Lodge No. 11

Woodbury, W C
appears as: Woodbury, W C; Woodbray, W C
pg 301 (1873 July 12) Union Lodge No. 7; pg 337 (1873 July 12) Union Lodge No. 7

Woodward, Robert J
pg 103 (1869 Apr 10); pg 107 (1869 May 8); pg 222 (1872 Feb 24) bill for for transporting J S Anderson to Missouri; pg 226 (1872 Apr 13) bill presented; pg 252 (1872 Dec 14) bill presented; pg 285 (1873 Apr 26) bill presented for postage stamps

Wright, Alpheus
appears as: Wright; Wright, A; Wright, Alpheus, Wright, Alpheus, Esq
offices held: Treas, JD, JW
pg 216 (1872 Jan 13); pg 219 (1872 Feb 10); pg 221 (1872 Feb 10); pg 260 (1873 Jan 11); pg 271 (1873 Feb 22); pg 273 (1873 Mar 1); pg 277 (1873 Mar 12); pg 283 (1873 Apr 12); pg 284 (1873 Apr 12); pg 284 (1873 Apr 19); pg 285 (1873 Apr 26); pg 286 (1873 Apr 26); pg 287 (1873 May 1); pg 287 (1873 May 3); pg 289 (1873 May 14); pg 290 (1873 May 19); pg 290 (1873 May 24); pg 291 (1873 May 24); pg 294 (1873 June 4); pg 295 (1873 June 4) offered resolution of tribute to the deceased to be printed in the St Louis and Philadelphia papers as well as the Boulder News; pg 297 (1873 June 24); pg 298 (1873 June 28); pg 300 (1873 July 2); pg 301 (1873 July 12); pg 302 (1873 July 19); pg 305 (1873 Aug 23); pg 306 (1873 Sept 13); pg 314 member; pg 336 (1872 Feb 24) member

Wright, P B
pg 338 (1873 Dec 27) Black Hawk Lodge No. 11

Wyman, C E
pg 332 (1874 Sept 26) Washington Lodge No. 12

Wymer, see Wimer, John A

Wyncoop, see Wynkoop, William C

Wynkoop, William C
appears as: Wyncoop, W C; Wynkoop, W C
pg 176 (1870 Dec 24); pg 182 (1871 Jan 28); pg 280 (1873 Mar 22); pg 285 (1873 Apr 26); pg 286 (1873 Apr 26); pg 337 (1873 Apr 26) *did not become a member of the Columbia Lodge

Columbia Lodge No. 14

Minute Book Vol 2, 1873–1879

The Columbia Lodge No. 14 Ancient Free & Accepted Masons was formally established in the town of Columbia (now called Ward) in 1867. As the number suggests, there were 13 other Masonic lodges established before the Columbia Lodge in places like Golden City (Lodge No. 1), Nevada (Nevadaville - Lodge No. 4), Denver (Lodge No. 5), Central (Central City - Lodge No. 6), Empire (Lodge No. 8) and Black Hawk (Lodge No. 11).

In 1868, the Columbia Lodge petitioned the Grand Lodge to move the lodge to Boulder. There was a contemporary lodge in Valmont that disolved and many of the members of that lodge became members of the Columbia Lodge. In the 1870s, a new lodge opened up in Longmont (St. Vrain Lodge No. 23), and another lodge opened in Boulder (Boulder Lodge No. 45).

Access to the early records of the Columbia Lodge was gracious granted to the Boulder Pioneers Project by Bruce Yellen, current President of the Columbia Lodge. The Boulder Pioneers Project is trying to determine who all of the residents of Boulder County were before Colorado became a state in 1876. As a part of that project, we have reached out to groups like the Masons who were helping to create lasting communities within the Boulder Valley for access to their records.

The Minute Book of the Columbia Lodge, Vol 2 1873-1879, contains not only references to the on-going activities of the Columbia Lodge, but mentions members of the community who provided services to the lodge; members of the community who were in need and were helped by the lodge; Masons from this lodge and others who died in Boulder and whose funerals were conducted by the lodge; the establishment of a cemetery in the community part of which was run by the Columbia Lodge, part of which was sold to the Odd Fellows, part of which was reserved for a potter's field; members of the community who purchased lots in the Masonic Cemetery; other organizations like the Odd Fellows who shared space and expenses with the Columbia Lodge, and much more. The Minute Book is a fascinating look at early life in Boulder.

As is to be expected, most of the mentions in the book pertain to the members of the lodge including who held which offices, who was present, who paid dues and who has asked for a "demit" and left the community for other places.

New members are often listed as visitors first along with the lodge where they are already a member. For the members, we have listed the offices they held, but not what role they played on each page where they were listed. Mostly, members were marked as "present" or shown as holding an office. Petitioners to the lodge often have their places of residence listed, and petitioners who are already Masons often have the name and number of their home lodges listed. These Masons often are listed as being "accompanied by a demit" meaning that they had been granted a release by their home lodge to apply to a new lodge in the place where they had settled.

Non-members' listings usually have more detail including the circumstances under which they were mentioned in the Minute Book, or where they might have been from. On occasion, motions were raised by members that contained interesting information about the community, and those listings are included.

Recording practices vary from Secretary to Secretary and accordingly, it is sometimes difficult to tell which Masons were simply visiting the lodge from out of town and which were members of the lodge who were present, but simply were not mentioned very often. There is a note written within this Minute Book from 1956 which affirms that it was the practice of the early Masons to allow visiting Masons to take the seat of an officer as a courtesy to that visiting Mason which adds a bit to the confusion. The terms visiting and present were not used consistently.

Not all visiting members were listed as visiting either. Often they were listed among the other Columbia Lodge members as "present." There are also cases of Masons who were members of other lodges in other states who had moved to Boulder, but not affiliated with the Columbia Lodge who attended meetings as visitors.Dates within the volume are listed year first, followed by month and day. This is an unconventional way to present dates, but it is the method that the Colorado State Archives uses in its databases, and we have chosen to follow that method here.

Legend to the listings.

Members

Known members of the Columbia Lodge No. 14.

Possible Members

People who have attended meetings of the membership at the lodge, but who have very few records indicating that they might be a visiting Mason from another lodge. In the following list of Columbia Lodge Masons, those names which could not be determined for certain to have been members have an asterisk before them. There was a list hand-written in pencil that was stuck into the book. The names of these men are also considered possible members.

Boulder

People who were in Boulder but non-members such as members of the Valmont Lodge, St Vrain Lodge, wives of members, deceased Masons who were not members of the lodge, businesses, vendors who provided services to the lodge, etc.

Non-Boulder

These people were mentioned in a commmunication from another lodge and were not associated with the Columbia Lodge.

An asterisk before names in the Membership List indicates a possible member.

If there are listings where the correct spelling could not be determined, the listing will contain both spellings, such as **Imil [Imel], David.**

Every effort has been made to assure that these listings are correct, however, extracting hand-written records can be tricky, and some listings may contain inaccuracies. We hope you enjoy as much as we have the discoveries we have made about early Boulder.

— The Boulder Pioneers Project

Members List from Vol 2

A__son, J G
Allen, Henly Wheaton
*Ambrose
Ames, Leeman C
Anderson, A A
Anderson, David B
Anderson, Erick J
Andrews, Elijah H
Austin, Schuyler D
*Bailey, John
*Bailey, M
Banning, J A
*Barker, William
Barney, Royal Sigbert
Barney, William M
Barrowman, William
Bartels, Henry
*Barter, Thomas
Barter, William
Baum, Henry M
Baxter, William
Belcher, Freeman
*Belford
Bemus, James E
Bently, W G
Berdell, Theodore
Berger, Andrew E
Beveridge, James
*Bigelow
*Bingham, Henry
*Blake
Bock, David
Bosworth, R W
*Bradley
Brainard, Thomas C
Breath, Samuel M
Brodie, John
Brown, Francis M
Brown, Thomas J
*Bruner, F F
Buchanan, George H
Budd, Sylvanus
Bunn, David
Bush, Arthur W
Buttles, John F

*possible member

Calahan [Callahan], Patrick
Campbell, John L
Campbell, Sanford B
Carmack, Thomas K
Carter, George W
*Caswell
Chase, George F
Clark, G A
Clow, David
Clow, Richard
Cluff, Chester P
Coffin, O C
Colborn, Joseph
Collins, R B
*Comb
Conroy, Pierre
Cook, George D
Corning, George C
Corson, William A
Coulson, William Wallace
Crow, Richard
Cullacott, John J F
*Curtis, W D
Danforth, W T
Davidson, [Charles B or W]
Davis, David W
Davis, John M
*Davis, Thomas
Dawley, James M
Deitz, Henry
Denham, Thomas
Develine, Edward W
Dexter, W W
Deyo, R H
*Dickerson
*Dickinson
Dimick, Erastus H
Donald, William
Donaldson, Charles B
Dow, J E
Dunagan, Elijah
Dunagan, Jackson J
Dunn, James
Durham, Thomas
Durnagan, Charles
*Eldred
Ellingham, John J

Ellingham, Robert
Ellis, Adelbert L
Emrick, H J
*Farwell
*Fields, A N
Foote, James B
*Fowler
French, S M
*Fulton
Gilbert, Clark W
*Gilbert, Richard
*Goodwin
Gorman, Michael
Goss, Abel
Goss, P D
Green, Henry
Green, William H
Groesbeck, John B
Guin, Spencer
Gutterson, Charles L
Guyage, Julius
H, D S
Halverson, Christian
Hamlin, Oliver T
*Hammer
*Hammond
*Hanson
Harker, Oliver H
Harmon, George D
Harris, Addison W
Harris, Barney
Harris, Myers B
Harvey, Christopher
*Haskins
Haswell, Theodore H
Hathaway, Mark
*Hawkins
Henry, Albert T
Henry, Oren H
Henry, Ormal E
Hernandez, Anthony R
Hill, Thomas J
Hinkle, John P
Hinman, Fred
Hockaday, Charles N
Hopkins, David L
Howell, C C

Howell, William R
Howse, W J L
Hunt, Fred A
Hunt, William K
*Hunter
*Inbody
Irwin, Joseph
Jackson, G W
*Johns
Johns, John H
Johnson, Seymour
Jones, Thomas J
Juneman, Frederick W
Kavanaugh, A A
*Kellogg
Kerr, David
Kessler, Marion
King, Robert
Kline, Marcus
Knox, John
Kohler, Frederick W
Kroll, Anson
LaPoint, George
Lawson, Alexander
Lea, Alfred E
Lester, James E
Lewis, James
Leyner, Peter A
*Loab
Logan, H
Logue
*Long
Longley, Thomas
Loyd, Joseph Jr
Luther, Henry E
Lykens, D J
Lytle, George
Maxwell, James P
Mayer, Gottlieb F
McCall, Nathaniel H
McCaslin, Matthew L
McClure, Edward P
McClure, George M
*McCormick
McCowan, J C
McDowell, John M
McIntosh, Lemuel
Mead, Marcus S
Meginnis, Daniel
Metcalf, Eli P
Meyring, Henry
Michaud, Theodore
Miller, David W
Mills, Abraham
Moffett, C M
Moffett, J C
Mooney, Michael
Morris, Webb
*Morton, Richard
Mulford, John Spencer
Munson
Neill, Lewis
Nichols, Charles L
Nichols, David H
Nichols, Ezra H
Nicholson, John W
*Norris
North, James M
*O'Conner
O'Hara, William
Parlin, David
*Parsons
*Patterson
Paul, Henry
Peryam, William T
Peters, Anson W
*Peterson
Philippi, Frederick W
Phillips, Ives
Pierce, Oscar
Pitts, Martin J
Pollock, James R
Quinn, [John L or T]
*Reynolds
Ritchie, J W
Robinson, Daniel A
Rompf, Charles
*Ross, W A
Ryalls, Thomas
Samuels, Henry C
Sawdey, Edgar
*Sawyer, H F
Schriver, J C
Scott, Samuel
Sears, Frank
Sears, William F
*Secor, William W
Seely, Eli
Severance, Isaac H
Sheets, Henry W
Sherratt, Charles
Sherwood, Clarence A
*Shortridge
Silver, S D
*Simmons
Slater, W C
Slaughter, B H
Slifer, Esrom G
Smith, Azon A
Smith, J Alden
Smith, Marinus G
Smith, Walter H
Smith, Winton
Snyder, Hanson
Sommers, Wilhelm
Southland, Judson D
Southland, W J
Squires, George C
St Clair, Joel F T
Stanton, John A
*Stephens
*Stevens
Stewart, Thomas C
Stuchell, C D
*Sullivan
Sutherland, Datus E
Tallman, Isaac T
Tarvin, E M
Tilney, Robert H
Titcomb, John S
Turner, Charles
Tyrell, Norman J
*Underwood, Henry M
Van Deren, Archibald J
Van Fleet, Charles G
Van Riper, Cornelius
Van Valkenberg, R J
Van, Clay M
Walker, Thomas C
Wallace, George
Wallace, William J
Walter, Thomas D
Washburn, Hiram E
*Waters, Lawrence W
Webster, George W
*Weil
Wellman, Luther C
Wellman, Sylvanus
Wharton, Joseph J
White, David S

____, Chase
pg 104 (1875 Dec 25) Black Hawk Lodge No. 11

____, William
pg 70 (1875 May 8) Black Hawk Lodge No. 11

A__, Alfred
pg 126 (1876 May 13) South Pueblo Lodge U.D.

A___son, J G
office held: SW
pg 275 (1879 Aug 23)

Abel, Alfred
pg 202 (1878 Jan 26) Denver Lodge No. 5

Adams
pg 64 (1875 Mar 11) chaplain for William Morton Large funeral

Adams, B C
pg 266 (1879 June 28) Occidental Lodge No. 20

Adams, Charles
pg 31 (1874 Apr 25) Doric Lodge U.D.

Adams, George H
pg 79 (1875 Aug 14) Central Lodge No. 6

Allen, Gay S
pg 111 (1876 Jan 2_)
*did not become a member of the Columbia Lodge

Allen, Henly Wheaton
appears as: Allen, H W
pg 64 (1875 Feb 27) petitioner of Waverly Lodge No. 54 of Appleton, WI

Allen, R S
pg 249 (1879 Feb 22) Ionic Lodge No. 34

Allman, S H
pg 43 (1874 Aug 22) Denver Lodge No. 5

Ambrose
pg 138 (1876 June 24) present

Ames
pg 135 (1876 June 10) visiting; pg 138 (1876 June 24) visiting

Ames, George C
pg 163 (1877 Feb 24); pg 167 (1877 Mar 24); pg 174 (1877 June 9); pg 178 (1877 July 14)
*did not become a member of the Columbia Lodge

Ames, Leeman C
appears as: Ames, Leeman C; Ames, Luman C
pg 212 (1878 Mar 9); pg 200 (1878 Jan 12); pg 204 (1878 Feb 9); pg 205 (1878 Feb 9); pg 206 (1878 Feb 13); pg 208 (1878 Feb 23); pg 211 (1878 Mar 9); pg 213 (1878 Mar 9); pg 214 (1878 Mar 15); pg 217 (1878 Apr 13); pg 218 (1878 Apr 13); pg 244 (1878 Dec 28)

Amesburg
pg 14 (1874 Jan 24) present

Ammis, E B
pg 266 (1879 June 28) Occidental Lodge No. 20

Anderson, [A A, David B, or Erick J]
pg 181 (1877 Aug 11) present

Anderson, A A
pg 82 (1875 Aug 28); pg 88 (1875 Sept 25); pg 88 (1875 Sept 25); pg 90 (1875 Oct 1)

Anderson, David B
appears as: Anderson, D B; Anderson, David B
pg 169 (1877 Apr 14); pg 176 (1877 June 23); pg 177 (1877 June 23); pg 178 (1877 July 14); pg 230 (1878 Aug 10); pg 240 (1878 Dec 14); pg 241 (1878 Dec 14); pg 241 (1878 Dec 14); pg 242 (1878 Dec 14); pg 257 (1879 May 10); pg 257 (1879 May 10); pg 258 (1879 May 10)

Anderson, Erick J
appears as: Anderson, E H; Anderson, E J; Anderson, Eric J
office held: JS
pg 157 (1877 Jan 13); pg 157 (1877 Jan 13); pg 161 (1877 Feb 10); pg 161 (1877 Feb 10); pg 161 (1877 Feb 10); pg 164 (1877 Feb 24); pg 164 (1877 Feb 24); pg 166 (1877 Mar 17); pg 168 (1877 Apr 14); pg 169 (1877 Apr 14); pg 170 (1877 Apr 21); pg 170 (1877 Apr 21); pg 179 (1877 July 28); pg 180 (1877 July 28); pg 182 (1877 Aug 11); pg 182 (1877 Aug 11); pg 182 (1877 Aug 11); pg 193 (1877 Dec 8); pg 196 (1877 Dec 8); pg 245 (1879 Jan 11); pg 245 (1879 Jan 11); pg 245 (1879 Jan 11); pg 271 (1879 July 12); pg 279 (1879 Sept 13); pg 266 (1879 June 28); pg 181 (1877 Aug 11)

Anderson, J A
pg 17 (1874 Feb 14)
*did not become a member of the Columbia Lodge

Banks, John W
pg 79 (1875 Aug 14) Central Lodge No. 6

Banning, J A
appears as: Banning; Banning, J A
office held: JD
pg 114 (1876 Feb 16); pg 115 (1876 Feb 26); pg 141 (1876 July 22) visiting; pg 176 (1877 June 23)

Bard, Richard
pg 245 (1879 Jan 11); pg 248 (1879 Feb 8); pg 258 (1879 May 10) WM authorized to give aid to brother Richard Bard who is reportedly sick and destitute; pg 272 (1879 July 12; re-paid money advanced him
*did not become a member of the Columbia Lodge

Barker, William
office held: Tiler
pg 226 (1878 June 22)

Barker, Mrs
pg 130 (1876 May 13) late Mrs Barker, deed for cemetery plot

Barney, Royal Sigbert
appears as: Barney; Barney, R S; Barney, Royal S
offices held: SS, JD, JW, Tiler, Secy, SD
pg 87 (1875 Sept 25); pg 90 (1875 Oct 9); pg 94 (1875 Nov 13); pg 95 (1875 Nov 13); pg 96 (1875 Nov 27); pg 98 (1875 Dec 3); pg 99 (1875 Dec 11); pg 88 (1875 Sept 25); pg 100 (1875 Dec 11); pg 103 (1875 Dec 12); pg 107 (1876 Jan 8); pg 110 (1876 Jan 2_); pg 112 (1876 Feb 12); pg 115 (1876 Feb 26); pg 116 (1876 Mar 4); pg 122 (1876 Apr 8); pg 126 (1876 May 13); pg 132 (1876 Mar 27); pg 134 (1876 May 31); pg 134 (1876 June 3); pg 135 (1876 June 10); pg 137 (1876 June 10); pg 137 (1876 June 17); pg 138 (1876 June 24) pg 140 (1876 July 8); pg 140 (1876 June 28); pg 141 (1876 July 22); pg 142 (1876 July 29); pg 143 (1876 Aug 26); pg 144 (1876 Oct 14); pg 146 (1876 Oct 14); pg 147 (1876 Oct 28); pg 148 (1876 Nov 11); pg 163 (1877 Feb 24); pg 164 (1877 Mar 10); pg 167 (1877 Mar 24); pg 168 (1877 Apr 14); pg 172 (1877 May 26); pg 174 (1877 June 9); pg 176 (1877 June 23); pg 179 (1877 July 18); pg 181 (1877 Aug 11); pg 183 (1877 Sept 1); pg 184 (1877 Sept 8); pg 186 (1877 Sept 8); pg 186 (1877 Sept 22); pg 187 (1877 Oct 13); pg 188 (1877 Oct 27); pg 190 (1877 Nov 10); pg 191 (1877 Nov 20); pg 193 (1877 Dec 8); pg 194 (1877 Dec 8); elected pg 195 (1877 Dec 8); pg 196 (1877 Dec 8); pg 198 (1877 Dec 22); pg 199 (1877 Dec 22); pg 203 (1878 Jan 26); pg 204 (1878 Feb 9); pg 206 (1878 Feb 13); pg 207 (1878 Feb 23); pg 209 (1878 Feb 27); pg 210 (1878 Mar 5); pg 211 (1878 Mar 9); pg 212 (1878 Mar 9); pg 217 (1878 Apr 13); pg 219 (1878 Apr 27); pg 221 (1878 May 11); pg 237 (1878 Nov 9); pg 239 (1878 Nov 23); pg 240 (1878 Nov 23); pg 240 (1878 Dec 14); pg 241 (1878 Dec 14); pg 242 (1878 Dec 14); pg 243 (1878 Dec 28); pg 244 (1879 Jan 11); pg 245 (1879 Jan 11); pg 246 (1879 Jan 25); pg 247 (1879 Feb 8); pg 249 (1879 Feb 22); pg 250 (1879 Mar 8); pg 251 (1879 Mar 22); pg 252 (1879 Mar 22) bill presented for coal; pg 253 (1879 Apr 12); pg 256 (1879 Apr 26); pg 257 (1879 May 10); pg 259 (1879 May 12); pg 259 (1879 May 24); pg 262 (1879 May 27); pg 263 (1879 June 10); pg 264 (1879 June 14); pg 266 (1879 June 28); pg 271 (1879 July 12); pg 272 (1879 July 26); pg 273 (1879 July 26); pg 273 (1879 Aug 9); pg 275 (1879 Aug 23); pg 279 (1879 Sept 13); pg 281 (1879 Sept 27); pg 283 (1879 Sept 30)

Barney, William M
appears as: Barney, W M
offices held: SS, SD, JD
pg 44 (1874 Sept 12); pg 114 (1876 Feb 16); pg 125 (1876 Apr 22); pg 144 (1876 Sept 16); pg 277 (1879 Aug 23)

Barnhurst, Geo
pg 58 (1874 Dec 26) bill presented

Barrowman, William
appears as: Barraman, William; Barrowman, Wm; Barrowman, William
offices held: SS
pg 242 (1878 Dec 14); pg 199 (1878 Jan 12); pg 207 (1878 Feb 23); pg 208 (1878 Feb 23); pg 210 (1878 Mar 5); pg 219 (1878 Apr 27); pg 220 (1878 Apr 27); pg 223 (1878 May 25); pg 224 (1878 May 25); pg 227 (1878 July 13)

Berger, Andrew E
appears as: Berger, A E
pg 82 (1875 Aug 28)

Betters, Jeremiah
pg 110 (1876 Jan 2_) Washington Lodge No. 12

Beverage, see Beveridge, James

Beveridge, James
appears as: Beverage; Beverage, J; Beveridge; Beveridge Wm (*this was probably a mistake by the Secretary and not a different person)
pg 1 (1873 Nov 8); pg 10 (1873 Dec 27); pg 11 (1873 Dec 27); pg 15 (1874 Jan 24); pg 20 (1874 Mar 14); pg 23 (1874 Mar 14); pg 24 (1874 Mar 19); pg 29 (1874 Apr 10); pg 30 (1874 Apr 10); pg 71 (1875 May 8); pg 112 (1876 Feb 12); pg 114 (1876 Feb 12) paid for lot 79, block B - Joseph Harden; pg 213 (1878 Mar 9); pg 224 (1878 May 25)

Bigelow
pg 62 (1875 Feb 13); pg 64 (1875 Mar 11); pg 102 (1875 Dec 12)

Bill, Raif A
pg 38 (1874 July 11) Laramie Lodge No. 18

Bingham, Henry
pg 88 (1875 Sept 25) petitioner

Birtsells, Col C H
pg 145 (1876 Oct 14) visiting from Union Lodge No. 5, Alexandria, Egypt; pg 146 (1876 Oct 14) gave a lecture on the origin and antiquity of Masonry and its present condition in Egypt, Palestine, etc.

Bixby & Wilder
pg 119 (1876 Mar 25) bill presented for printing; pg 150 (1876 Nov 25) bill presented for printing; pg 156 (1876 Dec 23) bill presented; pg 165 (1877 Mar 10) bill presented for printing; pg 194 (1877 Dec 8) bill presented for 500 circulars; pg 208 (1878 Feb 23) bill presented for printing; pg 239 (1878 Nov 23) bill presented for printing

Black Hawk Lodge
pg 255 (1879 Apr 12) sent money

Blackly
pg 148 (1876 Nov 11) Pueblo Lodge No. 17

Blake
pg 219 (1878 Apr 27) present

Blume, Charles
pg 158 (1877 Jan 28) King Solomon Lodge No. 30

Bock, David
appears as: Bock: Bock, D
offices held: WM, JW, SW, Tiler, Secy, SS, JS, SD
pg 1 (1873 Nov 8); pg 2 (1873 Nov 22); pg 4 (1873 Dec 13); pg 8 (1873 Dec 13); pg 9 (1873 Dec 27); pg 10 (1873 Dec 27); pg 11 (1873 Dec 27); pg 12 (1874 Jan 10); pg 14 (1874 Jan 24); pg 15 (1874 Jan 27); pg 17 (1874 Feb 14); pg 18 ((1874 Feb 20)); pg 19 (1874 Feb 28); pg 23 (1874 Mar 19); pg 25 (1874 Mar 28); pg 27 (1874 Mar 28); pg 28 (1874 Apr 4); pg 34 (1874 May 9); pg 36 (1874 May 23); pg 38 (1874 July 11); pg 39 (1874 July 28); pg 41 (1874 Aug 8) committee to take care of Bro Dexter; pg 42 (1874 Aug 22); pg 43 (1874 Sept 12); pg 47 (1874 Oct 14); pg 47 (1874 Oct 24); pg 48 (1874 Oct 24) bill presented to fix the stove pipe; pg 48 (1874 Nov 14); pg 49 (1874 Nov 14) motion to collaborate with the Odd Fellows to obtain an ante-room stove; pg 53 (1874 Dec 12); pg 57 (1874 Dec 26); pg 56 (1874 Dec 19); pg 58 (1874 Dec 26); pg 59 (1875 Jan 9); pg 62 (1875 Feb 13); pg 65 (1875 Mar 13); pg 66 (1875 Mar 27); pg 67 (1875 Mar 27) paid for ball tickets; pg 68 (1875 Apr 24); pg 70 (1875 Apr 24); pg 70 (1875 May 8); pg 73 (1875 June 12); pg 74 (1875 June 26); pg 78 (1875 July 29); pg 81 (1875 Aug 28); pg 81 (1875 Aug 7); pg 83 (1875 Aug 28); pg 86 (1875 Sept 16); pg 87 (1875 Sept 25); pg 88 (1875 Sept 25); pg 89 (1875 Sept 27); pg 90 (1875 Oct 1); pg 92 (1875 Oct 23); pg 91 (1875 Oct 9); pg 93 (1875 Oct 23); pg 94 (1875 Nov 13); pg 95 (1875 Nov 13); pg 96 (1875 Nov 27); pg 98 (1875 Dec 3); pg 98 (1875 Dec 11); pg 100 (1875 Dec 11); pg 103 (1875 Dec 12); pg 106 (1875 Dec 27); pg 107 (1876 Jan 8); pg 108 (1876 Jan 8); pg 110 (1876 Jan 19); pg 110 (1876 Jan 2_); pg 111 (1876 Jan 2_); pg 112 (1876 Feb 12); pg 114 (1876 Feb 16); pg 115 (1876 Feb 26); pg 115 (1876 Feb 26); pg 116 (1876 Mar 4); pg 119 (1876 Mar 25); pg 120 (1876 Mar 25); pg 121 (1876 April 1); pg 122 (1876 Apr 8); pg 123

Carmack, Thomas K
appears as: Carmack, K; Carmack, T K; Carmack, Thomas K
offices held: JD, JW
pg 94 (1875 Nov 13); pg 88 (1875 Sept 25); pg 89 (1875 Sept 27); pg 93 (1875 Oct 23); pg 95 (1875 Nov 13); pg 138 (1876 June 24); pg 176 (1877 June 23); pg 264 (1879 June 14) asked for a demit, granted a non-affiliate status for one year

Carnahan, J M
pg 223 (1878 May 25) bill presented

Carr, B L
appears as: Carr, Col B L; Carr, B L
pg 184 (1877 Sept 5) visiting Deputy Grand Master; pg 185 (1877 Sept 8) appointed as Deputy Grand Master to examine the lodge

Carrigan, D J
pg 130 (1876 May 13) deed for cemetery plot

Carrington, D J
pg 74 (1875 June 26) purchased cemetery lot

Carroll, A C
pg 185 (1877 Sept 8) Huerfano Lodge No. 27

Carter, George W
appears as: Carr; George W; Carter, G W
offices held: SD
pg 2 (1873 Nov 8); pg 72 (1875 June 12); pg 277 (1879 Aug 23)

Caspari, Joseph
pg 204 (1878 Feb 9) Union Lodge No. 7

Caswell
pg 158 (1877 Jan 28); pg 263 (1879 June 10)

Cavanaugh, see Kavanaugh, A A

Chamberlin, O
pg 29 (1874 Apr 10) Washington Lodge No. 12

Champion, H W
pg 3 (1873 Nov 22)
*did not become a member of the Columbia Lodge

Chase, George F
appears as: Chase; Chase, G F; Chase, George F
offices held: JW, Treas, SD, SW, Treas, JD
pg 4 (1873 Dec 13); pg 8 (1873 Dec 13); pg 9 (1873 Dec 27); pg 10 (1873 Dec 27); pg 12 (1874 Jan 10); pg 16 (1874 Feb 14); pg 19 (1874 Feb 28); pg 23 (1874 Mar 19); pg 25 (1874 Mar 28); pg 35 (1874 May 16); pg 36 (1874 May 23); pg 36 (1874 June 27); pg 47 (1874 Oct 24); pg 48 (1874 Nov 14); pg 49 (1874 Nov 14); pg 55 (1874 Dec 12); pg 56 (1874 Dec 26); pg 57 (1874 Dec 26); pg 58 (1874 Dec 26); pg 59 (1875 Jan 9); pg 60 (1875 Jan 23); pg 62 (1875 Feb 13); pg 64 (1875 Mar 11); pg 65 (1875 Mar 13); pg 66 (1875 Mar 27); pg 67 (1875 Apr 10); pg 71 (1875 May 22); pg 72 (1875 May 22); pg 73 (1875 June 26); pg 74 (1875 June 26) money paid for Nathaniel Hayden; pg 75 (1875 July 10); pg 76 (1875 July 24); pg 81 (1875 Aug 7); pg 81 (1875 Aug 28); pg 84 (1875 Sept 11); pg 86 (1875 Sept 16); pg 90 (1875 Oct 1); pg 91 (1875 Oct 20); pg 98 (1875 Dec 3); pg 98 (1875 Dec 11); pg 100 (1875 Dec 11); pg 101 (1875 Dec 11); pg 102 (1875 Dec 12); pg 103 (1875 Dec 12); pg 103 (1875 Dec 25); pg 106 (1875 Dec 27); pg 107 (1876 Jan 8); pg 108 (1876 Jan 8); pg 110 (1876 Jan 2_); pg 112 (1876 Feb 12); pg 115 (1876 Feb 26); pg 116 (1876 Mar 4); pg 117 (1876 Mar 11); pg 118 (1876 Mar 11); pg 119 (1876 Mar 25); pg 120 (1876 Mar 25); pg 122 (1876 Apr 8); pg 124 (1876 Apr 10); pg 125 (1876 Apr 22); pg 126 (1876 May 13); pg 127 (1876 May 13); pg 132 (1876 Mar 27); pg 134 (1876 May 31); pg 134 (1876 June 3); pg 137 (1876 June 17); pg 138 (1876 June 24); pg 141 (1876 July 22); pg 142 (1876 July 22); pg 142 (1876 July 29); pg 143 (1876 Aug 26); pg 144 (1876 Sept 16); pg 145 (1876 Oct 14); pg 147 (1876 Oct 28); pg 148 (1876 Nov 11); pg 149 (1876 Nov 25); pg 150 (1876 Nov 25); pg 152 (1876 Dec 9) bill presented for money advanced to a sick brother; pg 153 (1876 Dec 9); pg 154 (1876 Dec 12); pg 155 (1876 Dec 12); pg 155 (1876 Dec 23); pg 156 (1876 Dec 23); pg 157 (1877 Jan 13); pg 160 (1877 Feb 10); pg 162 (1877 Feb 14); pg 163 (1877 Feb 24); pg 164 (1877 Mar 10); pg 166 (1877 Mar 17); pg 167 (1877 Mar 24); pg 168 (1877 Apr 14); pg 169 (1877 Apr 14); pg 171 (1877 April 28); pg 171 (1877 May 12); pg 174 (1877 June 9); pg 176 (1877 June 23); pg 189 (1877 Nov 10); pg 191 (1877 Nov 20); pg 193 (1877 Dec 8); pg 194 (1877 Dec 8); pg 195 (1877 Dec 8);

Coffin, O C
pg 160 (1877 Feb 10) petitioner of Bear Canyon; pg 165 (1877 Mar 10); pg 166 (1877 Mar 17)

Coggens, Nelson J
pg 79 (1875 Aug 14) Central Lodge No. 6

Cohen, Herman
pg 250 (1879 Mar 8) Las Animas Lodge No. 28

Coin, Mrs James H
appears as: Coin, Mrs J H
pg 124 (1876 Apr 8) purchased cemetery lot

Colborn, Joseph
pg 33 (1874 May 7); pg 22 (1874 Mar 14); pg 24 (1874 Mar 26); pg 31 (1874 Apr 25); pg 32 (1874 Apr 25); pg 33 (1874 May 7); pg 58 (1874 Dec 26); pg 57 (1874 Dec 26) petitioner

Cole, J L
pg 207 (1878 Feb 23) King Solomon Lodge No. 30

Coleman, D
pg 22 (1874 Mar 14) Pueblo Lodge No. 17

Collett, James H
pg 192 (1877 Nov 20) Washington Lodge No. 12

Collins, R B
appears as: Collins; Collins, R B
pg 219 (1878 Apr 27); pg 225 (1878 June 8); pg 244 (1878 Dec 28); pg 251 (1879 Mar 22); pg 252 (1879 Mar 22)

Colorado House
pg 245 (1879 Jan 11) bill presented for board for the ball

Colorado University
pg 183 (1877 Sept 1) lodge to participate in the inaugural exercises at the University Bldg on 5 Sept 1877

Columbia Cemetery
pg 225 (1878 June 8) motion that the cemetery be resurveyed; pg 280 (1879 Sept 13) cemetery lots to be sold in 1/4 lots for $7.50, whole lots for $30. 1/4 lots above the ditch are to be $5, whole lots $20.

Colvin, W J
pg 85 (1875 Sept 11) Las Animas Lodge U.D.

Colyer, Rev Robert
pg 77 (1875 July 24) of Chicago in regard to the money paid to defray the funeral expenses of Bro W M Large; pg 243 (1878 Dec 28) Secy instructed to write to Rev Robert Colyer of Chicago regarding the funeral expenses of brother Large buried by this lodge some years since; pg 246 (1879 Jan 25) communication regarding the funeral expenses of Brother Large; pg 260 (1879 May 24) communication repaying in full $69 expended for funeral expenses for Bro. William M Large in 1875; pg 262 (1879 May 24) payment for Bro W M Large

Comb
pg 38 (1874 July 11); pg 40 (1874 Aug 1); pg 41 (1874 Aug 8)

Congdon, William
pg 125 (1876 Apr 22) Washington Lodge No. 12

Connor
pg 137 (1876 June 17) visiting

Connor, O
pg 151 (1876 Dec 2) visiting

Conroy, Pierre
pg 76 (1875 July 24); pg 82 (1875 Aug 28); pg 83 (1875 Sept 1); pg 84 (1875 Sept 1)

Conway
pg 132 (1876 Mar 27) visiting

Cook, George D
appears as: Cook; Cook, George D
offices held: JW, Treas
pg 110 (1876 Jan 19); pg 151 (1876 Dec 2) visiting; pg 152 (1876 Dec 9) visiting; pg 154 (1876 Dec 12); pg 155 (1876 Dec 23) visiting; pg 250 (1879 Mar 8) Secretary requested to contact Black Hawk Lodge in regards to his care; pg 259 (1879 May 12) payment on behalf of brother Cook from Black Hawk Lodge; pg 260 (1879 May 24) communication from Black Hawk lodge repaying in full funds for helping Bro. Cook; pg 248 (1879 Feb 8) is sick and destitute at Gold Hill, is to be returned to Boulder and cared for, member of Black Hawk Lodge; pg 250 (1879 Mar 8) bill presented for the board of J D Cook; pg 252 (1879 Mar 22) bill presented for the board of J D Cook; pg 253 (1879 Apr 12) bill presented for board of

J D Cook; pg 253 (1879 Apr 12) Black Hawk Lodge made a payment on his behalf

Cookman, William H

pg 279 (1879 Sept 13) Washington Lodge No. 12

Cooper, C W

pg 22 (1874 Mar 14) Pueblo Lodge No. 17

Cork

pg 149 (1876 Nov 25) visiting

Corning, George C

appears as: Corning; Corning, George C
offices held: Treas
pg 2 (1873 Nov 22); pg 3 (1873 Nov 22); pg 4 (1873 Dec 13); pg 5 (1873 Dec 13); pg 8 (1873 Dec 13); pg 9 (1873 Dec 27); pg 11 (1873 Dec 27); pg 12 (1874 Jan 10); pg 14 (1874 Jan 24); pg 19 (1874 Feb 28); pg 20 (1874 Feb 28); pg 20 (1874 Mar 14); pg 23 (1874 Mar 14); pg 26 (1874 Mar 28); pg 27 (1874 Mar 28); pg 28 (1874 Apr 4); pg 33 (1874 May 7); pg 39 (1874 July 28); pg 53 (1874 Dec 12); pg 54 (1874 Dec 12); pg 56 (1874 Dec 12); pg 83 (1875 Sept 1); pg 101 (1875 Dec 11); pg 115 (1876 Feb 26); pg 125 (1876 Apr 22); pg 145 (1876 Oct 14); pg 269 (1879 June 28)

Corson, William A

appears as: Corson; Corson, Wm; Corson, Wm A; Corson, William A
offices held: SS, SD, Secy, Grand Marshall, JW, Tiler, SW, JD
pg 1 (1873 Nov 8); pg 8 (1873 Dec 13); pg 9 (1873 Dec 27); pg 13 (1874 Jan 10); pg 16 (1874 Feb 14); pg 17 (1874 Feb 14) committee to take charge of the cemetery; pg 23 (1874 Mar 14); pg 26 (1874 Mar 28); pg 32 (1874 Apr 25); pg 32 (1874 Apr 25); pg 33 (1874 May 7); pg 38 (1874 June 27); pg 41 (1874 Aug 8) committee to take care of Bro Dexter; pg 48 (1874 Oct 24); pg 48 (1874 Nov 14); pg 49 (1874 Nov 14); pg 49 (1874 Nov 18); pg 51 (1874 Nov 28)motion to help the Secy, David H Nichols to complete his minutes as he is suffering from a severe and long-continued illness; pg 52 (1874 Dec 5) motion to investigate the propriety of having a party on St John's Day which falls on a Sunday; pg 55 (1874 Dec 12); pg 56 (1874 Dec 12); pg 64 (1875 Feb 27); pg 65 (1875 Mar 11); pg 66 (1875 Mar 27); pg 69 (1875 Apr 24) asked for a demit for A W Harris; pg 71 (1875 May 22); pg 72 (1875 May 22) motion to present the bills for fuel and lights; pg 84 (1875 Sept 11); pg 85 (1875 Sept 11); pg 91 (1875 Oct 20); pg 100 (1875 Dec 11) Grand Marshall; pg 101 (1875 Dec 11); pg 102 (1875 Dec 12); pg 110 (1876 Jan 2_); pg 112 (1876 Feb 12); pg 116 (1876 Mar 4); pg 117 (1876 Mar 4); pg 125 (1876 Apr 22); pg 126 (1876 May 13); pg 140 (1876 July 8); pg 152 (1876 Dec 9); pg 154 (1876 Dec 9); pg 167 (1877 Mar 24); pg 168 (1877 Apr 14); pg 169 (1877 Apr 14); pg 170 (1877 April 28); pg 171 (1877 April 28); pg 171 (1877 May 12); pg 172 (1877 May 26); pg 174 (1877 June 9); pg 177 (1877 July 14); pg 178 (1877 July 14); pg 181 (1877 Aug 11); pg 188 (1877 Oct 13); pg 193 (1877 Dec 8); pg 193 (1877 Dec 8); pg 194 (1877 Dec 8); pg 195 (1877 Dec 8); pg 198 (1877 Dec 22); pg 199 (1878 Jan 12); pg 200 (1878 Jan 12); pg 201 (1878 Jan 12); pg 202 (1878 Jan 26); pg 203 (1878 Jan 26); pg 204 (1878 Feb 9); pg 206 (1878 Feb 13); pg 210 (1878 Mar 5); pg 211 (1878 Mar 9); pg 212 (1878 Mar 9); pg 214 (1878 Mar 15); pg 215 (1878 Mar 23); pg 217 (1878 Apr 13); pg 219 (1878 Apr 27); pg 221 (1878 May 11); pg 223 (1878 May 25); pg 240 (1878 Dec 14); pg 242 (1878 Dec 14); pg 246 (1879 Jan 25); pg 249 (1879 Feb 22); pg 250 (1879 Mar 8); pg 251 (1879 Mar 22); pg 253 (1879 Apr 12); pg 254 (1879 Apr 12); pg 255 (1879 Apr 17); pg 256 (1879 Apr 26); pg 257 (1879 Apr 26); pg 257 (1879 May 10); pg 259 (1879 May 12); pg 259 (1879 May 24); pg 262 (1879 May 27); pg 264 (1879 June 14); pg 266 (1879 June 28); pg 271 (1879 July 12); pg 273 (1879 Aug 9); pg 274 (1879 Aug 9); pg 275 (1879 Aug 23); pg 278 (1879 Aug 29); pg 279 (1879 Sept 13)

Cosgrove, John

pg 75 (1875 July 10); pg 82 (1875 Aug 28)
*did not become a member of the Columbia Lodge

Cottonwood, David

pg 172 (1877 May 26) Washington Lodge No. 12

Coulborn, see Colborn, Joseph

Coulson, C M
pg 173 (1877 May 26) bill presented for bridge across the ditch in the cemetery

Coulson, John C
pg 45 (1874 Sept 26) Idaho Lodge UD

Coulson, William Wallace
appears as: Coulson, W W
pg 183 (1877 Sept 5)

Coulter, John A
pg 49 (1874 Nov 14) Washington Lodge No. 12

Coulter, John L
pg 176 (1877 June 23) Washington Lodge No. 12

Cox, S M
pg 198 (1877 Dec 22) Mount Moriah Lodge No. 15

Crabb, John Henry
pg 212 (1878 Mar 9) Central Lodge No 6

Craig, Alexander
pg 192 (1877 Nov 20) imposter posing as a mason

Craine, J E
pg 53 (1874 Dec 12) Nevada Lodge No. 4

Crook, J D
pg 163 (1877 Feb 24) Las Animas Lodge No. 28

Crow, Richard
appears as: Crow; Crow, Richard
offices held: JD, Treas, JW
pg 26 (1874 Mar 28); pg 28 (1874 Apr 4); pg 31 (1874 Apr 25); pg 35 (1874 May 16); pg 46 (1874 Oct 10); pg 47 (1874 Oct 10); pg 48 (1874 Oct 24); pg 52 (1874 Dec 5); pg 55 (1874 Dec 12); pg 73 (1875 June 12); pg 75 (1875 July 10); pg 76 (1875 July 24); pg 79 (1875 Aug 14); pg 81 (1875 Aug 7); pg 82 (1875 Aug 28); pg 83 (1875 Sept 1); pg 88 (1875 Sept 25); pg 101 (1875 Dec 11); pg 113 (1876 Feb 12); pg 120 (1876 Mar 25) read a telegram announcing the death of brother John H Johns in a mine at Caribou; pg 153 (1876 Dec 9); pg 198 (1877 Dec 22); pg 277 (1879 Aug 23); pg 280 (1879 Sept 13); pg 281 (1879 Sept 13)

Cullacott, John J F
appears as: Cullacott, J J F; Cullacott, John F; Callacott, John J; Callacott, J J F
offices held: SD
pg 181 (1877 Aug 11); pg 188 (1877 Oct 13); pg 189 (1877 Oct 27); pg 190 (1877 Nov 10); pg 191 (1877 Nov 10); pg 191 (1877 Nov 20); pg 192 (1877 Nov 20); pg 193 (1877 Nov 20); pg 240 (1878 Nov 23); pg 253 (1879 Apr 12); pg 254 (1879 Apr 12); pg 278 (1879 Aug 29)

Curtis, H A
pg 186 (1877 Sept 22) Weston Lodge

Curtis, W D
appears as: Curtis; Curtis, W D
pg 145 (1876 Oct 14) visiting; pg 147 (1876 Oct 28) visiting; pg 148 (1876 Nov 11) visiting; pg 155 (1876 Dec 23) visiting; pg 157 (1877 Jan 13) visiting; pg 167 (1877 Mar 24) visiting

Cutting
pg 43 (1874 Aug 22) Denver Lodge No. 5

Dabney & Russell
pg 258 (1879 May 10) bill presented for lumber and fence posts for the cemetery

Dabney, Charles
pg 26 (1874 Mar 28); pg 28 (1874 Mar 28)
*did not become a member of the Columbia Lodge

Daily & Smart
pg 39 (1874 July 11) bill presented for Visitors Register

Daily, John
pg 37 (1874 June 27) Washington Lodge No. 12

Dameven, N V
pg 159 (1877 Jan 28) Doric Lodge No. 25

Danford, see Danforth, W T

Danforth, W T
pg 102 (1875 Dec 12)

Darrah, Benjamin
pg 279 (1879 Sept 13) Washington Lodge No. 12

Davidson, [Charles B or W]
pg 49 (1874 Nov 18); pg 57 (1874 Dec 26)

Davis, B Y
pg 29 (1874 Apr 10) St Vrain Lodge No. 23

Davis
pg 177 (1877 July 14) visiting

granted to his present residence at Bradford, IL; pg 130 (1876 May 13)

Dickerson
pg 155 (1876 Dec 23) visiting

Dickerson
pg 247 (1879 Feb 8) present

Dickinson
pg 115 (1876 Feb 26) present

Dietz, see Deitz, Henry

Dimick, Erastus H
appears as: Dimick; Dimick E H; Dimmick, Erastus H; Dimmock, E H
pg 96 (1875 Nov 27) petitioner of Ottawa Lodge No. 126, Ottawa, KS; pg 104 (1875 Dec 25); pg 106 (1875 Dec 25); pg 107 (1876 Jan 8); pg 126 (1876 May 13); pg 145 (1876 Oct 14); pg 163 (1877 Feb 24); pg 186 (1877 Sept 22); pg 187 (1877 Sept 22) resolution presented to heartily sympathize with the temperance movement now in progress in this town; pg 269 (1879 June 28); pg 277 (1879 Aug 23)

Ditheridge, E D
pg 118 (1876 Mar 11) El Paso Lodge No. 13

Dodge, Horace O
appears as: Dodge, Dr; Dodge, H O
pg 92 (1875 Oct 20) the house where the body lay; pg 92 (1875 Oct 20) thanks for the kind care and attention to the deceased brother

Dodge, Horace O and Mrs (Laura Sturdevant)
appears as: Dodge, H O and Mrs
pg 93 (1875 Oct 23) thanks for the kind care and attention to the deceased brother

Donald, William
appears as: Donald; Donald Wm
offices held: Treas
pg 87 (1875 Sept 25); pg 138 (1876 June 24); pg 126 (1876 May 13); pg 198 (1877 Dec 22)

Donaldson, Charles B
appears as: Donaldson; Donaldson, C B; Donaldson, Charles B
pg 37 (1874 June 27); pg 39 (1874 July 28); pg 72 (1875 May 22); pg 74 (1875 June 26); pg 146 (1876 Oct 14); pg 148 (1876 Nov 11); pg 149 (1876 Nov 11); pg 149 (1876 Nov 25); pg 150 (1876 Nov 25); pg 151 (1876 Dec 2); pg 152 (1876 Dec 9); pg 153 (1876 Dec 9); pg 155 (1876 Dec 12); pg 172 (1877 May 26); pg 227 (1878 June 22); pg 245 (1879 Jan 11)

Dow, J E
appears as: Dow; Dow, J E
offices held: JS, JW
pg 147 (1876 Oct 28) visiting; pg 148 (1876 Nov 11); pg 149 (1876 Nov 25); pg 152 (1876 Dec 9); pg 153 (1876 Dec 9); pg 189 (1877 Nov 10); pg 191 (1877 Nov 20); pg 193 (1877 Dec 8); pg 196 (1877 Dec 8); pg 247 (1879 Jan 25); pg 250 (1879 Mar 8); pg 255 (1879 Apr 17); pg 256 (1879 Apr 26); pg 257 (1879 Apr 26); pg 259 (1879 May 12); pg 259 (1879 May 24); pg 264 (1879 June 14)

Down, John
pg 41 (1874 Aug 8) Black Hawk Lodge No. 11

Downing, C P
pg 177 (1877 July 14) El Paso Lodge No. 13

Downing, William S
pg 279 (1879 Sept 13) Washington Lodge No. 12

Draper, T W M
pg 279 (1879 Sept 13) Crystal Lake Lodge No. 34

Drew
pg 43 (1874 Aug 22) Denver Lodge No. 5

Drummond, David B
pg 119 (1876 Mar 25) King Solomon Lodge U.D.

Duffy, J B
pg 266 (1879 June 28) South Pueblo Lodge

Dunagan, Elijah
appears as: Dunagan; Dunagan, Elijah
pg 145 (1876 Oct 14); pg 153 (1876 Dec 9); pg 170 (1877 Apr 21); pg 195 (1877 Dec 8); pg 244 (1878 Dec 28)

Dunagan, Jackson J
appears as: Dunnagan, J A
offices held: SW
pg 143 (1876 Aug 26)

Dunlon, R F
pg 279 (1879 Sept 13) Las Animas Lodge No. 28

Dunn, James
appears as: Dunn; Dunn, James
offices held: Steward

pg 8 (1873 Dec 13); pg 17 (1874 Feb 14); pg 49 (1874 Nov 18); pg 113 (1876 Feb 12); pg 126 (1876 May 13); pg 269 (1879 June 28) has a new address; pg 277 (1879 Aug 23)

Dunnagan, see Dunagan, Elijah

Dunnagan, see Dunagan, Jackson J

Dunner, J R
pg 125 (1876 Apr 22) Black Hawk Lodge No. 11

Durham, Thomas
pg 227 (1878 June 22) member

Durley, Ben C
pg 138 (1876 June 24) Black Hawk Lodge No. 11

Durnagan, Charles
pg 280 (1879 Sept 13) member

Earl, William E
pg 230 (1878 Aug 10) Denver Lodge No. 5

Eckhardt, Otto
pg 204 (1878 Feb 9) Nevada Lodge No. 4

Eddy, Edward
pg 29 (1874 Apr 10) Washington Lodge No. 12

Edgrist, Andrew
pg 125 (1876 Apr 22) Doric Lodge No. 25

Edwards, Justin
pg 132 (1876 Mar 27) visiting

Edwards, J W
pg 204 (1878 Feb 9) Nevada Lodge No. 4

Eldred
pg 56 (1874 Dec 19) present

Eldred, Holden R
pg 79 (1875 Aug 14) Central Lodge No. 6

Ellet
pg 156 (1876 Dec 23) paid for cemetery lots

Ellingham, [John J or Robert]
pg 43 (1874 Sept 12); pg 66 (1875 Mar 27); pg 170 (1877 April 28); pg 171 (1877 May 12); pg 172 (1877 May 26); pg 183 (1877 Sept 1); pg 199 (1878 Jan 12); pg 202 (1878 Jan 26); pg 204 (1878 Feb 9); pg 207 (1878 Feb 23); pg 211 (1878 Mar 9); pg 212 (1878 Mar 9); pg 215 (1878 Mar 23); pg 246 (1879 Jan 25)

Ellingham, Charles E
pg 80 (1875 Aug 14) deceased; pg 81 (1875 Aug 7) deceased of Albany Lodge No. 566, IL, service held at the ME Church, burial at Columbia

Ellingham, John J
appears as: Ellingham, J J; Ellingham, John; Ellingham, John J
offices held: JD, SD
pg 8 (1873 Dec 13); pg 10 (1873 Dec 27); pg 12 (1874 Jan 10); pg 14 (1874 Jan 24); pg 16 (1874 Feb 14); pg 20 (1874 Mar 14); pg 67 (1875 Mar 27); pg 69 (1875 Apr 24) committee to draft resolutions for Samuel Renslow, deceased; pg 75 (1875 July 10); pg 87 (1875 Sept 25); pg 88 (1875 Sept 25); pg 97 (1875 Nov 27); pg 126 (1876 May 13); pg 158 (1877 Jan 13); pg 200 (1878 Jan 12); pg 202 (1878 Jan 26); pg 233 (1878 Sept 14); pg 237 (1878 Nov 9); pg 245 (1879 Jan 11); pg 250 (1879 Mar 8); pg 254 (1879 Apr 12)

Ellingham, Robert
appears as: Ellingham, R; Ellingham, Robert
offices held: JD, Tiler
pg 3 (1873 Nov 22); pg 13 (1874 Jan 10) requested to write to the lodge of Bro Taylor requesting help for his needy condition, bill presented for the support of brother C W Taylor; pg 24 (1874 Mar 26); pg 36 (1874 June 27); pg 38 (1874 June 27); pg 58 (1874 Dec 26); pg 73 (1875 June 12); pg 79 (1875 Aug 14); pg 80 (1875 Aug 14) cemetery lot; pg 126 (1876 May 13); pg 213 (1878 Mar 9); pg 251 (1879 Mar 8)

Elliott, S A
pg 266 (1879 June 28) Occidental Lodge No. 20

Ellis, Adelbert L
appears as: Ellis, A L; Ellis; Ellis, Adelbert L
offices held: Secy
pg 66 (1875 Mar 27) petitioner of Hamilton Lodge No. 35, Kansas; pg 70 (1875 May 8); pg 71 (1875 May 8); pg 101 (1875 Dec 11); pg 125 (1876 Apr 22); pg 126 (1876 May 13); pg 127 (1876 May 13); pg 129 (1876 May 13); pg 130 (1876 May 13); pg 131 (1876 May 13); pg 138 (1876 June 24); pg 277 (1879 Aug 23)

Emperor, William
pg 282 (1879 Sept 27) Weston Lodge No. 22

Emrick, H J
offices held: Treas
pg 42 (1874 Aug 15)

England, G A
pg 64 (1875 Mar 11) chaplain for William Morton Large funeral; pg 65 (1875 Mar 11); pg 81 (1875 Aug 7) funeral services conducted by Bro England; pg 92 (1875 Oct 20) brother and Reverend who performed the funeral rites; pg 232 (1878 Sept 14)

Esterbrook, A B
pg 256 (1879 Apr 26) Occidental Lodge No. 2

Euler, child
pg 276 (1879 Aug 23) a brother was appointed to take charge of the Masonic Cemetery and to confer with Mr. Euler concerning the removal of the body of Euler's child buried by mistake on a wrong lot.

Euler, Mr
pg 273 (1879 Aug 9) a question was raised upon the Euler lot matter whereby Mr Euler had already purchased a lot from the lodge only to find out that the same lot was in the Odd Fellows portion of the cemetery and already owned by someone else. He was granted a new deed and a different lot; pg 274 (1879 Aug 9) discussion continued; pg 276 (1879 Aug 23) a brother was appointed to take charge of the Masonic Cemetery and to confer with Mr. Euler concerning the removal of the body of Euler's child buried by mistake on a wrong lot.

Eusson, B W
pg 204 (1878 Feb 9) Nevada Lodge No. 4

Farwell
pg 56 (1874 Dec 19) present

Farwell, C B
pg 111 (1876 Jan 2_) Occidental Lodge No. 20

Farwell, Cy
pg 126 (1876 May 13) visiting

Feshler, Maus
pg 46 (1874 Oct 10) Black Hawk Lodge No. 11

Fields, A N
pg 232 (1878 Sept 14) petitioner; pg 234 (1878 Oct 12) petitioner

Fillian, Joseph A
pg 85 (1875 Sept 11) Idaho Springs Lodge U.D.

Finley, H M
pg 65 (1875 Mar 13) Pueblo Lodge No. 17

Fisher, L
pg 188 (1877 Oct 27) Las Animas Lodge No. 28

Fisher, Samuel
pg 192 (1877 Nov 20) Washington Lodge No. 12

Fleck, John W
pg 22 (1874 Mar 14) Pueblo Lodge No. 17

Foot, S C
pg 9 (1873 Dec 27) El Paso Lodge No. 13

Foote, James B
appears as: Foote; Foot; Foote, James B
offices held: JS
pg 132 (1876 Mar 27) visiting; pg 162 (1877 Feb 14); pg 256 (1879 Apr 26); pg 261 (1879 May 24); pg 262 (1879 May 27); pg 263 (1879 May 27); pg 263 (1879 June 10); pg 278 (1879 Aug 29)

Fornary, C C
pg 159 (1877 Jan 28) a communication from him was read

Fortune, Henry
pg 66 (1875 Mar 27) Huerfano Lodge U.D.

Foushee, A S
appears as: Foushee
pg 90 (1875 Oct 9) visiting

Fowler
pg 163 (1877 Feb 24) present

France, Matt
pg 12 (1874 Jan 10) El Paso Lodge No. 13

Francis, Henry
pg 239 (1878 Nov 23)
*did not become a member of the Columbia Lodge

French, S M
appears as: French; French, S M
offices held: SW
pg 138 (1876 June 24) visiting; pg 165 (1877 Mar 10) petitioner, along with a demit from Denver Lodge No. 5; pg 169 (1877 Apr 14); pg 170 (1877 April 28); pg 199 (1878 Jan 12); pg

*did not become a member of the Columbia Lodge

Goodwin
pg 183 (1877 Sept 5) present (probably M W Goodwin)

Goodwin, D H
pg 282 (1879 Sept 27) Weston Lodge No. 22

Goodwin, H
pg 260 (1879 May 24) St Vrain Lodge No. 23

Goodwin, John
pg 87 (1875 Sept 25) Washington Lodge No. 12

Gorman, Michael
pg 75 (1875 July 10); pg 80 (1875 Aug 14); pg 106 (1875 Dec 25)

Goss, [Abel or P D]
pg 18 (1874 Feb 20); pg 25 (1874 Mar 28); pg 28 (1874 Apr 4); pg 34 (1874 May 9); pg 36 (1874 May 23); pg 188 (1877 Oct 27)

Goss, Abel
appears as: Goss, A; Goss, Abel
offices held: Tiler, JD
pg 29 (1874 Apr 10); pg 31 (1874 Apr 25); pg 35 (1874 May 16); pg 37 (1874 June 27) petitioner from Paffumsic Lodge No. 27, St Johnsbury, VT; pg 41 (1874 Aug 8); pg 80 (1875 Aug 14); pg 89 (1875 Sept 27); pg 90 (1875 Oct 9); pg 197 (1877 Dec 19); pg 268 (1879 June 28); pg 274 (1879 Aug 9)

Goss, P D
offices held: JD, SD, Secy
pg 15 (1874 Jan 27); pg 20 (1874 Mar 14); pg 31 (1874 Apr 25); pg 35 (1874 May 16); pg 36 (1874 May 23); pg 42 (1874 Aug 15); pg 72 (1875 May 22) purchased cemetery lot; pg 91 (1875 Oct 20)

Gottlieb, David
pg 85 (1875 Sept 11) Las Animas Lodge U.D.

Goulding, W E
pg 25 (1874 Mar 28) Cheyenne Lodge No. 16

Grant, M N
pg 50 (1874 Nov 28) Laramie Lodge No. 18

Green, [Henry or William H]
appears as: Green, Greene
pg 12 (1874 Jan 10); pg 35 (1874 May 16); pg 39 (1874 July 28); pg 40 (1874 Aug 1); pg 40 (1874 Aug 8); pg 42 (1874 Aug 15); pg 42 (1874 Aug 22); pg 47 (1874 Oct 14); pg 50 (1874 Nov 28); pg 63 (1875 Feb 27); pg 65 (1875 Mar 13); pg 66 (1875 Mar 27); pg 67 (1875 Apr 10); pg 72 (1875 May 22); pg 75 (1875 July 10); pg 76 (1875 July 24); pg 86 (1875 Sept 16); pg 137 (1876 June 17); pg 138 (1876 June 24); pg 152 (1876 Dec 9); pg 183 (1877 Sept 1)

Green, David S
pg 79 (1875 Aug 14) Central Lodge No. 6

Green, Henry
appears as: Green, H; Green, Henry
offices held: SD, JD, JS
pg 4 (1873 Dec 13); pg 34 (1874 May 9); pg 40 (1874 Aug 1); pg 55 (1874 Dec 12); pg 56 (1874 Dec 12); pg 58 (1874 Dec 26); pg 64 (1875 Mar 11); pg 68 (1875 Apr 24); pg 81 (1875 Aug 7); pg 82 (1875 Aug 28); pg 82 (1875 Aug 28); pg 91 (1875 Oct 20); pg 139 (1876 June 24); pg 139 (1876 June 24); pg 146 (1876 Oct 14); pg 153 (1876 Dec 9); pg 154 (1876 Dec 9); pg 193 (1877 Dec 8); pg 195 (1877 Dec 8); pg 268 (1879 June 28); pg 272 (1879 July 12)

Green, William H
appears as: Green, W H
offices held: JW, JD, SW, Treas
pg 42 (1874 Aug 15); pg 49 (1874 Nov 18); pg 78 (1875 July 27); pg 79 (1875 Aug 14); pg 81 (1875 Aug 28); pg 83 (1875 Sept 1); pg 84 (1875 Sept 11); pg 89 (1875 Sept 27); pg 90 (1875 Oct 1); pg 90 (1875 Oct 9); pg 106 (1875 Dec 27); pg 134 (1876 June 3); pg 140 (1876 June 28)

Gregory, A J
pg 21 (1874 Mar 14) Laramie Lodge No. 18

Grey, C F
pg 279 (1879 Sept 13) South Pueblo Lodge

Griffin, Michael
pg 176 (1877 June 23) Black Hawk Lodge No. 11

Griffith, J S
pg 43 (1874 Aug 22) St Vrain Lodge No. 23

Grinnell, William E
pg 122 (1876 Apr 8) El Paso Lodge No. 13

Guyage, Julius
appears as: Guyage; Guyage, Julius
pg 74 (1875 June 26); pg 76 (1875 July 24); pg 77 (1875 July 24); pg 78 (1875 July 29); pg 78 (1875 July 29); pg 83 (1875 Sept 1)

H, D S
appears as: initials only D S H
offices held: JS
pg 184 (1877 Sept 8)

Haas, David
pg 164 (1877 Mar 10) Black Hawk Lodge No. 11

Hale, Caleb D
pg 160 (1877 Feb 10) Central Lodge No 6; pg 204 (1878 Feb 9) Central Lodge No 6

Hall, Gor F
pg 22 (1874 Mar 14) Pueblo Lodge No. 17

Hall, T A
pg 143 (1876 Aug 26); pg 147 (1876 Oct 28) petition withdrawn, physically disqualified from being made a mason

Halverson, Christian
appears as: Halverson; Halverson, Christian; Halvorson; Halvorson, C; Halvorson, Christian
offices held: JS, SS
pg 8 (1873 Dec 13); pg 9 (1873 Dec 27); pg 10 (1873 Dec 27); pg 17 (1874 Feb 14); pg 56 (1874 Dec 12); pg 114 (1876 Feb 16); pg 101 (1875 Dec 11); pg 145 (1876 Oct 14); pg 146 (1876 Oct 14); pg 152 (1876 Dec 9); pg 154 (1876 Dec 9); pg 154 (1876 Dec 12); pg 183 (1877 Sept 1); pg 193 (1877 Dec 8); pg 195 (1877 Dec 8); pg 198 (1877 Dec 22); pg 239 (1878 Nov 23); pg 240 (1878 Dec 14); pg 242 (1878 Dec 14); pg 254 (1879 Apr 12); pg 264 (1879 June 14); pg 275 (1879 Aug 23); pg 281 (1879 Sept 27)

Halvorson, see Halverson, Christian

Hamilton, Thomas
pg 90 (1875 Oct 1) visiting from Eureka Lodge No. 366, Union Mills, PA

Hamlin, Oliver T
appears as: Hamblin
pg 15 (1874 Jan 27)

Hammer
offices held: JS
pg 256 (1879 Apr 26); pg 262 (1879 May 27); pg 264 (1879 June 14)

Hammond
pg 247 (1879 Feb 8); pg 255 (1879 Apr 17)

Hammuch, E E
pg 172 (1877 May 26) Union Lodge No. 7

Hampson, W C
pg 157 (1877 Jan 13) visiting

Hanna & Humphrey
pg 190 (1877 Nov 10) bill presented for a hatchet; pg 199 (1877 Dec 22) bill presented for water cooler; pg 208 (1878 Feb 23) bill presented for coal oil

Hanna, Joseph P
pg 163 (1877 Feb 24) South Pueblo Lodge No. 31

Hanson
pg 268 (1879 June 28)

Harculs___, A
pg 126 (1876 May 13) Las Animas Lodge No. 28

Harden, Joseph
pg 114 (1876 Feb 12) purchased lot 79, block B - paid for by James Beverage

Hardenbrook, W A
pg 174 (1877 June 9); pg 177 (1877 July 14); pg 178 (1877 July 14)
*did not become a member of the Columbia Lodge

Harker, Oliver H
appears as: Harker; Harker, O H; Harker, Oliver H
pg 10 (1873 Dec 27) petitioner of Central Lodge No 6, CO Terr; pg 17 (1874 Feb 14); pg 19 (1874 Feb 28); pg 20 (1874 Feb 28); pg 57 (1874 Dec 26); pg 92 (1875 Oct 20); pg 94 (1875 Nov 13); pg 95 (1875 Nov 13); pg 101 (1875 Dec 11); pg 111 (1876 Jan 2_); pg 119 (1876 Mar 25); pg 120 (1876 Mar 25); pg 126 (1876 May 13); pg 129 (1876 May 13); pg 146 (1876 Oct 14); pg 159 (1877 Jan 28); pg 172 (1877 May 26); pg 173 (1877 May 26); pg 174 (1877 June 9) reports that the Fullerton family was given provisions but were in need of clothing. The committee

(1875 Oct 23); pg 94 (1875 Oct 23); pg 269 (1879 June 28); pg 156 (1876 Dec 23); pg 277 (1879 Aug 23)

Harwell, see Haswell, Theodore

Haskins
pg 102 (1875 Dec 12); Chaplain

Haslett
pg 43 (1874 Aug 22) Denver Lodge No. 5

Haswell, Theodore H
appears as: Harwell; Haswell; Haswell, Theodore H
pg 104 (1875 Dec 25); pg 118 (1876 Mar 11); pg 126 (1876 May 13); pg 170 (1877 Apr 21); pg 225 (1878 June 8); pg 239 (1878 Nov 23) a committee was formed to ascertain the true condition of brother Theodore Haswell's financial relation to this lodge; pg 242 (1878 Dec 14); pg 251 (1879 Mar 8)

Hatchinson, John
pg 122 (1876 Apr 8) Pueblo Lodge No. 17

Hathaway, Mark
appears as: Hathaway; Hathaway, Mark
offices held: JS
pg 57 (1874 Dec 26) petitioner from St Marks Lodge No. 63 of Woodstock, state of IL; pg 61 (1875 Jan 23); pg 135 (1876 June 10); pg 137 (1876 June 10); pg 138 (1876 June 24); pg 167 (1877 Mar 24); pg 246 (1879 Jan 25); pg 255 (1879 Apr 17); pg 257 (1879 May 10); pg 248 (1879 Feb 8); pg 259 (1879 May 12)

Hawkins
pg 142 (1876 July 29) present

Hayden, Joseph
pg 86 (1875 Sept 11) purchased cemetery lot 72, block B

Hayden, Nathaniel
pg 49 (1874 Nov 14); pg 54 (1874 Dec 12); pg 61 (1875 Jan 23); pg 74 (1875 June 26)
*did not become a member of the Columbia Lodge

Healy, Nathan M
pg 245 (1879 Jan 11); pg 248 (1879 Feb 8)
*did not become a member of the Columbia Lodge

Heat, Charles
pg 34 (1874 May 9) Cheyenne Lodge No. 16

Heberlein
pg 145 (1876 Oct 14) visiting

Heiter, Alois
pg 156 (1876 Dec 23) Del Norte Lodge No. 29

Heitter, Ed
pg 246 (1879 Jan 25) Del Norte Lodge No. 29

Helpstine, Henry H
pg 37 (1874 June 27) Cheyenne Lodge No. 16

Helton, B A
pg 41 (1874 Aug 8) Weston Lodge No. 22

Henry, [Albert T, Oren H, or Ormal E]
pg 33 (1874 May 7); pg 59 (1875 Jan 9); pg 65 (1875 Mar 11); pg 96 (1875 Nov 27); pg 114 (1876 Feb 16); pg 157 (1877 Jan 13); pg 163 (1877 Feb 24); pg 166 (1877 Mar 17); pg 168 (1877 Apr 14); pg 183 (1877 Sept 1); pg 191 (1877 Nov 20); pg 202 (1878 Jan 26); pg 209 (1878 Feb 27); pg 210 (1878 Mar 5); pg 211 (1878 Mar 9); pg 215 (1878 Mar 23); pg 219 (1878 Apr 27) visiting

Henry & Metcalf
pg 67 (1875 Mar 27) bill for hearse and buss for the funeral of late brother Wm M Large

Henry, Albert T
appears as: Henry, A T
offices held: JD, Treas
pg 214 (1878 Mar 15); pg 231 (1878 Aug 24); pg 245 (1879 Jan 11); pg 246 (1879 Jan 25); pg 250 (1879 Mar 8); pg 253 (1879 Apr 12); pg 255 (1879 Apr 17); pg 256 (1879 Apr 26); pg 262 (1879 May 27); pg 278 (1879 Aug 29)

Henry, Oren H
appears as: Henry O; Henry, O H
offices held: JW, Grand Master, SW, Secy, Treas, JD, Senior Grand Warden, SD
pg 1 (1873 Nov 8); pg 2 (1873 Nov 22); pg 3 (1873 Nov 22); pg 4 (1873 Dec 13); pg 5 (1873 Dec 13); pg 9 (1873 Dec 27); pg 10 (1873 Dec 27); pg 11 (1873 Dec 27) motion to send notices for those who owe payment for lots in the cemetery grounds; pg 13 (1874 Jan 10); pg 14 (1874 Jan 24); pg 22 (1874 Mar 14); pg 23 (1874 Mar 14); pg 23 (1874 Mar 14); pg 23 (1874 Mar

19); pg 24 (1874 Mar 19); pg 26 (1874 Mar 28); pg 27 (1874 Mar 28); pg 32 (1874 Apr 25); pg 34 (1874 May 9); pg 35 (1874 May 16); pg 38 (1874 July 11); pg 40 (1874 Aug 8); pg 43 (1874 Sept 12); pg 44 (1874 Sept 26); pg 45 (1874 Sept 26); pg 46 (1874 Oct 10); pg 47 (1874 Oct 24); pg 48 (1874 Oct 24); pg 49 (1874 Nov 14); pg 57 (1874 Dec 26); pg 59 (1875 Jan 9) motion to cancel the bill of Mr Barkhurst; pg 63 (1875 Feb 13); pg 64 (1875 Feb 27) motion that David Bunn be authorized to alter the gate at the cemetery grounds so that the Buss can pass through, and employ some one to flow a furrow on each side of the streets and allies in the cemetery grounds; pg 66 (1875 Mar 27); pg 67 (1875 Apr 10); pg 68 (1875 Apr 24); pg 69 (1875 Apr 24); pg 71 (1875 May 8); pg 71 (1875 May 22); pg 72 (1875 May 22) motion to rent the hall to the Boulder Chapter, Royal Arch Masons U.D.; pg 76 (1875 July 24); pg 77 (1875 July 24); pg 78 (1875 July 27); pg 81 (1875 Aug 7) bill presented for services performed by PM O H Henry; pg 83 (1875 Sept 1); pg 84 (1875 Sept 11); pg 86 (1875 Sept 16) motion to attend the corner stone laying as a lodge; pg 86 (1875 Sept 16); pg 88 (1875 Sept 25); pg 93 (1875 Oct 23); pg 96 (1875 Nov 27); pg 98 (1875 Dec 11); pg 99 (1875 Dec 11) read communication in thanks for good care of brother Wm F Sears, by Central Lodge No. 6; pg 100 (1875 Dec 11); pg 100 (1875 Dec 11); pg 101 (1875 Dec 11); pg 102 (1875 Dec 12); pg 107 (1876 Jan 8); pg 108 (1876 Jan 8); pg 109 (1876 Jan 8); pg 110 (1876 Jan 2_); pg 112 (1876 Feb 12); pg 117 (1876 Mar 11); pg 118 (1876 Mar 11); pg 119 (1876 Mar 25); pg 120 (1876 Mar 25); pg 121 (1876 April 1); pg 122 (1876 Apr 8); pg 123 (1876 Apr 8); pg 126 (1876 May 13); pg 126 (1876 May 13); pg 129 (1876 May 13); pg 154 (1876 Dec 9); pg 155 (1876 Dec 23); pg 156 (1876 Dec 23) motion to form a committee to secure a lot for a Masonic building; pg 170 (1877 April 28); pg 171 (1877 April 28); pg 193 (1877 Dec 8); pg 194 (1877 Dec 8) motion to have the body, buried in the alley of the cemetery to be removed and buried on a lot, and if the friends of the deceased fail to remove the same, that it be done at the expense of the lodge; pg 196 (1877 Dec 8); pg 270 (1879 June 28)

Henry, Ormal E

appears as: Henry, O E
offices held: SS, JD, JS, Treas, SD
pg 1 (1873 Nov 8); pg 4 (1873 Dec 13); pg 5 (1873 Dec 13) bill presented for coal; pg 8 (1873 Dec 13); pg 9 (1873 Dec 27); pg 10 (1873 Dec 27); pg 14 (1874 Jan 24); pg 16 (1874 Feb 14); pg 25 (1874 Mar 28); pg 26 (1874 Mar 28); pg 34 (1874 May 9); pg 36 (1874 May 23); pg 43 (1874 Sept 12); pg 50 (1874 Nov 28); pg 52 (1874 Dec 5); pg 56 (1874 Dec 19); pg 57 (1874 Dec 26); pg 62 (1875 Feb 13); pg 70 (1875 May 8); pg 71 (1875 May 8); pg 79 (1875 Aug 14); pg 96 (1875 Nov 27); pg 97 (1875 Nov 27) motion to make arrangements for the annual festival ball on St John's Day; pg 98 (1875 Dec 11); pg 103 (1875 Dec 12); pg 126 (1876 May 13); pg 138 (1876 June 24); pg 143 (1876 Aug 26); pg 152 (1876 Dec 9); pg 153 (1876 Dec 9); pg 154 (1876 Dec 9); pg 157 (1877 Jan 13); pg 158 (1877 Jan 28); pg 159 (1877 Jan 28); pg 163 (1877 Feb 24); pg 171 (1877 April 28); pg 172 (1877 May 26); pg 193 (1877 Dec 8); pg 195 (1877 Dec 8); pg 202 (1878 Jan 26); pg 217 (1878 Apr 13); pg 242 (1878 Dec 14); pg 246 (1879 Jan 25); pg 247 (1879 Jan 25) motion to remit the dues of David H Nichols to Dec 14, 1878; pg 250 (1879 Mar 8) communication from Silver Cliff stating that brother H C Samuels, a member of the lodge, was sick and destitute and asking for aid on his behalf, granted $25 to aid H C Samuels; pg 252 (1879 Mar 22) acknowledged the receipt of money for brother H C Samuels

Hepner, Jacob

pg 230 (1878 Aug 10) Washington Lodge No. 12

Herman, Max

pg 119 (1876 Mar 25); pg 127 (1876 May 13); pg 130 (1876 May 13); pg 257 (1879 Apr 26); pg 261 (1879 May 24)
*did not become a member of the Columbia Lodge

Hernandez, Anthony R

appears as: Hernandez; Hernandez, A; Hernandez, A R; Hernandez, Anthony
offices held: Tiler, SS, Secy
pg 145 (1876 Oct 14); pg 148 (1876 Nov 11); pg 149 (1876 Nov 25); pg 152 (1876 Dec 9);

pg 153 (1876 Dec 9); pg 155 (1876 Dec 23); pg 158 (1877 Jan 28); pg 160 (1877 Feb 10); pg 163 (1877 Feb 24); pg 164 (1877 Mar 10); pg 166 (1877 Mar 17); pg 167 (1877 Mar 24); pg 170 (1877 April 28); pg 171 (1877 May 12); pg 176 (1877 June 23); pg 177 (1877 July 14); pg 179 (1877 July 18); pg 179 (1877 July 28); pg 183 (1877 Sept 1); pg 190 (1877 Nov 10); pg 193 (1877 Dec 8); pg 195 (1877 Dec 8); pg 196 (1877 Dec 8); pg 197 (1877 Dec 19); pg 199 (1878 Jan 12); pg 202 (1878 Jan 26); pg 204 (1878 Feb 9); pg 206 (1878 Feb 13); pg 207 (1878 Feb 23); pg 209 (1878 Feb 27); pg 210 (1878 Mar 5); pg 211 (1878 Mar 9); pg 212 (1878 Mar 9); pg 214 (1878 Mar 15); pg 217 (1878 Apr 13); pg 219 (1878 Apr 27); pg 221 (1878 May 11); pg 223 (1878 May 25); pg 225 (1878 June 8); pg 226 (1878 June 22); pg 228 (1878 July 27); pg 229 (1878 Aug 10); pg 231 (1878 Aug 24); pg 232 (1878 Sept 14); pg 240 (1878 Dec 14); pg 242 (1878 Dec 14); pg 244 (1879 Jan 11); pg 247 (1879 Feb 8); pg 250 (1879 Mar 8); pg 253 (1879 Apr 12); pg 256 (1879 Apr 26); pg 257 (1879 Apr 26); pg 262 (1879 May 27); pg 263 (1879 May 27); pg 266 (1879 June 28); pg 271 (1879 July 12); pg 272 (1879 July 26); pg 273 (1879 Aug 9); pg 257 (1879 May 10); pg 259 (1879 May 24); pg 264 (1879 June 14)

Hewson, D H F
pg 75 (1875 July 10) Pueblo Lodge No. 17

Hicks, John P
pg 156 (1876 Dec 23) St Vrain Lodge No. 23

Hilburn, Edward A
pg 272 (1879 July 26) Rosita Lodge

Hill, Ezra P
pg 279 (1879 Sept 13) Washington Lodge No. 12

Hill, Thomas J
pg 44 (1874 Sept 26); pg 113 (1876 Feb 12) funeral in May 1873

Hinkle, John P
pg 243 (1878 Dec 28); pg 246 (1879 Jan 25); pg 247 (1879 Jan 25); pg 248 (1879 Feb 8); pg 190 (1877 Nov 10); pg 191 (1877 Nov 10)

Hinman, Fred
pg 193 (1877 Dec 8); pg 194 (1877 Dec 8); pg 197 (1877 Dec 19)

Hobson
pg 148 (1876 Nov 11) Pueblo Lodge No. 17

Hockaday, Charles N
appears as: Hockaday; Hockaday, C N; Hockiday; Hockaday, Charles N
offices held: JD, JW
pg 2 (1873 Nov 8); pg 4 (1873 Dec 13); pg 15 (1874 Jan 27); pg 29 (1874 Apr 10); pg 31 (1874 Apr 25); pg 46 (1874 Oct 10); pg 53 (1874 Dec 12); pg 57 (1874 Dec 26); pg 75 (1875 July 10); pg 94 (1875 Nov 13); pg 95 (1875 Nov 13); pg 101 (1875 Dec 11); pg 106 (1875 Dec 27); pg 108 (1876 Jan 8); pg 125 (1876 Apr 22); pg 127 (1876 May 13); pg 129 (1876 May 13); pg 138 (1876 June 24); pg 146 (1876 Oct 14); pg 157 (1877 Jan 13); pg 158 (1877 Jan 13); pg 174 (1877 June 9); pg 179 (1877 July 18); pg 210 (1878 Mar 5); pg 269 (1879 June 28); pg 273 (1879 July 26)

Hockiday, see Hockaday, Charles N

Hoffman, L A
pg 126 (1876 May 13) South Pueblo Lodge U.D.

Hollister, William
pg 4 (1873 Dec 13) Central Lodge No 6

Holme, Andrew
pg 188 (1877 Oct 27) Golden City Lodge No. 1

Holmes, Charles
pg 22 (1874 Mar 14) Pueblo Lodge No. 17; pg 37 (1874 June 27) Pueblo Lodge No. 17

Holstein, George B
pg 167 (1877 Mar 24); pg 173 (1877 May 26); pg 189 (1877 Oct 27); pg 192 (1877 Nov 20) *did not become a member of the Columbia Lodge

Holverson, see Halverson, Christian

Home, Edward
pg 126 (1876 May 13) South Pueblo Lodge U.D.

Hopkins, David L
appears as: Hopkins; Hopkins, D L; Hopkins, David L
offices held: JS, JD, SD, SW, JW, SS, Tiler, Treas

pg 83 (1875 Sept 1); pg 87 (1875 Sept 25); pg 89 (1875 Sept 27); pg 90 (1875 Oct 1); pg 103 (1875 Dec 12); pg 103 (1875 Dec 25); pg 115 (1876 Feb 26); pg 126 (1876 May 13); pg 135 (1876 June 10); pg 136 (1876 June 10); pg 137 (1876 June 10); pg 137 (1876 June 17); pg 138 (1876 June 24); pg 140 (1876 June 28); pg 147 (1876 Oct 28); pg 148 (1876 Nov 11); pg 149 (1876 Nov 25); pg 151 (1876 Dec 2); pg 152 (1876 Dec 9); pg 154 (1876 Dec 12); pg 155 (1876 Dec 23); pg 160 (1877 Feb 10); pg 170 (1877 Apr 21); pg 176 (1877 June 23); pg 179 (1877 July 28); pg 181 (1877 Aug 11); pg 183 (1877 Sept 1); pg 184 (1877 Sept 8); pg 186 (1877 Sept 22); pg 187 (1877 Sept 22); pg 187 (1877 Oct 13); pg 188 (1877 Oct 13); pg 189 (1877 Nov 10); pg 190 (1877 Nov 10); pg 191 (1877 Nov 20); pg 197 (1877 Dec 19); pg 199 (1878 Jan 12); pg 202 (1878 Jan 26); pg 207 (1878 Feb 23); pg 211 (1878 Mar 9); pg 212 (1878 Mar 9); pg 214 (1878 Mar 15); pg 215 (1878 Mar 23); pg 269 (1879 June 28); pg 277 (1879 Aug 23)

Horow, William
pg 87 (1875 Sept 25) Pueblo Lodge No. 17

Howell, C C
pg 230 (1878 Aug 10) petitioner accompanied by a demit from another lodge; pg 232 (1878 Sept 14); pg 233 (1878 Sept 14); pg 275 (1879 Aug 23)

Howell, William R
appears as: Howell; Howell, W R; Howell, Wm R; Howell, William R
offices held: WM, SW, JW
pg 1 (1873 Nov 8); pg 2 (1873 Nov 22); pg 4 (1873 Dec 13); pg 5 (1873 Dec 13); pg 8 (1873 Dec 13); pg 10 (1873 Dec 27); pg 15 (1874 Jan 27); pg 29 (1874 Apr 10); pg 36 (1874 June 27); pg 37 (1874 June 27); pg 42 (1874 Aug 22); pg 48 (1874 Nov 14); pg 49 (1874 Nov 14); pg 55 (1874 Dec 12)\; motion to send twenty dollars to the Erie Lodge; pg 56 (1874 Dec 12); pg 63 (1875 Feb 27); pg 76 (1875 July 24); pg 91 (1875 Oct 20); pg 98 (1875 Dec 11); pg 100 (1875 Dec 11); pg 101 (1875 Dec 11); pg 110 (1876 Jan 2_); pg 130 (1876 May 13); pg 152 (1876 Dec 9); pg 153 (1876 Dec 9); pg 154 (1876 Dec 9); pg 188 (1877 Oct 27); pg 199 (1878 Jan 12); pg 200 (1878 Jan 12); pg 201 (1878 Jan 12); pg 223 (1878 May 25); pg 265 (1879 June 14)

Howes, see Howse, W J L

Howse, W J L
appears as: Howes, W J L; Howse, W J L
offices held: SD, SS, SW, Tiler
pg 8 (1873 Dec 13); pg 14 (1874 Jan 24); pg 15 (1874 Jan 27); pg 16 (1874 Feb 14); pg 18 (1874 Feb 20); pg 20 (1874 Mar 14); pg 45 (1874 Sept 26); pg 87 (1875 Sept 25) inquiry about Bro. W J L Howes, from St Johns Lodge No. 209, London, Ontario; pg 101 (1875 Dec 11); pg 108 (1876 Jan 8) now residing in Ontario, Canada asking for demit

Hubbard, Mrs
pg 159 (1877 Jan 28) cemetery lot purchased

Hubbard, R M
pg 272 (1879 July 26) St Vrain Lodge No. 23

Hunt, [Fred A or William K]
pg 83 (1875 Sept 1); pg 122 (1876 Apr 8); pg 136 (1876 June 10)

Hunt, Fred A
appears as: Hunt, F A; Hunt, Fred A
offices held: JW
pg 123 (1876 Apr 8); pg 132 (1876 Mar 27); pg 133 (1876 Mar 27); pg 135 (1876 June 10); pg 135 (1876 June 10); pg 138 (1876 June 24); pg 155 (1876 Dec 23); pg 156 (1876 Dec 23); pg 197 (1877 Dec 19); pg 247 (1879 Jan 25)

Hunt, William K
appears as: Hunt, W K; Hunt, William H; Hunt, William K
pg 26 (1874 Mar 28) petitioner of St Johns Lodge No. 675 Ireland; pg 31 (1874 Apr 25); pg 32 (1874 Apr 25); pg 138 (1876 June 24); pg 139 (1876 June 24); pg 177 (1877 June 23); pg 181 (1877 Aug 11); pg 265 (1879 June 14); pg 268 (1879 June 28)

Hunter
pg 181 (1877 Aug 11) present

Hunter, Andrew
pg 143 (1876 Aug 26); pg 150 (1876 Nov 25) *did not become a member of the Columbia Lodge

Huntington, A J
pg 282 (1879 Sept 27) Weston Lodge No. 22

Hyder, David
pg 152 (1876 Dec 9) petitioner of Caribou; pg 157 (1877 Jan 13); pg 164 (1877 Feb 24)

Inbody
pg 115 (1876 Feb 26); pg 126 (1876 May 13) visiting

Inskus, V S
pg 22 (1874 Mar 14) Pueblo Lodge No. 17

Insurance Company of North America
pg 125 (1876 Apr 22); bill presented for insurance

Irwin, Joseph
appears as: Irwin; Irwin, Joseph
pg 73 (1875 June 12); pg 78 (1875 July 27); pg 78 (1875 July 27); pg 87 (1875 Sept 25); pg 88 (1875 Sept 25); pg 89 (1875 Sept 27); pg 109 (1876 Jan 8); pg 217 (1878 Apr 13); pg 218 (1878 Apr 13); pg 242 (1878 Dec 14)

Jackson, Alex
pg 99 (1875 Dec 11) Central Lodge No 6

Jackson, G W
appears as: Jackson; Jackson, G M
pg 48 (1874 Oct 24); pg 50 (1874 Nov 28); pg 51 (1874 Nov 28); pg 73 (1875 June 12); pg 98 (1875 Dec 3); pg 181 (1877 Aug 11); pg 267 (1879 June 28)

Jackson, John
pg 4 (1873 Dec 13); pg 13 (1874 Jan 10)
*did not become a member of the Columbia Lodge

Jay
pg 177 (1877 July 14) visiting

Jeffrey, Francis
pg 204 (1878 Feb 9) Nevada Lodge No. 4

Job, James R
pg 272 (1879 July 26) Washington Lodge No. 12

Johns
pg 135 (1876 June 10) visiting; pg 138 (1876 June 24) visiting; pg 145 (1876 Oct 14) visiting; pg 151 (1876 Dec 2) visiting; pg 152 (1876 Dec 9) visiting; pg 154 (1876 Dec 12); pg 166 (1877 Mar 17); pg 171 (1877 May 12) visiting; pg 177 (1877 July 14)

Johns, J B
pg 57 (1874 Dec 26) Washington Lodge No. 12

Johns, John H
appears as: Johns; Johns, J H; Johns, John H
pg 74 (1875 June 26); pg 76 (1875 July 24); pg 82 (1875 Aug 28); pg 83 (1875 Sept 1); pg 84 (1875 Sept 1); pg 87 (1875 Sept 25); pg 88 (1875 Sept 25); pg 93 (1875 Oct 23); pg 94 (1875 Oct 23); pg 96 (1875 Nov 27); pg 97 (1875 Nov 27); pg 120 (1876 Mar 25) deceased in a mining accident in Caribou

Johnson, Alexander
pg 132 (1876 Mar 27) Washington Lodge No. 12

Johnson, Charles W
pg 79 (1875 Aug 14) Central Lodge No. 6

Johnson, H A
pg 260 (1879 May 24) Central Lodge No. 6

Johnson, Seymour
pg 127 (1876 May 13); pg 138 (1876 June 24); pg 139 (1876 June 24); pg 144 (1876 Sept 16)

Johnstone, Alex
pg 65 (1875 Mar 13) Doric Lodge No. 25

Jones, Abel E
pg 282 (1879 Sept 27) Denver Lodge No. 5

Jones, E Paul
pg 79 (1875 Aug 14) Central Lodge No. 6

Jones, J M
pg 152 (1876 Dec 9) petitioner of Valmont; pg 157 (1877 Jan 13); pg 158 (1877 Jan 13); pg 225 (1878 June 8); pg 227 (1878 July 13)
*did not become a member of the Columbia Lodge

Jones, J W
pg 260 (1879 May 24) Union Lodge No. 7

Jones, Samuel E
pg 207 (1878 Feb 23) King Solomon Lodge No. 30

Jones, Thomas J
appears as: Jones; Jones, Thomas; Jones, Thomas J
offices held: Treas

(1876 Dec 9); pg 240 (1878 Nov 23); pg 240 (1878 Dec 14); pg 242 (1878 Dec 14)

Kessler, Marion
appears as: Kessler; Kessler, Marion
offices held: SS, JS, JD, SD
pg 94 (1875 Nov 13); pg 104 (1875 Dec 25); pg 106 (1875 Dec 25); pg 110 (1876 Jan 19); pg 119 (1876 Mar 25); pg 120 (1876 Mar 25); pg 121 (1876 Mar 25); pg 121 (1876 Mar 25); pg 132 (1876 Mar 27); pg 133 (1876 Mar 27); pg 134 (1876 May 31); pg 134 (1876 June 3); pg 135 (1876 June 10); pg 138 (1876 June 24); pg 154 (1876 Dec 12); pg 155 (1876 Dec 12); pg 159 (1877 Jan 28); pg 163 (1877 Feb 24); pg 164 (1877 Mar 10); pg 176 (1877 June 23); pg 179 (1877 July 28); pg 181 (1877 Aug 11); pg 184 (1877 Sept 8); pg 188 (1877 Oct 27); pg 189 (1877 Nov 10); pg 191 (1877 Nov 20); pg 198 (1877 Dec 22); pg 199 (1877 Dec 22); pg 202 (1878 Jan 26); pg 204 (1878 Feb 9); pg 206 (1878 Feb 13); pg 207 (1878 Feb 23); pg 211 (1878 Mar 9); pg 212 (1878 Mar 9); pg 215 (1878 Mar 23); pg 217 (1878 Apr 13); pg 219 (1878 Apr 27); pg 221 (1878 May 11); pg 238 (1878 Nov 9); pg 247 (1879 Feb 8); pg 266 (1879 June 28); pg 273 (1879 Aug 9)

Kiel, A E
pg 190 (1877 Nov 10) visiting of Joppa Lodge No. 136, Monhore, IA

Kier, see Kerr, David

Kilbourne, J V
pg 156 (1876 Dec 23) King Solomon Lodge No. 30

King, Robert
appears as: King; King, Robert
pg 69 (1875 Apr 24); pg 74 (1875 June 26); pg 76 (1875 July 24) petitioner of Cambria Lodge No. 152, WI; pg 82 (1875 Aug 28); pg 84 (1875 Sept 11); pg 101 (1875 Dec 11); pg 138 (1876 June 24); pg 193 (1877 Dec 8); pg 195 (1877 Dec 8); pg 266 (1879 June 28); pg 269 (1879 June 28); pg 272 (1879 July 12)

Klein, see Kline, Marcus

Kline, Marcus
appears as: Klein, M; Kline; Kline, Marcus
offices held: JS, JD, Treas, JW
pg 160 (1877 Feb 10) petitioner of Boulder; pg 165 (1877 Mar 10); pg 166 (1877 Mar 17); pg 168 (1877 Apr 14); pg 169 (1877 Apr 14); pg 170 (1877 Apr 21); pg 170 (1877 April 28); pg 171 (1877 April 28); pg 172 (1877 May 12); pg 172 (1877 May 26); pg 177 (1877 July 14); pg 179 (1877 July 18); pg 181 (1877 Aug 11); pg 183 (1877 Sept 1); pg 183 (1877 Sept 5); pg 184 (1877 Sept 8); pg 186 (1877 Sept 22); pg 187 (1877 Oct 13); pg 188 (1877 Oct 27); pg 189 (1877 Oct 27); pg 191 (1877 Nov 20); pg 193 (1877 Dec 8); pg 195 (1877 Dec 8); pg 197 (1877 Dec 19); pg 198 (1877 Dec 22); pg 199 (1878 Jan 12); pg 200 (1878 Jan 12); pg 201 (1878 Jan 12); pg 202 (1878 Jan 26); pg 204 (1878 Feb 9); pg 206 (1878 Feb 13); pg 207 (1878 Feb 23); pg 209 (1878 Feb 27); pg 210 (1878 Mar 5); pg 211 (1878 Mar 9); pg 212 (1878 Mar 9); pg 214 (1878 Mar 15); pg 215 (1878 Mar 23); pg 217 (1878 Apr 13); pg 219 (1878 Apr 27); pg 221 (1878 May 11); pg 223 (1878 May 25); pg 225 (1878 June 8); pg 226 (1878 June 22); pg 227 (1878 July 13); pg 228 (1878 July 27); pg 229 (1878 Aug 10); pg 231 (1878 Aug 24); pg 232 (1878 Sept 14); pg 234 (1878 Oct 12); pg 235 (1878 Oct 26); pg 237 (1878 Nov 9); pg 239 (1878 Nov 23); pg 240 (1878 Dec 14); pg 242 (1878 Dec 14); pg 243 (1878 Dec 28); pg 245 (1879 Jan 11); pg 246 (1879 Jan 25); pg 247 (1879 Feb 8); pg 249 (1879 Feb 22); pg 250 (1879 Mar 8); pg 251 (1879 Mar 8)

Klein, Mrs Annie
pg 135 (1876 June 3) paid for cemetery plot

Knight, William M
pg 91 (1875 Oct 9) Doric Lodge No. 25

Knox, John
pg 8 (1873 Dec 13); pg 101 (1875 Dec 11); pg 154 (1876 Dec 9); pg 199 (1878 Jan 12); pg 200 (1878 Jan 12); pg 242 (1878 Dec 14)

Koehler, see Kohler, Frederick W

Kohler, Frederick W
appears as: Koehler; Kohler; Kohler, F W; Kohler, Frederick W
pg 2 (1873 Nov 22); pg 3 (1873 Nov 22); pg 8 (1873 Dec 13); pg 37 (1874 June 27); pg 38 (1874 June 27); pg 43 (1874 Sept 12); pg 44

105 (1875 Dec 25) deceased, memoriam, "a valuable member of the third estate"

Luther, Mrs A O
pg 130 (1876 May 13) deed for cemetery plot

Lykens, D J
pg 83 (1875 Aug 28) has become a member of another lodge

Lyner, see Leyner, Peter A

Lyon, H H
pg 279 (1879 Sept 13) Washington Lodge No. 12

Lyons, Mrs
pg 13 (1874 Jan 10) bill presented for the support of brother C W Taylor

Lytle, George
appears as: Lytle; Lytle, George
pg 16 (1874 Feb 14); pg 26 (1874 Mar 28) petitioner of Black Hawk lodge No. 11, Territory of Colorado; pg 31 (1874 Apr 25); pg 32 (1874 Apr 25); pg 47 (1874 Oct 24); pg 101 (1875 Dec 11); pg 134 (1876 June 3); pg 151 (1876 Nov 25) purchased lot 68, Block B, Columbia Cemetery; pg 152 (1876 Dec 9); pg 154 (1876 Dec 9); pg 163 (1877 Feb 24); pg 172 (1877 May 26); pg 264 (1879 June 14); pg 265 (1879 June 14)

M E Church
pg 163 (1877 Feb 24) bill presented for use of church hall for lecture

Mack, Henry
pg 95 (1875 Nov 13); pg 104 (1875 Dec 25); pg 106 (1875 Dec 25); pg 136 (1876 June 10); pg 141 (1876 July 8); pg 160 (1877 Feb 10) petitioner of Gold Hill; pg 165 (1877 Mar 10)
*did not become a member of the Columbia Lodge

Mackey, see Macky, Andrew J

Mackintosh, see McIntosh, Lemuel

Macky, Andrew J
appears as: Mackey, A J; Macky; Macky A J
pg 158 (1877 Jan 13) asked to lecture before the lodge; pg 171 (1877 April 28) notified lodge of expiration of insurance on lodge furniture, etc.; pg 171 (1877 May 12) bill presented [unreadable]; pg 183 (1877 Sept 1) addressed the lodge on the Scottish Rites of masonry; pg 225 (1878 June 8) bill presented; pg 258 (1879 May 10) bill presented for insurance

Maginnes, see Meginnis, David

Maginnis, see Meginnis, David

Markley, W G
pg 279 (1879 Sept 13) Las Animas Lodge No. 28

Martin, Charles H
pg 275 (1879 Aug 23) Washington Lodge No. 12

Marx, Sigmond [Sigmund]
pg 37 (1874 June 27) Occidental Lodge No. 20; pg 79 (1875 Aug 14) Occidental Lodge No. 20

Mason, S A
pg 167 (1877 Mar 24) Mount Morial Lodge No. 15

Masters, Thomas
pg 87 (1875 Sept 25); pg 94 (1875 Nov 13); pg 95 (1875 Nov 13)
*did not become a member of the Columbia Lodge

Mattison, C
pg 25 (1874 Mar 28) Occidental Lodge No. 20

Maxwell, A D
pg 172 (1877 May 26) El Paso Lodge No. 13

Maxwell, D
pg 66 (1875 Mar 27) El Paso Lodge No. 13

Maxwell, James P
appears as: Maxwell; Maxwell, J P; Maxwell, James P
offices held: SW, WM, JD, JW
pg 4 (1873 Dec 13); pg 8 (1873 Dec 13); pg 19 (1874 Feb 28); pg 20 (1874 Mar 14); pg 23 (1874 Mar 14); pg 27 (1874 Mar 28); pg 28 (1874 Apr 4); pg 29 (1874 Apr 10); pg 31 (1874 Apr 25); pg 32 (1874 Apr 25); pg 33 (1874 May 7); pg 34 (1874 May 9); pg 38 (1874 July 11); pg 39 (1874 July 28); pg 45 (1874 Sept 26) delegate to the Grand Lodge; pg 48 (1874 Nov 14); pg 49 (1874 Nov 14); pg 49 (1874 Nov 18); pg 52 (1874 Dec 5); pg 53 (1874 Dec 12); pg 55 (1874 Dec 12) motion to appoint a committee to confer with the ditch company regarding the ditch running through the cemetery; pg 56 (1874 Dec 19); pg 58 (1874 Dec 26); pg 60 (1875 Jan 23); pg 62

(1875 Feb 13); pg 63 (1875 Feb 27); pg 64 (1875 Mar 11); pg 65 (1875 Mar 13); pg 66 (1875 Mar 27); pg 67 (1875 Apr 10); pg 69 (1875 Apr 24); pg 76 (1875 July 24); pg 78 (1875 July 27); pg 81 (1875 Aug 7); pg 87 (1875 Sept 25); pg 88 (1875 Sept 25); pg 90 (1875 Oct 9); pg 91 (1875 Oct 9); pg 91 (1875 Oct 20); pg 92 (1875 Oct 20) acting WM at the cemetery for the funeral; pg 92 (1875 Oct 23); pg 94 (1875 Nov 13); pg 95 (1875 Nov 13); pg 98 (1875 Dec 11); pg 100 (1875 Dec 11); pg 101 (1875 Dec 11); pg 102 (1875 Dec 12); pg 103 (1875 Dec 25); pg 106 (1875 Dec 27); pg 107 (1876 Jan 8); pg 108 (1876 Jan 8); pg 110 (1876 Jan 19); pg 110 (1876 Jan 2_); pg 112 (1876 Feb 12); pg 114 (1876 Feb 16); pg 115 (1876 Feb 26); pg 116 (1876 Mar 4); pg 117 (1876 Mar 11); pg 119 (1876 Mar 25); pg 121 (1876 April 1); pg 122 (1876 Apr 8); pg 124 (1876 Apr 10); pg 125 (1876 Apr 22); pg 125 (1876 Apr 22); pg 126 (1876 May 13); pg 130 (1876 May 13); pg 131 (1876 May 16); pg 137 (1876 June 17); pg 138 (1876 June 24); pg 140 (1876 July 8); pg 141 (1876 July 8); pg 142 (1876 July 29); pg 144 (1876 Oct 14); pg 145 (1876 Oct 14); pg 147 (1876 Oct 28); pg 151 (1876 Dec 2); pg 155 (1876 Dec 12); pg 156 (1876 Dec 23); pg 167 (1877 Mar 24); pg 168 (1877 Apr 14); pg 169 (1877 Apr 14); pg 172 (1877 May 12); pg 174 (1877 June 9); pg 174 (1877 June 9); pg 176 (1877 June 23); pg 177 (1877 July 14); pg 178 (1877 July 14); pg 181 (1877 Aug 11); pg 181 (1877 Aug 11); pg 188 (1877 Oct 13); pg 193 (1877 Dec 8); pg 196 (1877 Dec 8); pg 198 (1877 Dec 22); pg 199 (1877 Dec 22); pg 207 (1878 Feb 23); pg 217 (1878 Apr 13); pg 227 (1878 July 13); pg 235 (1878 Oct 26); pg 237 (1878 Nov 9); pg 240 (1878 Dec 14); pg 242 (1878 Dec 14); pg 243 (1878 Dec 28); pg 249 (1879 Feb 22); pg 250 (1879 Mar 8); pg 253 (1879 Apr 12); pg 255 (1879 Apr 17); pg 256 (1879 Apr 26); pg 257 (1879 Apr 26); pg 257 (1879 May 10); pg 259 (1879 May 12); pg 260 (1879 May 24); pg 266 (1879 June 28); pg 270 (1879 June 28) officers to confer with Bro J P Maxwell about reducing the rent for the lodge; pg 279 (1879 Sept 13); pg 283 (1879 Sept 27)

Mayer, Gottlieb F
appears as: Mayer; Mayer, G F; Mayer, Gottlieb
offices held: Treas
pg 223 (1878 May 25); pg 226 (1878 June 22); pg 227 (1878 June 22); pg 227 (1878 July 13); pg 228 (1878 July 13); pg 228 (1878 July 27); pg 229 (1878 July 27); pg 231 (1878 Aug 24); pg 237 (1878 Nov 9); pg 238 (1878 Nov 9); pg 244 (1878 Dec 28)

Maynard, J L
pg 145 (1876 Oct 14) Golden City Lodge No. 1

McAllister
pg 167 (1877 Mar 24) visiting; pg 255 (1879 Apr 17) visiting

McAllister, J T
pg 166 (1877 Mar 17) visiting

McBride, D N
pg 66 (1875 Mar 27) Huerfano Lodge U.D.

McBride, Sam
pg 148 (1876 Nov 11) Pueblo Lodge No. 17

McCall, Nathaniel H
appears as: McCall
pg 116 (1876 Mar 4)

McCaslin, Matthew L
appears as: McCaslin; McCaslin, M L
offices held: JD
pg 29 (1874 Apr 10); pg 55 (1874 Dec 12); pg 101 (1875 Dec 11); pg 164 (1877 Feb 24); pg 206 (1878 Feb 13); pg 270 (1879 June 28)

McClure, [Edward P or George M]
pg 35 (1874 May 16) present

McClure, Edward P
appears as: McClure; McClure, E P
pg 82 (1875 Aug 28); pg 258 (1879 May 10); pg 260 (1879 May 24)

McClure, George M
pg 10 (1873 Dec 27)

McClure, H
pg 185 (1877 Sept 8) Mt Moriah Lodge No. 15

McCombe, John
pg 253 (1879 Apr 12) Ionic Lodge No. 34

McCormick
pg 40 (1874 Aug 1) present

McCowan, J C
pg 1 (1873 Nov 8); pg 2 (1873 Nov 8)

McDowell, John M
appears as: McDowell; McDowell, J M
offices held: Treas, JS, Tiler, SS
pg 92 (1875 Oct 23); pg 97 (1875 Nov 27); pg 98 (1875 Dec 3); pg 103 (1875 Dec 25); pg 105 (1875 Dec 25); pg 107 (1875 Dec 27); pg 107 (1876 Jan 8); pg 109 (1876 Jan 8); pg 110 (1876 Jan 2_); pg 112 (1876 Feb 12); pg 115 (1876 Feb 26); pg 117 (1876 Mar 11); pg 119 (1876 Mar 25); pg 122 (1876 Apr 8); pg 125 (1876 Apr 22); pg 126 (1876 May 13); pg 132 (1876 Mar 27); pg 135 (1876 June 10); pg 137 (1876 June 10); pg 137 (1876 June 17); pg 138 (1876 June 24); pg 142 (1876 July 29); pg 147 (1876 Oct 28); pg 149 (1876 Nov 25); pg 152 (1876 Dec 9); pg 154 (1876 Dec 12); pg 155 (1876 Dec 23); pg 156 (1876 Dec 23); pg 160 (1877 Feb 10); pg 162 (1877 Feb 14); pg 163 (1877 Feb 24); pg 164 (1877 Mar 10); pg 166 (1877 Mar 17); pg 167 (1877 Mar 24); pg 168 (1877 Apr 14); pg 170 (1877 Apr 21); pg 170 (1877 April 28); pg 171 (1877 May 12); pg 172 (1877 May 26); pg 195 (1877 Dec 8); pg 241 (1878 Dec 14) requesting a demit; pg 242 (1878 Dec 14)

McGanphy, William
pg 279 (1879 Sept 13) Ouray Lodge U.D.

McGovern, Andy
pg 200 (1878 Jan 12) Pueblo Lodge No. 17

McIntosh & Van
pg 123 (1876 Apr 8) bill presented for chimneys

McIntosh, Lemuel
appears as: Mackintosh; McIntosh; McIntosh, L; McIntosh, Lemuel
pg 29 (1874 Apr 4); pg 40 (1874 Aug 1); pg 43 (1874 Sept 12); pg 47 (1874 Oct 24); pg 74 (1875 June 26); pg 86 (1875 Sept 11) purchased cemetery lot 71, block B; pg 101 (1875 Dec 11); pg 114 (1876 Feb 12) lot 80, block B - paid for by Joseph J Wharton; pg 126 (1876 May 13); pg 141 (1876 July 22); pg 269 (1879 June 28); pg 277 (1879 Aug 23)

McLeod, John W
pg 85 (1875 Sept 11) Union Lodge No. 7

Mead, Marcus S
appears as: Mead; Mead, M S; Mead, Marcus; Mead, Marcus S
offices held: JD, JW, SS, JD, Secy, Treas
pg 115 (1876 Feb 26); pg 120 (1876 Mar 25); pg 124 (1876 Apr 10); pg 131 (1876 May 13); pg 131 (1876 May 16); pg 134 (1876 May 31); pg 135 (1876 June 10); pg 137 (1876 June 17); pg 138 (1876 June 24); pg 140 (1876 June 28); pg 154 (1876 Dec 9); pg 170 (1877 Apr 21);pg 179 (1877 July 18); pg 186 (1877 Sept 22); pg 188 (1877 Oct 27); pg 189 (1877 Nov 10); pg 191 (1877 Nov 10); pg 213 (1878 Mar 9); pg 217 (1878 Apr 13); pg 226 (1878 June 22); pg 246 (1879 Jan 25); pg 247 (1879 Jan 25); pg 259 (1879 May 24); pg 262 (1879 May 27); pg 278 (1879 Aug 29)

Meginnis, Daniel
appears as: Maginnes, David; Maginnis; Maginnis, Daniel; Meginnis; Meginnis, Daniel
pg 65 (1875 Mar 13) bill presented for coffin and case for brother Wm M Large; pg 162 (1877 Feb 14) undertaker where the body lay; pg 273 (1879 July 26); pg 276 (1879 Aug 23) appointed to take charge of the Masonic Cemetery and to confer with Mr. Euler concerning the removal of the body of Euler's child buried by mistake on a wrong lot; pg 278 (1879 Aug 29); pg 280 (1879 Sept 13) Secretary to look up the cemetery book and notes of lots sold and turn them over to Meginnis who now has charge of the cemetery; pg 281 (1879 Sept 27); pg 282 (1879 Sept 27); pg 283 (1879 Sept 30); pg 284 (1879 Sept 30)

Metcalf, Eli P
appears as: Metcalf;
offices held: SD, JD, JW, SS
pg 13 (1874 Jan 10) bill presented for 1 1/2 tons of coal; pg 23 (1874 Mar 19); pg 30 (1874 Apr 10); pg 40 (1874 Aug 1); pg 47 (1874 Oct 24); pg 49 (1874 Nov 18); pg 50 (1874 Nov 28); pg 53 (1874 Dec 12); pg 59 (1875 Jan 9); pg 60 (1875 Jan 23); pg 61 (1875 Jan 23); pg 62 (1875 Feb 13); pg 63 (1875 Feb 27); pg 64 (1875 Feb 27); pg 66 (1875 Mar 27); pg 67 (1875 Apr 10); pg 68 (1875 Apr 24); pg 71 (1875 May 22); pg 72 (1875 May 22); pg 78 (1875 July 29); pg 88 (1875 Sept 25); pg 96 (1875 Nov 27); pg 101

(1875 Dec 11); pg 115 (1876 Feb 26); pg 143 (1876 Aug 26); pg 148 (1876 Nov 11); pg 145 (1876 Oct 14); pg 151 (1876 Dec 2); pg 152 (1876 Dec 9); pg 154 (1876 Dec 9); pg 156 (1876 Dec 23); pg 157 (1877 Jan 13); pg 158 (1877 Jan 28); pg 159 (1877 Jan 28); pg 160 (1877 Feb 10); pg 163 (1877 Feb 24); pg 164 (1877 Mar 10); pg 165 (1877 Mar 10); pg 167 (1877 Mar 24); pg 171 (1877 April 28); pg 193 (1877 Dec 8); pg 194 (1877 Dec 8); pg 195 (1877 Dec 8); pg 198 (1877 Dec 22); pg 199 (1878 Jan 12); pg 200 (1878 Jan 12); pg 202 (1878 Jan 26); pg 204 (1878 Feb 9); pg 210 (1878 Mar 5); pg 211 (1878 Mar 9); pg 212 (1878 Mar 9); pg 214 (1878 Mar 15); pg 217 (1878 Apr 13); pg 219 (1878 Apr 27); pg 270 (1879 June 28)

Meyer, see Mayer, Gottlieb

Meyring, Henry
appears as: Meyring; Meyring, Henry
pg 171 (1877 April 28); pg 174 (1877 June 9); pg 175 (1877 June 9); pg 177 (1877 June 23); pg 177 (1877 June 23); pg 179 (1877 July 28); pg 180 (1877 July 28); pg 180 (1877 July 28); pg 181 (1877 Aug 11); pg 182 (1877 Aug 11); pg 184 (1877 Sept 8); pg 185 (1877 Sept 8); pg 186 (1877 Sept 8); pg 186 (1877 Sept 8); pg 188 (1877 Oct 27); pg 199 (1877 Dec 22); pg 240 (1878 Nov 23); pg 254 (1879 Apr 12)

Michaud, Theodore
pg 76 (1875 July 24); pg 82 (1875 Aug 28); pg 83 (1875 Sept 1); pg 84 (1875 Sept 1)

Middleton
pg 151 (1876 Dec 2) visiting

Miller, David F
pg 31 (1874 Apr 25) Doric Lodge U.D.

Miller, David W
pg 83 (1875 Aug 28) has become a member of another lodge; pg 147 (1876 Oct 14) demit granted

Miller, George C
pg 168 (1877 Apr 14) Idaho Springs Lodge No. 26

Miller, Henry J
pg 181 (1877 Aug 11) Collins Lodge No. 19

Miller, Lafayette
pg 198 (1877 Dec 22); pg 202 (1878 Jan 26); pg 203 (1878 Jan 26)
*did not become a member of the Columbia Lodge

Miller, Lewis
pg 142 (1876 July 22); pg 146 (1876 Oct 14) withdrew his petition for membership to return to his former home

Milliken, Robert
pg 204 (1878 Feb 9) Nevada Lodge No. 4

Millman, Mrs
pg 216 (1878 Mar 23) F W Juneman made a motion to aid Mrs Millman with $15 as she is sick and destitute

Mills, Abraham
appeared as: Mills; Mills, Abram
pg 25 (1874 Mar 28); pg 80 (1875 Aug 14); pg 98 (1875 Dec 11); pg 100 (1875 Dec 11); pg 101 (1875 Dec 11)

Mitchell, Samuel
pg 37 (1874 June 27) Pueblo Lodge No. 17

Mock, Joseph
pg 37 (1874 June 27) Cheyenne Lodge No. 16

Moffett, [C M or J C]
pg 261 (1879 May 24); pg 283 (1879 Sept 27)

Moffett, C M
pg 261 (1879 May 24)

Moffett, J C
appears as: Moffitt, J C; Moffett, J C
pg 256 (1879 Apr 26); pg 263 (1879 June 10)

Moffitt, see Moffett, J C

Moncton, A C
pg 272 (1879 July 26) St Vrain Lodge No. 23

Montgomery, J H
pg 185 (1877 Sept 8) Idaho Springs Lodge No. 26

Mooney, Michael
appears as: Mooney; Mooney, Michael; Moony, Michael
pg 193 (1877 Dec 8); pg 200 (1878 Jan 12); pg 201 (1878 Jan 12); pg 264 (1879 June 14); pg 265 (1879 June 14)

Moore
pg 138 (1876 June 24) visiting

Morgridge, A
pg 46 (1874 Oct 10) bill presented for chimney cleaning

Morgridge, William O
pg 73 (1875 June 12) bill presented for oil

Morris
pg 237 (1878 Nov 9) visiting

Morris, Webb
appears as: Morris; Morris, Webb
offices held: SD
pg 12 (1874 Jan 10); pg 43 (1874 Sept 12); pg 227 (1878 July 13)

Morton, John
pg 156 (1876 Dec 23) Algonquin Lodge No 256, IL

Morton, Richard
pg 46 (1874 Oct 10); pg 60 (1875 Jan 9); pg 61 (1875 Jan 23)

Moser, Christopher
pg 151 (1876 Nov 25) purchased lot 50, Block C, Columbia Cemetery

Moyle, J B
pg 87 (1875 Sept 25) Washington Lodge No. 12

Moynahan, T J
pg 232 (1878 Sept 14) bill presented

Mulford, John Spencer
appears as: Mulford, Mulford, J S
offices held: JD, JS
pg 41 (1874 Aug 8); pg 86 (1875 Sept 16); pg 87 (1875 Sept 25); pg 137 (1876 June 17)

Munley, Joseph
pg 200 (1878 Jan 12) Washington Lodge No. 12

Munroe, Hugh
pg 72 (1875 May 22) Golden City Lodge No. 1

Munson
pg 33 (1874 May 7)

Munson, George C
pg 260 (1879 May 24) Central Lodge No. 6

Murray, Bernard
pg 119 (1876 Mar 25) Mt Morial Lodge No. 15

Mustin, Ed
pg 65 (1875 Mar 13) bill presented for a dressing gown

Myler, Stephen
pg 186 (1877 Sept 22) Weston Lodge

Nance, Thomas
pg 87 (1875 Sept 25) Washington Lodge No. 12

Naphyes, Benj F
pg 37 (1874 June 27) Washington Lodge No. 12

Nash, T D
pg 260 (1879 May 24) Central Lodge No. 6

Neal, see Neill, Lewis

Neill, Lewis
appears as: Neal; Neill, Lewis; Neil, Lewis; Neill
office held: Tiler
pg 201 (1878 Jan 12); pg 203 (1878 Jan 26); pg 203 (1878 Jan 26) committee found him to be a master mason; pg 204 (1878 Feb 9) to be given $5 over the amount ordered to be paid him by the lodge; pg 207 (1878 Feb 23) communication from Summit City Lodge No. 170, Fort Wayne, IN indicating that he is a brother in good standing; pg 221 (1878 May 11) communication to his lodge requesting a contribution for his support; pg 229 (1878 July 27) motion to disallow the payment of $5 per week until further notice; pg 244 (1878 Dec 28) Secy instructed to write to Summit City Lodge, IN in regard to the care of brother Lewis Neill; pg 246 (1879 Jan 25); pg 251 (1879 Mar 22); pg 253 (1879 Apr 12); pg 254 (1879 Apr 12) Secretary requested to contact the Grand Lodge in IN in requesting payment for relief of brother Lewis Neill which his lodge as so far neglected to pay; pg 255 (1879 Apr 17); pg 256 (1879 Apr 26); pg 259 (1879 May 24); pg 277 (1879 Aug 23) Secretary ordered to look for correspondence with his lodge at Fort Wayne, IN in order to bring the matter before the Grand Lodge in this state; pg 280 (1879 Sept 13) Secretary to find correspondence in relation to him and his lodge in Fort Wayne

Newton, J D
pg 57 (1874 Dec 26) Golden City Lodge No. 1

Nichols, [Charles L, David H or Ezra H]
pg 13 (1874 Jan 10); pg 36 (1874 May 23); pg 49 (1874 Nov 18); pg 160 (1877 Feb 10)

Nichols, Charles L
appears as: Nichols, C L; Nichols, Charles L
pg 14 (1874 Jan 24) petitioner of Lawson Ridge Lodge No. 415, IL; pg 22 (1874 Mar 14); pg 23 (1874 Mar 14); pg 268 (1879 June 28)

Nichols, David H
appears as: Nichols, D H; Nichols, David H
offices held: Secy
pg 1 (1873 Nov 8); pg 2 (1873 Nov 8); pg 2 (1873 Nov 22); pg 3 (1873 Nov 22); pg 4 (1873 Dec 13); pg 8 (1873 Dec 13); pg 9 (1873 Dec 27); pg 11 (1873 Dec 27); pg 12 (1874 Jan 10); pg 13 (1874 Jan 10); pg 14 (1874 Jan 24); pg 15 (1874 Jan 24); pg 15 (1874 Jan 27); pg 18 (1874 Feb 20); pg 20 (1874 Mar 14); pg 23 (1874 Mar 14); pg 24 (1874 Mar 26); pg 25 (1874 Mar 28); pg 28 (1874 Mar 28); pg 29 (1874 Apr 10); pg 30 (1874 Apr 10); pg 31 (1874 Apr 25); pg 33 (1874 Apr 25); pg 33 (1874 May 7); pg 34 (1874 May 9); pg 35 (1874 May 9); pg 36 (1874 June 27); pg 38 (1874 June 27); pg 38 (1874 July 11); pg 39 (1874 July 11); pg 40 (1874 Aug 8); pg 41 (1874 Aug 8); pg 42 (1874 Aug 22); pg 43 (1874 Aug 22); pg 43 (1874 Sept 12); pg 44 (1874 Sept 12); pg 44 (1874 Sept 26); pg 45 (1874 Sept 26) elected to be an alternate delegate to the Grand Lodge in Denver on the 29th of September; pg 46 (1874 Oct 10); pg 47 (1874 Oct 10); pg 53 (1874 Dec 12); pg 55 (1874 Dec 12); pg 56 (1874 Dec 12); pg 57 (1874 Dec 26); pg 58 (1874 Dec 26); pg 59 (1875 Jan 9); pg 60 (1875 Jan 23); pg 61 (1875 Jan 23); pg 62 (1875 Feb 13); pg 63 (1875 Feb 13); pg 63 (1875 Feb 27); pg 64 (1875 Feb 27); pg 64 (1875 Mar 11); pg 65 (1875 Mar 11); pg 65 (1875 Mar 13); pg 66 (1875 Mar 13); pg 66 (1875 Mar 27); pg 67 (1875 Mar 27); pg 67 (1875 Apr 10); pg 68 (1875 Apr 10); pg 70 (1875 May 8); pg 71 (1875 May 8); pg 71 (1875 May 22); pg 72 (1875 May 22); pg 73 (1875 June 12); pg 74 (1875 June 26); pg 75 (1875 July 10); pg 76 (1875 July 24); pg 77 (1875 July 24); pg 79 (1875 Aug 14); pg 80 (1875 Aug 14); pg 81 (1875 Aug 7); pg 101 (1875 Dec 11); pg 109 (1876 Jan 8); pg 111 (1876 Jan 2_); pg 113 (1876 Feb 12); pg 152 (1876 Dec 9); pg 247 (1879 Jan 25); pg 260 (1879 May 24); pg 265 (1879 June 14); pg 267 (1879 June 28); pg 277 (1879 Aug 23); pg 280 (1879 Sept 13); pg 282 (1879 Sept 27)

Nichols, Ezra H
appears as: Hichols, E H; Nichols, Ezra H
offices held: SS, JD, Tiler, Steward, JS
pg 8 (1873 Dec 13); pg 10 (1873 Dec 27); pg 12 (1874 Jan 10); pg 28 (1874 Apr 4); pg 36 (1874 May 23); pg 55 (1874 Dec 12); pg 56 (1874 Dec 26); pg 58 (1874 Dec 26); pg 62 (1875 Feb 13); pg 63 (1875 Feb 27); pg 69 (1875 Apr 24); pg 72 (1875 June 12); pg 84 (1875 Sept 11); pg 86 (1875 Sept 16); pg 87 (1875 Sept 25); pg 103 (1875 Dec 25); pg 115 (1876 Feb 26); pg 116 (1876 Mar 4); pg 126 (1876 May 13); pg 132 (1876 Mar 27); pg 134 (1876 June 3); pg 138 (1876 June 24); pg 269 (1879 June 28); pg 277 (1879 Aug 23)

Nicholson, John W
appears as: Nicholson; Nicholson, J W
offices held: JS, JD, Treas, Tiler, SS
pg 111 (1876 Jan 2_); pg 116 (1876 Feb 26); pg 117 (1876 Mar 4); pg 119 (1876 Mar 25); pg 121 (1876 Mar 25); pg 122 (1876 Apr 8); pg 123 (1876 Apr 8); pg 124 (1876 Apr 8); pg 126 (1876 May 13); pg 132 (1876 Mar 27); pg 138 (1876 June 24); pg 145 (1876 Oct 14); pg 146 (1876 Oct 14); pg 147 (1876 Oct 28); pg 148 (1876 Nov 11); pg 152 (1876 Dec 9); pg 154 (1876 Dec 9); pg 155 (1876 Dec 23); pg 171 (1877 April 28); pg 172 (1877 May 26); pg 177 (1877 July 14); pg 179 (1877 July 18); pg 181 (1877 Aug 11); pg 183 (1877 Sept 1); pg 189 (1877 Nov 10); pg 190 (1877 Nov 10); pg 197 (1877 Dec 19); pg 198 (1877 Dec 22); pg 204 (1878 Feb 9); pg 205 (1878 Feb 9); pg 207 (1878 Feb 23); pg 209 (1878 Feb 27); pg 210 (1878 Mar 5); pg 217 (1878 Apr 13); pg 253 (1879 Apr 12); pg 254 (1879 Apr 12); pg 255 (1879 Apr 12); pg 263 (1879 June 10)

Normandean, Edmund
pg 256 (1879 Apr 26) Idaho Springs Lodge No. 26

Norris
pg 210 (1878 Mar 5) present

Pettis & Co
pg 123 (1876 Apr 8) bill presented for ballot box

Philippi, Frederick W
appears as: Philippi, Philippi, Fred; Philippi, Frederick W; Phillipi, Fred
offices held: JD
pg 229 (1878 Aug 10); pg 232 (1878 Sept 14); pg 234 (1878 Oct 12); pg 235 (1878 Oct 12); pg 235 (1878 Oct 26); pg 236 (1878 Oct 26); pg 239 (1878 Nov 23); pg 240 (1878 Dec 14); pg 242 (1878 Dec 14); pg 244 (1879 Jan 11); pg 245 (1879 Jan 11); pg 246 (1879 Jan 25); pg 247 (1879 Feb 8); pg 249 (1879 Feb 22); pg 250 (1879 Mar 8); pg 251 (1879 Mar 22); pg 253 (1879 Apr 12); pg 255 (1879 Apr 17); pg 256 (1879 Apr 26); pg 257 (1879 Apr 26); pg 257 (1879 May 10); pg 259 (1879 May 12); pg 259 (1879 May 24); pg 262 (1879 May 27); pg 263 (1879 June 10); pg 264 (1879 June 14); pg 266 (1879 June 28); pg 271 (1879 July 12); pg 272 (1879 July 26); pg 273 (1879 July 26); pg 273 (1879 Aug 9); pg 278 (1879 Aug 29); pg 279 (1879 Sept 13); pg 281 (1879 Sept 27)
Phillipi, see Philippi Frederick W

Phillips Bros
pg 46 (1874 Oct 10) bill presented for sundries

Phillips, Ives
appears as: Phillips; Phillips, Ives
pg 62 (1875 Feb 13); pg 64 (1875 Mar 11); pg 98 (1875 Dec 11); pg 101 (1875 Dec 11) donation made; pg 102 (1875 Dec 12); pg 105 (1875 Dec 25) donation made; pg 247 (1879 Feb 8); pg 255 (1879 Apr 17)

Picket, Edwin J
pg 215 (1878 Mar 23) Occidental Lodge No. 2

Pierce, Oscar
pg 185 (1877 Sept 8) communication from Elk City, PA; pg 187 (1877 Sept 22) Central City Lodge No. 1

Pierson, Hollis K
pg 279 (1879 Sept 13) Washington Lodge No. 12

Pitts, Martin J
pg 181 (1877 Aug 11); pg 188 (1877 Oct 13); pg 189 (1877 Oct 27)

Platte
pg 219 (1878 Apr 27) visiting

Polk, Alfred S
pg 148 (1876 Nov 11) King Solomon Lodge No. 30

Pollock, James R
appears as: Pollock; Pollock, J R; Pollock, James R
offices held: JD, JS, SW, SD, Treas
pg 167 (1877 Mar 24) visiting; pg 187 (1877 Sept 22); pg 190 (1877 Nov 10); pg 191 (1877 Nov 10); pg 192 (1877 Nov 20); pg 229 (1878 Aug 10); pg 254 (1879 Apr 12); pg 257 (1879 May 10); pg 259 (1879 May 24); pg 262 (1879 May 24); pg 262 (1879 May 27); pg 263 (1879 June 10); pg 264 (1879 June 14); pg 266 (1879 June 28); pg 271 (1879 July 12); pg 272 (1879 July 26); pg 275 (1879 Aug 23); pg 279 (1879 Sept 13); pg 280 (1879 Sept 13) elected to attend the Grand Lodge in Denver as proxy; pg 281 (1879 Sept 27)

Poor, George
pg 154 (1876 Dec 9) purchased cemetery lot

Porter, J R
pg 192 (1877 Nov 20) Washington Lodge No. 12

Pound, Frank
pg 178 (1877 July 14) bill presented for nursing bro Fullerton

Powell, James S
pg 85 (1875 Sept 11) Weston Lodge No. 22; pg 138 (1876 June 24) Weston Lodge No. 22

Pratt, M A
pg 123 (1876 Apr 8) Pueblo Lodge No. 17

Quaintance, S D
pg 29 (1874 Apr 10) Black Hawk Lodge No. 11

Quinn, [John L or T J]
pg 47 (1874 Oct 24) present

Quinn, George P
pg 260 (1879 May 24) Central Lodge No. 6

Rear, A B
pg 45 (1874 Sept 26) Washington Lodge No. 12

Redding & Co.
pg 256 (1879 Apr 26) communication regarding collars ordered for officers

211 (1878 Mar 9); pg 212 (1878 Mar 9); pg 214 (1878 Mar 15); pg 215 (1878 Mar 23); pg 217 (1878 Apr 13); pg 219 (1878 Apr 27); pg 232 (1878 Sept 14); pg 239 (1878 Nov 23); pg 264 (1879 June 14); pg 269 (1879 June 28); pg 277 (1879 Aug 23)

Roges, C D
pg 200 (1878 Jan 12) Collins Lodge No. 19

Rompf, Charles
pg 164 (1877 Mar 10) communication from Nelson Lodge No. 80 West Virginia

Rood, A
pg 54 (1874 Dec 12) bill presented for hardware

Root, D W C
pg 21 (1874 Mar 14) El Paso Lodge No. 13

Roper & Nesbit
pg 260 (1879 May 24) bill presented for living hive

Roseburg, Arington
pg 145 (1876 Oct 14) Huerfano Lodge No. 27

Rosenbloom, Isaac
pg 4 (1873 Dec 13) Central Lodge No 6

Ross, Frank A
pg 271 (1879 July 12) Olive Branch Lodge No. 32

Ross, W A
office held: JD
pg 209 (1878 Feb 27)

Russell, Horace M
pg 3 (1873 Nov 22) Union Lodge No. 7

Russell, John S
pg 253 (1879 Apr 12) Ionic Lodge No. 34

Ruttencutter, William C
pg 279 (1879 Sept 13) Washington Lodge No. 12

Ryalls, Thomas
pg 83 (1875 Aug 28)

Sackett, Thomas G
pg 279 (1879 Sept 13) Washington Lodge No. 12

Sagendorf, Andrew
pg 70 (1875 May 8) Denver Lodge No. 5

Sampson, A J
pg 141 (1876 July 22) visiting

Samuels, Henry C
appears as: Samuels; Samuels, H C; Samuels, Henry C
offices held: Tiler
pg 168 (1877 Apr 14) communication from Palestine Lodge No. 481, Ballard Cty, KY; pg 176 (1877 June 23); pg 181 (1877 Aug 11); reply from Palestine Lodge No. 481, Ballard Cty, KY; pg 190 (1877 Nov 10); pg 197 (1877 Dec 19); pg 204 (1878 Feb 9); pg 219 (1878 Apr 27); pg 225 (1878 June 8); pg 249 (1879 Feb 22); pg 250 (1879 Mar 8) communication from Silver Cliff stating that brother H C Samuels, a member of the lodge, was sick and destitute and asking for aid on his behalf; pg 252 (1879 Mar 22) acknowledged the receipt of money for brother H C Samuels

Samuelson, William
pg 172 (1877 May 26) Washington Lodge No. 12

Sanders, George
pg 122 (1876 Apr 8) Central Lodge No. 6

Savory, Oscar
pg 198 (1877 Dec 22); pg 202 (1878 Jan 26); pg 203 (1878 Jan 26)
*did not become a member of the Columbia Lodge

Sawdey, Edgar
appears as: Sawdey; Sawdey, Edgar; Sawdy; Sawdy E; Sawdy, Edgar
offices held: JD, Secy, SD, Treas
pg 4 (1873 Dec 13) petitioner from Freemont Lodge No. 15; pg 14 (1874 Jan 24); pg 55 (1874 Dec 12); pg 94 (1875 Nov 13); pg 96 (1875 Nov 27); pg 100 (1875 Dec 11); pg 101 (1875 Dec 11); pg 106 (1875 Dec 27); pg 107 (1875 Dec 27); pg 107 (1876 Jan 8); pg 110 (1876 Jan 2_); pg 112 (1876 Feb 12); pg 115 (1876 Feb 26); pg 135 (1876 June 10); pg 142 (1876 July 22); pg 154 (1876 Dec 9); pg 155 (1876 Dec 23); pg 183 (1877 Sept 5); pg 193 (1877 Dec 8); pg 196 (1877 Dec 8); pg 198 (1877 Dec 22); pg 202 (1878 Jan 26); pg 219 (1878 Apr 27); pg 223 (1878 May 25); pg 248 (1879 Feb 8)

pg 16 (1874 Feb 14); pg 26 (1874 Mar 28); pg 28 (1874 Mar 28); pg 28 (1874 Apr 4); pg 29 (1874 Apr 4); pg 31 (1874 Apr 25); pg 32 (1874 Apr 25); pg 33 (1874 Apr 25); pg 34 (1874 May 9); pg 35 (1874 May 16); pg 55 (1874 Dec 12); pg 57 (1874 Dec 26); pg 70 (1875 May 8); pg 73 (1875 June 12); pg 76 (1875 July 24); pg 78 (1875 July 27); pg 81 (1875 Aug 7); pg 81 (1875 Aug 28); pg 90 (1875 Oct 1); pg 98 (1875 Dec 11); pg 101 (1875 Dec 11); pg 113 (1876 Feb 12); pg 132 (1876 Mar 27); pg 153 (1876 Dec 9); pg 195 (1877 Dec 8); pg 198 (1877 Dec 22); pg 242 (1878 Dec 14); pg 253 (1879 Apr 12)

Short, George W
pg 22 (1874 Mar 14) Pueblo Lodge No. 17

Shortreed, Thomas
pg 53 (1874 Dec 12) Cheyenne Lodge No. 16

Shortridge
pg 49 (1874 Nov 18) present

Sigwood, Christ
pg 260 (1879 May 24) St Vrain Lodge No. 23

Sileck, A
pg 29 (1874 Apr 10) Washington Lodge No. 12

Silver, S D
appears as: Silver; Silver, S D
offices held: JD, SS
pg 10 (1873 Dec 27) petitioner of St Johns Lodge No. 113, KS; pg 26 (1874 Mar 28); pg 28 (1874 Mar 28); pg 92 (1875 Oct 23); pg 101 (1875 Dec 11); pg 103 (1875 Dec 25); pg 106 (1875 Dec 27); pg 267 (1879 June 28); pg 277 (1879 Aug 23); pg 280 (1879 Sept 13); pg 281 (1879 Sept 13)

Simmons
pg 94 (1875 Nov 13) present; pg 275 (1879 Aug 23) present

Simpson, John H
pg 108 (1876 Jan 8); pg 113 (1876 Feb 12)
*did not become a member of the Columbia Lodge

Skinner
pg 132 (1876 Mar 27) visiting

Slater, W C
pg 82 (1875 Aug 28)

Slaughter, B H
pg 82 (1875 Aug 28)

Slifer, Esrom G
appears as: Slifer, E J; Slifer, E S; Slifer, Eiren
pg 83 (1875 Aug 28); pg 164 (1877 Feb 24); pg 193 (1877 Dec 8); pg 195 (1877 Dec 8) asking to cancel back dues and give him a demit; pg 196 (1877 Dec 8)

Sloan
pg 43 (1874 Aug 22) Denver Lodge No. 5

Smails, John D
appears as: Smails, J D; Smails, John D
pg 69 (1875 Apr 24) Black Hawk Lodge No. 11; pg 215 (1878 Mar 23) Black Hawk Lodge No. 11

Smith, [Azon A, J Alden, Marinus G, or Walter H]
pg 18 (1874 Feb 20); pg 60 (1875 Jan 23); pg 65 (1875 Mar 13); pg 66 (1875 Mar 27); pg 72 (1875 May 22); pg 75 (1875 July 10); pg 79 (1875 Aug 14); pg 86 (1875 Sept 16); pg 91 (1875 Oct 20); pg 96 (1875 Nov 27); pg 98 (1875 Dec 11); pg 102 (1875 Dec 12); pg 103 (1875 Dec 12); pg 116 (1876 Mar 4); pg 130 (1876 May 13); pg 167 (1877 Mar 24); pg 172 (1877 May 26); pg 174 (1877 June 9); pg 186 (1877 Sept 22); pg 191 (1877 Nov 20); pg 199 (1878 Jan 12); pg 202 (1878 Jan 26); pg 209 (1878 Feb 27); pg 239 (1878 Nov 23); pg 278 (1879 Aug 29)

Smith, Azon A
appears as: Smith, A A; Smith, Azon A
pg 16 (1874 Feb 14) petitioner of Here__ Lodge No. 142, MO; pg 26 (1874 Mar 28); pg 28 (1874 Mar 28); pg 37 (1874 June 27); pg 75 (1875 July 10); pg 76 (1875 July 24); pg 82 (1875 Aug 28); pg 87 (1875 Sept 25); pg 88 (1875 Sept 25); pg 106 (1875 Dec 25); pg 113 (1876 Feb 12); pg 151 (1876 Dec 2); pg 215 (1878 Mar 23) communication from Wyanet Lodge No. 231 of Wyanet, IL containing a bill for burial expenses of the wife of brother A A Smith; pg 227 (1878 June 22); pg 248 (1879 Feb 8) now residing in Leadville asking for demit

Smith, D Tom
pg 185 (1877 Sept 8) Union Lodge No. 7

Sneal, James H
pg 22 (1874 Mar 14) Collins Lodge No. 19

Snedecor, Isaac D
pg 253 (1879 Apr 12) bill presented for work on the cemetery

Snell, James
pg 38 (1874 June 27)
*did not become a member of the Columbia Lodge

Snowdon, David Harry
pg 174 (1877 June 9) has tried to pass himself off as a mason, Washington Lodge No. 12

Snyder, Hanson
appears as: Snyder; Snyder, Hanson
pg 16 (1874 Feb 14); pg 17 (1874 Feb 14); pg 18 (1874 Feb 20); pg 34 (1874 May 9); pg 36 (1874 May 23); pg 56 (1874 Dec 12); pg 144 (1876 Aug 26); pg 268 (1879 June 28); pg 277 (1879 Aug 23); pg 280 (1879 Sept 13); pg 281 (1879 Sept 13)

Sodenstrom, Andrew
appears as: Sodenstrom, Andrew; Soderstrom, Andrew
pg 122 (1876 Apr 8) Black Hawk Lodge No. 11; pg 164 (1877 Mar 10) Black Hawk Lodge No. 11

Sodenstrom, Dolan
pg 122 (1876 Apr 8) Black Hawk Lodge No. 11

Soderstrom, see Sodenstrom, Andrew

Solander, David
pg 62 (1875 Feb 13) bill presented for repairing the secretary desk

Solander, Lane
pg 253 (1879 Apr 12) bill presented for hauling material

Solomon, Joseph
pg 264 (1879 June 14) Denver Lodge No. 5

Sommers, Wilhelm
appears as: Somers, W; Sommers, Wilh; Sommers, Wilhelm
pg 82 (1875 Aug 28); pg 95 (1875 Nov 13); pg 101 (1875 Dec 11); pg 111 (1876 Jan 2_); pg 156 (1876 Dec 23); pg 196 (1877 Dec 8); pg 269 (1879 June 28); pg 277 (1879 Aug 23)

Sorrell, E J
pg 146 (1876 Oct 14); pg 153 (1876 Dec 9)
*did not become a member of the Columbia Lodge

Southerland, D E, see Sutherland, Datus E

Southland, D E, see Sutherland, Datus E

Southland, [Judson D or W J]
pg 135 (1876 June 10); pg 149 (1876 Nov 25); pg 151 (1876 Dec 2); pg 152 (1876 Dec 9); pg 170 (1877 Apr 21); pg 170 (1877 April 28); pg 172 (1877 May 26); pg 174 (1877 June 9); pg 183 (1877 Sept 1); pg 209 (1878 Feb 27); pg 211 (1878 Mar 9); pg 212 (1878 Mar 9)

Southland, Judson D
appears as: Southerland, J D; Southland, J D; Southland, Judson; Southland; Southerland, J D
offices held: SS, JD, Tiler
pg 43 (1874 Sept 12); pg 46 (1874 Oct 10); pg 47 (1874 Oct 10); pg 47 (1874 Oct 14); pg 50 (1874 Nov 28); pg 51 (1874 Nov 28); pg 52 (1874 Nov 28); pg 52 (1874 Dec 5); pg 53 (1874 Dec 12); pg 54 (1874 Dec 12); pg 56 (1874 Dec 19); pg 73 (1875 June 12); pg 101 (1875 Dec 11); pg 114 (1876 Feb 16); pg 126 (1876 May 13); pg 140 (1876 July 8); pg 163 (1877 Feb 24); pg 168 (1877 Apr 14); pg 203 (1878 Jan 26); pg 234 (1878 Oct 12); pg 235 (1878 Oct 26); pg 248 (1879 Feb 8)

Southland, W J
pg 108 (1876 Jan 8); pg 154 (1876 Dec 9)

Sparks, O T
pg 204 (1878 Feb 9) Nevada Lodge No. 4

Springer, Arnold
pg 256 (1879 Apr 26) South Pueblo Lodge

Squires, Frederick A
appears as: Squires, F A; Squires, Fred A
pg 5 (1873 Dec 13) bill presented for sundries; pg 99 (1875 Dec 11) bill for oil, matches; pg 58 (1874 Dec 26) bill presented

Squires, George C
appears as: Squires, G C; Squires, George C
pg 8 (1873 Dec 13); pg 63 (1875 Feb 13); pg 10 (1873 Dec 27); pg 101 (1875 Dec 11); pg 115 (1876 Feb 26); pg 154 (1876 Dec 9); pg 269

137 (1876 June 17); pg 142 (1876 July 29); pg 179 (1877 July 28); pg 181 (1877 Aug 11); pg 187 (1877 Oct 13); pg 223 (1878 May 25); pg 226 (1878 June 22); pg 228 (1878 July 27); pg 232 (1878 Sept 14); pg 239 (1878 Nov 23); pg 249 (1879 Feb 22); pg 253 (1879 Apr 12); pg 257 (1879 May 10); pg 259 (1879 May 12); pg 262 (1879 May 27); pg 264 (1879 June 14); pg 266 (1879 June 28); pg 272 (1879 July 26); pg 273 (1879 Aug 9); pg 281 (1879 Sept 27); pg 282 (1879 Sept 27)

Sutherland, J D, see Southland, Judson D

Sweet, J K
pg 186 (1877 Sept 22) Mt Moriah Lodge No. 15

Talbot, Mrs
pg 66 (1875 Mar 13) bill presented for washing aprons

Tallman, Isaac T
appears as: Tallman; Tallman, Isaac T
pg 100 (1875 Dec 11) petitioner of Streater Lodge No. 607, Streator, IL; pg 111 (1876 Jan 2_); pg 112 (1876 Feb 12); pg 113 (1876 Feb 12); pg 138 (1876 June 24); pg 161 (1877 Feb 10); pg 246 (1879 Jan 25); pg 247 (1879 Jan 25)

Tanner, N R
pg 167 (1877 Mar 24) Mount Morial Lodge No. 15

Tarvin, E M
appears as: Tarvin; Tarvin, E M
pg 82 (1875 Aug 28) petitioner Rev E M Tarvin; pg 88 (1875 Sept 25); pg 90 (1875 Oct 1); pg 103 (1875 Dec 25); pg 105 (1875 Dec 25); pg 107 (1875 Dec 27); pg 115 (1876 Feb 26); pg 116 (1876 Feb 26); pg 120 (1876 Mar 25); pg 132 (1876 Mar 27); pg 152 (1876 Dec 9); pg 154 (1876 Dec 9); pg 162 (1877 Feb 14); pg 168 (1877 Apr 14); pg 236 (1878 Oct 26); pg 245 (1879 Jan 11)

Taylor, C W
pg 13 (1874 Jan 10) taken care of by Mrs Lyons

Taylor, Eugene
pg 30 (1874 Apr 10); pg 48 (1874 Oct 24); pg 53 (1874 Dec 12); pg 54 (1874 Dec 12)
*did not become a member of the Columbia Lodge

Taylor, R S
pg 9 (1873 Dec 27) El Paso Lodge No. 13

Teiyise, Mr
pg 21 (1874 Mar 14) Nevada Lodge No. 4

Thompson
pg 134 (1876 June 3) visiting

Thompson, A R
pg 239 (1878 Nov 23) Crystal Lake Lodge of Lake City

Thompson, G B
pg 145 (1876 Oct 14) Washington Lodge No. 12

Thompson, Henry Clay
appears as: Thompson, H C
pg 152 (1876 Dec 9) bill presented for coal oil; pg 173 (1877 May 26) bill presented for oil, chimneys

Thompson, James
pg 226 (1878 June 22)
*did not become a member of the Columbia Lodge

Thompson, Rev Nathan
appears as: Thompson, Rev N
pg 65 (1875 Mar 11) minister for the funeral of William Morton Large, held at the Congregational Church

Tilleny, William H
pg 112 (1876 Feb 12) Golden City Lodge No. 1

Tillett, H R
pg 282 (1879 Sept 27) Weston Lodge No. 22

Tilney, Robert H
appears as: Tilney; Tilney, R H; Tilney, Robert H
offices held: JD, SD
pg 118 (1876 Mar 11); pg 123 (1876 Apr 8); pg 124 (1876 Apr 10); pg 131 (1876 May 13); pg 131 (1876 May 16); pg 132 (1876 Mar 27); pg 134 (1876 May 31); pg 135 (1876 June 10); pg 137 (1876 June 10); pg 137 (1876 June 17); pg 138 (1876 June 24); pg 148 (1876 Nov 11); pg 151 (1876 Dec 2); pg 152 (1876 Dec 9); pg 154 (1876 Dec 9); pg 154 (1876 Dec 12); pg 155 (1876 Dec 23); pg 156 (1876 Dec 23); pg 157 (1877 Jan 13); pg 158 (1877 Jan 28); pg 160 (1877 Feb 10); pg 162 (1877 Feb 14); pg 164 (1877 Mar 10); pg 167 (1877 Mar 24); pg 170 (1877 Apr 21); pg 170 (1877 April 28); pg

171 (1877 May 12); pg 172 (1877 May 26); pg 176 (1877 June 23); pg 179 (1877 July 18); pg 183 (1877 Sept 1); pg 183 (1877 Sept 5); pg 186 (1877 Sept 22); pg 193 (1877 Dec 8); pg 195 (1877 Dec 8); pg 199 (1878 Jan 12); pg 202 (1878 Jan 26); pg 217 (1878 Apr 13); pg 239 (1878 Nov 23); pg 240 (1878 Nov 23); pg 240 (1878 Dec 14); pg 242 (1878 Dec 14); pg 243 (1878 Dec 28); pg 244 (1879 Jan 11); pg 246 (1879 Jan 25); pg 247 (1879 Feb 8); pg 249 (1879 Feb 22); pg 250 (1879 Mar 8); pg 251 (1879 Mar 22); pg 253 (1879 Apr 12); pg 256 (1879 Apr 26); pg 257 (1879 Apr 26); pg 259 (1879 May 12); pg 259 (1879 May 24); pg 260 (1879 May 24); pg 272 (1879 July 26); pg 273 (1879 July 26); pg 273 (1879 Aug 9); pg 275 (1879 Aug 23); pg 276 (1879 Aug 23); pg 279 (1879 Sept 13); pg 280 (1879 Sept 13) elected to attend the Grand Lodge in Denver as proxy; pg 281 (1879 Sept 27); pg 282 (1879 Sept 27)

Titcomb, John S

appears as: Titcomb; Titcomb, J S; Titcomb, John S

offices held: WM, SD, Secy, JW, SW, JD

pg 2 (1873 Nov 22); pg 19 (1874 Feb 28); pg 54 (1874 Dec 12) bill presented for plot of cemetery; pg 63 (1875 Feb 27) petitioner of Occidental Lodge No. 20 of Greeley, Colo Terr; pg 67 (1875 Mar 27); pg 70 (1875 May 8); pg 71 (1875 May 22); pg 72 (1875 June 12); pg 74 (1875 June 26); pg 75 (1875 July 10); pg 78 (1875 July 27); pg 80 (1875 Aug 14); pg 81 (1875 Aug 7); pg 81 (1875 Aug 28); pg 82 (1875 Aug 28); pg 83 (1875 Aug 28) appointed Secretary to finish the term in the Secretary's absence; pg 83 (1875 Sept 1); pg 84 (1875 Sept 1); pg 84 (1875 Sept 11); pg 85 (1875 Sept 11) proxy to the Grand Lodge; pg 86 (1875 Sept 11); pg 86 (1875 Sept 16); pg 87 (1875 Sept 25); pg 88 (1875 Sept 25); pg 89 (1875 Sept 25); pg 90 (1875 Oct 9); pg 91 (1875 Oct 9); pg 91 (1875 Oct 20); pg 92 (1875 Oct 20); pg 92 (1875 Oct 23); pg 94 (1875 Oct 23); pg 94 (1875 Nov 13); pg 95 (1875 Nov 13); pg 96 (1875 Nov 27); pg 97 (1875 Nov 27); pg 98 (1875 Dec 3); pg 99 (1875 Dec 11); pg 98 (1875 Dec 11); pg 100 (1875 Dec 11); pg 101 (1875 Dec 11); pg 102 (1875 Dec 12); pg 102 (1875 Dec 12); pg 103 (1875 Dec 25); pg 106 (1875 Dec 25); pg 107 (1876 Jan 8); pg 108 (1876 Jan 8); pg 109 (1876 Jan 8); pg 110 (1876 Jan 2_); pg 112 (1876 Jan 2_); pg 112 (1876 Feb 12); pg 113 (1876 Feb 12); pg 114 (1876 Feb 12); pg 115 (1876 Feb 26); pg 116 (1876 Feb 26); pg 117 (1876 Mar 11); pg 118 (1876 Mar 11); pg 119 (1876 Mar 25) bill presented for guilding the "G" and telegrams; pg 120 (1876 Mar 25); pg 121 (1876 Mar 25); pg 121 (1876 April 1); pg 122 (1876 Apr 8); pg 122 (1876 April 1); pg 123 (1876 Apr 8); pg 124 (1876 Apr 8); pg 124 (1876 Apr 10); pg 126 (1876 May 13); pg 130 (1876 May 13); pg 131 (1876 May 16); pg 132 (1876 Mar 27); pg 133 (1876 Mar 27); pg 134 (1876 May 31); pg 134 (1876 June 3); pg 135 (1876 June 3); pg 135 (1876 June 10); pg 136 (1876 June 10); pg 137 (1876 June 10); pg 137 (1876 June 17); pg 138 (1876 June 24); pg 139 (1876 June 24); pg 140 (1876 July 8); pg 141 (1876 July 8); pg 141 (1876 July 22); pg 142 (1876 July 22); pg 142 (1876 July 29); pg 143 (1876 July 29); pg 143 (1876 Aug 26); pg 144 (1876 Oct 14); pg 145 (1876 Oct 14); pg 147 (1876 Oct 14); pg 147 (1876 Oct 28); pg 148 (1876 Oct 28); pg 148 (1876 Nov 11); pg 149 (1876 Nov 11); pg 149 (1876 Nov 25); pg 150 (1876 Nov 25); pg 151 (1876 Dec 2); pg 152 (1876 Dec 9); pg 153 (1876 Dec 9); pg 154 (1876 Dec 9); pg 154 (1876 Dec 12); pg 155 (1876 Dec 12); pg 155 (1876 Dec 23); pg 156 (1876 Dec 23); pg 157 (1877 Jan 13); pg 158 (1877 Jan 28); pg 151 (1876 Nov 25); pg 151 (1876 Dec 2); pg 160 (1877 Feb 10); pg 162 (1877 Feb 14) performed the ceremonies at the cemetery; pg 163 (1877 Feb 24); pg 164 (1877 Mar 10); pg 166 (1877 Mar 17); pg 167 (1877 Mar 24); pg 171 (1877 May 12); pg 173 (1877 May 26); pg 174 (1877 June 9); pg 176 (1877 June 23); pg 177 (1877 July 14); pg 181 (1877 Aug 11); pg 183 (1877 Sept 5); pg 185 (1877 Sept 8); pg 188 (1877 Oct 27); pg 193 (1877 Dec 8); pg 195 (1877 Dec 8); pg 197 (1877 Dec 19); pg 199 (1878 Jan 12); pg 201 (1878 Jan 12); pg 207 (1878 Feb 23); pg 209 (1878 Feb 27) ceremonies at the cemetery performed by J S Titcomb; pg 217 (1878 Apr 13); pg 218 (1878 Apr 13); pg 226 (1878 June 22) motion to pay $67 for surveying the cemetery; pg 227 (1878 June 22); pg 231 (1878 Aug 24); pg 232 (1878 Sept 14); pg 233 (1878 Sept 14); pg 234 (1878

Oct 12); pg 235 (1878 Oct 26); pg 237 (1878 Nov 9); pg 239 (1878 Nov 23); pg 240 (1878 Nov 23); pg 240 (1878 Dec 14); pg 242 (1878 Dec 14); pg 243 (1878 Dec 28); pg 244 (1878 Dec 28); pg 244 (1879 Jan 11); pg 245 (1879 Jan 11) bill presented for ball expenses; pg 246 (1879 Jan 25); pg 247 (1879 Jan 25); pg 247 (1879 Feb 8); pg 248 (1879 Feb 8); pg 249 (1879 Feb 22); pg 250 (1879 Mar 8); pg 251 (1879 Mar 8); pg 251 (1879 Mar 22); pg 252 (1879 Mar 22); pg 253 (1879 Apr 12); pg 255 (1879 Apr 12); pg 255 (1879 Apr 17); pg 256 (1879 Apr 26); pg 257 (1879 Apr 26); pg 257 (1879 May 10); pg 258 (1879 May 10); pg 259 (1879 May 24); pg 260 (1879 May 24); pg 262 (1879 May 24); pg 263 (1879 June 10); pg 264 (1879 June 14); pg 265 (1879 June 14); pg 266 (1879 June 28); pg 270 (1879 June 28); pg 281 (1879 Sept 27); pg 282 (1879 Sept 27); pg 283 (1879 Sept 27)

Trevastor, Thomas J
pg 88 (1875 Sept 25); pg 113 (1876 Feb 12) *did not become a member of the Columbia Lodge

Trewewail, Edwin
pg 125 (1876 Apr 22) Washington Lodge No. 12

Trury, John
pg 110 (1876 Jan 2_) Washington Lodge No. 12

Turner, Charles
appears as: Turner; Turner, Charles
offices held: Marshall; WM, JW, SD, Treas, JD
pg 9 (1873 Dec 27) petitioner from Amity Lodge No. 323, NY; pg 14 (1874 Jan 24); pg 22 (1874 Mar 14); pg 52 (1874 Dec 5); pg 79 (1875 Aug 14); pg 98 (1875 Dec 11); pg 101 (1875 Dec 11); pg 102 (1875 Dec 12); pg 119 (1876 Mar 25); pg 121 (1876 Mar 25); pg 125 (1876 Apr 22); pg 126 (1876 May 13); pg 127 (1876 May 13); pg 130 (1876 May 13); pg 134 (1876 May 31); pg 138 (1876 June 24); pg 151 (1876 Dec 2); pg 152 (1876 Dec 9); pg 153 (1876 Dec 9); pg 155 (1876 Dec 23); pg 156 (1876 Dec 23); pg 157 (1877 Jan 13); pg 158 (1877 Jan 28); pg 159 (1877 Jan 28); pg 160 (1877 Feb 10); pg 161 (1877 Feb 10) motion to pay $8250 for lot 12, block 97; pg 163 (1877 Feb 24); pg 164 (1877 Mar 10); pg 166 (1877 Mar 17); pg 167 (1877 Mar 24); pg 168 (1877 Apr 14); pg 170 (1877 Apr 21); pg 171 (1877 April 28); pg 171 (1877 May 12); pg 172 (1877 May 26); pg 174 (1877 June 9); pg 176 (1877 June 23); pg 177 (1877 July 14); pg 178 (1877 July 14) motion to write to Wood County Lodge No. 112, OH on behalf of brother John M Davis; pg 183 (1877 Sept 1); pg 183 (1877 Sept 5); pg 184 (1877 Sept 8); pg 188 (1877 Oct 27); pg 189 (1877 Oct 27); pg 189 (1877 Nov 10); pg 190 (1877 Nov 10); pg 191 (1877 Nov 20); pg 192 (1877 Nov 20); pg 193 (1877 Dec 8); pg 194 (1877 Dec 8); pg 195 (1877 Dec 8); pg 196 (1877 Dec 8); pg 199 (1878 Jan 12); pg 202 (1878 Jan 26); pg 204 (1878 Feb 9); pg 206 (1878 Feb 13); pg 209 (1878 Feb 27) motion to extend thanks to the visiting members in attendance at the funeral; pg 211 (1878 Mar 9); pg 212 (1878 Mar 9); pg 214 (1878 Mar 15); pg 215 (1878 Mar 23); pg 217 (1878 Apr 13); pg 219 (1878 Apr 27); pg 221 (1878 May 11); pg 223 (1878 May 25); pg 225 (1878 June 8); pg 226 (1878 June 22); pg 228 (1878 July 27); pg 229 (1878 Aug 10); pg 230 (1878 Aug 10); pg 232 (1878 Sept 14); pg 235 (1878 Oct 26); pg 240 (1878 Dec 14); pg 242 (1878 Dec 14); pg 244 (1879 Jan 11); pg 245 (1879 Jan 11); pg 246 (1879 Jan 25); pg 247 (1879 Feb 8); pg 257 (1879 May 10); pg 259 (1879 May 12); pg 259 (1879 May 24); pg 260 (1879 May 24); pg 262 (1879 May 24); pg 262 (1879 May 27); pg 263 (1879 June 10); pg 264 (1879 June 14); pg 266 (1879 June 28); pg 271 (1879 July 12); pg 272 (1879 July 26); pg 273 (1879 July 26); pg 273 (1879 Aug 9); pg 275 (1879 Aug 23); pg 276 (1879 Aug 23); pg 278 (1879 Aug 29); pg 279 (1879 Sept 13); pg 281 (1879 Sept 27); pg 282 (1879 Sept 27); pg 283 (1879 Sept 30)

Turner, Lewis E
pg 76 (1875 July 24) Washington Lodge No. 12

Turner, W H
pg 69 (1875 Apr 24) Black Hawk Lodge No. 11

Tuttle, Capt A A
pg 168 (1877 Apr 14) warning from Las Animas Lodge No. 28 that this man is a dead beat

Tuttle, Cephas
pg 111 (1876 Jan 2_) Pueblo Lodge No. 17; pg 112 (1876 Feb 12) Pueblo Lodge No. 17

Tyrell, Norman J
appears as: Tyrell; Tyrell, N J
offices held: SS, JS
pg 10 (1873 Dec 27); pg 13 (1874 Jan 10); pg 14 (1874 Jan 24); pg 18 (1874 Feb 20); pg 26 (1874 Mar 28); pg 42 (1874 Aug 15); pg 52 (1874 Dec 5); pg 56 (1874 Dec 19); pg 57 (1874 Dec 26); pg 59 (1875 Jan 9); pg 60 (1875 Jan 23); pg 63 (1875 Feb 13); pg 101 (1875 Dec 11); pg 154 (1876 Dec 9); pg 155 (1876 Dec 12); pg 196 (1877 Dec 8); pg 245 (1879 Jan 11); pg 250 (1879 Mar 8) communication from N J Tyrell from Silver Cliff stating that brother H C Samuels, a member of the lodge, was sick and destitute and asking for aid on his behalf

Underwood, Henry M
pg 26 (1874 Mar 28) bill presented for ledgers; pg 27 (1874 Mar 28) brother of Kenosha, WI

Urso, Camilla
pg 251 (1879 Mar 22) lodge dismissed to attend the concert of Camilla Urso, the celebrated violinist

Van Deren, Archibald J
appears as: Van Deren; Van Deren, A J
pg 126 (1876 May 13); pg 145 (1876 Oct 14); pg 190 (1877 Nov 10)

Van Fleet, Charles G
appears as: Van Fleet; Van Fleet, Charles G
pg 237 (1878 Nov 9); pg 241 (1878 Dec 14); pg 243 (1878 Dec 28); pg 255 (1879 Apr 17); pg 273 (1879 Aug 9); pg 276 (1879 Aug 23); pg 281 (1879 Sept 27)

Van Riper, Cornelius
appears as: Van Riper; Van Riper C
offices held: SD, JD, JW, Treas
pg 1 (1873 Nov 8); pg 4 (1873 Dec 13); pg 14 (1874 Jan 24); pg 16 (1874 Feb 14); pg 19 (1874 Feb 28); pg 25 (1874 Mar 28); pg 26 (1874 Mar 28) petitioner of N___ Station Lodge No. 682 of NY, communication from Lodge No 682, NY about his standing; pg 31 (1874 Apr 25); pg 32 (1874 Apr 25); pg 33 (1874 Apr 25); pg 36 (1874 June 27); pg 37 (1874 June 27); pg 38 (1874 July 11); pg 42 (1874 Aug 22); pg 43 (1874 Sept 12); pg 46 (1874 Oct 10); pg 57 (1874 Dec 26); pg 62 (1875 Feb 13); pg 67 (1875 Apr 10); pg 73 (1875 June 12); pg 94 (1875 Nov 13); pg 101 (1875 Dec 11); pg 172 (1877 May 12); pg 257 (1879 May 10)

Van Valkenberg, see Van Valkenburg, R J

Van Valkenberg, R J
appears as: Van Valkenberg, R J; Van Valkenburg, R J; Van Vaulkenberg
pg 14 (1874 Jan 24); pg 29 (1874 Apr 10); pg 69 (1875 Apr 24) committee to draft resolutions for Samuel Renslow, deceased; pg 188 (1877 Oct 13); pg 210 (1878 Mar 5)

Van, Clay M
appears as: Van; Van, C M; Van, Clay M
offices held: JW, SD, Secy, SW, JD, Steward, SS
pg 1 (1873 Nov 8); pg 2 (1873 Nov 22); pg 4 (1873 Dec 13); pg 8 (1873 Dec 13); pg 9 (1873 Dec 27); pg 10 (1873 Dec 27); pg 14 (1874 Jan 24); pg 15 (1874 Jan 27); pg 16 (1874 Feb 14); pg 18 (1874 Feb 20); pg 19 (1874 Feb 28); pg 20 (1874 Mar 14); pg 23 (1874 Mar 19); pg 24 (1874 Mar 26); pg 25 (1874 Mar 28); pg 26 (1874 Mar 28); pg 28 (1874 Apr 4); pg 29 (1874 Apr 10); pg 31 (1874 Apr 25); pg 33 (1874 May 7); pg 36 (1874 May 23); pg 38 (1874 June 27); pg 39 (1874 July 28); pg 40 (1874 Aug 1); pg 40 (1874 Aug 8); pg 42 (1874 Aug 15); pg 46 (1874 Oct 10); pg 47 (1874 Oct 14); pg 48 (1874 Oct 24); pg 48 (1874 Nov 14); pg 49 (1874 Nov 18); pg 50 (1874 Nov 28); pg 52 (1874 Dec 5); pg 53 (1874 Dec 12); pg 55 (1874 Dec 12); pg 56 (1874 Dec 19); pg 56 (1874 Dec 26); pg 58 (1874 Dec 26); pg 59 (1875 Jan 9); pg 60 (1875 Jan 23); pg 63 (1875 Feb 27); pg 64 (1875 Feb 27); pg 64 (1875 Mar 11); pg 65 (1875 Mar 13); pg 66 (1875 Mar 27); pg 68 (1875 Apr 24); pg 69 (1875 Apr 24); pg 70 (1875 May 8); pg 73 (1875 June 26); pg 75 (1875 July 10); pg 76 (1875 July 24); pg 76 (1875 July 24); pg 81 (1875 Aug 7); pg 82 (1875 Aug 28); pg 87 (1875 Sept 25); pg 88 (1875 Sept 25); pg 89 (1875 Sept 27); pg 90 (1875 Oct 1); pg 90 (1875 Oct 9); pg 91 (1875 Oct 9); pg 91 (1875 Oct 20); pg 92 (1875 Oct 23); pg 93 (1875 Oct 23); pg 94 (1875 Nov 13); pg 95 (1875 Nov 13); pg 96 (1875 Nov 27); pg 97 (1875 Nov 27); pg 98 (1875 Dec 3); pg 101 (1875 Dec 11); pg 102 (1875 Dec 12); pg 103 (1875 Dec 25); pg 107 (1876 Jan 8); pg 108 (1876 Jan 8); pg 110 (1876 Jan 19); pg 112 (1876 Feb 12); pg 113 (1876 Feb 12); pg 114 (1876

Feb 16); pg 115 (1876 Feb 26); pg 116 (1876 Mar 4); pg 117 (1876 Mar 11); pg 118 (1876 Mar 11); pg 119 (1876 Mar 25); pg 121 (1876 April 1); pg 122 (1876 Apr 8); pg 123 (1876 Apr 8); pg 124 (1876 Apr 10); pg 125 (1876 Apr 22); pg 132 (1876 Mar 27); pg 134 (1876 May 31); pg 134 (1876 June 3); pg 267 (1879 June 28); pg 274 (1879 Aug 9); pg 276 (1879 Aug 23) granted a demit, and dues remitted

Vance, Emery J
pg 79 (1875 Aug 14) Central Lodge No. 6

Vandework, Elmer
pg 163 (1877 Feb 24) Collins Lodge No. 19

Veach
pg 148 (1876 Nov 11) Pueblo Lodge No. 17

Vincent, Benson, T
pg 79 (1875 Aug 14) Central Lodge No. 6

Wait, Mrs A L
pg 120 (1876 Mar 25) communication from Trio Lodge No. 57 of Rock Island, IL in reference to the case of Mrs A L Wait of Sunshine

Walch, A L
pg 275 (1879 Aug 23) bill presented for a lamp shade and wicks

Waldron, John M
pg 96 (1875 Nov 27) Huerfano Lodge No. 27

Walker, George
pg 63 (1875 Feb 27) Washington Lodge No. 12; pg 104 (1875 Dec 25) Washington Lodge No. 12

Walker, Thomas C
appears as: Walker; Walker, T C; Walker, Thomas C
pg 31 (1874 Apr 25); pg 34 (1874 May 9); pg 41 (1874 Aug 8); pg 42 (1874 Aug 15); pg 44 (1874 Sept 12); pg 76 (1875 July 24); pg 77 (1875 July 24); pg 79 (1875 Aug 14); pg 80 (1875 Aug 14); pg 87 (1875 Sept 25); pg 88 (1875 Sept 25); pg 114 (1876 Feb 12); pg 187 (1877 Sept 22); pg 233 (1878 Sept 14); pg 268 (1879 June 28); pg 268 (1879 June 28); pg 277 (1879 Aug 23)

Wallace, [George or William J]
pg 209 (1878 Feb 27); pg 225 (1878 June 8) motion to print the sermon of Bro Wallace given on Sunday the 2nd of June in the interests of masonry; pg 237 (1878 Nov 9)

Wallace, George
pg 228 (1878 July 27); pg 229 (1878 July 27) to deliver the lecture at the next Grand Lodge; pg 232 (1878 Sept 14); pg 233 (1878 Sept 14); pg 245 (1879 Jan 11); pg 255 (1879 Apr 17)

Wallace, William J
appears as: Wallace, W J; Wallace; Wallace, William J
offices held: JS, JD, SS
pg 4 (1873 Dec 13); pg 8 (1873 Dec 13); pg 10 (1873 Dec 27); pg 16 (1874 Feb 14); pg 18 (1874 Feb 20); pg 20 (1874 Mar 14); pg 23 (1874 Mar 14); pg 25 (1874 Mar 28); pg 29 (1874 Apr 10); pg 55 (1874 Dec 12); pg 71 (1875 May 8); pg 72 (1875 May 22); pg 73 (1875 June 12); pg 112 (1876 Jan 2_); pg 208 (1878 Feb 23); pg 246 (1879 Jan 25); pg 267 (1879 June 28); pg 271 (1879 July 12); pg 272 (1879 July 12)

Walter, Thomas D
pg 10 (1873 Dec 27); pg 11 (1873 Dec 27); pg 15 (1874 Jan 27); pg 32 (1874 Apr 25); pg 33 (1874 Apr 25); pg 34 (1874 May 9); pg 35 (1874 May 16); pg 72 (1875 May 22);

Walters, John
pg 31 (1874 Apr 25) Doric Lodge U.D.

Wangelin & Tilney
pg 250 (1879 Mar 8) bill presented for printing

Ward, Ross
pg 64 (1875 Feb 27) paid for 1/4 cemetery lot

Warrant, J H
pg 22 (1874 Mar 14) Pueblo Lodge No. 17

Warren, Thomas F
pg 53 (1874 Dec 12) Nevada Lodge No. 4

Warren, W D L
pg 279 (1879 Sept 13) Las Animas Lodge No. 28

Washburn, Hiram E
appears as: Washburn; Washburn, H E; Washburne, H E
offices held: Secy, Treas, SW
pg 210 (1878 Mar 5); pg 246 (1879 Jan 25); pg 251 (1879 Mar 22); pg 255 (1879 Apr 17); pg 259 (1879 May 12); pg 262 (1879 May 24) refreshments provided by Bro Hiram E Washburn; pg 278 (1879 Aug 29); pg 283 (1879 Sept 30); pg 284 (1879 Sept 30)

Wilson, [Benjamin F or John M]
pg 110 (1876 Jan 2_); pg 112 (1876 Feb 12); pg 116 (1876 Mar 4); pg 132 (1876 Mar 27); pg 134 (1876 May 31); pg 158 (1877 Jan 28); pg 159 (1877 Jan 28); pg 160 (1877 Feb 10); pg 163 (1877 Feb 24); pg 166 (1877 Mar 17); pg 167 (1877 Mar 24); pg 172 (1877 May 26); pg 184 (1877 Sept 8); pg 186 (1877 Sept 22); pg 189 (1877 Nov 10); pg 191 (1877 Nov 20); pg 202 (1878 Jan 26); pg 207 (1878 Feb 23); pg 211 (1878 Mar 9); pg 212 (1878 Mar 9); pg 215 (1878 Mar 23); pg 240 (1878 Dec 14); pg 261 (1879 May 24)

Wilson, Benjamin F
appears as: Wilson, B F
offices held: JS, Tiler
pg 108 (1876 Jan 8); pg 113 (1876 Feb 12); pg 114 (1876 Feb 16); pg 117 (1876 Mar 11); pg 118 (1876 Mar 11); pg 120 (1876 Mar 25); pg 121 (1876 April 1); pg 122 (1876 April 1); pg 122 (1876 Apr 8); pg 126 (1876 May 13); pg 134 (1876 June 3); pg 135 (1876 June 10); pg 137 (1876 June 17); pg 138 (1876 June 24); pg 141 (1876 July 22); pg 142 (1876 July 29); pg 145 (1876 Oct 14); pg 149 (1876 Nov 25); pg 151 (1876 Dec 2); pg 152 (1876 Dec 9); pg 154 (1876 Dec 9); pg 164 (1877 Mar 10); pg 168 (1877 Apr 14); pg 176 (1877 June 23); pg 193 (1877 Dec 8); pg 196 (1877 Dec 8); pg 253 (1879 Apr 12) communication from Lovelaceville, KY enquiring about brother B F Wilson; pg 269 (1879 June 28); pg 277 (1879 Aug 23)

Wilson, Frank
offices held: JD, Tiler
pg 225 (1878 June 8); pg 227 (1878 July 13)

Wilson, John M
appears as: Wilson, J M; Wilson, John M; Willson, J M; Willson, John M
offices held: WM, SD, SW, Tiler, Treas, JW
pg 1 (1873 Nov 8); pg 2 (1873 Nov 22); pg 3 (1873 Nov 22); pg 4 (1873 Dec 13); pg 8 (1873 Dec 13); pg 10 (1873 Dec 27); pg 12 (1874 Jan 10); pg 14 (1874 Jan 24); pg 15 (1874 Jan 27); pg 16 (1874 Feb 14); pg 16 (1874 Feb 14); pg 19 (1874 Feb 28); pg 23 (1874 Mar 19); pg 24 (1874 Mar 26); pg 25 (1874 Mar 28); pg 31 (1874 Apr 25); pg 33 (1874 May 7); pg 34 (1874 May 9); pg 35 (1874 May 16); pg 36 (1874 May 23); pg 36 (1874 June 27); pg 37 (1874 June 27); pg 38 (1874 July 11); pg 39 (1874 July 28); pg 40 (1874 Aug 1); pg 40 (1874 Aug 8); pg 42 (1874 Aug 15); pg 42 (1874 Aug 22); pg 44 (1874 Sept 12); pg 44 (1874 Sept 26); pg 45 (1874 Sept 26) delegate to the Grand Lodge; pg 46 (1874 Oct 10); pg 47 (1874 Oct 14); pg 47 (1874 Oct 24); pg 48 (1874 Nov 14); pg 49 (1874 Nov 18); pg 50 (1874 Nov 28); pg 52 (1874 Dec 5); pg 53 (1874 Dec 12); pg 55 (1874 Dec 12); pg 56 (1874 Dec 19); pg 58 (1874 Dec 26); pg 59 (1875 Jan 9); pg 60 (1875 Jan 23); pg 67 (1875 Apr 10); pg 68 (1875 Apr 24); pg 69 (1875 Apr 24); pg 70 (1875 May 8); pg 71 (1875 May 22); pg 72 (1875 June 12); pg 73 (1875 June 12); pg 75 (1875 July 10); pg 76 (1875 July 24); pg 78 (1875 July 27); pg 78 (1875 July 29); pg 79 (1875 Aug 14); pg 81 (1875 Aug 7); pg 81 (1875 Aug 28); pg 83 (1875 Sept 1); pg 84 (1875 Sept 11); pg 86 (1875 Sept 16); pg 87 (1875 Sept 25); pg 88 (1875 Sept 25); pg 89 (1875 Sept 27); pg 90 (1875 Oct 1); pg 90 (1875 Oct 9); pg 91 (1875 Oct 20); pg 92 (1875 Oct 23); pg 94 (1875 Nov 13); pg 96 (1875 Nov 27); pg 98 (1875 Dec 3); pg 98 (1875 Dec 11); pg 102 (1875 Dec 12); pg 103 (1875 Dec 12); pg 103 (1875 Dec 25); pg 106 (1875 Dec 27); pg 107 (1876 Jan 8); pg 108 (1876 Jan 8); pg 110 (1876 Jan 19); pg 114 (1876 Feb 16); pg 115 (1876 Feb 26); pg 115 (1876 Feb 26); pg 119 (1876 Mar 25); pg 121 (1876 April 1); pg 122 (1876 Apr 8); pg 123 (1876 Apr 8); pg 134 (1876 June 3); pg 136 (1876 June 10); pg 137 (1876 June 17); pg 138 (1876 June 24); pg 139 (1876 June 24); pg 142 (1876 July 29); pg 144 (1876 Sept 16); pg 145 (1876 Oct 14); pg 146 (1876 Oct 14); pg 151 (1876 Dec 2); pg 152 (1876 Dec 9); pg 155 (1876 Dec 23); pg 160 (1877 Feb 10); pg 160 (1877 Feb 10); pg 163 (1877 Feb 24); pg 164 (1877 Mar 10); pg 165 (1877 Mar 10); pg 168 (1877 Apr 14); pg 169 (1877 Apr 14); pg 183 (1877 Sept 1); pg 187 (1877 Sept 22); pg 187 (1877 Oct 13); pg 188 (1877 Oct 13); pg 193 (1877 Dec 8); pg 193 (1877 Dec 8); pg 203 (1878 Jan 26) motion to provide brother Lewis Neill with $5 per week until the next regular meeting of the lodge; pg 216 (1878 Mar 23); pg 223 (1878 May 25); pg 234 (1878 Oct 12); pg 235 (1878 Oct 26); pg

241 (1878 Dec 14); pg 243 (1878 Dec 28); pg 245 (1879 Jan 11); pg 246 (1879 Jan 25); pg 253 (1879 Apr 12); pg 256 (1879 Apr 26); pg 257 (1879 Apr 26); pg 257 (1879 May 10); pg 259 (1879 May 12); pg 259 (1879 May 24); pg 262 (1879 May 24); pg 262 (1879 May 27); pg 263 (1879 June 10); pg 264 (1879 June 14); pg 266 (1879 June 28); pg 275 (1879 Aug 23); pg 277 (1879 Aug 23); pg 278 (1879 Aug 29); pg 281 (1879 Sept 27); pg 283 (1879 Sept 30)

Wimer, John A

appears as: Wimer; Wimer, J A;
offices held: JD, SS, JS, Steward
pg 28 (1874 Apr 4); pg 40 (1874 Aug 8); pg 47 (1874 Oct 10); pg 55 (1874 Dec 12); pg 58 (1874 Dec 26); pg 62 (1875 Feb 13); pg 67 (1875 Apr 10); pg 78 (1875 July 29); pg 81 (1875 Aug 7); pg 87 (1875 Sept 25); pg 88 (1875 Sept 25); pg 91 (1875 Oct 20); pg 94 (1875 Nov 13); pg 98 (1875 Dec 3); pg 100 (1875 Dec 11); pg 101 (1875 Dec 11); pg 103 (1875 Dec 25); pg 110 (1876 Jan 19); pg 112 (1876 Feb 12); pg 116 (1876 Mar 4); pg 126 (1876 May 13); pg 134 (1876 May 31); pg 134 (1876 June 3); pg 135 (1876 June 10); pg 138 (1876 June 24); pg 144 (1876 Oct 14); pg 146 (1876 Oct 14); pg 157 (1877 Jan 13); pg 160 (1877 Feb 10); pg 166 (1877 Mar 17); pg 170 (1877 April 28); pg 191 (1877 Nov 20); pg 193 (1877 Dec 8); pg 195 (1877 Dec 8); pg 240 (1878 Dec 14); pg 242 (1878 Dec 14); pg 254 (1879 Apr 12)

Wolff, Mrs

pg 67 (1875 Mar 27) purchased cemetery lot

Wood, Gardner P

appears as: Wood; Wood, G P; Wood, Gardner P
offices held: JD
pg 12 (1874 Jan 10); pg 13 (1874 Jan 10); pg 28 (1874 Apr 4); pg 48 (1874 Oct 24); pg 61 (1875 Jan 23); pg 62 (1875 Feb 13); pg 83 (1875 Sept 1); pg 152 (1876 Dec 9); pg 154 (1876 Dec 9); pg 205 (1878 Feb 9); pg 240 (1878 Dec 14); pg 242 (1878 Dec 14); pg 270 (1879 June 28)

Woodruff & Squires

pg 175 (1877 June 9) to provide material help to the Fullerton family and send bills to the lodge; pg 176 (1877 June 23) bill presented for merchandise for Mrs Fullerton

Woodward, Robert J

appears as: Woodward, R J
pg 30 (1874 Apr 10) bill presented for stamps; pg 58 (1874 Dec 26) bill presented; pg 75 (1875 July 10) bill presented for stationery, postage, stamps; pg 10 (1873 Dec 27) bill presented for postage stamps; pg 163 (1877 Feb 24) bill for stamps; pg 167 (1877 Mar 24) bill presented for envelopes; pg 172 (1877 May 12) bill presented for envelopes; pg 178 (1877 July 14) bill presented

Woodward, William

pg 162 (1877 Feb 14) committee to ascertain the lodge where he belonged; pg 162 (1877 Feb 14) lodge convened to attend the funeral of this brother, deceased, a member of a lodge in MN

Wright, Alpheus

appears as: Wright; Wright, Alpheus; Wright, A
offices held: WM, Treas, SD, SW, JW, Secy, JD
pg 1 (1873 Nov 8); pg 4 (1873 Dec 13); pg 24 (1874 Mar 26); pg 26 (1874 Mar 28); pg 28 (1874 Apr 4); pg 29 (1874 Apr 4); pg 33 (1874 May 7); pg 36 (1874 June 27); pg 38 (1874 June 27); pg 41 (1874 Aug 8); pg 40 (1874 Aug 1); pg 45 (1874 Sept 26) elected to be an alternate delegate to the Grand Lodge in Denver on the 29th of September; pg 48 (1874 Nov 14); pg 52 (1874 Dec 5); pg 53 (1874 Dec 12); pg 55 (1874 Dec 12); pg 56 (1874 Dec 26); pg 57 (1874 Dec 26); pg 58 (1874 Dec 26); pg 59 (1875 Jan 9); pg 64 (1875 Mar 11); pg 65 (1875 Mar 13); pg 69 (1875 Apr 24); pg 70 (1875 Apr 24); pg 70 (1875 May 8); pg 71 (1875 May 8); pg 74 (1875 June 26); pg 75 (1875 July 10); pg 76 (1875 July 24); pg 81 (1875 Aug 7); pg 81 (1875 Aug 28); pg 83 (1875 Sept 1); pg 84 (1875 Sept 11); pg 85 (1875 Sept 11) proxy to the Grand Lodge; pg 86 (1875 Sept 16); pg 87 (1875 Sept 25); pg 88 (1875 Sept 25); pg 90 (1875 Oct 1); pg 91 (1875 Oct 9); pg 95 (1875 Nov 13); pg 96 (1875 Nov 27); pg 97 (1875 Nov 27); pg 98 (1875 Dec 3); pg 98 (1875 Dec 11); pg 100 (1875 Dec 11); pg 101 (1875 Dec 11); pg 102 (1875 Dec 12); pg 103 (1875 Dec 12); pg 103 (1875 Dec 25); pg 105 (1875 Dec 25); pg 107 (1876 Jan 8); pg 108 (1876 Jan 8); pg 110 (1876 Jan 2_); pg 111 (1876 Jan 2_); pg 112 (1876 Feb 12); pg 114 (1876 Feb

Columbia Lodge No. 14

Cash Book, 1875–1884

The Cash book shows each dues payment of members plus payments for cemetery lots and bills generated on behalf of the lodge for materials or services. There are several loose leaf pages that were inserted in the volume that did not have page numbers that are also included.

There are a number of places where members are listed as stricken from the rolls. Reasons for being stricken are not always given but include the death of a member or when a member has moved from the area and has been granted a demit from the Lodge.

Dates within the volume are listed year first, followed by month and day. This is an unconventional way to present dates, but it is the method that the Colorado State Archives uses in its databases.

Legend to the listings.

Members
Known members of the Columbia Lodge No. 14.

Possible Members
People who have attended meetings of the membership at the lodge, but who have very few records indicating that they might be a visiting Mason from another lodge. In the following list of Columbia Lodge Masons, those names which could not be determined for certain to have been members have an asterisk before them. There was a list hand-written in pencil that was stuck into the book. The names of these men are also considered possible members.

Boulder
People who were in Boulder but non-members such as members of the Valmont Lodge, St Vrain Lodge, wives of members, deceased Masons who were not members of the lodge, businesses, vendors who provided services to the lodge, etc.

Non-Boulder
These people were mentioned in a commmunication from another lodge and were not associated with the Columbia Lodge.

If there are listings where the correct spelling could not be determined, the listing will contain both spellings, such as **Imil [Imel], David.**

Every effort has been made to assure that these listings are correct, however, extracting hand-written records can be tricky, and some listings may contain inaccuracies. We hope you enjoy as much as we have the discoveries we have made about early Boulder.

— The Boulder Pioneers Project

Members List from the Cash Book

Allison, William H
Ames, Leeman C
Anderson, A A
Anderson, Daniel C
Anderson, David B
Anderson, Erick J
Andrews, Elisha H
Austin, Schuyler D
Banks, Francis B
Bard, Richard
Barney, Royal S
Barney, William M
Barrowman, William
Bartels, Henry
Baum, Henry M
Berger, Andrew E
Beveridge, James
Beveridge, William
Bigger, Robert A
Blake, Frank O
Bock, David
Border, Samuel B
Bradfield, Zachariah
Brainard, Thomas C
Broadie, John
Brookfield, Alfred A
Brown, Samuel C
Brown, Thomas J
Brurrayr
Buchanan, George W
Budd, Sylvanus
Bullard, Frank D
Bunn, David
Bush, Arthur W
Buttles, John F
Calahan, Patrick
Campbell, John L
Campbell, Sanford B
Carmack, Thomas K
Carter, George W
Casey, Robert
Chambers, John S
Chase, Byron E
Chase, George F
Church, John L
Clark, G A
Clow, David
Clow, Richard
Cluff, Chester P
Coffin, Onsville C
Colborn, Joseph
Collie, J
Collins
Collins, R B
Conroy, Pierre
Corning, George C
Corson, William A
Crow, Richard
Cullacott, John J
Darrow, V H
Davey, Joseph J
Davidson, William
Davis, Charles
Davis, David
Davis, John
Dawley, James M
Deitz, Henry
Denham, Thomas
Deyo, R H
Dimick, Erastus H
Dodge, Horace O
Dolloff, John W
Donaldson, Charles B
Dow, J E
Downer, Sylvester S
Drumm, Henry
Dunagan, Elijah
Dunn, James
Earhart, W R
Ellingham, John J
Ellingham, Robert
Ellis, Adelbert L
Farwell, C D
Fonda, George F
Foote, James B
Fox, M P
French, S M
Gilbert, Clark W
Gillam, W H
Glessner, Charles E
Goodwin, N W
Gorman, Michael
Goss, Abel
Green, Henry
Groesbeck, John B
Grund, John C
Gutterson, Charles L
Guyaze, Julius
Halverson, Christian
Harker, Oliver H
Harmon, George D
Harney, Chris
Harris, Addison W
Harris, Barney
Harris, Myers
Harvey, Christopher
Haswell, Theodore
Hathaway, Mark
Henry, Albert T
Henry, Oren H
Henry, Ormal E
Hernandez, Anthony R
Hinkle, John P
Hinman, Fred
Hockaday, Charles N
Holstein, George B
Hopkins, David L
Howse, W J L
Howell, C C
Howell, William R
Howse, W J L
Hunt, Fred A
Hunt, William K
Hutchinson, Daniel J
Hyder, David
Irwin, Joseph
Jackson, George W
Jeffers, Albert
Jester, William
Johns, John H
Johnson, Seymour
Johnson, Thomas C
Johnston, James J
Johnston, William J
Jones, Thomas J
Jones, Thomas R
Juneman, Frederick W
Kelley, James A
Kempton, James
Kerr, David
Kessler, Marion

King, Robert
Kline, Marcus
Knox, John
Kohler, Frederick W
Kroll, Anson
Langley, Thomas
Lawson, Alexander
Lea, Alfred E
Lester, James E
Leyner, Peter A
Lippoldt, Henry
Lockwood, Fred
Longley, Thomas
Low, Theodore
Lowman, E E
Loyd, Joseph
Lytle, George
Maxwell, James P
Mayer, Gottlieb F
McAllister, Ira
McBride, R T
McCaslin, Matthew L
McClure, Edward P
McDowell, John M
McIntosh, Lemuel
Mead, Marcus S
Meginnis, Daniel
Metcalf, Eli P
Meyring, Henry
Michant, Theodore
Mills, Abraham
Minks, George W
Moffett, J C
Mooney, Michael
Nichols, Charles L
Nichols, David H
Nichols, Ezra H
Nicholson, John W
North, James M
O'Hara, William
Owen, Thomas R, Jr
Parlin, David
Paul, Henry
Peryam, William T
Peters, Anson W
Peterson, Andrew
Philippi, Frederick
Phillips, Ives
Phillips, N M
Pitts, Martin J
Pollock, James R
Ritchie, John W
Rittenwater, Alex Jr
Robertson, G B
Robinson, Daniel A
Rogers, Platt
Rouse, Sterling D
Rowen, William F
Ryalls, Thomas
Safely, Alexander F
Samuels, H Clay
Sawdey, Edgar
Schriver, J C
Schroeder, Dederick
Scott, Samuel
Severance, Isaac H
Sheets, Henry W
Sherratt, Charles
Sherwood, Clarence A
Silver, S D
Simpson, John S
Slater, William C
Slaughter, Benjamin H
Slifer, Esrom G
Smith, Azon A
Smith, J Alden
Smith, J W
Smith, Marinus G
Smith, Walter H
Snyder, Hanson
Sommers, Wilhelm
Soule, Albert G
Spencer, Charles L
Squires, George C
Squires, Phineas L
St Clair, Joel F T
Stanton, John A
Stewart, Thomas C
Strasburger, Mathias
Styles, Eugene M
Sutherland, Judson
Tallman, Isaac T
Tarvin, E M
Thomas, Squires J
Tilney, Robert H
Tipple, George L
Titcomb, Hiram R
Titcomb, John S
Turner, Charles
Tyrell, Norman J
Van Fleet, Charles G
Van Riper, Cornelius
Van, Clay M
Viele, James B
Walker, Ed S
Walker, Thomas C
Walker, Thomas D
Wallace, George
Wallace, William J
Welderding, H J
Wellman, Luther C
Wellman, Sylvanus
Wharton, Joseph J
White, David S
White, William W
Whitney, George H
Wigginton, John W
Wilder, Eugene
Wilkins, Cornelius
Williams, George W
Williams, John T
Wilson, Benjamin F
Wilson, George W
Wilson, John M
Wilson, Thomas V
Wimer, John A
Wood, Gardner P
Wright, Alpheus
Yates, Isaiah
Yates, Joseph

Allison, William H
pg 220 (1880 Dec 11) Boulder, payments 11 Dec 1880 - Dec 1884

Ames, Leeman C
appears as: Ames, Leeman C; Ames, L C
pg 12 (1878 Feb 13) paid; pg 12 (1878 Mar 15) paid; pg 12 (1878 Mar 23) paid; pg 13 (1878 Dec 28); pg 16 (1880 Jan 17) paid; pg 186 (1878 Feb 13) Salt Lake City (Denver crossed out), payments 13 Feb 1878 - Dec 1884

Anderson, A A
pg 1 (1875 Oct 1) paid; pg 82 (1875 Oct 1) payment 1 Oct 1875

Anderson, Daniel C
pg 238 (1881 Aug 13) Leadville (Sugar Loaf crossed out), 13 Aug 1881 - Dec 1884

Anderson, David B
appears as: Anderson, D B; Anderson, D B
pg 14 (1879 May 10) paid; pg 15 (1879 Dec 13) paid; pg 198 (1878 Aug 10) Summerville, payments 10 Aug 1878 - Dec 1884

Anderson, Erick J
appears as: Anderson, E J
pg 9 (1877 Feb 10) paid; pg 9 (1877 June 4); pg 10 (1877 Aug 11) paid; pg 11 (1877 Dec 8) paid; pg 13 (1879 Jan 11); pg 16 (1879 Dec 27) paid; pg 170 (1877 Feb 24) Boulder, payments 24 Feb 1877 - 9 Feb 1884

Andrews, Elija H
appears as: Andrews, E H, Andrews, Elisha H
pg 6 (1876 Dec 9) paid; pg 11 (1877 Dec 8) paid; pg 16 (1879 Dec 27) paid; pg 156 (1876 Dec 9) Leadville, payments 9 Dec 1876 - 27 Dec 1879

Austin, E A
pg 14 (1879 Nov 8) cemetery lot; pg 276 (1879 Nov 8) cemetery lot

Austin, Schuyler D
appears as: Austin, A D; Austin, Schuyler D
pg 1 (1875 Nov 27) paid; pg 18 (1880 Aug 14) paid; pg 83 (1875 Dec 11) payments, 11 Dec 1875 - 23 Aug 1879

Aztlan Lodge
pg 3 (1876 Feb 26) paid

B H Lodge #11
pg 13 (1879 Apr 12) cook

Babcock, William
appears as: Babcock, Wm
pg 14 (1879 Nov 8) cemetery lot; pg 276 (1879 Nov 8) cemetery lot

Banks, Francis B
appears as: Banks, F B
pg 226 (1880 Dec 11) payments 11 Dec 1880 - Dec 1884

Bard, Richard
appears as: Bard, R; Bard, Dr
pg 17 (1880 May 22) paid; pg 18 (1880 Oct 23) paid

Barney, Royal S
appears as: Barney, R S; Barney, Royal S
pg 1 (1875 Dec 3) paid; pg 4 (1876 June 10) paid; pg 11 (1877 Dec 8) paid; pg 85 (1875 Dec 11) Boulder, payments 11 Dec 1875 - Dec 1884

Barney, William M
pg 116 (1874 Dec 14) payments 14 Dec 1874 - 8 Dec 1877 - demitted to become a charter member of St Vrain Lodge No. 23

Barrowman, William
pg 12 (1878 Mar 5) paid; pg 187 (1878 Mar 5) Erie, payments 5 Mar 1878 - 20 Sept 1882 - demitted to become a charter member of Garfield Lodge No. 50, Erie

Bartels, Henry
pg 11 (1877 Dec 19) paid; pg 12 (1878 Feb 9) paid; pg 193 (1877 Dec 19) payments 19 Dec 1877 - 10 June 1882

Baum, Henry M
pg 52 (1874 Dec 14) payments 14 Dec 1874 - 24 Nov 1877 - demitted

Ben Hayman Ice
pg loose sheet (1887 Aug 13) bill presented; pg loose sheet (1887 Oct 22) bill presented

Berger, Andrew E
pg 108 (1874 Dec 14) payments 14 Dec 1874 - 28 Aug 1875

Berlin & Co
pg loose sheet (1886 Jan 9) bill for chimneys; pg loose sheet (1886 June 12) bill for taxes

Berlin, Isaac
appears as: Berlin, I
pg 276 (1877 Mar 24) cemetery lot

Bertin, G
pg 9 (1877 Mar 24) 1/4 Cemetery lot

Beveridge, James
appears as: Beverage, James; Beveridge, James
pg 3 (1876 Feb 12) paid; pg 31 (1874 Jan 24) payments 24 Jan 1874 - Dec 1884

Beveridge, William
pg 12 (1878 Mar 9) paid

Bigger, Robert A
pg 274 (1884 May 15) Salina, payments 15 May 1884 - Dec 1884

Black Hawk Lodge
pg 14 (1879 May 12) paid

Blake, Frank O
pg 104 (1884 July 1) payments 1 July 1884 - 22 Nov 1884

Bloomfield, L S
appears as: Bloomfield, L S; Bloomfield
pg 17 (1880 Mar 13) cemetery lot; pg 276 (1880 Mar 13) cemetery lot

Bock, David
pg 142 (1875 Dec 11) payments 11 Dec 1875 - 27 Aug 1881

Border, Samuel B
appears as: Border, S B
pg 259 (1882 Sept 9) Boulder, payments 9 Sept 1882 - Dec 1884

Bottoms, S S
pg 18 (1880 July 10) cemetery lot; pg 18 (1880 Aug 14) cemetery lot; pg 276 (1880 July 10) cemetery lot

Boulder Chapter No. 7
pg 1 (1875 Dec 10) paid; pg 3 (1876 Feb 26) paid; pg 3 (1876 Mar 4) paid; pg 13 (1879 Mar 22) rent; pg 16 (1879 Dec 27) rent; pg 17 (1880 Mar 13) rent; pg 18 (1880 June 12) rent; pg 249 (1882 June 1) payments 1 June 1882 - Dec 1884

Boulder Lodge No. 45
pg loose sheet (1887) rent paid; pg 252 (1882 Apr 1) payments 1 Apr 1882 - Dec 1884

Bradfield, Zachariah
pg 254 (1882 Dec 24) payments 24 Dec 1882 - Dec 1884

Brainard, Thomas C
pg 63 (1875 Apr 10) payment on 10 Apr 1875

Broadie, John
pg 2 (1875 Dec 11) paid; pg 5 (1876 Dec 9) paid; pg 16 (1879 Dec 27) paid; pg 90 (1875 Dec 11) Erie, payments 11 Dec 1875 - Dec 1884

Brookfield, Alfred A
appears as: Brookfield, A A
pg 49 (1873 May 1) payment on 1 May 1873

Brown, S C & Co
pg loose sheet (1887 Dec 10) bill for 6 box lights; pg loose sheet (1886 Dec 27) bill for banquet

Brown, Samuel C
pg 65 (1884 July 1) payments 1 July 1884 - Dec 1884

Brown, Thomas J
appears as: Brown, T J; Brown, Thomas J
pg 9 (1877 Mar 10) paid; pg 10 (1877 June 9) paid; pg 15 (1879 Dec 13) paid; pg 172 (1877 Mar 10) Salina, Newark, NJ, payments 10 May 1877 - 22 Sept 1883 - demitted

Brurrayr [??]
pg 19 (1880 Nov 30) paid

Buchanan, George W
pg 6 (1876 Dec 12) paid; pg 9 (1877 Feb 10) paid; pg 9 (1877 Mar 24) paid; pg 10 (1877 Dec 8) rent; pg 19 (1880 Nov 30) paid; pg 169 (1876 Dec 13) Postseville, Sevier Cty, UT (Jamestown crossed out), payments 13 Dec 1876 - Dec 1884

Budd, Sylvanus
pg 2 (1875 Dec 11) paid; pg 10 (1877 Dec 8) rent; pg 15 (1879 Dec 13) paid; pg 93 (1875 Dec 11) Niwot, payments 11 Dec 1875 - Dec 1884

Bullard, Frank D
pg 245 (1884 Dec 10) payments 10 Dec 1881 - died 29 Oct 1882

Bunn, David
pg 2 (1875 Dec 11) paid; pg 4 (1876 Nov 25) paid; pg 13 (1879 Jan 25); pg 17 (1880 Feb 28)

paid; pg 48 (1873 May 14) payments 14 May 1873 - 27 Aug 1881 - demitted

Bush, Arthur W
appears as: Bush, A W; Bush, Arthur W
pg 4 (1876 Apr 1) paid; pg 5 (1876 Dec 9) paid; pg 68 (1875 Dec 11) Boulder, payments 11 Dec 1875 - 23 Aug 1879

Buttles, John F
pg 164 (1876 Dec 9) payments 9 Dec 1876 - 23 Aug 1879

Calahan, Patrick
appears as: Calahan, Pat; Calahan, Patrick
pg 12 (1878 Mar 9) paid; pg 191 (1878 Mar 9) payments 9 Mar 1878 - 24 Aug 1878

Campbell, John L
appears as: Campbell, John L; Campbell, J L
pg 3 (1876 Feb 16) paid; pg 3 (1876 Mar 4) paid; pg 4 (1876 Apr 1) paid; pg 6 (1876 Dec 9) paid; pg 16 (1879 Dec 27) paid; pg 150 (1876 Feb 16) Red Cliff (Denver crossed out), payments 15 Feb 1876 - Dec 1884

Campbell, Sanford B
appears as: Campbell, S B
pg 4 (1876 Nov 25) paid ; pg 67 (1875 Dec 11) payments 11 Dec 1875 - 25 Nov 1876 - demitted

Carmack, Thomas K
appears as: Carmack, T K; Carmack, Thomas K
pg 84 (1875 Dec 11) Salina, Boulder, payments 11 Dec 1875 - Dec 1884; pg 15 (1879 Dec 13) paid

Carter, George W
pg 97 (1870 June 11) payments, 11 June 1870 - 23 Aug 1879

Casady, see Cassaeday, N

Casey, Robert
pg 164 (1883 Aug 11) payments 11 Aug 1883 - Dec 1884

Cassaeday, N
appears as: Cassaeday, N; Casady, N
pg loose sheet (1887 Mar 12) bill for gasoline; pg loose sheet (1887 Nov 26) bill for gasoline; pg loose sheet (1886 Dec 25) bill for gasoline

Chambers, John S
pg 239 (1881 Apr 9) Louisville, payments 9 Apr 1881 - Dec 1884

Chase, Byron E
pg 231 (1881 Mar 26) Boulder, payments 26 Mar 1881 - Dec 1884

Chase, George F
pg 2 (1875 Dec 11) deposit by Treasurer; pg 3 (1876 Jan 22) deposit by Treasurer; pg 3 (1876 Jan 8) deposit by Treasurer; pg 3 (1876 Feb 12) deposit by Treasurer; pg 3 (1876 Feb 17) deposit by Treasurer; pg 3 (1876 Feb 26) deposit by Treasurer; pg 3 (1876 Mar 11) deposit by Treasurer; pg 4 (1876 Apr 8) deposit by Treasurer; pg 4 (1876 Apr 11) deposit by Treasurer; pg 4 (1876 May 31) deposit by Treasurer; pg 4 (1876 June 3) deposit by Treasurer; pg 4 (1876 June 17) deposit by Treasurer; pg 4 (1876 June 24) deposit by Treasurer; pg 4 (1876 July 22) deposit by Treasurer; pg 4 (1876 July 29) deposit by Treasurer; pg 4 (1876 Nov 11) deposit by Treasurer; pg 5 (1876 Nov 25) deposit by Treasurer; pg 5 (1876 Dec 2) deposit by Treasurer; pg 5 (1876 Dec 9) deposit by Treasurer; pg 6 (1876 Dec 12) deposit by Treasurer; pg 6 (1876 Dec 23) deposit by Treasurer; pg 9 (1877 Feb 10) deposit by Treasurer; pg 9 (1877 Mar 10) deposit by Treasurer; pg 9 (1877 Mar 24) deposit by Treasurer; pg 9 (1877 May 12) deposit by Treasurer; pg 9 (1877 June 8) deposit by Treasurer; pg 10 (1877 Aug 11) deposit by Treasurer; pg 10 (1877 Nov 10) deposit by Treasurer; pg 10 (1877 Dec 22) deposit by Treasurer; pg 11 (1877 Dec 8) paid; pg 12 (1878 Jan 26) deposit by Treasurer; pg 12 (1878 Feb 13) deposit by Treasurer; pg 12 (1878 Mar 9) deposit by Treasurer; pg 12 (1878 Mar 23) deposit by Treasurer; pg 12 (1878 Apr 8) deposit by Treasurer; pg 14 (1879 May 24) deposit by Treasurer; pg 14 (1879 May 31) deposit by Treasurer; pg 14 (1879 June 25) deposit by Treasurer; pg 14 (1879 Oct 25) deposit by Treasurer; pg 14 (1879 Nov 8) deposit by Treasurer; pg 14 (1879 Nov 28) deposit by Treasurer; pg 16 (1879 Dec 13) deposit by Treasurer; pg 16 (1879

Crosby Bros
pg loose sheet (1886 Dec 27) music for banquet

Crow, Richard
pg 2 (1875 Dec 11) paid; pg 16 (1880 Dec 13) paid; pg 43 (1873 Mar 12) Boulder, payments - 12 Mar 1873 - Dec 1884

Cullacott, John J
appears as: Cullicott, J J F; Callicott, J J; Callicott, John J, Cullicott, John J
pg 10 (1877 Oct 27) paid; pg 10 (1877 Nov 10) paid; pg 15 (1879 Dec 13) paid; pg 177 (1877 Oct 27) Salina, payments 27 Oct 1877 - Dec 1884

Darrow, V H
pg 236 (1881 May 31) payment 31 May 1881 - 14 Jan 1884

Davey, Joseph J
pg 161 (1883 Apr 28) payments 28 Apr 1883 - 23 July 1884

Davidson, William
pg 260 (1882 Sept 9) Boulder, payments 9 Sept 1882 - Dec 1884

Davis, Charles
pg 250 (1882 Jan 14) Crisman, payments 14 Jan 1882 - Dec 1884

Davis, David
pg 12 (1878 Mar 23) paid; pg 13 (1879 Mar 26); pg 33 (1874 Apr 4) payments 4 Apr 1874 - Dec 1884

Davis, John
pg 1 (1875 Nov 27) paid; pg 5 (1876 Dec 9) paid; pg 10 (1877 Dec 8) rent; pg 13 (1878 Dec 28); pg 15 (1879 Dcc 13) paid; pg 127 (1875 Dec 11) Valmont, payments 11 Dec 1875 - Dec 1884

Dawley, James M
appears as: Dawley, J M; Dawley, James M
pg 11 (1877 Dec 10) paid; pg 50 (1874 Dec 14) payments 14 Dec 1874 - 8 June 1878 - demitted

Day, C W
appears as: Day, C; Day, C W
pg 17 (1880 May 22) cemetery lot; pg 276 (1880 May 22) cemetery lot

Day, Horatio
appears as: Day, H; Day, Horatio
pg 17 (1880 May 22) cemetery lot; pg 276 (1880 May 22) cemetery lot

Deitz, Henry
appears as: Deitz, Henry; Dietz, Henry
pg 10 (1877 Dec 8) rent; pg 14 (1879 June 21) paid; pg 15 (1879 Dec 13) paid; g 17 (1880 May 22) paid; pg 181 (1877 Dec 8) payments 8 Dec 1877 - 10 Jan 1882 - demitted

Denham, Thomas
pg 14 (1879 June 10) paid; pg 180 (1877 Dec 8) Boulder, payments 8 Dec 1877 - Dec 1884

Deyo, R H
pg 1 (1875 Nov 13) paid; pg 3 (1875 Dec 16) paid; pg 3 (1875 Dec 25) paid; pg 4 (1876 May 13); pg 86 (1875 Nov 13) payments - 13 Nov 1875 - 16 Dec 1875, see page 125
pg 125 (1875 Nov 13) payments 13 Nov 1875 - 13 May 1876 - demitted

Dimick, Erastus H
pg 157 (1876 Dec 9) payments, 9 Dec 1876 - 23 Aug 1879

Dodge, Horace O
appears as: Dodge, H O
pg 18 (1880 Oct 26) paid; pg 19 (1880 Nov 13) paid; pg 19 (1880 Nov 27) paid; pg 225 (1880 Oct 26) Boulder, payments 26 Oct 1880 - Dec 1884

Dolloff, John W
pg 263 (1883 May 18) payments 18 May 1883 - Dec 1884

Donaldson, Charles B
appears as: Donaldson, C B; Donaldson, Charles B
pg 4 (1876 Nov 11) paid; pg 5 (1876 Dec 2) paid; pg 6 (1876 Dec 12) paid; pg 13 (1879 Jan 11); pg 16 (1880 Jan 10) paid; pg 163 (1876 Nov 11) payments 11 Nov 1876 - Dec 1884

Dow, J E
pg 11 (1877 Dec 8) paid; pg 13 (1879 Jan 25); pg 15 (1879 Dec 13) paid; pg 167 (1877 Dec 8) payments 8 Dec 1877 - 9 Dec 1882 - demitted

Downer, Sylvester S
appears as: Downer, S S; Downer, Sylvester S
pg 17 (1880 Feb 28) paid; pg 17 (1880 Mar 17) paid; pg 17 (1880 Mar 27) paid; pg 217 (1880 Feb 28) Boulder, payments 28 Feb 1880 - Dec 1884

Drumm, Henry
pg 17 (1880 Feb 17) paid; pg 17 (1880 Mar 2) paid; pg 17 (1880 Mar 13) paid; pg 216 (1880 Feb 17) Boulder, payments 17 Feb 1880 - Dec 1884

Dunagan, Elijah
appears as: Dunnagan, E; Dunnagan, Elijah
pg 10 (1877 Dec 8) rent; pg 16 (1880 Jan 17) paid; pg 13 (1878 Dec 28) paid; pg 185 (1877 Dec 8) Nederland, payments 8 Dec 1877 - Dec 1884, died Apr 1884

Dunn, James
pg 122 (1875 Dec 11) payments 11 Dec 1875 - 23 Aug 1879

Dunnagan, see Dunagan, Elijah

Earhart, W R
appears as: Earheart, W R
pg 258 (1881 Dec 24) payments 24 Dec 1881 - Dec 1884

Earheart, see Earhart, W J

Edison, Mrs
pg 17 (1880 May 22) cemetery lot; pg 276 (1880 May 22) cemetery lot

Ellingham, John J
appears as: Ellingham, J J; Ellingham, John J
pg 1 (1875 Nov 27) paid; pg 9 (1877 Jan 1) paid; pg 13 (1879 Jan 11); pg 18 (1880 Sept 11) paid; pg 123 (1875 Dec 11) Rosita, payments 11 Dec 1875 - Dec 1884

Ellingham, Robert
pg 12 (1878 Mar 9) paid; pg 13 (1879 Mar 8); pg 18 (1880 Sept 11) paid; pg 132 (1876 Dec 9) Boulder, payments 9 Dec 1876 - 9 Aug 1884

Ellis, Adelbert L
appears as: Ellis, A L
pg 2 (1875 Dec 11) paid; pg 74 (1875 Dec 11) Leadville, payments 11 Dec 1875 - 23 Aug 1879, reinstated and demit granted 25 Aug 1883

Farwell, C D
pg 261 (1883 Feb 10) payments 10 Feb 1883 - Dec 1884

Floyd, W S
pg 16 (1880 Jan 24) cemetery lot; pg 276 (1880 June 10) cemetery lot

Fonda, George F
pg 265 (1883 June 30) payments 30 June 1883 - Dec 1884

Foote & Gould
pg loose sheet (1886 Dec 27) bill for banquet; pg loose sheet (1887) were paid

Foote, James B
appears as: Foote, J B; Foote, June B
pg 14 (1879 June 10) paid; pg 208 (1879 May 27) payments 27 May 1879 - Dec 1884

Fox, M P
pg 237 (1881 May 31) payments 31 May 1881 - Dec 1884

French, S M
pg 13 (1879 Mar 22) paid on note; pg 182 (1877 Dec 8) payments 8 Dec 1877 - 23 Aug 1879, demitted 12 Feb 1881

Fullerton, Mrs
pg 12 (1878 Feb 9) paid; pg 276 (1878 Feb 9) cemetery lot

Gilbert, Clark W
pg 3 (1875 Dec 11) paid; pg 18 (1880 July 24) paid; pg 18 (1880 Aug 28) paid; pg 40 (1874 Aug 1) payments, 1 Aug 1874 - 28 Aug 1880

Gillam, W H
pg 244 (1881 Dec 10) Boulder, payments 10 Dec 1881 - 9 Feb 1884 - demitted

Glessner, Charles E
pg 233 (1881 Apr 13) Boulder, payments 13 Apr 1881 - Dec 1884

Goodall, David J
appears as: Goodall, D J; Goodall
pg 4 (1876 May 27) cemetery lot; pg 276 (1876 May 27) cemetery lot

Goodwin, N W
pg 247 (1881 Dec 10) Boulder, payments 10 Dec 1881 - Dec 1884

Gorman, Michael
pg 3 (1875 Dec 25) paid

Goss, Abel
pg 11 (1877 Dec 17) paid; pg 60 (1874 Dec 14) payments 14 Dec 1874 - 27 Aug 1881

Graves, Daniel C
appears as: Graves, D C
pg 18 (1880 Aug 14) cemetery lot

Green, Henry
appears as: Green H; Green, Henry
pg 5 (1876 Dec 9) paid; pg 4 (1876 June 24) paid; pg 110 (1874 Dec 14) Boulder, payments 14 Dec 1874 - Dec 1884

Groesbeck, John B
appears as: Groesbeck, J B; Groesbeck, John B
pg 1 (1875 Dec 3) paid; pg 5 (1876 Dec 9) paid; pg 57 (1874 Dec 14) payments 14 Dec 1874 - 8 June 1878 - demitted

Grund, John C
appears as: Grund, J C
pg 256 (1882 Dec 24) payments 24 Dec 1882 - Dec 1884

Gutterson, Charles L
appears as: Gutterson, C L; Gutterson, Charles L
pg 4 (1876 May 31) paid; pg 4 (1876 June 28) paid; pg 4 (1876 July 29) paid; pg 5 (1876 Dec 9) paid; pg 10 (1877 June 9) Secretary from 9 June 1877 - 8 Dec 1877; pg 11 (1877 Dec 8) Secretary from 8 Dec 1877 - 19 Dec 1988; pg 12 (1877 Dec 22) Secy from 23 Dec 1877 - 23 Mar 1878; pg 155 (1876 May 31) St Johns, Apache Cty, Arizona, payments 31 May 1876 - 27 Aug 1881, reinstated 22 Apr 1882 - Dec 1884

Guyage, Julius
appears as: Guyaze, Julius
pg 65 (1875 July 29) payment 29 July 1875

Halverson, Christian
appears as: Halvorson, C; Halverson, Christian; Halverson, Chris
pg 3 (1875 Dec 11) paid; pg 6 (1876 Dec 9) paid; pg 10 (1877 Dec 8) rent; pg 15 (1879 Dec 13) paid; pg 118 (1875 Dec 11) Ward, payments 11 Dec 1875 - Dec 1884

Halvorson, see Halverson, Christian

Harker, Oliver H
appears as: Harker, O H; Harker, Oliver H
pg 10 (1877 Dec 8) rent; pg 2 (1875 Dec 11) paid; pg 16 (1880 Jan 10) paid; pg 53 (1874 Dec 14) payments 14 Dec 1874 - 12 Feb 1881 - demitted

Harmon, George D
appears as: Harmon, George D; Harmon, G D
pg 2 (1875 Dec 11) paid; pg 3 (1876 Feb 12) paid; pg 9 (1877 Feb 10) paid; pg 14 (1879 June 17) paid; pg 16 (1880 Jan 10) paid; pg 17 (1880 May 8) paid; pg 131 (1874 Dec 14) Boulder, payments 14 Dec 1874 - Dec 1884

Harney, Chris
pg 1 (1875 Sept 1) paid

Harris, Addison W
appears as: Harris, A W
pg 3 (1876 Jan 8) paid; pg 120 (1875 Apr 24) payments 24 Apr 1875 - 8 Jan 1876 - demitted

Harris, Barney
pg 223 (1878 Nov 9) payment 9 Nov 1878

Harris, Myers
appears as: Harris, Myers; Harris, M; Harris, Meyers
pg 2 (1875 Dec 11) paid; pg 6 (1876 Dec 9) paid; pg 10 (1877 Dec 8) rent; pg 13 (1879 Jan 11) paid; pg 15 (1879 Dec 13) paid; pg 138 (1875 Dec 11) Boulder, payments 11 Dec 1875 - Dec 1884; pg 173 (1877 Mar 17) mentioned in the record of Marcus Kline

Harvey, Christopher
appears as: Harvey, Chris; Harvey, Christopher
pg 1 (1875 Sept 11) paid; pg 1 (1875 Sept 25) paid; pg 1 (1875 Oct 23) paid; pg 6 (1876 Dec 23) paid; pg 76 (1875 Sept 1) payments 1 Sept 1875 - 23 Aug 1879

Haswell, Theodore
pg 9 (1877 Apr 20); pg 13 (1879 Mar 8); pg 15 (1879 Dec 13) paid; pg 92 (1874 Dec 14) payments, 14 Dec 1874 - 23 Jan 1881

Hathaway, Mark
pg 4 (1876 June 10) paid; pg 13 (1879 Feb 8); pg 15 (1879 Dec 13) paid; pg 69 (1875 Dec 11) Boulder, payments 11 Dec 1875 - Dec 1884

Hayden
pg 1 (1875 Sept 11) cemetery lot; pg 276 (1875 Sept 11) cemetery lot

Hayman, see Ben Hayman Ice

Henry, Albert T
appears as: Henry, A T
pg 260 (1882 Oct 14) payments 14 Oct 1882 - Dec 1884

Henry, Oren H
appears as: Henry, O H; Henry, Oren H
pg 2 (1875 Dec 11) paid; pg 5 (1876 Dec 9) paid; pg 11 (1877 Dec 8) paid; pg 14 (1879 June 24) paid; pg 100 (1875 Dec 11) Golden, payments 11 Dec 1875 - Dec 1884

Henry, Ormal E
appears as: Henry, O E; Henry, Ormal E; Henry, Oramel, E
pg 1 (1875 Nov 27) paid; pg 5 (1876 Dec 9) paid; pg 10 (1877 Dec 8) rent; pg 16 (1879 Dec 27) paid; pg 133 (1874 Dec 14) payments 14 Dec 1874 - 14 Feb 1880 - demitted

Hernandez, Anthony R
appears as: Hernandez, A; Hernandez, Anthony
pg 11 (1877 Dec 8) paid; pg 16 (1880 Jan 10) paid; pg 168 (1877 Dec 8) payments 8 Dec 1877 - 10 Jan 1882 - demitted

Hinkle, John P
pg 13 (1879 Feb 8) paid; pg 201 (1879 Feb 8) payment 8 Feb 1879, see pg 181

Hinman, Fred
appears as: Hinmon, Fred
pg 10 (1877 Nov 10) paid; pg 11 (1877 Dec 19) paid; pg 192 (1877 Dec 19) payment 19 Dec 1877

Hinmon, see Hinman, Fred

Hockaday, Charles N
appears as: Hockaday, C N; Hockaday, Charles N
pg 1 (1875 Nov 13) paid; pg 2 (1875 Dec 11) paid; pg 9 (1877 Jan 13) paid; pg 15 (1879 Dec 13) paid; pg 129 (1875 Nov 12) Boulder, payments 12 Nov 1875 - Dec 1884

Holstein, George B
appears as: Holstein, George B; Holstein, G B
pg 16 (1879 Dec 27) paid; pg 16 (1880 Jan 10) paid; pg 16 (1880 Jan 17) paid; pg 17 (1880 Feb 28) paid; pg 18 (1880 Sept 25) paid; pg 215 (1879 Dec 27) Boulder, payments 27 Dec 1879 - Dec 1884

Hopkins, David L
appears as: Hopkins, D L; Hopkins, David L
pg 6 (1876 Dec 9) paid; pg 160 (1876 Dec 9) payments 9 Dec 1876 - 23 Aug 1879, reinstated 12 Aug 1882 - Dec 1884

Howe, see Howse, W J L

Howell, C C
pg 16 (1880 Jan 10) paid; pg 195 (1879 Sept 14) payments 14 Sept 1879 - 10 Jan 1882 - demitted

Howell, William R
appears as: Howell, Wm R; Howell, William R
pg 2 (1875 Dec 11) paid; pg 5 (1876 Dec 9) paid; pg 12 (1878 Jan 12) paid; pg 14 (1879 June 14) paid; pg 136 (1875 Dec 11) Erie, payments 11 Dec 1875 - 20 Dec 1882 - demitted to become a Charter member of Garfield Lodge No. 50, Erie

Howse, W J L
appears as: Howes, W J L
pg 2 (1875 Dec 11) paid; pg 143 (1875 Dec 11) payment 11 Dec 1875 made by A Wright, demitted 8 Jan 1876

Hubbard, Mr
pg 9 (1877 Jan 21) cemetery lot

Hubbard, Mrs
pg 276 (1877 Jan 24) cemetery lot

Hunt, Fred A
pg 6 (1876 Dec 23) paid; pg 11 (1877 Dec 10) paid; pg 13 (1879 Jan 25);; pg 16 (1880 Jan 24) paid; pg 159 (1876 Dec 9) Cuihuiriahic, Chihuahua, Mexico (Denver crossed out), payments 9 Dec 1876 - Dec 1884

Hunt, William K
appears as: Hunt, W K; Hunt, William K
pg 4 (1876 June 24) paid; pg 10 (1877 June 23) paid; pg 14 (1879 June 14) paid; pg 15 (1879 Dec 13) paid; pg 58 (1874 Dec 14) Leadville, payments 14 Dec 1874 - 25 Aug 1883

Hutchinson, Daniel J
appears as: Hutchinson, D J
pg 258 (1882 Sept 9) Boulder, payments 9 Sept 1882 - Dec 1884

Hyder, David
pg 9 (1877 Feb 24) paid; pg 171 (1877 Feb 24) payment 24 Feb 1877

Irwin, Joseph
appears as: Irwin, Joseph; Irwin, Jo
pg 1 (1875 Sept 27) paid; pg 3 (1876 Jan 8) paid (Wilder); pg 17 (1880 Mar 13) paid; pg 64 (1875 July 27) Osborne, payments 27 July 1875 - Dec 1884

Jackson, George W
appears as: Jackson, George W; Jackson, G W
pg 14 (1879 Oct 11) paid; pg 16 (1879 Dec 27) paid; pg 66 (1875 Dec 11) payments 11 Dec 1875 - 27 Dec 1879 - demitted

Jeffers, Albert
appears as: Jeffries, Albert
pg 271 (1884 Feb 9) payments 9 Feb 1884 - Dec 1884

Jeffries, see Jeffers, Albert

Jester, William
pg 228 (1880 Dec 11) Boulder, payments 11 Dec 1880 - Dec 1884

Johns, John H
appears as: Johns, John H; Johns, J H
pg 1 (1875 Sept 1) paid; pg 1 (1875 Oct 23) paid; pg 77 (1875 Sept 1) payments 1 Sept 1875 - 27 Nov 1875, killed in mine at Caribou, 17 Mar 1876

Johnson, J T
pg 276 (1880 June 10) cemetery lot

Johnson, Seymour
pg 4 (1876 Sept 16) paid; pg 162 (1876 Spet 16) Sugar Loaf, payments 16 Sept 1876 - Dec 1884

Johnson, Thomas C
pg 274 (1884 Apr 17) Gold Hill, payments 17 Apr 1884 - Dec 1884

Johnston, James J
appears as: Johnston, J I; Johnton, James J
pg 16 (1880 Jan 10) cemetery lot; pg 257 (1882 Sept 24) payments 27 May 1882 - 24 Dec 1882

Johnston, William J
pg 235 (1881 Apr 26) Boulder, payments 26 Apr 1881 - Dec 1884

Jones, Thomas J
appears as: T J; Jones, Thomas; Jones, Thomas J
pg 3 (1875 Dec 25) paid; pg 4 (1876 Apr 1) paid; pg 4 (1876 Apr 11) paid; pg 9 (1877 Jan 13) paid; pg 10 (1877 Dec 8) rent; pg 15 (1879 Dec 13) paid; pg 70 (1875 Dec 11) payments 11 Dec 1875 - 28 June 1879; pg 113 (1874 Dec 14) Valmont, payments 14 Dec 1874 - 11 Dec 1880 - dues remitted for life

Jones, Thomas R
pg 242 (1880 Dec 11) Valmont, payments 11 Dec 1880 - 20 Sept 1882 - demitted to become a Charter member of Garfield Lodge No. 50, Erie

Juneman, Frederick W
appears as: Juneman, F W
pg 2 (1875 Dec 11) paid; pg 5 (1876 Nov 25) paid; pg 15 (1879 Dec 13) paid; pg 39 (1874 Dec 12) payments 12 Dec 1874 - 11 Dec 1880 - demitted

Kelley, James A
pg 262 (1883 Feb 13) Crisman, payments 13 Feb 1883 - Dec 1884

Kempton, James
pg 17 (1880 Mar 13) paid; pg 17 (1880 Mar 29) paid; pg 17 (1880 Apr 10) paid; pg 218 (1880 Mar 13) Magnolia, payments 13 Mar 1880 - Dec 1884

Kerr, David
pg 2 (1875 Dec 11) paid; pg 6 (1876 Dec 9) paid; pg 16 (1880 Jan 10) paid; pg 141 (1874 Dec 14) Louisville, payments 14 Dec 1874 - Dec 1884

Kessler, Marion
pg 3 (1876 Jan 19) paid; pg 4 (1876 Mar 25) paid; pg 4 (1876 May 27); pg 6 (1876 Dec 12) paid; pg 12 (1877 Dec 22) paid; pg 18 (1880 June 12) paid; pg 149 (1876 Jan 19) Boulder, payments 19 Jan 1876 - Dec 1884

King, Robert
pg 2 (1875 Dec 11) paid; pg 10 (1877 Dec 8) rent; pg 75 (1875 Dec 11) Boulder, payments 11 Dec 1875 - Dec 1884

Klein, see Kline, Marcus

Kline, Marcus
appears as: Kline, Marcus; Kline, M
pg 4 (1876 June 3) paid; pg 9 (1877 Mar 17) paid; pg 9 (1877 Apr 14) paid; pg 9 (1877 May 12); pg 10 (1877 Dec 8) rent; pg 15 (1879 Dec 13) paid; pg 173 (1877 Mar 17) care M Harris, Boulder, Leadville, payments 17 Mar 1877 - Dec 1884

Knox, John
pg 2 (1875 Dec 11) paid; pg 5 (1876 Dec 9) paid; pg 16 (1879 Dec 27) paid; pg 145 (1875 Dec 11) Erie, payments 11 Dec 1875 - Dec 1884

Kohler, Frederick W
appears as: Kohler, F W; Kohler, Frederick W, Kohler, Fred
pg 1 (1875 Dec 3) paid; pg 4 (1876 Nov 25) paid; pg 10 (1877 Dec 8) rent; pg 15 (1879 Dec 13) paid; pg 19 (1880 Nov 27) paid; pg 137 (1875 Dec 11) Boulder, payments 11 Dec 1875 - Dec 1884

Kroll, Anson
pg 214 (1880 Dec 24) Boulder, payments 24 Dec 1880 - Dec 1884

Lake, George E
appears as: Lake
pg 276 (1880 Feb 28) cemetery lot

Langley, Thomas
pg 14 (1879 Sept 27) paid

Large, William Morton
appears as: Large, W M
pg 14 (1879 May 24) funeral expenses paid for by Robert Collyer

Lawson, Alexander
appears as: Lawson, Alex; Lawson, Alexander
pg 13 (1879 Apr 12); pg 14 (1879 May 24) paid; pg 202 (1878 Oct 26) Ward, payments 26 Oct 1878 - 24 May 1879 - dead in Scotland

Lea, Alfred E
appears as: Lea, A E; Lea, Alfred E
pg 4 (1876 Nov 25) paid; pg 16 (1879 Dec 27) paid; pg 46 (1872 Nov 27) Boulder, payments 27 Nov 1872 - Dec 1884

Leeland, Mrs
pg 17 (1880 Apr 10) cemetery lot; pg 276 (1880 Apr 10) cemetery lot

Lehman, Gilbert
appears as: Lehman, Gilbert; Lehman, G
pg 16 (1880 Dec 13) cemetery lot; pg 276 (1879 Dec 13) cemetery lot

Lester, James E
appears as: Lester, J E; Lester, James E
pg 14 (1879 May 12) paid; pg 14 (1879 June 14) paid; pg 15 (1879 Dec 13) paid; pg 71 (1875 Dec 11) payments 11 Dec 1875 - 28 June 1879; pg 205 (1879 May 12) payments 12 May 1879 - Dec 1884

Leyner, Peter A
appears as: Leyner, P A; Leyner, Peter A
pg 5 (1876 Dec 9) paid; pg 15 (1879 Dec 13) paid; pg 95 (1875 June 12) Canfield, payments 12 June 1875 - Dec 1884

Lippoldt, Henry
pg 264 (1883 Aug 25) payment 25 Aug 1883

Lockwood, Fred
pg 269 (1884 Jan 17) payments 17 Jan 1884 - Dec 1884

Longer, John
pg 4 (1876 July 8) cemetery lot; pg 276 (1876 July 8) cemetery lot

Longley, Thomas
pg 16 (1879 Dec 27) paid; pg 17 (1880 May 22) paid; pg 211 (1879 Sept 27) Ward, payments 27 Sept 1879 - Dec 1884

Lowes, see Low, Theodore

Low, Theodore
pg 257 (1883 Apr 28) payments 28 Apr 1883 - 23 July 1884

Lowman, E E
pg 244 (1884 Apr 12) payments 12 Apr 1884 - Dec 1884

Loyd, Joseph
pg 157 (1883 Feb 10) payments 10 Feb 1883 - Dec 1884

Lytle, George
pg 2 (1875 Dec 11) paid; pg 5 (1876 Nov 25) cemetery lot; pg 6 (1876 Dec 9) paid; pg 14

(1879 June 14) paid; pg 59 (1874 Dec 14) Boulder, payments 14 Dec 1874 - Dec 1884; pg 276 (1876 Nov 25) cemetery lot

Markeley, see Markley, M

Markley, M
pg 17 (1880 Mar 13) cemetery lot; pg 276 (1880 Mar 13) cemetery lot

Maxwell, James P
appears as: Maxwell, James P; Maxwell, J P
pg 2 (1875 Dec 11) paid; pg 11 (1877 Dec 8) paid; pg 15 (1879 Dec 13) paid; pg 16 (1880 Dec 13) cemetery lot; pg 130 (1874 Dec 14) Boulder, payments 14 Dec 1874 - Dec 1884; pg 276 (1879 Dec 13) cemetery lot

Mayer, Gottlieb F
appears as: Mayer, Gottlieb; Mayer, G F
pg 13 (1878 Dec 28); pg 15 (1879 Dec 13) paid; pg 197 (1878 June 22) Salina, payments 22 June 1878 - Dec 1884

McAllister, Ira
appears as: McAllister, S T
pg 255 (1882 Dec 24) payments 24 Dec 1882 - Dec 1884

McBride, R T
pg 267 (1883 Nov 24) Langford, CO, payments 24 Nov 1883 - Dec 1884

McCaslin, Matthew L
appears as: McCaslin, M L
pg 2 (1875 Dec 11) paid; pg 9 (1877 Feb 24) paid; pg 12 (1878 Feb 13) paid; pg 15 (1879 Dec 13) paid; pg 135 (1875 Dec 11) Longmont, payments 11 Dec 1875 - Dec 1884

McClure, Edward P
pg 109 (1874 Dec 14) payments 14 Dec 1874 - 28 Aug 1875, reinstated 8 Nov 1879 - demitted

McDowell, John M
appears as: McDowell, J M; McDowell, John M
pg 1 (1875 Dec 3) paid; pg 3 (1875 Dec 27) paid; pg 3 (1876 Jan 8) paid; pg 4 (1876 June 10) paid; pg 10 (1877 Dec 8) rent; pg 148 (1875 Dec 3) payments 3 Dec 1875 - 14 Dec 1878 - demitted

McIntosh, Lemuel
appears as: McIntosh; McIntosh, Lemuel
pg 1 (1875 Sept 11) cemetery lot; pg 2 (1875 Dec 11) paid; pg 111 (1875 Dec 11) payments 11 Dec 1875 - 28 Aug 1879, reinstated 26 Feb 1887; pg 276 (1875 Sept 11) cemetery lot

Mead, Marcus S
appears as: Mead, M S; Mead, Marcus S
pg 4 (1876 Apr 11); pg 4 (1876 May 16); pg 4 (1876 June 17) paid; pg 5 (1876 Dec 9) paid; pg 12 (1878 Mar 9) paid; pg 13 (1879 Jan 25); pg 15 (1879 Dec 13) paid; pg 154 (1876 Apr 10) Boulder, payments 10 Apr 1876 - Dec 1884

Meginnis, Daniel
appears as: Maginnes, D; Maginnes, Daniel; Meginnis, Daniel
pg 14 (1879 Oct 4) paid; pg 14 (1879 Oct 11) paid; pg 15 (1879 Dec 13) paid; pg 210 (1879 Aug 29) Boulder, 29 Aug 1879 - Dec 1884

Metcalf, Eli P
appears as: Metcalf, E P; Metcalf, Eli P
pg 2 (1875 Dec 11) paid; pg 6 (1876 Dec 9) paid; pg 10 (1877 Dec 8) rent; pg 14 (1879 June 20) paid; pg 14 (1879 Nov 8) paid; pg 29 (1873 Mar 1) Boulder, payments 1 Mar 1873 - 8 Dec 1883; pg 261 (1883 Jan 27) Boulder, payments 27 Jan 1883 - Dec 1884

Meyring, Henry
pg 10 (1877 June 23) paid; pg 10 (1877 Aug 11) paid; pg 10 (1877 Sept 8) paid; pg 12 (1877 Dec 22) paid; pg 15 (1879 Dec 13) paid; pg 176 (1877 June 23) Salina, payments 23 June 1877 - Dec 1884

Michaud, Theodore
appears as: Michant, Theodore
pg 1 (1875 Sept 1) paid; pg 78 (1875 Sept 1) payment 1 Sept 1875; pg 276 (1880 Apr 10) cemetery lot

Michel, Jo
pg 17 (1880 Apr 10) cemetery lot

Mills, Abraham
appears as: Mills, Abram
pg 2 (1875 Dec 11) paid; pg 96 (1874 Dec 14) payments 14 Dec 1874 - 11 Dec 1875 - demitted

Minks, George W
pg 18 (1880 July 24) paid; pg 18 (1880 Aug 14) paid; pg 18 (1880 Aug 28) paid; pg 221 (1880

July 24) Louisville, payments 24 July 1880 - Dec 1884

Moffett, J C
pg 14 (1879 June 10) paid; pg 18 (1880 Oct 9) paid; pg 209 (1879 June 10) payments 10 June 1879 - 9 Oct 1880

Mooney, Michael
pg 12 (1878 Jan 12) paid; pg 14 (1879 June 14) paid; pg 194 (1878 Jan 12) paymrnts 12 Jan 1878 - 14 June 1878

Moore, Thomas M
appears as: Moore, Thomas M, Moore, T M
pg 18 (1880 July 10) cemetery lot; pg 276 (1880 July 10) cemetery lot

Morton Lumber
pg 249 (24 Feb 1883) paid

Mosher, C
appears as: Mosher, C; Moser, C
pg 5 (1876 Nov 25) cemetery lot; pg 276 (1876 Nov 25) cemetery lot

Mt Sinai Commandery
pg 253 (1882 Apr 1) payments 1 Apr 1882 - Dec 1884; pg loose sheet (1887) rent paid

Newton & Kaeldy
pg loose sheet (1886 Dec 27) bill for banquet

Nichols, Charles L
pg 55 (1874 Dec 14) payments, 14 Dec 1874 - 28 June 1879

Nichols, David H
appears as: Nichols, D H; Nichols, David H
pg 2 (1875 Dec 11) paid; pg 124 (1876 Dec 9) Boulder, payments 9 Dec 1876 - Dec 1884

Nichols, Ezra H
pg 91 (1875 Dec 11) payments 11 Dec 1875 - 28 June 1879

Nicholson, John W
appears as: Nicholson, J W, Nicholson, John W
pg 3 (1876 Mar 4) paid; pg 4 (1876 Mar 25) paid; pg 4 (1876 Apr 1) paid; pg 5 (1876 Dec 9) paid; pg 12 (1878 Feb 9) paid; pg 13 (1879 Apr 12); pg 152 (1876 Mar 4) Boulder, payments 4 Mar 1876 - Dec 1884

North, James M
appears as: North, J M; North, James M
pg 13 (1879 Apr 17) paid; pg 14 (1879 Nov 8) paid; pg 16 (1880 Dec 13) paid; pg 204 (1879 Apr 17) Boulder, 17 Apr 1874 - Dec 1884

Odd Fellows
pg 3 (1875 Dec 25) paid

O'Hara, William
appears as: O'Hara, Wm; O'Hara, William
pg 11 (1877 Dec 19) paid; pg 12 (1878 Feb 9) paid; pg 12 (1878 Mar 9) paid; pg 13 (1879 Mar 8); pg 16 (1880 Jan 17) paid; pg 189 (1877 Dec 19) 203 Santa Fe St, payments 19 Dec 1877 - 8 Mar 1884 - demitted

Owen, Thomas R, Jr
pg 63 (1884 May 24) payments, 24 May 1884 - Dec 1884

Parlin, David
pg 2 (1875 Dec 11) paid; pg 114 (1874 Dec 14) payments 14 Dec 1874 - 23 Aug 1879

Paul, Henry
pg 17 (1880 Mar 13) paid; pg 101 (1876 Dec 9) Idaho Springs, payments 9 Dec 1876 - 23 Aug 1879, reinstated 13 Mar 1880 - 26 Apr 1884 - demitted

Pell, William G
appears as: Pell, W G
pg 16 (1880 Feb 14) cemetery lot; pg 276 (1880 Feb 14) cemetery lot

Peryam, William T
pg 144 (1875 Dec 11) payments 11 Dec 1875 - 23 Aug 1879

Peters, Anson W
appears as: Peters, A W; Peters, Anson W
pg 14 (1879 Apr 26) paid; pg 18 (1880 June 12) paid; pg 119 (1874 Dec 14) Silver City, NM, payments 14 Dec 1874 - Dec 1884

Peterson, Andrew
pg 262 (1883 Feb 27) Magnolia, payment 27 Feb 1883

Philippi, Frederick
appears as: Phllipi, Fred; Philippi, Fred; Philippi, Frederick
pg 14 (1879 Nov 8) donation; pg 15 (1879 Dec 13) paid; pg 19 (1880 Nov 16) paid; pg 199 (1878 Sept 14) Boulder, payments 14 Sept 1878 - Dec 1884

Schroeder, Dederick
pg 241 (1881 June 25) payment 25 June 1881

Scott, Samuel
appears as: Scott, Sam
pg 30 (1874 Jan 11) payments 11 Jan 1874 - 28 June 1879

Severance, Isaac H
appears as: Severance, I H; Severance, Isaac H
pg 14 (1879 May 24) paid; pg 18 (1880 Sept 11) paid; pg 206 (1879 Dec 13) Frisco, Summit Cty, payments 13 Dec 1879 - 23 Dec 1883

Sheets, Henry W
appears as: Sheets, H W
pg 17 (1880 Mar 13) paid; pg 184 (1877 Dec 8) Boulder, payments 8 Dec 1877 - Dec 1884

Sherratt, Charles
pg 12 (1878 Mar 5) paid; pg 15 (1879 Dec 13) paid; pg 188 (1878 Mar 5) Erie, payments 5 Mar 1878 - 20 Sept 1882 - demitted to become a charter member of Garfield Lodge No. 50, Erie

Sherwood, Clarence A
appears as: Sherwood, C A
pg 2 (1875 Dec 11) paid; pg 10 (1877 Dec 8) rent; pg 15 (1879 Dec 13) paid; pg 35 (1874 Apr 4) Leadville, payments 1874 Apr 4 - 16 July 1883 - demitted

Silver, S D
pg 3 (1875 Dec 11) paid; pg 54 (1874 Dec 14) Leadville, payments 14 Dec 1874 - Dec 1884, 27 Aug 1881, 26 Aug 1882 - reinstated

Simpson, John S
pg 272 (1884 Feb 9) payments 9 Feb 1884 - Dec 1884

Slater, William C
pg 104 (1874 Dec 14) payments 14 Dec 1874 - 28 Aug 1875

Slaughter, Benjamin H
pg 107 (1874 Dec 14) payments 14 Dec 1874 - 28 Aug 1875

Slifer, Esrom G
appears as: Slifer, E G; Slifer, Esrom, G
pg 11 (1877 Dec 8) paid; pg 115 (1874 Dec 14) payments 14 Dec 1874 - 8 Dec 1877 - demitted

Smith, Azon A
appears as: Smith, A A; Smith, Azon A
pg 3 (1875 Dec 25) paid; pg 5 (1876 Dec 2) paid; pg 13 (1879 Feb 8); pg 56 (1874 Dec 14) payments 14 Dec 1874 - 8 Feb 1879 - demitted

Smith, J Alden
pg 11 (1877 Dec 8) paid; pg 165 (1877 Dec 8) Boulder, payments 8 Dec 1877 - Dec 1884

Smith, J W
pg 268 (1883 Dec 13) payments 13 Dec 1883 - Dec 1884

Smith, Marinus G
appears as: Smith, M G; Smith, Marinus G
pg 5 (1876 Nov 25) paid; pg 99 (1876 Dec 9) Boulder, payments 9 Dec 1876 - 13 Sept 1879, dues remitted for life from 11 Dec 1880

Smith, Nelson K
appears as: Smith, N K
pg 16 (1880 Jan 24) cemetery lot; pg 276 (1880 June 10) cemetery lot

Smith, Walter H
pg 2 (1875 Dec 11) paid; pg 126 (1874 Dec 14) payments 14 Dec 1874 - 23 Aug 1879

Snyder, Hanson
pg 4 (1876 Aug 26) paid; pg 37 (1871 Apr 14) died at Leadville, 27 Oct 1879, payments 14 Apr 1871 - 14 Dec 1878

Sommers, Wilhelm
pg 3 (1875 Dec 11) paid; pg 6 (1876 Dec 23) paid; pg 11 (1877 Dec 8) paid; pg 103 (1874 Dec 14) payments, 14 Dec 1874 - 23 Aug 1879

Soule, Albert G
appears as: Soule, A G
pg 266 (1883 Sept 8) payments 8 Sept 1883 - Dec 1884

Southland, Judson
appears as: Southland, Judson; Southland, J D; Southland, Jud
pg 2 (1875 Dec 11) paid; pg 5 (1876 Dec 9) paid; pg 12 (1878 Jan 26) paid; pg 13 (1879 Feb 8); pg 17 (1880 Mar 13) paid; pg 62 (1874 Oct 14) Platteville, Boulder, payments 14 Oct 1874 - Dec 1884

Spencer, Charles L
pg 232 (1881 Apr 9) Boulder, payments 9 Apr 1881 - Dec 1884

Squires, George C
pg 2 (1875 Dec 11) paid; pg 5 (1876 Dec 9) paid; pg 128 (1875 Dec 11) Boulder, payments 11 Dec 1875 - Dec 1884

Squires, Phineas L
appears as: Squires, P L
pg loose sheet (1886 Dec 27) bill for banquet

St Clair, Joel F T
appears as: St Clair, J F T; St Clair, Joel F T
pg 16 (1880 Jan 10) paid; pg 166 (1877 Dec 8) Gold Hill, Boulder, payments 8 Dec 1877 - Dec 1884

St Johns Festival
pg 3 (1876 Jan 8) paid

Stanton, John A
pg 102 (1874 Dec 14) payments 14 Dec 1874 - 14 Aug 1875

Stewart, Thomas C
pg 2 (1875 Dec 11) paid; pg 38 (1874 Dec 12) Boulder, payments 12 Dec 1874 - Dec 1884

Strasburger, Mathias
appears as: Strasburger, M
pg 18 (1880 Oct 9) paid; pg 19 (1880 Nov 13) paid; pg 19 (1880 Nov 27) paid

Styles, Eugene M
appears as: Styles, E M
pg 234 (1884 Apr 13) Burlington, VT, payments 13 Apr 1881 - 9 Feb 1884, demitted

Sutherland, see Southland, Judson

Tallman, Isaac T
appears as: Tallman, I T; Tallman, Isaac T
pg 9 (1877 Feb 10) paid; pg 13 (1879 Jan 25); pg 15 (1879 Dec 13) paid; pg 158 (1876 Dec 9) payments 9 Dec 1876 - 1 Mar 1881 - demitted

Tarvin, E M
pg 1 (1875 Oct 1) paid; pg 3 (1875 Dec 27) paid; pg 3 (1876 Feb 26) paid; pg 5 (1876 Dec 9) paid; pg 13 (1879 Jan 11); pg 81 (1875 Oct 1) payments - 1 Oct 1875 - 27 Aug 1881, reinstated 26 Aug 1882 - Dec 1884

Thomas, Squires J
appears as: Thomas, Square J
pg 275 (1884 Apr 26) payments 26 Apr 1884 - Dec 1884

Tilney, Robert H
appears as: Tilney, R H; Tilney, Robert H
pg 4 (1876 Apr 11); pg 4 (1876 May 16); pg 4 (1876 June 3) paid; pg 5 (1876 Dec 9) paid; pg 10 (1877 Dec 8) rent;; pg 15 (1879 Dec 13) paid; pg 153 (1876 Apr 10) Boulder, payments 10 Apr 1876 - 9 Feb 1884

Tipple, George L
appears as: Tipple, George L; Tippet, George L
pg 227 (1880 Dec 24) payments 24 Dec 1880 - Dec 1884

Titcomb, Hiram R
pg 240 (1881 Sept 10) Boulder, payments 10 Sept 1881 - Dec 1884

Titcomb, John S
appears as: Titcomb, John S; Titcomb, J S
pg 1 (1875 Sept 1) Secy 1 Sept 1875 - 10 Dec 1875; pg 1 (1875 Nov 27) paid; pg 5 (1876 Nov 25) paid; pg 10 (1877 Dec 8) rent; pg 13 (1877 Dec 28) deposit by Treasurer; pg 13 (1878 Apr 12) deposit by Treasurer; pg 13 (1878 Apr 17) deposit by Treasurer; pg 13 (1878 Dec 28) Secy from 23 Dec 1878 - 17 Apr 1879; pg 13 (1878 Jan 27) deposit by Treasurer; pg 13 (1878 Feb 8) deposit by Treasurer; pg 13 (1878 Mar 8) deposit by Treasurer; pg 14 (1879 Apr 26) Secy from 26 Apr 1879 - 1 Dec 1879; pg 14 (1879 Nov 8) paid; pg 15 (1879 Dec 13) Secy from 13 Dec 1879 - 13 Dec 1879; pg 16 (1879 Dec 13) Secy from 13 Dec 1879 - 14 Feb 1880; pg 17 (1880 Feb 14) Secy from 14 Feb 1880 - 22 May 1880; pg 18 (1880 May 22) Secy from 22 May 1880 - 26 Oct 1880; pg 18 (1880 Aug 28) paid; pg 19 (1880 Nov 13) Secy from 13 Nov 1880 - 26 Mar 1881; pg 73 (1875 Dec 11) Boulder, payments 11 Dec 1875 - Dec 1884; pg 276 (1875 Sept 11) deposits for cemetery 11 Sept 1875 - 14 Aug 1880

Turner, Charles
pg 2 (1875 Dec 11) paid; pg 4 (1876 Mar 25) paid; pg 11 (1877 Dec 8) paid; pg 15 (1879 Dec 13) paid; pg 51 (1874 Dec 14) payments 14 Dec 1874 - Dec 1884

Tyrell, Norman J
appears as: Tyrell, N J; Tyrell, Norman J
pg 3 (1875 Dec 11) paid; pg 5 (1876 Dec 9) paid; pg 11 (1877 Dec 8) paid; pg 13 (1879 Jan 11); pg 147 (1875 Dec 11) payments 11 Dec 1875 - Dec 1884

Van Fleet, Charles G
pg 15 (1879 Dec 13) paid; pg 212 (1879 Dec 13) Boulder, payments 13 Dec 1879 - Dec 1884

Van Riper, Cornelius
appears as: Van Riper, C; Van Riper, Cornelius
pg 2 (1875 Dec 11) paid; pg 9 (1877 May 2); pg 16 (1879 Dec 27) paid; pg 36 (1874 Dec 14) Boulder, payments 14 Dec 1874 - Dec 1884

Van, Clay M
appears as: Van, C M; Van, Clay M
pg 3 (1875 Dec 11) paid; pg 74 (1879 Aug 23) amount for A L Ellis charged to C M Van; pg 146 (1875 Dec 11) payments 11 Dec 1875 - 23 Aug 1879 - demitted; pg 243 (1880 Dec 11) Boulder, payments 11 Dec 1880 - Dec 1884

Viele, James B
pg 248 (1881 Nov 26) Boulder, payments 26 Nov 1881 - 22 Nov 1884

Walker, Ed S
pg 209 (1884 Aug 23) payment 9 Aug 1884 - 23 Aug 1884

Walker, Thomas C
pg 3 (1876 Feb 12) paid; pg 10 (1877 Sept 8) paid; pg 41 (1874 Aug 15) 380 Delganey St, Denver, payments 15 Aug 1874 - 25 Aug 1883 - demitted

Walker, Thomas D
pg 18 (1880 July 10) paid; pg 18 (1880 July 24) paid; pg 34 (1874 Jan 27) payments 27 Jan 1874 - Dec 1884 - reinstated

Wallace, George
pg 13 (1879 Jan 11); pg 17 (1880 Apr 24) paid; pg 200 (1878 Dec 14) payments 14 Dec 1878 - 10 Jan 1882 - demitted

Wallace, William J
appears as: Wallace, W J; Wallace, William J
pg 3 (1876 Jan 22) paid; pg 12 (1878 Mar 23) paid; pg 140 (1875 May 8) Pilot Point, Denton Cty, TX, payments 8 May 1875 - 25 Aug 1883

Welderding, H J
pg 245 (1884 May 15) payment 15 May 1884

Wellman, Luther C
appears as: Wellman, L C; Wellman, Luther C
pg 5 (1876 Dec 9) paid; pg 10 (1877 Nov 10) paid; pg 13 (1879 Mar 8); pg 139 (1875 Dec 11) payments 11 Dec 1875 - Dec 1884

Wellman, Sylvanus
appears as: Wellman, Sylvanus; Wellman, S
pg 5 (1876 Dec 9) paid; pg 15 (1879 Dec 13) paid; pg 10 (1877 Nov 10) paid; pg 17 (1880 Mar 27) cemetery lot; pg 134 (1875 Dec 11) Boulder, payments 11 Dec 1875 - Dec 1884; pg 276 (1880 Mar 27) cemetery lot; pg loose sheet (1886 Jan 23) bill for coal; pg loose sheet (1887 Feb 26) bill for coal; pg loose sheet (1887 Nov 26) bill presented for coal

Westlake, W B
appears as: Westlake
pg 1 (1875 Oct 9) cemetery lot 48 section D; pg 276 (1875 Oct 9) cemetery lot

Wharton, Joseph J
appears as: Wharton, Joseph J; Wharton, J J
pg 3 (1876 Feb 12) paid; pg 11 (1877 Dec 19) paid; pg 13 (1879 Feb 8); pg 16 (1880 Jan 24) paid; pg 89 (1875 Dec 12) Erie, payments 12 Dec 1875 - Dec 1884

White, David S
pg 213 (1879 Dec 13) payments 13 Dec 1879 - Dec 1884

White, William W
pg 273 (1884 Apr 12) payments 12 Apr 1884 - Dec 1884

Whitney, George H
pg 72 (1884 July 1) payments, 1 July 1884 - Dec 1884

Wigginton, John W
pg 106 (1874 Dec 14) payments 14 Dec 1874 - 28 Aug 1875, dues remitted 11 Nov 1882, died 12 May 1883

Wilder, Eugene
appears as: Wilder, Eugene; Wilder
pg 2 (1875 Dec 11) paid; pg 3 (1876 Jan 8) paid for Joseph Irwin; pg 3 (1876 Mar 25) paid; pg 11 (1877 Dec 8) paid; pg 13 (1878 Dec 28); pg

14 (1879 Nov 8) donation; pg 15 (1879 Dec 13) paid; pg 61 (1874 Dec 14) Boulder, payments 14 Dec 1874 - Dec 1884

Wilkins, Cornelius
pg 161 (1876 Dec 9) payments 9 Dec 1876 - we Aug 1879

Williams, George W
pg 9 (1877 May 26); pg 18 (1880 May 22) paid; pg 175 (1877 May 26) payment made 26 May 1877

Williams, John T
appears as: Williams, T J; Williams, J T; Williams, John T
pg 12 (1878 Mar 9) paid; pg 12 (1878 Mar 23) paid; pg 17 (1880 Feb 28) paid; pg 190 (1878 Mar 9) Garfield, Chaffee Cty, payments 9 Mar 1878 - Dec 1884

Wilson, Benjamin F
pg 3 (1876 Feb 16) paid; pg 3 (1876 Mar 4) paid; pg 4 (1876 Apr 1) paid; pg 5 (1876 Dec 9) paid; pg 11 (1877 Dec 8) paid; pg 17 (1880 Mar 13) paid; pg 18 (1880 Oct 23) paid; pg 151 (1876 Feb 16) payments 16 Feb 1876 - 23 Aug 1879, reinstated 13 Mar 1880 - 23 Oct 1880 - demitted

Wilson, George W
pg 71 (1884 June 28) payments 28 June 1884 - Dec 1884

Wilson, John M
appears as: Wilson, J M; Wilson, John M
pg 5 (1876 Dec 2) paid; pg 12 (1878 Mar 23) paid; pg 14 (1879 May 24) paid; pg 14 (1879 Oct 11) paid; pg 18 (1880 Sept 11) paid; pg 98 (1876 Dec 9) Boulder, payments 9 Dec 1876 - Sept 1884

Wilson, Thomas V
pg 246 (1881 Dec 10) Boulder, payments 10 Dec 1881 - Dec 1884

Wimer, John A
appears as: Wymer, J A; Wymer, John A; Wimer, J A
pg 1 (1875 Dec 3) paid; pg 2 (1875 Dec 11) paid; pg 9 (1877 Mar 17) paid; pg 10 (1877 Dec 8) rent; pg 19 (1880 Nov 27) paid; pg 44 (1873 Apr 5) Boulder, payments 5 Apr 1873 - Dec 1884

Wood, Gardner P
appears as: Wood, G P; Wood, Gardner P
pg 6 (1876 Dec 9) paid; pg 12 (1878 Feb 9) paid pg 87 (1873 July 26) Sugar Loaf, payments - 26 July 1873 - Dec 1884

Wright, Alpheus
pg 2 (1875 Dec 11) paid; pg 5 (1876 Nov 25) paid; pg 10 (1877 Dec 8) rent; pg 47 (1873 Mar 1) Boulder, payments 1 Mar 1873 - Dec 1884; pg 143 (1875 Dec 11) made payment for W J L Howes

Wright, Henry
pg 17 (1880 Mar 13) cemetery lot; pg 276 (1880 Mar 13) cemetery lot

Wymer, see Wimer, John A

Yates, D C
pg 276 (1880 Aug 14) cemetery lot

Yates, Isaiah
pg 14 (1879 May 24) paid; pg 15 (1879 Dec 13) paid; pg 18 (1880 Oct 9) paid; pg 207 (1879 May 24) Boulder, payments 24 May 1879 - Dec 1884

Yates, Joseph
pg 230 (1881 Jan 22) Boulder, payments 22 Jan 1881 - 26 Jan 1884

Columbia Lodge No. 14

Visitors Book, 1874–1886

The Visitors Book of the Columbia Lodge, 1874-1886, contains a list of the visitors to the Columbia Lodge, some of whom stayed in Boulder and became members of the Columbia Lodge.

The listings follow the same customs as were established in the Minute books.

Legend to the listings.

Members
Visitors who became known members of the Columbia Lodge No. 14.

Possible Members
Visitors who were mentioned in the Minute Books of the Columbia Lodge whose membership could not be determined.

Boulder
People who identified as being members of one of the other local lodges - St Vrain Lodge No. 23 in Longmont, or the other Boulder Lodge No. 45.

Non-Boulder
These visitors were identified with lodges in places other than Boulder County who were not identified as having become members in the Minute Books.

An asterisk before names in the Membership List indicates a possible member.

If there are listings where the correct spelling could not be determined, the listing will contain both spellings, such as Imil [Imel], David.

Every effort has been made to assure that these listings are correct, however, extracting handwritten records can be tricky, and some listings may contain inaccuracies. We hope you enjoy as much as we have the discoveries we have made about early Boulder.

— The Boulder Pioneers Project

Members List from the Visitor's Book

Allison, W H
Austin, Schuyler D
*Barter, Thomas
Barter, William
Bemus, James E
Carmack, Thomas K
Clow, Richard
Cook, George D
Denham, Thomas
Develine, Edward W
Dow, J E
Dunagan, Elijah
French, S M
Gilbert, Richard
Henry, Albert T
Hernandez, Anthony
Jeffers, Albert
Johnston, James J
*Kavanaugh, A M [A A]
King, Robert
Kroll, Anson
Lake, George E
McAllister, J T
Newnam, Eedward B
Parker, Charles E
Safely, Alexander F
Samuels, Henry C
*Sawyer, N F [H F]
Sears, William F
*Secor, W W
Severance, Isaac H
Sheets, Henry W
*Simmons, John
Simpson, John H
St Clair, Joel F T
Stanton, J W [J A]
*Stuchell, G D
Tallman, Isaac T
Tipple, George L
Van Fleet, Charles G
Washburn, Hiram E
*Yankee, William H

*possible member

Alexander, F E
pg 11 (1882 Jan 14) Mexico NY No. 136

Allen, John
pg 13 (1883 Feb 24) Tregenna No. 1272 St Ives, England

Allen, Robert B
pg 15 (1885 Nov 14) Parker City PA No. 521

Allison, W H
pg 14 (1883 Dec 22) Boulder No. 45

Austin, Schuyler D
appears as: Austin, S D
pg 1 (1874 July 28)Washington Lodge No. 12 Georgetown

Bactery, J
pg 1 (1874 July 28) Golden Lodge No. 1

Bagley, J A Jr
pg 15 (1885 Nov 14) Catshill NY No. 468

Bailey, Elias
pg 12 (1883 Feb 10) Longmont; pg 13 (1883 Feb 24) Longmont No. 23

Bailey, John C
appears as: Bailey J C
pg 8 (1879 Aug 9) St Vrain No. 23; pg 13 (1883 Sept 8) St Vrain No. 23

Baker, Thomas
pg 10 (1880 Nov 13) Minneapolis No. 19

Ballard, Frank D
pg 4 (1876 Dec 2) Joseph ____ Boston, MA

Banks, F B
pg 9 (1880 Aug 28) Marengo, IA No. 114

Barney, M G
pg 3 (1876 June 24) York No. 35 NE

Barqese, P A
pg 6 (1878 Jan 26) Butler Mo No. 265

Barr, R S
pg 11 (1881 July 23) Adel, IA

Barter, Thomas
pg 5 (1876 Dec 12) Kenosha, WI No. 67

Barter, William
pg 5 (1877 Jan 13) Golden Lodge No. 1

Bartlett, Reuel
pg 10 (1881 Mar 26) Centre Midland

Baylor, John M
pg 15 (1885 Dec 26) Gould No. 542 IL

Bemus, James E
appears as: Bemus, J E
pg 12 (1882 Aug 26) Boulder No. 45; pg 12 (1882 Nov 25) Boulder No. 45

Bentley, K G
pg 6 (1878 Aug 1) Occidental No. 20 Greeley

Bergheim, Jonas
pg 6 (1877 Nov 10) Evening Starr Lodge No. 44 Hormell, IA; pg 8 (1879 Dec) Evening Star Lodge No. 44 Rorwellsonts; pg 9 (1880 Mar 27) Evening Star, No. 44, Howellsville, NY

Birtsollo, C H
pg 4 (1876 Oct 14) Alexandria, Egypt

Blanchard, E P
pg 5 (1877 June 29) Doric Lodge No. 127 Monson, ME

Bound, B F
pg 8 (1879 Aug 9) New Albany, IN No 338

Bowes, J E
pg 10 (1880 Nov 27) Monroe No 143, Brookford, NY

Boyd, _ H
pg 13 (1883 Feb 24) Mt Vernon, No 64, Norwalk, OH

Bradfield, T
pg 9 (1880 June 26) Calhoun Lodge No. 182, MO

Bradley, A
pg 15 (1885 Sept 12) Walton NY No. 559

Bradley, Fred
pg 13 (1883 Feb 24) Boulder No. 45

Bradley, James
pg 7 (1879 June 14) Tebo No 68, Clinton MO

Breitung, Edward
pg 4 (1876 Oct 14) Negawnee, MI No. 202

Brenning, H S
pg 14 (1883 Dec 22) Grent Lodge, Porwood, MA

Brokabe, H William
pg 1 (1875 July 10) Kensington Lodge No. 211 Philadelphia, PA

Brooks, Anson
pg 1 (1874 July 11) Denver No.5

Brower, N G
pg 5 (1877 Jan 13) Denver No.5

Bunam, E B
pg 8 (1879 Aug 9) St Vrain No. 23

Burchill, Art
pg 4 (1876 Dec 2) Ishpenning No. 314 MI

Butter, Thomas
pg 8 (1879 Aug 9) St Vrain No. 23

Buziak, W C
pg 6 (1878 Aug 10) Lincoln Center, KS

Cantrell, J L
pg 11 (1882 Jan 14) Olive Lodge No. 181 KS

Carmack, Thomas K
appears as: Carmack, T K pg 1 (1874 July 11) Fort Richerson No. 320

Casey, Robert
pg 13 (1883 Feb 24) Mt Carmet No. 245

Cassinger, H A
pg 12 (1882 Nov 25) Boulder, No. 45

Catongher, D
pg 3 (1876 Aug 26) Elk Folds, KS, Mount No. 126

Chase, N W
pg 7 (1879 Apr 17) Montpelier, Vt, Aurora

Cirode, W T
pg 14 (1884 May 15) South Memphis No. 118

Clarke, L A, MD
pg 2 (1875 Sept 17) Center No. 23 Indianapolis, IN

Closter, Harry
pg 8 (1879 Aug 9) Warwick Lodge No 544

Clow, Richard
pg 1 (1874 July 28) Saint John Lodge No. 121

Clymer, P S
pg 11 (1881 July 23) Council Grove KS No. 36

Cochran, Samuel
pg 4 (1876 Oct 28) Winfield MI No. 197

Cohen, D
pg 9 (1880 Oct 9) Laffaquill No. 171 NY

Colton, Allen L
pg 12 (1882 Sept 2) Ionia No 36 Iona, MI

Conner, C W
pg 3 (1876 June 17) Burlington IA Malta No. 318

Conroy, James C
appears as: Conroy, J C; Conroy, James C pg 2 (1876 May 27) Straton No. 607, IL; pg 2 (1875 Oct 9) Straton, IL No. 607

Conway, A J
pg 14 (1884 Oct 11) Pitkin No. 40

Cook, George D
pg 4 (1876 Dec 2) 11 (Black Hawk?)

Coombe, Henry
pg 1 (1874 July 11) Moralitz No. 186

Cox, Thomas M
pg 14 (1884 May 15) Xenia IL Lodge NO. 485

Cresswell, J S
pg 5 (1877 June 29) Potos Lodge No. 131

Crook, Elam
pg 2 (1876 Mar 4) Hastings, MI No. 52

Crowell, A N
pg 12 (1882 Nov 25) Denver No.5

Curtis, W D [W W]
pg 4 (1876 Oct 14) Lewiston, ME Ashlar pg 5 (1877 Jan 13) Ashlar No. 105 Lewiston, ME

Dabney, Charles
pg 11 (1882 Jan 14) Boulder No. 45; pg 13 (1883 Feb 24) Boulder No. 45; pg 14 (1883 Dec 22) Boulder No. 45

Dale, Alexander
pg 11 (1881 July 23) Grand Rapids, MI

Danford, Thomas
appears as: Danford, Thomas
pg 12 (1882 Nov 25) Boulder No. 45; pg 12 (1883 Feb 10) Boulder No. 45

Davies, D W
pg 7 (1879 July 12) Topeka, KA No. 17

Davis, C H
pg 2 (1876 Apr 17) Baraboo No. 34

Davis, John M
pg 5 (1877 June 29) Wood Cow No. 112, Bowling Green

Davis, John M
pg 10 (1881 Mar 26) Golden Age

Dawson, Wm I G
pg 4 (1876 Dec 2) Northumberland Lodge No. 17 NB Canada

De Groot, Cornelius
pg 1 (1875 July 10) The Hague Union

Denham, Thomas
appears as: Denham, T
pg 3 (1876 Nov 9) Gentreyville No. 195

Develine, Edward W
appears as: Develine, E W pg 4 (1876 Dec 2) Rubicon Lodge No. 237 Toledo, OH

Develine, J W
pg 4 (1876 Dec 2) Mt Vernon, No 64, Norwalk, OH; pg 10 (1880 Nov 27) Mt Vernon, No 64, Norwalk, OH

Dickerson, R E
pg 5 (1876 Dec 12) Occidental No. 20 Greeley

Dickey, J M
pg 6 (1877 Oct 27) Shenango, PA, Prince Lodge No. 475

Dickinson, E W
pg 12 (1883 Feb 10) Wm C Hobles Lodge, Eureka IL

Dickson, L H
pg 8 (1879 Aug 9) St Vrain No. 23

Dolloff, A W
pg 13 (1883 Feb 24) Evergreen No. 92, Stevens Point, WI

Dow, J E
pg 4 (1876 Oct 28) Boulder, Peoria No. 7 IL

Dunagan, Elijah
appears as: Dunagan, E
pg 3 (1876 Nov 9) Gentreyville No. 195

Duncan, Charles C
pg 13 (1883 Feb 24) Praineville No. 554 IN

Dunnagan, P H
pg 10 (1880 Nov 27) Central Lodge No. 6

Ebeling, Wm J
pg 5 (1876 Dec 12) Lafayette No. 123 Lafayette, IN

Edwards, Justin
pg 2 (1876 Mar 27) Golden Lodge No. 1

Eldred, Holden R
appears as: Eldred, Holden R
pg 7 (1878 Oct 26) Central Lodge No. 2; pg 8 (1879 Dec) Central Lodge No. 6

Entwistle, Thomas
pg 5 (1877 Jan 13) Black Hawk No. 11

Eubanks, J C
pg 11 (1881 July 23) Bainbridge, OH

Euozens, A
pg 10 (1881 May 28) Laramie No. 48

Evans, H C
pg 14 (1884 Nov 22) Jersey City, Enterprise No. 48

Ewing, L
pg 9 (1880 July 24) Marine Lodge No. 353, IL

Fairhurst, William
pg 4 (1876 Dec 2) Black Hawk No. 11

Fourier, C C
pg 5 (1876 Dec 12) Prince Asthern Sardey Sh___ No. 685 RM

Foushee, A S
pg 2 (1875 Oct 9) Denver No.5

French, S M
pg 3 (1876 June 24) Denver No.5

Frick, Oran O
pg 8 (1879 Aug 9) Ortonorth, MI No 329

Fuller, J G
pg 8 (1879 Aug 9) Mattawan Lodge No 268 MI; pg 8 (1879 Dec) No 268 MI

Fulton, A G
pg 9 (1880 Mar 27) Union Lodge No. 71, Ripley, OH

Fulton, Frank
pg 7 (1879 Feb 8) Garden City No. 141 Chicago

Fulton, L M
pg 11 (1882 Jan 14) Western Star No. 174 KS

Gage, L G
pg 13 (1883 Feb 24) Evans No. 524 Evanston, IL

Gay, Edward B
pg 4 (1876 Oct 14) Marquette, MI No. 101

Gibbs, W J
pg 10 (1880 Nov 27) Fidelity No. 51 Ithaca NY

Gilbert, Richard
pg 8 (1879 Aug 9) ; pg 12 (1883 Feb 10) Boulder No. 45

Gill, John H, C.E.
pg 1 (1874 July 25) Arlington No. 346, Rolla, MO

Gilman, W L
pg 15 (1885 Dec 26) Boulder, A__ N___ No. 1

Goodwin, A W
pg 10 (1881 Mar 26) Woodstock Lodge No. 11

Goodwin, H L
pg 6 (1878 Feb 19) Denver, Union No. 7

Gravelle, A L
pg 13 (1883 Sept 8) Boulder No. 45

Gravelle, H B
pg 13 (1883 Dec 22) Boulder No. 45

Green, William H
appears as: Green, Wm H pg 1 (1874 July 11) Mound No. 122 Laylonnee

Greene, Jay L
pg 14 (1884 Nov 22) Eagle No. 43, Red Cliff, CO

Greene, Oscar Fitz Allen
pg 1 (1874 July 28) Boulder Sterin the West Lodge

Haffner, D N
pg 10 (1880 Nov 27) Whartonvalle No. 162

Halbert, W W
pg 9 (1880 Mar 27) No. 225 Allegany, Fraundohlt, NY

Halbrook, C M
pg 9 (1880 Aug 28) St Croix No. 46

Hammer, A W
pg 7 (1879 Feb 22) Adams Lodge No. 63

Hammond, L H
pg 7 (1878 Nov 9) Friendship No. 7, Clupualut, RI

Hampson, W C
pg 5 (1877 Jan 13) LaKey No. 221 IL

Harrington, W C
pg 9 (1880 Mar 27) Morning Flower No. 71, West Rupert; pg 10 (1881 Feb 26) Morning Flower No. 71, West Rupert

Hasmet, J A
pg 12 (1882 June 24) San Joaquin No. 19 Stockton, CA

Hasson, W F C
pg 13 (1883 Sept 8) Robert Burns No. 63 Newport, KY

Hawkins, B E
pg 3 (1876 July 22) Stubenville No. 45 OH

Hayenlochs, Reichold
pg 11 (1882 Jan 14) Cheyenne Lodge NO. 1

Heberking, Adolf
pg 4 (1876 Oct 14) Ishpenning No. 314 MI

Henry, Albert T
appears as: Henry, A T
pg 8 (1879 Dec) Occidental Lodge No. 56

Hernandez, Anthony
pg 4 (1876 Oct 14) Williamsport, IN; pg 4 (1876 Nov 25) Williamsport, IN No. 38

Hoben, A
pg 11 (1881 July 23) Cohaes Lodge No. 116

Holbrook, C M
pg 13 (1883 Dec 22) St Croix No. 46

Hollingsworth, W R
pg 13 (1883 Feb 24) Russell No. 154 IL

Hollingworth, H P
pg 12 (1882 Nov 25) Russell No. 154 IL

Hook, W A
pg 2 (1876 May 27) Attica No. 462 Attica, NY

Howell, C C
pg 6 (1878 Aug 10) Amma, IL

Hull, Samuel
pg 4 (1876 Dec 2) Demoin Lodge No. 180 MO

Humphreys, John
pg 9 (1880 Aug 28) Mt Moriah No. 15

Hunter, W T
pg 1 (1875 Sept 17) Potosi No. 131 Potosi, MO

Hurry, A T
pg 7 (1878 Oct 26) Occidental No. 20 Greeley

Hyle, W W
pg 14 (1884 June 17) Eureka Lodge No. 76 MO

James, G
pg 3 (1876 June 24) Trene Orrayu, No. 16 NY

Jeanaver, John
pg 7 (1879 Aug 9) Crescent Lodge No. 25 Cedar Rapids; pg 8 (1879 Aug 9) Crescent Lodge No. 25 Cedar Rapids

Jeffers, Albert
pg 13 (1883 Feb 24) Otseningo No. 435 Binghampton; pg 13 (1883 Sept 8) Otseningo No. 435 Binghampton

Johnston, J P
pg 6 (1878 Aug 1) Sharon Lodge No. 250, Sharon, PA; pg 7 (1878 Oct 26) Sharon Lodge No. 250, Sharon, PA; pg 9 (1880 Mar 27) Sharon Lodge No. 250, Sharon, PA

Johnston, James J
pg 8 (1879 Dec) Sharon Lodge No. 250, Sharon, PA; pg 10 (1880 Nov 27) Sharon No. 250 Sharon, PA

Jones, R M
pg 6 (1878 Aug 1) Haynesville, MO

Jones, T R
pg 7 (1879 Aug 9) Brazil Lodge No. 204 Brazil IN

Jones, W W
pg 9 (1880 Mar 27) Aunty Lodge No 83 Huntington

Judd, D H
pg 9 (1880 July 24) Marine Lodge No. 353, IL

Karana, R Jr
pg 2 (1875 Oct 9) Retreat, TX No. 138

Kavanaugh, A M
*could be A A Kavanaugh
pg 7 (1878 Oct 12) Cass No. 39

Kavanaugh, R F
pg 5 (1877 Jan 13) Retreat, TX No. 138

Kellogg, G M
pg 15 (1885 Dec 26) Boulder, Lounsett No. 34

Kellogg, George A
pg 13 (1883 Feb 24) Nevada No. 99 IA

Kendrick, A T
pg 13 (1883 Aug 25) Dewitt, No. 59 Dewitt, MO

Kiel, A E
pg 6 (1877 Nov 10) Joppa No. 186 Montrose, IA

King, Robert
appears as: King, R
pg 1 (1874 July 25) Cambria Lodge No. 152, WI

Kroll, Anson
pg 6 (1878 Aug 10) Sharon Walworth No 136

Lake, George E
pg 14 (1884 Nov 29) Pitkin No. 40

Law, Theodore
pg 12 (1882 Aug 26) Demited from Gentryville No. 625

Leakin, D
pg 6 (1878 Sept 14) Hiram No 362, Gashoka, MO

Lee, George
pg 10 (1881 Mar 26) Berlin, MI

Leland, Theo
pg 2 (1875 Oct 23) Denver No.5

Lillibridge, C E
pg 2 (1876 May 27) Tadmore No. 225 IA

Litton, J B
pg 14 (1884 Oct 11) Buckeye City No. 286 Antioch

Long, H
pg 2 (1876 Mar 27) Western Star No. 100, Benton, IA

Macky, A J
pg 12 (1882 Nov 25) Boulder No. 45; pg 14 (1883 Dec 22) Boulder No. 45

Manwaring, P B
pg 11 (1882 June 24) Denver No.5

McAllister, G T
pg 5 (1877 Jan 13) Franklin Lodge NO. 6, Lebanon MO

McAllister, J T
pg 8 (1879 Dec) Franklin, NH No. 6

McCall, N H
pg 10 (1880 Nov 27) Central Lodge No. 6

McCluney, Uriah
pg 14 (1884 Nov 29)

McColloon, Crusie
pg 15 (1886 Mar 27) Perserverance No. 92, Louisiana, MO

McGaffey, D R
pg 14 (1885 Sept 12) Orient No. 51 Topeka, KS

McIntosh, D
pg 3 (1876 June 24) Great Lights No. 181 Dewich, PA

McLaughlin, S K
pg 3 (1876 May 27) Pt Pleasant No. 360 OH

Middleton, John
pg 4 (1876 Dec 2) O&O Franz No 656 IL

Midland, H G
pg 3 (1876 July 22) Pacific No 29 KS

Mitchell, J P
pg 4 (1876 Dec 2) Peryance No. 237 MI

Moecker, H
pg 11 (1882 Jan 14) Luce No. 439 Quincy, IL

Montgomery, P W
pg 6 (1878 Jan 26) Canton, IA NO. 202

Moon, T H
pg 6 (1878 Aug 1) Council Grove KS No. 36

Moore, T M
pg 3 (1876 June 24) Charthano, IL, 523

Moorhead, John
pg 13 (1883 Feb 24) Boulder No. 45

Morris, S D
pg 6 (1878 Apr 13) Evening Star, No. 94, Cuba NM; pg 7 (1878 Oct 26) St Louis Evening Star

Mugford, J
pg 14 (1884 May 24) Fowey, England No. 977

Newnam, Eedward B
pg 14 (1884 May 15) St Vrain No. 23

Norris, J W
pg 5 (1877 Jan 13) Red Oak Lodge No. 162 IA

Norton, S B
pg 9 (1880 Mar 2) Union Lodge No. 7

O'Connor, James
pg 4 (1876 Dec 2) Delaware Cty, IN No 265

Olmstead, A O
pg 14 (1884 Apr 2) Lisbon Lodge, MI

Osborne, H B
pg 12 (1882 Nov 25) Excelsion No. 257

Parker, Charles E
pg 4 (1876 Dec 2) Denver No.5

Parker, E A D
pg 10 (1881 Apr 23) Nelson No. 77, Nelson, NE; pg 11 (1881 July 23) Nelson No. 77, Nelson, NE

Parker, W H
pg 12 (1883 Feb 10) Monument No. 96, Houston, ME

Parkinson, B E
pg 2 (1876 May 27) Fairmont No. 45, NE

Parson, G H
pg 1 (1874 July 11) Mound No. 122 Laylonnee

Partlett, Reuel
pg 9 (1880 Feb 5) Midland MI Centre Lodge

Partridge, E M
pg 7 (1879 May 11) Hunda Sta No 682 NY

Passel, James L
pg 14 (1884 July 26) White River Lodge No. 332, Shoals IN

Pattridge, George
pg 5 (1877 June 29) MM St Johns Lodge Hamilton Ontario Canada West

Paulson, Martin
pg 6 (1878 Mar 23) Chesterfield No. 445, Chesterfield, IA

Pemnan, James
pg 7 (1879 Feb 22) Shenandoah Lodge No. 511

Perrin, E S
pg 2 (1876 May 13) Portland, MI

Phillips, Ives
pg 7 (1879 Feb 8) Aurora Lodge Fitchburg, MA

Platt, O H
pg 5 (1877 June 9) Rankton Lodge No. 1 Lakota, TX

Platt, O H
pg 7 (1878 Oct 26) Franklin Lodge NO. 6, Lebanon MO

Pokings, Henry
pg 3 (1876 June 24) Dodgeville No. 119 WI

Pollock, James R
appears as: Pollock, J R
pg 5 (1877 Jan 13) Elm Spring Lodge No. 155, AR

Power, I W
pg 1 (1874 July 28) Madena Mt Miredema No. 31

Pray, J Q
pg 6 (1878 Jan 26) Portage O, Wood Cty, No. 112

Rent, T B
pg 3 (1876 May 27) Summerfield, OH No. 425

Reynolds, George D
pg 1 (1875 Sept 17) Boulder - Tuscan No. 60, MO

Robbins, D P
pg 5 (1877 June 9) Cambridge Covenant Lodge No. 1173 PA

Roberts, J E
pg 14 (1884 Nov 29) Kansas City Lodge, No. 220

Ross, W W
pg 3 (1876 Aug 26) Idaho Springs No. 26

Russell, J Willard
pg 11 (1881 July 23) Adel, IA

Safely, Alexander F
appears as: Safely, A F
pg 11 (1882 Jan 14) Ionic No. 35 Leadville; ;pg 12 (1882 Nov 25) Ionic No. 35 Leadville; pg 13 (1883 Feb 24) Ionic No. 35 Leadville

Sampson, A J
pg 3 (1876 July 22) Canon City, Mt Moriah No. 16

Sampson, J H
pg 10 (1881 May 28) Western Star No. 21

Samuels, Henry C
appears as: Samuels, H C pg 5 (1877 June 29) Palestine Lodge No. 481 Ballard Cty, KY

Sawyer, N F
*could be H F Sawyer
pg 2 (1876 May 13) Central Lodge No. 2

Schroudt, A J
pg 7 (1879 June 28) Oclow No. 148 N Dak

Scott, William
pg 1 (1874 July 11) Munda Station No 682

Sears, William F
appears as: Sears, Wm F pg 1 (1875 July 10) Central Lodge No. 2; pg 1 (1874 July 28) Central Lodge No. 2

Secor, W W
pg 10 (1880 Oct 26) St Vrain No. 23

Severance, Frances H
pg 6 (1878 Oct 12) Idaho Springs No. 26

Severance, Isaac H
pg 7 (1878 Oct 26) Idaho Springs No. 26

Sheasman, H A
pg 9 (1880 July 24) Maine Perigo No. 104

Sheets, Henry W
pg 2 (1876 Mar 4) Nemiach, MO U.D.; pg 3 (1876 May 27) Olney Lincoln Co, MO

Simmons, John
pg 2 (1875 Oct 23) Hazel Green Lodge, WI

Simpson, John H
appears as: Simpson, John; Simpson, J H
pg 2 (1875 Sept 17) Western Star No. 21 Youngstown, OH; pg 7 (1878 Nov 9) Louisville No. 28 Youngstown, OH; pg 9 (1880 Aug 28) Western Star No. 21

Simpson, William
appears as: Simpson, Wm pg 10 (1881 Mar 26) Western Star OH

Skinner, A T W
pg 2 (1876 May 27) Lincoln Park, 611 Chicago, IL

Smith, Powell H
pg 6 (1878 May 11) Harman, MO

Spangler, G W
pg 14 (1884 May 24) Albany, IL No. 566

Spangler, I W
pg 8 (1879 Aug 9) Albany No 566 Albany, IL

St Clair, Joel F T
pg 4 (1876 Oct 28) Linn Wood No. 167

Stanton, J A
pg 4 (1876 Oct 14) Nevada No. 4

Stark, A E
pg 9 (1880 Mar 27) Metropolitan Lodge No. 49, Dubuque, IA

Stevens, George E
pg 4 (1876 Oct 14) Pueblo Lodge

Stevens, James
pg 2 (1876 May 13) Lodge No. 45 Pittsburg, PA

Stockwell, E J
pg 11 (1882 Jan 14) Kingston Lodge NO. 266 IL

Stover, W C
pg 3 (1876 June 17) Collins No. 19 CO

Strauss, M
pg 9 (1880 Mar 27) Maska No. 420, St Louis, MO

Stroud, H E
pg 14 (1884 Nov 29) Mesa NO. 55, Grand Junction, CO

Stuchell, Charles D
appears as: Stuchell, C D [G D]
pg 1 (1875 Mar 28) Tuscola ILL No. 382

Sulye, Charles
pg 15 (1885 Dec 26) St John NB Hibernia No. 3

Sutter, G M
pg 6 (1878 Feb 19) Black Hawk No. 11

Tallman, Isaac T
pg 2 (1875 Oct 9) Straton, IL No. 607

Tankersley, E D
pg 8 (1879 Aug 9) Valley Grove No 336 AR

Teller, William
pg 15 (1885 Sept 12) Central Lodge No. 6

Tennar, John
pg 8 (1879 Aug 9) Crescent Lodge No. 25 Cedar Rapids

Thayer, Arch F
pg 2 (1876 Mar 4) Clotham, IL No. 523

Thiel, Math.
pg 14 (1884 June 17) Rosita Lodge No. 36

Thompson, H C
pg 3 (1876 May 27) Mound No. 122

Tipple, George L
appears as: Tipple, G L
pg 3 (1876 June 24) Monitor Lodge No. 330

Titley, G W
pg 15 (1886 Mar 27) Golden City No. 1

Treffinor, William H
pg 12 (1883 Feb 10) Black Hawk No. 11

Trussell, A J
pg 10 (1880 Oct 26) Jackson No. 60

Tucker, Thomas
pg 9 (1880 Aug 28) Ashler No. 3

Turner, F F
pg 7 (1879 July 12) Boulder

Van Fleet, Charles G
pg 7 (1878 Nov 9) Boulder, Peter Williamson No 323

Virgin, W T
pg 9 (1880 Oct 26) Matta Lodge No. 218 IA

Waggoner, A J
pg 1 (1875 July 10) Morning Star Lodge No. 20 Beloit WI

Walker, H B
pg 6 (1878 Aug 10) Washington, No 53, Nashville, IL

Ward, Elijah
pg 9 (1880 Mar 27) Washington Lodge No. 6

Ward, J C
pg 2 (1875 Oct 23) Ishpenning No. 314 MI

Washburn, Hiram E
appears as: Washburn, H E
pg 7 (1879 Feb 22) St Vrain No. 23; pg 8 (1879 Aug 9) St Vrain No. 23; pg 10 (1881 Feb 26) St Vrain No. 23; pg 10 (1880 Oct 26) St Vrain No. 23; pg 10 (1880 Nov 27) St Vrain No. 23; pg 11 (1882 Jan 14) St Vrain No. 23; pg 12 (1882 Nov 25) St Vrain No. 23; pg 13 (1883 Feb 24) St Vrain No. 23

Webster, G M
pg 8 (1879 Aug 9) St Vrain No. 23

Welch, A D
pg 8 (1879 Dec) Boulder

Wheaton, E A
pg 11 (1882 Jan 14) Star in the East, New Bedford, MA

White, H A
pg 11 (1882 Jan 14) Western Star No. 174 KS

White, James
pg 3 (1876 July 22) Pine Bluff No. 9 AR

Williams, H
pg 3 (1876 June 24) Broknaha Kinsington No. 211 Philadelphia, PA

Williams, R H
pg 2 (1876 May 27) St Vrain No. 23

Willoughby, Euth
pg 1 (1874 July 11) Union No. 7

Wilson, G W
pg 11 (1882 Jan 14) NiWot Longmont CO

Wilson, Thomas
pg 9 (1880 Feb 5) Safnia, OH No 324

Winger, S G
pg 6 (1878 Feb 19) Washington Lodge No. 5, Atchison, KS

Wirt, Samuel E
pg 14 (1884 Nov 29) Unity Lodge No. 682

Witten, D P
pg 1 (1874 July 25) Occidental No. 20 Greeley

Wolf, M W
pg 5 (1877 June 23) Wm B Warren No. 209 Chicago

Yankee, William H
pg 3 (1876 July 22) Sedalia No. 36 MO

Index

B

C

D

E

F

G

H

I

J

K

L

M

N

O

P

Q

R

S

T

Y

www.ingramcontent.com/pod-product-compliance
Lightning Source LLC
LaVergne TN
LVHW080320110826
845155LV00026B/165

* 9 7 8 1 8 7 9 5 7 9 5 7 6 *